# PIAGETIAN PERSPECTIVE FOR PRESCHOOLS
## A Thinking Book for Teachers

RUTH SAUNDERS

ANN M. BINGHAM-NEWMAN

PRENTICE-HALL, INC., ENGLEWOOD CLIFFS, NEW JERSEY 07632

Library of Congress Cataloging in Publication Data

Saunders, Ruth A.
    Piagetian perspective for preschools.

    Includes bibliographies and index.
        1.  Piaget, Jean, 1896–      .    2.  Education, Preschool.
3.  Child development.      I.  Bingham-Newman, Ann M.,
(date).      II.  Title.
LB775.P492S28 ̲1984          372'.21          83-13796
ISBN 0-13-675009-5

Editorial/production supervision and
    interior design: Virginia M. Livsey
Cover design: Wanda Lubelska Design
Manufacturing buyer: Harry P. Baisley


Illustrations produced from drawings
made by Hoai, Nam, and Phong Nguyen
during their preschool years.

Printed in the United States of America

10  9  8  7  6  5  4  3  2  1


ISBN 0-13-675009-5


Prentice-Hall International, Inc., *London*
Prentice-Hall of Australia Pty. Limited, *Sydney*
Editora Prentice-Hall do Brasil, Ltda., *Rio de Janeiro*
Prentice-Hall Canada Inc., *Toronto*
Prentice-Hall of India Private Limited, *New Delhi*
Prentice-Hall of Japan, Inc., *Tokyo*
Prentice-Hall of Southeast Asia Pte. Ltd., *Singapore*
Whitehall Books Limited, *Wellington, New Zealand*

# CONTENTS

# PREFACE

This book expresses our conviction that there is something fundamentally and importantly right about the Piagetian perspective for understanding development. Like all theories, Piaget's theory has grown and changed. There are, and will continue to be, disagreements over theoretical details and implications for application. Major revisions may lie in wait. But there is no doubt that the theoretical perspective has been tremendously fruitful for work with young children.

Our aim in this book is to help you, the reader, construct your own understanding of the theory and its applications. What we offer is neither a comprehensive comparison of theories nor a Piagetian "how-to" manual. Rather, we have tried to convey the ideas and attitudes we think crucial to the Piagetian perspective while helping you to actively integrate the theory into your own work with children. Numerous thought-provoking exercises throughout the text are designed to cultivate a healthy questioning attitude toward the theory and toward our interpretation of it. Detailed examples and suggestions illustrate the enormous potential we've found in Piaget's theory. We have put the theory to use in devising daily schedules, planning activities, arranging the classroom, observing and interpreting behavior, interacting effectively with children, setting goals for children, and working with other adults.

The more we have learned about applying Piaget's theory, the more we have realized the significance of the focus on mechanisms of development. Our key words for a Piagetian classroom are activity, diversity, change, and intellectual honesty—not classification, seriation, and number. The tremendous value of descriptions of stage-related understandings in infralogical and logico-mathematical knowledge lies in the guidance they give for choosing challenging materials and stimulating interaction strategies. The emphasis in this book reflects this realization.

As we have worked with preschool children, teachers, parents, administrators, nurses, and college students, we have become increasingly impressed by the fact that many of the basic theoretical principles that apply to children's development also apply to adult understandings. We have tried, as much as is possible in a written work, to do with you the kind of thing we hope you will do with children. We have included questions and exercises to help you do your own thinking about children, classroom activities, teaching strategies, and theory. Discussions of theory have been interspersed with thoughts about applications. The Teacher Tasks that appear throughout the book are exercises that have helped us and the adults we've worked with to transform an acquaintance with theoretical jargon into active understanding.

This book has its roots in the early 1970s when, as graduate students in child development at the University of Wisconsin-Madison, we were first introduced to Piaget's theory. The impact on our understanding and interpretation of children's behavior was immediate and far-reaching. Here was a comprehensive theory that gave insights into the sometimes charming, sometimes frustrating behaviors so well known to those who work with young children. Here was a way to understand why certain traditional activities were so effective and others so ineffective. Shortly thereafter we began a three-year research project involving the development and evaluation of a Piagetian-based preschool program and the intensive teacher-education component needed to make the program work. As the teachers' reluctance to take on the burden of theory yielded to excitement and enthusiasm, we knew we had a book to write. Since then, a variety of extensions of that original project, in a variety of places, have deepened our understanding of children and of the people who work with them.

## ACKNOWLEDGMENTS

This book would never have gone beyond the preoperational stage without the help and friendship of many people throughout the years. We extend our thanks to: Frank H. Hooper, for introducing us to Piaget's theory and putting the initial research project on its feet; the student teachers and graduate assistants at the University of Wisconsin Preschool Laboratory, for their willingness to put in long hours, for their ideas and activity plans, and especially for their patience as we stumbled through our early attempts to change the way we taught young children; the many teachers, students, and workshop participants over the years, for the insistence on concrete examples, which kept us intellectually honest; colleagues at the Institute for Research in Human Development at Educational Testing Service, for helpful and challenging discussions; the children at the University of Wisconsin Preschool Laboratory, at the Child Care Research Center at Educational Testing Service, and at the houses of friends and family, for providing numerous delightful examples of sensorimotor and preoperational thinking and for teaching us how to teach; Jane Goldman, Joan Ershler, Irv Sigel, Rhoda McShane Becher, Audrey J. Crandall, and Mary Alice Paul for their valuable comments on the structure and organization of various drafts of this book; and the many other good friends and colleagues who provided continued support and encouragement. We owe special thanks to Emily Nguyen, without whose delight in each new chapter and firm conviction that others ought to see the completed work, this book would have remained a file drawer of notes and unfinished chapters. Finally, we thank Lawrence Levy, for the adaptability and good humor that saw the work through to the end.

Madison, Wisconsin                                                          Ruth Saunders
January 1983

# 1 INTRODUCTION

## AN INTRODUCTION TO THE PIAGETIAN POINT OF VIEW

If you've been around preschoolers, you've heard comments like these:

> When I grow up, I'm going to be a daddy.
> No, you're not. You'll be a mom.
> I can't be a mom. I already have a mom.

or

> These are the same size because they're orange.

or

> I'm not four and a half years old. I'm just four and a half.*

*These are direct quotes from children at the University of Wisconsin preschool laboratory.

What do they mean? Are they more than just cute examples of the struggles children are having with language? Why are they so different from the mistakes that foreign-language speakers make in learning English? What lies behind such apparent absurdities?

In the early part of this century, the Swiss psychologist Jean Piaget began to take such comments seriously. He asked himself what lay behind such seemingly absurd statements. Through a combination of observations, clinical interviews, and carefully designed experiments, Piaget concluded that children's language can provide useful insights into a different way of thinking. Piaget, his coworkers in Geneva, and numerous British and American researchers inspired by his ideas have undertaken careful studies of children's language and behaviors. Results of these studies have led them to believe that children's systems of thought, their ways of knowing, are quite different from adult systems.

Let's stop for a moment and think of what the implications of such a conclusion might be. They run deep. An implication discussed frequently by those familiar with Piaget's theory is that, since children are not capable of understanding information the way adults do, information must be thoughtfully selected, skillfully presented, and carefully matched to the child's level. This suggests that content should be presented in different ways according to each child's stage of development (that is, sensorimotor, preoperational, concrete operational, and formal operational—see Chapter 2). This is certainly true. If we are interested in content, we ought to present it in a way the child can understand. But Piaget's theory has something even more radical than that to say. It tells us that the *kind* of information we make available to the child and the precise way we make it available can do more than to make a particular concept comprehensible. These factors *actually influence when and how developmental progress is made.*

Remember, it is not just that the child knows *less* than the adult. The child uses a *different system* for interpreting the world. To get a feel for what this means, imagine a starfish trying to figure out the notions of "left" and "right." Such notions hardly fit into the world view of a radially symmetrical creature. Now try to imagine what it would be like to *be* a starfish—what it would be like not to have a left and right side. Or imagine trying to give a starfish directions to the neighborhood laundromat. Hard, isn't it? This is the kind of problem that faces us if, as Piaget tells us, children really do have a different system from ours.

As if this were not enough, Piaget's theory points to an even greater difficulty. Let's accept the view that children in our classrooms have a different system of thought than we adults do, and let's try to imagine those same children some fifteen to twenty years into the future. They will have changed into adults—with adult ways of thinking. The changes they will undergo are no less surprising than the change from an egg to a baby chick or from a caterpillar to a butterfly. The children's ways of thinking will have undergone *qualitative* change. This needs some explaining.

If the change were merely in the amount of information (or number of facts) one had acquired, it would be easy to explain. Just as a pile of sand can be built up a grain at a time, so the change could be brought about through a gradual and continuous process of adding individual facts or pieces of information. But the change is not only in amount or number. The change Piaget refers to is a change in what is done with the information. Development involves change in the *organization* of information. How do we explain that?

Freud (and Erikson) have viewed similar transformations in the realm of psychosexual development as genetically preprogrammed. Regardless of how well, or how poorly, an individual has developed within a stage, when the genetic alarm clock rings, it's on to the next stage, ready or not. Is this how it works with intellectual development? Piaget's answer, though he has sometimes been misinterpreted on this point, is a resounding *No*. Rather, he proposes an embryological explanation. Just as the unborn fetus develops "normally" only under very restricted environmental conditions (the right amount and timing of hormones, the appropriate temperature range, and so on), so the child's intellect develops "normally" only in the appropriate environment. And we adults are an important part of that environment. Thus it behooves us to take a thorough look at how the child and the environment interact.

In Piaget's view, children *construct* systems of knowing. As the word "construct" suggests, children use available materials and arrange them into some form. "Materials" is a metaphor, of course. What we're really talking about are children's perceptions of the world. When they look at the world around them, children notice some details and overlook others. They use the details they notice to construct explanations, theories, about how things work in the world. In many ways, their theories are like houses they construct with windows from which to look out on the world. What they see (what features of the world they notice) will depend on the size and location of their windows. If they remodel their houses so that the windows are changed, they will notice different features of reality.

Children may not know what their final theory will be—they don't know how they will decide to remodel their building or how many times they will rearrange it. Piaget proposes that children will make several major revisions before the house and windows are suitable—before children have constructed an explanation of reality that is adapted to the world of human beings in today's society. So long as there are plenty of appropriate materials and enough time for building, however, children continue to work diligently at the task, arranging and rearranging the parts, but stopping now and then to admire their handiwork or to peer out the windows at the different views each new structure affords.

Such periods of enjoying the view are not wasteful. Far from it. It is their new perspective on the world that inspires children to undertake the next revision. "Ah, what a lovely view of the footpath. But where are all those people getting the apples they're munching? There must be an apple tree just out of my view. Hmm

. . . If I could think of a way to get a window in just the right place, I'll bet I could see the path and the apple tree. . . . Oh! What a marvelous stone! Now, why didn't I notice it before? . . . Perhaps I could add it to the west wall and make a picture window over there with a view of the apple tree. . . . But then, of course, I'd want to move the tower over a bit and build a loft over here. . . . Perhaps I could do away with the tower altogether and use its bricks for a new stairway. . . . And if I just had a piece of wood like so . . ."

Will the child find the right piece of wood? And where did that marvelous stone come from? You guessed it. *We,* the teachers, parents, friends, and relatives, *we,* the other human beings in the child's world, clever folk that we are, *we* rolled the stone as far as we could so that it might be seen from the window. Of course, we had to have a pretty good idea of what the child's structure was like, before our efforts with the heavy stone could have a chance of paying off. We knew it was risky. We took our cues from the child's comments about the view—comments such as, "From here it looks like 'these are the same size because they're orange' "—and we made an educated guess about the location of the windows. We put together clues about what the child's structure was like from the comments and behaviors we observed. We also counted on our oft-called-on ability to lure the child to the window. We wouldn't leave that to chance. Of course there was always the possibility that even if we were right about the child's structure, the view from the child's windows, and our ability to get the child to take a look at the footpath—even with all this in our favor—there was still the possibility that the child might not be puzzled about where the path originated. The view might simply be acknowledged and then ignored.

Shall we reveal our secret? We had also carried an enticing bit of driftwood over by the back door, we placed a wheelbarrow full of bricks over by the sagging porch support, and you can guess who it was who went by on the footpath, conspicuously munching apples. But enough. The rest of this book is designed to tell it all: how we tactfully point out a weak supporting wall, how we choose materials that will suggest a new arrangement (sometimes major, sometimes minor), how we try to get the materials noticed just when the restless remodeling urge is building up, how we make our guesses about the structure from the child's comments on the world as seen through his windows, and how we kindly let the child know that the view from those windows really isn't quite adequate.

Before we get to work on understanding and applying theory, let's take a moment to check where we've been and to make sure no one has taken a wrong turn. We have claimed that the child sees the world through different windows than we do. Another way of putting this is to say that the child has a different theory about the world than adults do, or that the child uses a different system for making sense out of available information. This means that information we may see as both obvious and crucial for understanding a particular phenomenon is neither obvious nor considered important to the child. In fact, it may not even be accessible. Sometimes the use of a theory can blind one to "obvious" facts—facts that are perfectly clear to someone with a different theory. This is true for the theories we adults adhere to as well as for the theories of a young child.

This approach is markedly different from the traditional view in American education, a view that, fortunately, is beginning to fade. The traditional view is that the mind is a *tabula rasa,* a blank slate on which experiences make nice, neat, and unalterable imprints. Philosophers and historians of science (such as Thomas Kuhn), developmental psychologists (including, of course, Piaget and his followers), and even literary critics (such as I. A. Richards) are abandoning this oversimplified approach to mental activity. Numerous writers with an influence on today's educational practices share Piaget's general orientation. Don't be surprised if you hear the voices of John Dewey, Haim Ginot, James Hymes, Daniel Jordan, Clark Moustakas, or Carl Rogers speaking to you from between the lines of this book. Your ears are not deceiving you. We are under no compulsion to confine ourselves to what has been set forth by Piaget himself when we apply the theory. (And it is a good thing we don't, since relatively few of his efforts have been devoted to a careful analysis of how theory should be applied to education.)

We can make use of the ideas of a great many modern thinkers and still avoid the mistake made in believing (to return to our metaphor) that the child inhabits the same kind of a building that we do and just hasn't gotten around to exploring the upper stories and the broader, more accurate view offered by the windows up there—the kind of windows we adults look through. Rather, as Piaget's theory points out, the child's mind inhabits a different kind of building altogether. The child can't see what we see because a child's house doesn't have the windows that ours does. The child has to construct a *new* building, with *new* windows, in order to understand the world in the way that adults in Western society typically do.

> *To present an adequate notion of learning one first must explain how the subject manages to construct and invent, not merely how he repeats and copies.*
>
> *Piaget, 1970, p. 714*

This realization has a profound influence on what it means to "really listen" to what children have to tell us. True, they are describing the same world we are, but the part they see is decidedly different. Remember the old story about the blind men and the elephant? (If you don't, you might try looking in any collection of classic tales from India—or look at Lillian Quigley's version for young children.) Children's comments, especially their interpretations and explanations for what they think, are eye opening. Chapters 2 and 5 are designed to give guidelines for how to listen—what to pay attention to and how to make sense of what you hear and see. The theory guides not only our teaching of young children, but also our whole interpretation of what they are about. Don't let the heavy theoretical reading in those chapters get you down. Human beings are very complex creatures. If we are going to attempt to understand them, we are going to have to climb a few hills and painstakingly cut our way through some dense thickets.

## WHAT DIFFERENCE DOES A THEORY MAKE?

### That's All Very Well in Theory, but Will It Work in Practice?

Suppose you grant that the child has a unique view of reality. What difference does this make in teaching? Children still need to learn to talk, to read, to write, to count, and all the other things we've been teaching them for years. Theoreticians come and go, one educational fad is followed by another, and still we go on essentially the same as we always did. Don't we end up doing pretty much the same thing regardless of whether we listen to John Locke or to Piaget? Going back to our metaphor again, what is the *practical* difference between leading a child through a shared building (pointing out the view from each room as we come to it) and helping the child to construct new buildings with new windows (helping the child to redo the whole structure)?

Such skepticism is not easy to dispel. There are differences—and pervasive ones—but they are subtle. They have to do with how we listen to children and interpret what they say. This influences how far we push in a particular concept area, how we treat nonadult responses (or, to put it in the old terminology, "wrong" answers), and when we introduce new ideas. We are probably not far off base in saying that the traditional goal in teaching has been to present ideas and information clearly and simply, so that children understand each step. The goal when one adheres to Piagetian theory is nearly the opposite. Just when children have comfortably settled in to a way of understanding things (and after they have had a chance to admire his handiwork), we introduce a new piece of information (remember the marvelous stone?), which requires the construction of a whole new perspective—a new building with new windows.

Suppose, for example, that Petra has decided that there are two kinds of things in the world: the kind that drip off the table and the kind that stay where they are put. Then suppose Petra gets a chance to play with silly putty. At first it seems to be a substance of the second kind; it can be shaped, bounced like a ball, broken into pieces, and so forth. When she leaves a little piece sitting near the edge of the table for a while, however, a strange thing happens. The silly putty seems to be like substances of the first kind. Something must be wrong. Could it be that there are three kinds of substances in the world? Or maybe she should start all over and find a new way to draw the boundary between kinds of substances.

### Can't a Theory Hinder as Well as Help?

So maybe the theory does make a practical difference, but didn't we just say a little while ago that theory can blind us to the facts? How on earth, then, can we advocate using a theory to guide teaching?

It cannot be denied that a theory can be dangerous. So can the Indian water buffalo. And yet, the survival of many Asian societies depends on the use of that beast for working in rice paddies. Like the water buffalo, the theory can be yoked and put to work *for* us, instead of against us. But how? How can we reap the advantages without falling prey to the dangers? First of all, we need to know the nature of the beast. Then we are in a position to figure out how to yoke it.

It is in the nature of theories to have uncertain status as far as truth is concerned. Theories are not unalterable facts (though they have a sneaky way of appearing to be so unless we watch them carefully). They are hypotheses about the world. Yes, some of the hypotheses *may* turn out to be true, but since we do not yet know which are the true ones and which are the false, we are well advised to keep them under the watchful eye of the skeptic in us.

A second characteristic of theories is their blissful ignorance of practical concerns. If they are going to be of any help to educational practice, we'll have to make the connections for them. We'll have to use good judgment in how to actually organize the classroom and our interactions in it. We'll have to sort through our bag of ideas and techniques (or someone else's bag if ours is still fairly empty) for those most likely to enhance our implementation of theory. We may have to try out a few variations before we get the best use out of the theory, but if we persist, we can find a way to make the theory helpful in meeting our needs. We want it to work for us, after all—not the other way around. In Chapter 8 we explore some ideas for how to use the theory in planning activities for children. Chapter 7 discusses some ideas we've already used for classroom organization, management, and interaction strategies. Remember, these are things that worked for *us*. You need to find what works for *you*.

Characteristic number three of theories is that they're revisable. Children don't care what the theory says. They'll go on doing what they do even if the theory strictly forbids it, calls it impossible, or rears back in astonishment. If this happens, it is the *theory* that needs changing. As mediators between the developing intelligence of the child and the environment that both shapes and is shaped by the child, teachers are in an ideal position to contribute to modifications of the theory. We can observe in detail the effects of what we do, how we do it, and when we do it. We can clarify the relationship between developmental processes and specific kinds of experiences. Our unique position, however, does not make theory revision an offhand affair. The beast balks and sulks. It doesn't always listen to us. We think twice before we attempt major modifications. Nonetheless, it is *we* who have the final say, not the theory.

We have admitted that a theory *can* obscure our view of what's really happening—*but only if we let it!* If we ignore every bit of evidence that runs counter to the theory, if we always dismiss contrary evidence as some kind of an illusion, if we stop asking ourselves how we might refine the theory here and there, if we stop searching for new and better ways to relate theory to practice, if we stop evaluating the effects of using the theory, if *this* is how we use a theory, then certainly we are letting the theory blind us. Fortunately, none of these is necessary when we apply theory to practice.

If we use it wisely, Piaget's theory can provide a way of seeking answers to the questions asked in any approach to education—quesions such as: What abilities or thought processes must the child have in order to make sense of the information we give? What do children's answers mean in terms of their grasp of subject material? How much should we strain to teach certain concepts to certain age groups? How can we expand a child's applications of newly acquired abilities and knowledge? What effect will specific learnings have on later development and learning? By proposing hypotheses about the mechanisms of developmental change and the limits of understanding at any particular stage, Piaget's theory provides guidelines and promising leads for us to use in our search for answers. In addition, it generates new questions. We no longer assume, for example, that if we simply demonstrate how to pick out all of the sixteen blue blocks from a pile of twenty-nine colored blocks, the child can repeat the behavior with new materials (or even with the same ones at a later date). We no longer take for granted the child's understanding of the basis for what we demonstrated. It has become legitimate to ask about the different ways a child might view a particular situation and how children's views might differ from those of an adult. Are you getting a feeling that maybe the old theories caused a little blindness? They did. *Remember, the theory can help us, but only if we make it!*

Theory can help *us* become more effective *learners.* It can give us a framework within which to do our own critical thinking about what children say and do. Our answer to why a child refuses to share, for example, is directly tied to what we decide to do about the situation. The theory can guide both steps. We need to be wary of the theory beast, but with proper handling, it can do wonders for our planning, our actual work with children, and our assessment of how things went.

## DISPELLING SOME DOUBTS

### I Don't Know About All This Cognitive Stuff
### . . . Can't Young Children Just Enjoy Life?

Piaget's theory is about logical thinking, isn't it? What about personality, morality, a sense of responsibility? What about making friends and learning to get along with others? Where's the place for sensory development and creative learning—not to mention art and music? And don't forget physical development. What's so great about being logical?

Whew! These are all questions deserving of more space than we have to give. Let us, then, sketch out a possible plan of defense to be filled out as we explore this theory beast further and think about how we might tame it.

First of all, you're entirely right. Piaget's theory does not explain (or even attempt to explain) all aspects of development. Now, suppose we use the theory in such a way that everything we do in the classroom must be specified by the theory. Sounds suspiciously like a case of blindness, doesn't it—the kind of blindness caused by our failure to get the yoke on the beast? Part of making the theory work for us is knowing its *limitations.*

Oops! Watch that pothole! Don't fall into the mistaken notion that Piaget's theory has nothing to say about anything except "purely intellectual activities"— whatever those are. Nearly everything we do involves *some* thinking. Take Nina, for example, who has trouble passing out napkins at juice time. Maybe she has perceptual problems, maybe she just isn't well coordinated, or maybe she purposely neglects to give one to Matthew, who hasn't let her participate in his block-building activities lately. Piaget's theory provides us with yet another possible interpretation. Possibly Nina doesn't yet think in terms of systematically pairing one napkin with each child. She can do it for one or two, but beyond that, when she doesn't come out right, she has no system of one-to-one correspondence to help her out of the difficulty. We teachers can use the theory to give us new questions to ask about behavior, new directions to go in, but we are left with the ultimate responsibility of deciding which hypothesis to accept.

Are you surprised to find juice time viewed as a time for intellectual development? Juice times are great for working on children's developing systems for figuring out how to make sure everyone gets what they need—a cracker, a cup, a napkin, and the like. It is often a time of togetherness, a time when there is strong motivation to resolve problems of how to distribute things fairly, and a time for pleasant social interchange. All of these factors make it ideal for intellectual games. Here are a few examples to illustrate the kinds of things that can be done:

(1) Guessing games based on foods: "I spy something that makes a crunch when you chew it; can you quess what it is?" or "I spy something that bends easily but doesn't break." To make the game more challenging, the questions can be asked about foods or properties not present in the immediate surroundings. One can ask such questions as, "I'm thinking of something that's green, that our guinea pig likes to eat, and that might make a pretty good drumstick. What do you think it could be?"

(2) Generating ideas (within constraints): "Let's think of things we can eat that are smaller than this grape"; or "What different kinds of animals might like to eat the kind of snack we're having today?"

(3) Questions related to amounts: "Would you still have just as much to eat if you broke your cracker in half?" or "Now we each have a handful of raisins. How can we be sure we have exactly the same amount?"

If you put your mind to it, you can probably think of many more. We'll also have more to say about why these activities are so beneficial, when we examine the theory in greater detail. For now, let's just take them as examples of what we're talking about.

In case the examples have taken us off the path a bit, let's try another situation to show how theory can be made useful in more areas than the stereotyped intellectual ones. If you've done much work with preschool children, you're familiar with the sudden nightmare epidemics: "But Henry never used to have nightmares. What frightening experience could he have had recently?" Freudian theory offers the most elaborate explanations for this phenomenon, but Piaget's theory can add a bit of insight too. According to Piaget's theory, the explanation might go something like this. Henry has recently acquired the ability to imagine situations he's never experienced. In addition, he can look ahead to what the outcomes might be like. He can imagine how much it would hurt if someone really sawed him in half. It is the ability to think about something that has not been experienced that enables the child to have fears of this type. Piaget's theory has nothing to say, however, about why Henry's nightmares are about being sawed in half and Margaret's are about being eaten by a lion.

To get a little clearer on the theory's limitations, let's look at a case where it is not particularly helpful. Consider this situation:

Yoshiko has been crying softly since her daddy left about ten minutes ago. You have patiently explained to her that her daddy will be back after juice time. Yoshiko wails, "I know he'll be back, but I just want him now." "Daddies can't stay at school," you patiently explain. "I know," she says with some exasperation, "but I *want* him to."

We could try to analyze this in terms of the child's unique system of thought. We could try to find some misunderstanding that is responsible for Yoshiko's sadness. Somehow, this doesn't seem to be a very fruitful approach. Instead, what we need are some ways to help Yoshiko cope with the feeling of sadness. We would do well to turn to other theories or to our own experience and good sense. We can take our theory beast for walks around the classroom—there are a surprising number of places where it might make itself useful—but we mustn't let it get away from us.

More will be said about all this in later chapters. These are issues worth returning to again and again.

### Maybe Kids Need Logic, But They'll Develop It Anyway. Why Teach It?

The counterpart to this question is, "Since development normally proceeds this way, why not accelerate the whole process? Sooner is better, right?" Wrong! When you've finished this book, you'll understand why it is so hard to hold back the scream of frustration when such words are heard. Both of these questions reflect a grave misunderstanding of Piaget's theory. Don't feel bad if one or both of these questions is on your mind. Keep them there as you read the explanation of Piagetian theory given in Chapters 2 and 5. Allow us to expend a few words on the subject here as well, however, lest the long wait without any hints at all lead you to forget the questions.

What is overlooked in the first question can be brought out by applying it to physical development. It is like asking, "Most children grow bigger and stronger normally, so why worry about what (or whether) we feed them?" Obviously, it matters what we feed them. The difference in stature attained by Japanese-Americans who reached puberty while living in the U.S. and those who grew up in Japan during the 1940s is a striking example of the importance of the environment. Like physical development, intellectual development is subject to the environment. Hereditary endowments place some limits on both of these areas of development, but it takes an environment to actualize the potential. Different kinds of environments influence how, and to what extent, potentials are actualized.

Intellectual development doesn't just happen by itself. We help it happen. Our interactions with the child, the experiences we provide, and the way we help the child make use of those experiences, provide the food needed for intellectual development. We don't teach logical development the way we might teach the letters of the alphabet, but we have a major role in facilitating its progress.

How can we accept all this and not advocate acceleration of the process? Why isn't sooner better? Perhaps you've already answered these questions yourself by extending the analogy with physical development. Certainly few would claim that better physical development means the attainment of adult stature at age five. As Piaget likes to point out (1970, p. 713), kittens accomplish in three months what it takes human infants nine months to accomplish. But look how far kittens progress intellectually! You don't see many cats reading Shakespeare or solving algebraic equations.

Intellectual development has an optimal pace, according to Piaget. We're not sure exactly what the pace is—it differs for each individual—but the educational goal is to help *each* child develop at an optimal rate. For some children this may mean stepping up the pace. Some children may be able to whiz through the building process of intellectual development if only the appropriate materials and inducements are offered. Others may need help in making their initial structures more solid before they begin remodeling. Or they may need help in taking a good look out their windows before they decide their present structure could use some revision. What inspires one child to build a new, more adequate structure may be ignored by another. Or it may be used to remodel the present structure without changing the view from the windows.

Unfortunately, we cannot give any child specific advice. We can infer approximate locations of the windows from the child's descriptions of the view (if we know how to *elicit* the descriptions and how to *listen* to them when given). We may know some of the building materials the child has used (a stack of bricks, the long wooden boards, and so forth). We may even know some of the furniture the child has acquired. Alas, we can know all this and still not know how they are arranged. Are the bricks used to make the floor, the walls, or the fireplace? Are all the chairs in one room, or are tables and chairs put together? How has the furniture been changed—painted, legs shortened? We can't even be sure of the relation between the floor and the windows once we have a good idea of where the windows are. Maybe the child has to stand on a bureau to peer out the window. How long it would take to get a complete description of each four-year-old's four years' worth of collecting, arranging, and rearranging!

Add to all this the fact that tastes differ, that what sparks an idea in one individual may do nothing for another, and that there are an exceedingly large number of ways to build a structure with a particular view. Attempts to accelerate development for a classroom full of children are doomed to failure. What we *can* do is to create an environment that helps children with a variety of personalities, previous experiences, and styles of building to develop at a variety of optimal rates. Chapters 4, 7, and 8 give some guidelines for how this can be done. It isn't easy— few worthwhile endeavors are—but the results are well worth the effort.


### But My Teaching Is Effective. Won't a Theory Ruin Me?

Some people seem to be natural teachers. They're sensitive to what children do and do not understand. They're perceptive. They have the knack for finding out just the right thing to help children learn. Won't a theory stifle this natural ability, making them stilted, artificial, and self-conscious in the classroom? Others have become very effective teachers after a long period of conscientious effort. Maybe the theory would have been helpful when they were just beginning, but now it seems a waste of time and effort.

These are all legitimate concerns. Trying a new theory may indeed take us back a few steps in our teaching skills. It is a struggle to keep theoretical guidelines in our heads while keeping up with the immediate demands of working with real, live children. It'll take practice. Things we previously did automatically now require a little hesitation and rethinking. For a while we may indeed be a little stilted, a little self-conscious. We'll find ourselves in situations where we know how we would have handled things, but we're not sure whether that way follows from the theory. That's all right. That's part of learning. Just like the child remodeling the structure so as to gain a broader view of the world, we'll know that we want a change and we'll have a fuzzy idea of how things ought to turn out, but we'll have many uncertainties as to how to get from what we have to what we want to have.

We'll have to temporarily give up some of the advantages of our present way of teaching in order to incorporate them into the new system. The loss is only temporary, though. It will take a little time to get the new system established, but when we do, we will have enhanced our natural abilities and added to our painstakingly acquired store of knowledge about how to help children grow. The momentary setback *is* momentary.

Some of us may be lucky. We may get the desired system on our first try. Most of us, however, will probably have to modify our structure several times before we're where we want to be. How soon we get there depends on where we start, the environment we work in (the suggestions we get from books and people and the help we get in assessing what we're doing at each level of our understanding), and which ideas or suggestions "click" for each of us.

A recurring part of this process is assessing where we are. Perhaps much of what we're already doing follows from Piaget's theory. After all, we're working with children on a daily basis. The same information that helped Piaget to formulate his theory is available to us every day—if we know how to get it and how to use it. It would not be unduly surprising if many of our observations and interpretations of children's behavior coincided with Piaget's. The trick is to organize them—to weed out the misleading ones, to separate those that depend on a particular arrangement of events from those of a more universal application, and to systematize the helpful ones so that they can be used to guide our teaching. This is where the theory can help. Since our notion of what our final teaching system will look like is somewhat fuzzy, we'll have to scrutinize very carefully the systems we develop. We'll know how good they are by watching their effects on children. For pointers on how to do this, see Chapter 9.

### Theory May Be Okay for the Old Hands, but for New Teachers, It's Too Much.

Maybe experienced teachers who already know how to work with children can tackle a new theory, but for new teachers, it's too much. New teachers are too busy getting to know what children are like and how to manage a group of them, to be able to incorporate theory into their practice.

Take care! The theory beast may be slipping by without letting us take a good look at it. Grab hold of it for a moment, and let's see whether it might be put to work for beginning teachers.

It is certainly true that successful use of the theory depends on good teaching. It is also true, as pointed out in the previous section, that the use of the theory influences our teaching. Theory is not simply something extra to be learned after we have mastered the basics of working with young children. It actively influences such mastery and colors the interpretations we make of children's behavior and classroom interactions. The theory can influence our system of values and can suggest alternative means to the goals we set, as well as simply providing knowledge of intellectual development.

Use of the theory in initial teaching experiences can help foster habits of careful observation, of constant assessment of children's abilities, of thorough analysis of classroom procedures, of careful planning, of continuous self-evaluation, of evaluating goals in terms of observations and theoretical insight, and of active participation in children's intellectual activities. New teachers can use the theory to help them understand children and the teaching-learning process.

You may be thinking that regardless of how valuable it may be, combining theory with one's first teaching experience is extremely demanding. You're right; it is demanding. But it is also exciting. Student teachers in the Piagetian program developed by the authors at the University of Wisconsin were careful to point out to us how much extra work they were doing. We agreed. It was demanding, frustrating at times, but worth it for all of us. The deeper we got into theory, the more exciting it became. Teachers went through periods of not interacting with children at all, for fear of doing the wrong things, and periods of doing too many of the right things, but at the wrong times. Eventually, a balance of sorts was reached. One is never finished with a process such as this. The longer we teach, the more progress we can make—*can* make, *if* we are willing to work at it.

## WILL ALL VOLUNTEERS PLEASE TAKE TWO STEPS FORWARD?

If we take Piaget's theory to heart, we are going to have to do some extensive rethinking of our educational environments. The numerous and varied attempts to apply Piaget's theory to education are testimony to the difficulty of the task. Although Piagetian theory has given inspiration to many practitioners (including teachers, curriculum designers, toy manufacturers, and specialists in work with mentally or physically handicapped), few attempts have been made to thoroughly integrate theory and practice. Initial attempts to apply Piaget's theory to early education sought primarily to add new concepts to those already taught in schools. Thus, instead of simply teaching arithmetic, one would add units on classification and seriation to the curriculum. Programs such as that developed by Lavatelli

(1970), the early version of Kamii's program (1972), and Weikart's cognitively oriented curriculum (Weikart, Adcock, and McClelland, 1971) used this kind of approach. More recent attempts, notably those by Kamii and DeVries (1976; 1978) and Forman and Hill (1980) have made more extensive use of the theory in providing the very foundations for the educational environment.

Piaget's writing style is notoriously difficult to read; his theory is abstract, complex, and still evolving (all of which make for difficulties in interpretation); and the theory is a theory of normal cognitive development—not a theory of how educational practices may or may not enhance development. It is no wonder that there has been confusion over exactly what the implications for education are. Whatever the implications are, however, they are not a laissez-faire approach to classroom teaching. If we are to have a favorable effect on development, we will need to spend time learning to understand children as well as curriculum material, and we will have to find ways to help children become actively involved in whatever experiences are offered. This is a huge task.

Piaget's theory tells us more than simply that children think differently than adults do. It tells us how their thinking differs and how we can recognize each child's level. It does *not* tell us specifically how we can help. Rather, it gives some suggestions and guidelines, some pointers on how (and when) we can help the child see a need to rebuild and how (and when) to assess the new structure. The use of Piaget's theory won't magically transform teaching from an art to a science. What it will do is to give us better tools with which to practice our art.

One final caution. Once you are acquainted with the theory, you may not want to let it go. Its usefulness and good sense make it an enticing companion. Are you still bent on going? Very well, then, but take these words of advice. The first part will be the hardest. You may find yourself resisting the effort it takes to become acquainted with our elusive theory beast. You may have to retravel the first part of the path several times before the beast is tamed and you and the theory have established a satisfactory relationship. Take heart. A good relationship is worth pursuing.

We have attempted in this book to help you understand the basic principles of Piagetian theory so that you can apply them to your work with children. Chapters 2, 3, and 5 are devoted to this task. Be careful, though! Some of the principles are easily misinterpreted, and have been by a great number of educators. Chapters 4 and 6 are intended to provide a bridge for crossing the gap between theory and practice. Make sure you use this bridge to cross the gap. It is a little narrow and sways a bit in the wind, but it crosses at the right place. If you find yourself wanting to widen and stabilize it, go right ahead. Chapter 10, in fact, provides some of the tools you'll need for this task; the suggested works on Piagetian theory can help you place appropriate supports on the theory side of the bridge. Most of the rest of the chapters supply examples of the theory in practice—the teacher role (Chapter 7), activity ideas (Chapter 8, as well as examples throughout the book), and how to evaluate what you're doing (Chapter 9). Don't neglect to do the Teacher Tasks distributed throughout the chapters. They are questions and exercises that have been the most helpful to us and to teachers we've worked with, in our efforts to understand and apply Piagetian theory in meaningful ways.

To use this book to make a better environment for your children, you will have to add your own creativity, sensitivity, and experience. It won't be easy. The path is largely uphill, and you will not get to the top the same person you were when you started.

P.S. The view is worth it.

## REFERENCES

FORMAN, GEORGE E., and FLEET HILL. *Constructive Play: Applying Piaget in the Preschool* (Monterey, Cal.: Brooks/Cole Publishing Company, 1980).

KAMII, CONSTANCE. "An Application of Piaget's Theory to the Conceptualization of a Preschool Curriculum," in *The Preschool in Action: Exploring Early Childhood Programs,* ed. Ronald K. Parker (Boston: Allyn and Bacon, 1972).

KAMII, CONSTANCE, and RHETA DeVRIES. *Physical Knowledge in Preschool Education: Implications of Piaget's Theory* (Englewood Cliffs, N.J.: Prentice-Hall, Inc., 1978).

KAMII, CONSTANCE, and RHETA DeVRIES. *Piaget, Children, and Number* (Washington, D.C.: National Association for the Education of Young Children, 1976).

LAVATELLI, CELIA S. *Piaget's Theory Applied to an Early Childhood Curriculum* (Boston: American Science and Engineering, 1970).

PIAGET, JEAN. "Piaget's Theory," in *Carmichael's Manual of Child Psychology,* Vol. 1. 3rd ed., ed. Paul H. Mussen (New York: John Wiley and Sons, Inc., 1970).

QUIGLEY, LILLIAN F. *The Blind Men and the Elephant,* illus. Janice Holland (New York: Charles Scribner's Sons, 1959).

WEIKART, DAVID P., LINDA ROGERS, CAROLYN ADCOCK, and DONNA McCLELLAND. *The Cognitively Oriented Curriculum* (Washington, D.C.: National Association for the Education of Young Children, 1971).

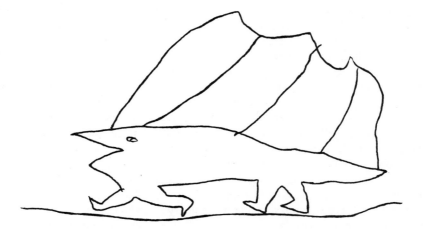

# 2

# THE
# THEORY
# BEAST

## PRELIMINARY REMARKS

Establishing a close relationship with the theory beast is no easy task, but it is absolutely essential if you and the theory are to work well together. There are two major obstacles to overcome in developing a good working relationship. First of all, the theory is a complex creature. Just when you think you've got it all figured out, it reveals another side of its personality, and you've got to revise your expectations. Secondly, it is growing and changing—it is still in its adolescence. Descriptions made of it during its infancy are only partially true of the theory in its present state. The result of all this is that descriptions of the theory vary considerably. The theory knows how to show its best side to onlookers and is sophisticated enough to judge what different onlookers are most likely to appreciate (or be shocked by—the theory beast can be as vain and as mischievous as any human being). Furthermore, some features of the theory were more prominent in its infancy than they are now (and vice versa). Descriptions of it will vary according to when the observer became acquainted with it, why the observer wanted to become acquainted with it, and what previous theories the observer had known before.

Fortunately, in spite of these variations, it is possible for us to identify some of the beast's basic personality traits and physical features. Various descriptions of the theory emphasize different details, but enough of the basic characteristics come through to enable us to identify all the descriptions as being descriptions of the same creature. The characterization of the theory in this chapter undoubtedly reflects the authors' own biases and interests—we do, after all, have a very special reason for making its acquaintance: we want it to work with us in educational settings. We will concentrate, however, on describing the features that have remained with the theory throughout its development from the 1920s to 1980.

Our aim in this chapter is to present a sketch of the theory such that you will be able to draw well-founded implications for education and such that when and if you read Piaget's own works (and those of his close associates), you will have a framework to build upon—something to modify by making qualifying statements here and there, by adding details where appropriate, by stressing now the importance of this principle, now of that one, and so forth. Although the introduction of some technical words is unavoidable, we will try to keep the use of theoretical jargon to a minimum. What we want, after all, is to help you be able to apply the theory intelligently in uncharted territory. Facility with high-sounding theoretical terms won't help you do that.

We will be emphasizing general characteristics of the theory to give you a feel for the overall approach. We have elaborated on particular features, sometimes be-

cause of their relevance for education and sometimes because we feel they are easily misunderstood (or are at least open to a variety of understandings, some of which we feel are more accurate or more fruitful than others).

This chapter will probably be most helpful to you if you first read it through quickly just to get a feel for the theory. Then, with several careful rereadings, question the generalizations that are made, ask yourself how it all fits together, and most importantly, try to put the concepts and explanations into your own words. Here's a Teacher Task for you to think about as you read, but don't worry if you can't do it until you've read through the chapter at least twice.

*TEACHER TASK 2-1*

---

Pick two key concepts from this chapter and explain them to someone who has not read the chapter and is unfamiliar with Piaget's theory. Use words the other person is thoroughly familiar with and really try to make him or her understand what the concept is and why it is important. (This is an important task. We will be making use of the understanding you gain for the Teacher Task presented at the end of this chapter, as well as throughout the rest of the book.)

---

## THE THEORY BEAST: FIRST IMPRESSIONS

In getting acquainted with the theory beast, it will be helpful to look for answers to three general questions. First, what is it about the beast that makes it a theory rather than simply a blow-by-blow description of intellectual development, or perhaps a recipe book for education? Second, what is the theory a theory about? Where are its boundaries? Does it explain human emotions and personality traits as well as intellectual development? And what, if anything, does it say about motivation? Finally, we will want to know the general orientation toward the subject matter of the theory.

### What Makes It a Theory?

As you recall from Chapter 1, we can't be sure of a theory's truth status. In addition, theories are generally ignorant of the practical details needed for application. Our theory is no exception. As you read the rest of the book, watch for concepts that need elaboration, extension, and ties with observable behaviors before being useful to you in your role as a teacher. You'll be the one to make those elaborations and extensions and ties! Also, watch for statements that don't fit with your experience and intuitions. There are aspects of the theory you'll want to test for yourself. They *may* not be true.

One word of caution, though, if you're serious about embarking on the intellectually demanding task of revising and testing the theory. This is no simple task. If you observe behaviors that don't seem to fit with the theory, ask yourself, "Is the theory wrong, or have I misunderstood it?" You'll want to check Piaget's own writings to answer this question. Flavell (1963) will also be a big help. Also, think about whether there have been any factors operating in what you observed that could account for the discrepant results. If you do decide that the theory is wrong, think about what impact the error you discovered has on other principles of the theory. A theory is a cohesive system, after all. A change in one part is likely to have numerous repercussions elsewhere. If the effect of the change you propose is to contradict your experiences relative to other parts of the theory, then maybe there is some error in your observation. If not, maybe you've found a change worth making.

### What Is It a Theory About?

#### *Intelligence*

Fundamentally, Piaget's theory is a theory of intellectual functioning in developing human beings; it is a theory about how we humans think. It attempts to explain both what we do to gain knowledge of the particular facts we claim to know and what we do with the knowledge we have gained. Although our theory concentrates its descriptive and explanatory efforts on intellectual abilities, it does so in order to gain understanding of real, live human beings, creatures with physical capabilities and personality traits as well as intellectual abilities. Our theory of intellectual abilities will have some implications for how we interpret other aspects of human functioning, but, as we have pointed out in Chapter 1, it does not give all the answers. To understand the part played by our particular theory in explaining human functioning as a whole and in understanding the interconnections among different types of functioning, we will have to get a feel for what the different types are.

Psychologists generally speak of three major domains of human functioning: the affective (or socio-emotional) domain, the psychomotor (or physical) domain, and the cognitive (or intellectual) domain. The characterizations that follow are meant to give you a very general idea of these three domains. They are not meant as rigorous definitions.

Generally, the affective domain includes feelings, emotions, moods, and temperament. Such things as self-concept, reactions to success and failure, the way one deals with frustration, the ability to give to others or to receive from them, one's particular interests, and feelings such as anger, fear, joy, sorrow, anxiety, and boredom are all part of the affective side of an individual.

The psychomotor domain includes physical skills, general physical coordination, reaction times, and neuromuscular control over various parts of the body (including control over such things as arm movements, the tiny eye movements involved in ordinary perception, and the movements involved in producing speech sounds). Abilities to move easily through space, to balance, to run, and to hop, as well as eye-hand coordination and muscle strength, are all part of the psychomotor domain.

The cognitive domain will become clearer as we examine it through the eyes of our theory beast, but for now think of it as including such things as the ability to play the twenty-questions game, the knowledge of how to do long division, the understandings and skills needed for reading and writing, the ability to judge relative distances, and the ability to remember stories (or television shows) in sequence.

Now that we have separated these three aspects of human functioning, let's put them back together. Consider three-year-old Jessica, who has decided that she'd like (affective domain) to ride the tricycle that Josh happens to be riding. She runs over to Josh and begins to pull him off (psychomotor domain). Jessica is *not* being deliberately selfish or rude (affective domain). Children of her age, and Jessica is no exception, tend to see things only from their own perspectives (*cognitive* domain). The thought hasn't even entered her mind (cognitive domain) that Josh wants to stay on the tricycle. As far as she's concerned, he is simply an obstacle to her goal of getting herself on the tricycle (cognitive domain). If this incident had taken place when Jessica was ten years old, we would be much more likely to interpret her behaviors as revealing selfishness or rudeness—or perhaps revealing that she was in a bad mood, had a grudge against Josh, and so on.

So, an incident that is frequently interpreted primarily as revealing affective features of an individual turns out to involve all three domains. Furthermore, the interpretations we give to certain of Jessica's behaviors (as revealing that she is being selfish or rude, for example) are influenced by what cognitive abilities we attribute to her.

Since the consideration of the interactions among the three domains is crucial in our applications of theory, let's look at another example. Suppose we see four-year-old Jamie pouring juice into a cup and letting it spill over the top. Is he trying to get attention (affective domain)? Is he having problems with physical coordination (psychomotor domain)? Or is he testing a hypothesis about relationships between containers and volumes of liquids (cognitive domain)? Clearly, what we know about Jamie from our other contacts with him will be important in determining how we interpret this incident. If we know he generally has good fine-motor coordination, we might suspect that he's testing a hypothesis—particularly if his eyes are focused on his own activity and not on teachers or other children.

*TEACHER TASK 2-2*

---

(1) For each interpretation suggested in the example of Jamie, list some hypothetical behaviors or characteristics that would, had you observed them, support the interpretation.

(2)   To experience for yourself the interplay of the different domains, climb up on an eight-foot-high fence, stairway, or box. Now look down and consider jumping off. See if you can separate your intellectual, emotional, and physical responses. Can you experience how your emotional response is influencing your physical response? How about the role played by your intellectual assessment of the task relative to your physical capabilities?

Our theory, being only in its adolescence, generally takes for granted the existence of intimate connections among the three domains. Its occasional halfhearted attempts to specify some of the connections and its faith in the motivational role played by certain cognitive events suggest that in its more mature years, the theory may extend its explanatory efforts to the affective and psychomotor domains. We who apply and test the theory as it is *now*, however, can afford neither to wait for the theory to mature nor to take the existence of connections for granted. We look at physical, emotional beings engaged in thought. There is work ahead for us.

### Development

So far we have discussed one striking feature of our theory—its concern with intellectual functioning, or cognition. There is a second feature, equally important, which now deserves our attention. Our theory is concerned with human beings who grow and develop, who *change* in the way they think. The theory tackles two major problems in development:

(1)   What changes are there in children's ways of thinking and in what they think about as they grow into adults?
(2)   How do the changes occur? What are the mechanisms of change?

In addressing these problems, the theory focuses on universal characteristics of developmental change. That is, the theory tries to discover cognitive changes and mechanisms of cognitive change that are common to every normal human being. In finding these universal features, the theory has had to take individual differences into account. It has had to recognize, for example, that although Carl's favorite toy is a set of keys and Eric's is a plastic fish, each of these infants is able to recognize a toy (so long as it is his own favorite toy) when it is partially hidden under a cloth. The theory has had to adjust for individual differences in such a way that its principles are general enough to apply to all normal human beings, in spite of their differences. In so doing, it has also had to dispense with precise measures of chronological age as fail-proof indicators of how one thinks. In the search for generalizations, the theory has been forced to conclude that although every human being goes through the same changes in the same sequence and as a result of the same mechanisms, the time it takes to go through the change varies from one individual to the next.

Notice that the theory does not address itself to the question of *how much* intelligence a person has. Instead, it focuses on *what kind* of intelligence someone has. Two children of the same age can simultaneously make one of the developmental changes our theory describes, yet one child will be viewed as the more intelligent by her friends and teachers. There may be explanations for such differences lurking somewhere deep in the theory, but so far, they have not shown themselves.

What about the implications of these features of our theory? Perhaps the most striking implication is that we who wish to make use of the theory are left with an enormous task. It is all very well for the theory to ignore individual differences for the sake of obtaining universal generalizations, but for those of us who wish to apply the theory, knowledge of individual differences and how they relate to the general principles is crucial. As users of the theory, we will want to be very sensitive to those individual differences and to consider them carefully as we try to fit theoretical generalizations to specific cases, each slightly (but importantly) different from the other. This is a good issue to keep in the back of your mind as you read and think about the rest of the book.

> *In the process of application something more than the theory is always involved. Thus, one does not move directly from astronomy to navigation without concern for tides, prevailing winds, and the location of lighthouses . . .*
>
> *Hilgard, 1964, p. 402*

## GENERAL THEORETICAL ORIENTATION

### Biological Foundations

So far we have claimed that the theory itself is constantly changing and developing; that the theory's primary concern is and has always been in the intellectual functioning of human beings; and that the theory is concerned with developmental changes in intellectual functioning. In this section we will be looking especially hard at the theory's general orientation toward these concerns.

Because our theory beast was raised and educated by a man who showed early interests in biology and philosophy (many of Piaget's earliest publications—about twenty-five of them—were on mollusks, and he very nearly completed a doctorate in philosophy as well as in psychology), it is not surprising that the theory draws heavily on biological explanations and concepts in interpreting philosophically and psychologically significant aspects of intelligence. The theory's background shows up in two central characteristics that have been part of the theory all through its life. These are:

(1)   Its description of *qualitatively distinct stages* of human intelligence; and
(2)   Its *interactionist explanation of changes* in the way humans think.

Both of these characteristics reflect the biological concepts with which the theory was raised. The first reflects the biologist's interest in, and acceptance of, both continuities and discontinuities in development. Modern genetics, for example, while acknowledging the discontinuity between a human infant and its parents (the infant is a distinct individual), points to a continuity in genetic material (the infant starts life with chromosomes from both of its parents). A somewhat similar story can be told for a caterpillar that becomes a pupa and then a butterfly. There is continuity, in that a single individual has undergone the changes, yet the overt forms are so different as to make one almost doubt the underlying continuity. The changes in shape are not best described in terms of continuous change, such as longer here, wider there. Rather, what seems to have taken place is a total reorganization. The butterfly has the same genetic material as the caterpillar, and, like the caterpillar, it has to adjust to an external environment—to move, to eat, to maintain the functioning of its cells—but it is totally different in form (or structure) and in the specific behaviors it uses to meet its needs.

The second central characteristic of our theory reflects the biologist's interest in the process of *adaptation* and its outcomes. Most living organisms look very different at the beginning of their lives than they do at later points. Furthermore, the way they look is influenced by their environment. Tadpoles never grow into elephants by being taken out of the pond and placed on a grassy plain in Africa, but variations in size and strength in mature frogs depend in part on the quality and quantity of food they've eaten, the amount of sunlight that has reached the pond, and so forth.

As an example of the part adaptation plays in developing organisms, consider maple trees. Young maple seedlings start out with soft, flexible stems and delicate green leaves spread out under the dense shade of their parent plants. The dense shade is just what they need to lengthen their stems and develop some woody tissue. (Less fortunate seedlings that have sprouted in strong sunlight have a rough go of it; they may not even manage to survive.) As the shaded seedlings respond to their favorable environment, their character changes. Their stems grow into solid tree trunks, and their leaves begin to toughen and become a stronger green. As this happens, they simultaneously find room for their own highest branches, with their tender growing tips, in the bright sunlight their parents inhabit. Though they will make even further adaptations to the intense sunlight they are now exposed to (by adjusting the size of tiny openings on their leaves, for example), they are ready for the new demands. They are prepared to take the appropriate actions in response to the challenge. Some of these changes, such as the elongation of the stem, would occur even in unfavorable environments. Others, such as the darkening of the leaf color and the adjustment of the leaf openings, occur only in response to the environment—and only when the plant is developmentally ready to respond in that fashion to the environmental demands.

Our maple-tree story is one of constant interaction between a developing organism and its environment. Our young seedling has been so constituted as to grow well in dense shade and not in strong sunlight. Yet it had to be developing in such a way as to be prepared to survive in bright sunlight when it outgrew the shade its parents had provided. This is the kind of relationship Piaget has in mind when he speaks of developmental changes being the result of the interaction between maturational (or hereditary) factors and environmental (or experiential) factors. Neither factor is more important than the other. Both are essential. The problem for the theory is to specify the nature of the interaction.

Perhaps you are convinced that qualitative change and adaptation are useful notions when applied to biological processes. But why, you may wonder, should we transport these notions into psychology? After all, the claim that there are qualitatively distinct levels of human thinking is a strong one, and it certainly does not enjoy universal agreement among psychologists. Many people are willing to go along with developmental differences in *how much* individuals know as they grow older, but they resist the idea that there are differences in the very system they use for thinking and acquiring knowledge. Yet Piaget has insisted on the latter. To see why our theory stands firm on this issue, let's look at some ways in which psychological development is analogous to biological development.

### From Biology to Psychology

Suppose that we do decide to transport the biological notions. What kinds of things will correspond to the organizational changes the caterpillars went through? What kinds of *psychological* adaptation is there? And, apart from the person doing the thinking, what exactly is it that stays the same throughout the qualitative cognitive changes? Our theory provides some answers to these questions, but to see why they arise in the first place, let's see why Piaget might have found the idea of stages so appealing in describing cognitive development.

Take a look at Sarah at six months of age and again when she is nine years old. There is something shared in the two glimpses we have of her. She has always been an alert, active child. And notice how persistent she is in trying to reach that teething ring at age six months. At nine years of age she's just as persistent in her attempts to figure out why she can't get her hand out of the cookie jar, when she so easily slid it in.

There's much in common, but there's also a considerable difference in Sarah at the two different ages. In fact, six-month-old Sarah is, in many ways, more similar to her six-and-a-half-month-old cousin, Susy, than she is to herself eight and a half years later. The infants, Susy and Sarah, both quickly lose interest in toys when the toys are completely hidden; both immediately put in their mouths any object they can grasp (and both try to grasp everything they see); and both try to prolong interesting sights (Sarah has learned to make noise by shaking a rattle and tries shaking movements to make other sounds, such as her mother's voice, continue. Susy has learned to pull a ring attached to a mobile hanging over her crib to make one of the clowns visible to her, and she tries the pulling motion to make other sights, such as her father's face, linger in her view).

There is something shared by all of Sarah and Susy's behaviors at six months of age that is not found in the behaviors of nine-year-old Sarah. That unspecified something seems to characterize six-month-old Sarah's general approach to her environment, both her attempts to respond to it and her efforts to make sense of it. Is it just that at six months, Sarah knows many fewer facts about the world than she does eight and a half years later? Surely that isn't enough to explain the fundamental difference we see in the way Sarah gets her mother to satisfy her needs for food at the two different ages. When six-month-old Sarah wants Mommy to bring food, she cries that special I-want-food cry. If the accumulation of facts and knowledge of the English language were the important variables responsible for the difference in Sarah's behavior at nine years of age, we'd expect the cry to give way to the plea, "Please, Mom, give me some cookies." Instead, the older Sarah waltzes into the living room, compliments her mother on the blouse she is wearing, mentions how envious her school friends were of the delicious cookies that were packed in her lunch today, and finally suggests that if her mother would like to join her in an afternoon tea party—with real tea cakes—she'd be delighted to set the table.

There are continuities, of course. Both Sarahs found a way to communicate a specific want when the object required for satisfying the want was not around. Both would have tried again—with variations—had their initial efforts failed. Both adjust their behaviors according to the specific situation. The infant Sarah, for example, cries loudly or softly depending on whether or not her mother is in sight. The child Sarah goes directly to her mother and then adjusts her behaviors according to the way her mother responds to her.

Piaget's careful observations of behavior and his ingenuity in devising situations for eliciting different types of behavior have revealed even more startling differences in the behaviors of children at different ages—differences even the most hard-core learning theorist can't ignore. Nearly everyone who has looked carefully for the behavioral differences Piaget described, has found them. The problem comes in interpreting and explaining the evidence. The theory has to account for both the continuities and the differences in the sets of behaviors. To do so it has distinguished three components of intelligence: content, function, and structure. An understanding of the differences, which Piaget has taken great pains to specify, is essential in understanding what kind of stages we are talking about and why they are so important to those who wish to apply Piaget's theory.

### Content, Function, and Structure

Think of yourself as a dedicated child-watcher. You see children moving and behaving in all sorts of ways—running, talking, learning to read, lifting blocks, dipping brushes in paints, working puzzles, and so forth. The actual behaviors you see form the *content* of intelligent action. Differences in behaviors constitute differences in content. In our earlier example, Sarah's shaking motion is different in content from Susy's pulling motions, though both motions may be interpreted as achieving similar goals and as reflecting similar understandings. Sarah's I-want-food cries are different in content from Sarah's tea-party suggesion, though both are used to get food.

The second thing you'll notice in your child-watching frame of mind is that children often modify and refine their behaviors. Any intelligent action is characterized by the constant adjustment of behaviors in response to environmental contingencies. An infant reaching out to grasp a parent's finger adjusts the stretch of its arm according to the distance between it and the finger. A twelve-year-old adjusts the amount of her teasing according to her assessment of her teacher's mood. This characteristic of intelligent action reveals the *function* of intelligence—what intelligence does. It is this universal component of intelligent activity that Piaget claims is responsible for the development of qualitatively different organizations of mental activity. The functional component, the process for continual adaptation to an ever-changing environment, is a permanent characteristic of intelligence at all the different stages. Yet its operation is what leads to the major reorganization in structure, the third component of intelligence. (We'll be getting back to this notion of function later in this chapter, when we explore in some detail the mechanisms for change.)

*Structures* are the organizational properties of intelligent actions. They are the patterns or rules of thought that are responsible for the behavioral content we child-watchers observe. We can't see the structures, and since none of us is directly aware of our own structures of thought, we can hardly expect children to describe their structures to us. We infer the existence of organizational properties in order to account for underlying similarities in behavior at given points in the life-span.

The notion of content, as our theory makes use of it, is fairly straightforward. Its relation to function and structure, however, gets fairly intricate. We'll be exploring that relationship throughout the book wherever we make connections between what we see children doing (content) and what we can infer about how the child is thinking (structure and function) and whenever we consider what cognitive outcomes are likely (structure and function) when we engage children in various activities (content). The notions of structure and function, however, warrant some more elaborate explanation. Structure plays a particularly strong role in the notion of qualitatively distinct stages, a topic we'll take up in the next section. Function is most important in explanations of developmental change; it will be further explored in the last section of this chapter, where we will look at mechanisms of change.

## THE NOTION OF STAGES

### The Differences Among the Stages

Our theory has claimed that there are distinct stages in intellectual development and that each stage is characterized by a distinct organization (or structure) that underlies observable features of intelligent action. Each stage, our theory tells us, is characterized by a specific way of thinking, of acquiring and using information about the world. In fact, Piaget (1971a, p. 3) has said that "every time we use the term intelligence, which has no meaning on its own, we shall need to define what level of development we are talking about. . . ." The levels he has in mind for human beings are the following three stages, briefly characterized:

(1) *The Sensorimotor Stage*—thinking with actions. At this stage, to think about previous experiences is to replay the actions one performed during that experience. To think about the future *is* to perform the actions one will be performing later on. To think about an object *is* to act the way one acts when in contact with that object. Most children in this stage of intellectual development are between the ages of birth and two years.

(2) *The Concrete Operations Stage*—thinking with organized mental procedures, called operations, and applying these procedures to what one is presently experiencing or to what one has already experienced (and remembers). At this stage, children have transformed (or *interiorized,* in Piaget's term) their physical actions into mental operations. In the transformation process, they have extended their repertoire of procedures and have reorganized their capabilities. In addition, they have developed the ability to use words and images and can now use their mental operations on such mental symbols. Many children aged seven to eleven years are in this stage.

(3) *The Formal Operations Stage*—thinking with sophisticated mental procedures (operations) and applying them to abstract notions. At this stage, children, or adults, can apply their system of thought to mere possibilities (to what might be) as well as to actual events and experiences (to what is or was). They can even think about their own thought. Their ways of thinking are organized in a way described by Piaget as isomorphic to the groups and lattices of logical algebra. Some children move into this stage at about eleven years of age. Others are sixteen or older.

In the foregoing descriptions, brief and oversimplified as they are, you may have noticed two kinds of differences among the stages. In the shift from Stage 1 to Stage 2, overt actions have been transformed (interiorized) into mental actions (operations). In the shift from Stage 1 to 2 *and* in the shift from Stage 2 to 3, there have been reorganizations of previous ways of thinking. These reorganizations occur through a process Piaget calls *reflective abstraction.* The nature of this process reveals some of the important distinctions among the different stages. Basically, the process is a *nonrandom* procedure, which *coordinates* both physical actions and mental operations (the latter being in large part nothing more than previously established coordinations of actions) in such a way that previous structures (or organizations) are *integrated* into the more elaborate structures that characterize the later stages (see Piaget, 1971a, p. 320, and pp. 2-13).

There is some danger here of being misled by the choice of terminology and by Piaget's emphasis on children's active role in their own cognitive development. One might be tempted to think that the changes are consciously made. This is not so. What Piaget is describing is the amazing amount of organization that exists without our being aware of it. The nature of the different stages and the processes for developmental change are not open to introspection. They have to be inferred from the behaviors we see, both our own behaviors and the behaviors of others. The word "reflective" in "reflective abstraction" is used to indicate the nonrandomness of the procedure—*not* to suggest that we can be directly aware of the process.

In our description of the levels of intellectual development, we have left out many important details, in order to highlight the qualitative differences among the stages. We'll be examining some of the important qualifications to be added to these descriptions in Chapter 5, where we take a long, hard look at the lengthy transitional period between the sensorimotor stage and the concrete operations stage. This transitional period is generally called the preoperational period and is occasionally even referred to as a stage in its own right. Because it is transitional, we'll be looking closely at the descriptions of the stages on either side of it. The formal operations stage will get short shrift in this book, since we are devoting our energies to the preoperational child. However, there is some fascinating work done on this last, ultimate stage of intellectual development. If you are interested, you might want to look at some of the references listed at the end of the chapter.

### The Similarities Among the Stages

In this chapter we will address general stage characteristics. We will want to know what it is about any stage that makes it a distinct stage rather than a transitional period or part of another stage. We will also want to know about any features of the stages that might influence our use of the notion in education.

In identifying stages, our theory has always kept two criteria in mind. First, the inferred organization underlying behaviors counts as a stage only if the organization has a certain form. It must constitute an integrated whole characterized by structural properties. There must be no loose ends, so to speak—no rules for thinking that are independent of the rest of the system. Piaget calls such an integrated system a "structure d'ensemble." Second, the organized wholes must appear in an invariant sequence. All human beings, regardless of their cultural backgrounds or individual experiences, must be in the sensorimotor stage before they are in the concrete operations stage, and in the latter before they are in the formal operations stage. This feature of the stages has been well borne out by cross-cultural studies, which, though they find differences in the ages at which each stage is reached, nearly always find the same developmental sequence (see Modgil and Modgil, 1976).

Our theory has not been content with simply identifying these stages, however. The reason for searching them out in the first place was to help explain the remarkable changes in the intellectual life of human beings as they grow from helpless infants into sophisticated adults. The stages are interesting if they are described in enough detail to be useful in helping us interpret and influence children's cognitive development. There are three additional features common to all the stages that are helpful for us to know. The stages are *hierarchical,* they involve both a *period of formation* and a *period of attainment,* and they are characterized by something called *décalages.*

The stages are hierarchical in the sense that the structures of earlier stages become integrated into the structures of later ones. Much of the sensorimotor infant's use of physical movements as a way of thinking remains a possibility for children at the concrete operations stage and even for adults in the formal operations stage. It is a good thing that this is so. Driving a car, for example, may involve sensorimotor intelligence in the use of the clutch, the use of concrete operations in judging whether or not to go through the intersection when the light is yellow, and the use of formal operations in driving defensively to avoid possible accidents.

This feature of cognitive development, that later stages incorporate the structures of earlier ones, suggests that not only is there continuity in the transitions from one stage to the next, but also that there is a reasonableness about the change. Piaget views the stages as a series of successive approximations toward an internal organization that matches an external one—the latter being the logico-mathematical structures described by mathematicians. The organization at each stage contains transformation rules, which, in combination with the appropriate experiences and environmental demands, will result in a new level of organization (integrating the previous level, of course).

The process of organizational change is a long and laborious one, which requires considerable experience with the external environment. The result is that each stage involves a lengthy formation period as well as a period of attainment. Remember our analogy to the construction of a house in Chapter 1? The period of formation corresponds to the busy arranging and rearranging of the picture window, the tower, and the stairway. The period of attainment corresponds to the pauses made to admire one's handiwork or to peer out at the new views offered by new windows. The new views, of course, stimulate new remodeling efforts. It is the combination of what's outside the house and how the house is built (especially the location of its windows) that leads to further remodeling.

The lengthy formation period for each stage often reveals itself through what are called *décalages,* or, literally translated, uncouplings. One might expect the *structure d'ensemble* to reveal itself all at once. After all, didn't we say that the structures had to be tightly integrated, with no loose ends? In this case, our expectations are not fulfilled. It turns out that even with a tightly knit structure, specific information and practice in a specific content area are required for the structural properties to be applied to that area. A child who realizes that the amount of water doesn't change when water is transferred from one container to another may not yet realize that the weight of the water will also stay the same. The same kinds of mental operations are required for each realization, but children do not apply their operational abilities to both problems simultaneously. This lack of simultaneity in the application of abilities to different content areas, this absence of couplings among content areas, is referred to as *horizontal décalage*—"horizontal" because the applications are all at one level of organization (at one stage); *"décalage"* because what we might expect to be one unified application of structure turns out to be disconnected applications, each content area uncoupled from the next.

Whenever our different amounts of experience with various content areas results in these horizontal *décalages,* the organizational tendencies of our thought work to bring the applications of the structure into a balance. Thus horizontal *décalages* can be evened out throughout the period of attainment—they can, that is, if the appropriate experiences are provided.

(If the discussion so far hasn't sent thoughts of educational implications whizzing through your head, this is probably a good time for you to take a break. Play a game of tennis or listen to some music for a while. You've been reading some heavy stuff and your brain may need a change of pace. It takes time and patience to tame the theory beast—and sometimes the time required is time away from the theory. When you come back to reread this section, you'll likely be ready to think through some of the implications.)

Before we leave our discussion of stages, let's look at a second kind of *décalage,* the vertical kind. In this kind of uncoupling, sophisticated thought within a specific content area is uncoupled from less sophisticated thought in the same area. We'll adapt one of Flavell's (1963) examples to illustrate this notion. Davy, a twenty-month-old infant, can find his way around the house, intelligently adjusting his path to avoid the blocks left in the center of the room this morning or to find the newspapers that were on the couch but are now on the table. Even with all this expertise in handling complex spatial relations, however, Davy cannot make sense of maps or diagrams of the space he knows so well. When he reaches the stage of concrete operations, however, he can deal with the same content in a totally new way. He can read and draw maps. He can deal with that content on the plane of thought as well as on the plane of action. Does this tell you something about classroom goals and objectives for particular content areas? It should!

The Teacher Task below will help you assess how your relationship with the theory is progressing. As you do the task, remember the key features for the stages we've been discussing:

organization (or structure) and integrated wholes
invariant sequence of stages
hierarchical integration of structures from previous stages
formation and attainment periods
horizontal and vertical *décalages*

*TEACHER TASK 2-3*

The stage notion has some important implications for education. Think of at least two and explain to someone how your suggestions follow from the theory.

Hint: Avoid such pitfalls as thinking that because there is an invariant sequence of development, educators don't have to worry about developmental change. They do have to concern themselves with it—the question is, in what way?

## MECHANISMS OF DEVELOPMENT

Our observations of human behavior suggest distinct organizational changes in intelligence. How is it, then, that human beings move from one level of organization to another? Piaget's answer is that we *construct* the new systems of thought. At the heart of his account of the construction process is the notion of function. As we saw earlier, the function of intelligence is what intelligence does. What it does is to regulate actions so that they adjust for subtle differences in the ever-fluctuating demands of the environment. Somehow, says our theory, this constant adjustment can result in major organizational changes. Let's see how this works.

We'll be looking at three key concepts: organization, adaptation, and equilibration. Let's look at them first at given points in development. An infant's responses to its environment reflect an underlying organization, or way of thinking about the world. Given that organization, however, the infant is constantly required to adapt to new input from the outside world. Toby, an infant who knows how to suck a nipple, is presented with a rattle. He uses his sucking know-how to explore the rattle. That is, he *assimilates* the rattle to his sucking abilities. Since the rattle is different in shape and size from the nipple he is used to, however, he has to adjust, or *accommodate,* his sucking action to the new size and shape. A four-year-old has a different mental organization than the infant but is still required to adapt to the world. Four-year-old Natalie who knows that daddies can cook breakfast, mow the lawn, and take children to the zoo sees her father paddling a canoe. To make sense of what she sees, she has to *assimilate* her observation of the man in the canoe to her notions of what daddies are and what they can do. Since she has never seen this particular behavior before, her notion of what daddies can do does not include canoeing. She has to change her notion by expanding it to include a new fact about daddies. This is the way she *accommodates* to what she sees. The two processes of assimilation and accommodation are part of every adaptive response to the environment.

*TEACHER TASK 2-4*

> Find someone to do this task with you. Place a cup, book, or whatever object you wish, on an empty table. Now pull up a chair and sit down so that you can reach out and pick up the object. Reach out several times, so that you are used to how far you have to reach and what movements your hands and fingers make in grasping the object. Now close your eyes and ask your partner to substitute a new object in place of the first one. Keeping your eyes closed, reach out and pick up the new object. Notice the adjustments you have to make in picking up the new object.
>
> If you have trouble experiencing the adjustments you have to make, try this activity with a variety of new objects, some similar to the first, some very different in size, shape, and/or texture. You might also want to try slight variations in the position of the new objects.

These two processes, however, are not always in perfect balance. Sometimes, as in flights of fancy, assimilation is dominant—that beat-up chair can be assimilated to any notion you wish, from a test pilot's cockpit to a bear's cave. At other times, as in efforts at precise imitation, accommodation holds sway. In such cases, one attempts to match one's behaviors to an external model with a minimum of creative interpretation. By themselves, neither pure fantasy nor rigid imitation are adaptive. A balance between the two must be maintained if a human being is to be able to engage in intelligent encounters with the environment. The process for maintaining the balance is called *equilibration.*

For an individual who has a given level of mental organization and who is engaged in a particular kind of behavior (such as stacking various toys), the process of equilibration helps maintain the balance required for intelligent interactions with the world. As its name suggests, it serves to bring the living, thinking system into equilibrium with its immediate environment. It does this by balancing the processes of assimilation and accommodation. Because developing human beings, unlike simple thermostats (whose functioning also depends on equilibration processes), must find equilibria at higher and higher levels of organization, the equilibration process has two other jobs to do. It ensures interactions among subsystems of thought (or schemata) at any given stage, so that eventually the horizontal *décalages* are evened out, and it provides a balance between the processes of differentiation and integration that lead to organizational change. The three applications of the equilibration process work together to enable intelligence to function in its usual way throughout development. That is, they enable our intelligence to help us *adapt* to the environment.

Don't be troubled at finding this notion of equilibration hard to understand. You are not alone. American psychologists have been particularly puzzled by this concept, and though it has been a central one for our theory beast throughout its life, it is only in Piaget's later works (particularly *Biology and Knowledge* [1971] and *The Development of Thought: Equilibration of Cognitive Structures* [1977]) that he has offered explicit characterizations of it. You're on the right track if you think of it basically as a balancing process that operates on three different kinds of things. It balances the assimilation and accommodation processes that go on whenever an individual interacts intelligently with the environment and so adapts to it. It balances the internal subsystems within any given organizational level (or stage) so that advances in basic understandings gained within a specific content area are eventually applied to other content areas (remember the horizontal *décalage*). And it balances the different kinds of relationships that can tie subsystems (schemata) together in an integrated whole (a *structure d'ensemble*) or break them apart in preparation for a new level of organization. Some people (for instance, Langer, 1969; Turiel, 1969 and 1974; Strauss, 1972, and even Piaget, 1977, p. 18) have found it helpful to think of the first kind of equilibration as external equilibration, since it involves the relation of the internal (mental) organization to the external environment. The second two kinds are then viewed as internal equilibration, since they involve the relations among internal mental processes and organizations.

Another way to think of these three balancing acts is to note that the first two are closely tied to within-stage modifications—to refinements and elaborations of intelligence at a particular level of organization. The third is more directly related to the transition from one stage to the next. However, all three are constant companions of cognitive activity. In fact, although our theory describes distinct stages of intellectual development, it views each stage as a dynamic organization of mental activity—*not* as a resting place where a child can spend a few years recuperating from the exhausting, but ultimately successful, struggle to escape from the preceding stage. As Inhelder, a close associate of Piaget's for many years, has emphasized (1956), each qualitatively distinct level of organization constitutes *at the same time* both the attainment of one stage and the starting point for the next. Or, as Piaget (1970, p. 140) puts it, "There is no structure apart from construction." What constitutes a good balance will vary somewhat from stage to stage, and sometimes a good balance between subsystems will be sacrificed for the sake of adapting to specific environmental demands, but both adaptation—the tendency to adjust thoughts and behaviors to the demands of the environment—and the push toward internal organization are always present. In fact, the tendencies toward adaptation and organization are often called the functional invariants in Piaget's system (see Flavell, 1963; Ginsburg and Opper, 1969).

TEACHER TASK 2-5

Before going on to the next section, check your understanding with the following questions.

(1) How are the concepts of assimilation and accommodation related to each of these other concepts: adaptation, organization, equilibration, and structure?

(2) Think of an example of a horizontal *décalage*. Tell it to someone else who has read this chapter and see if that person agrees that it is an appropriate example.

## THE IMPETUS FOR CHANGE

Apart from simply existing as general tendencies, the two functional invariants, adaptation and organization, play an important motivational role in cognitive development. The tendency for a structure (schema) to assimilate anything and everything it can and the push toward an internal organization are the driving forces behind each individual's construction of knowledge, both within and across stages. According to our theory, it is in the nature of structures (or schemata) to be active, to do what they are capable of doing. When a schema cannot act (that is, when there are no relevant behaviors for it to govern), the individual feels an intellectual need. One is motivated either to search for objects in the external world that can be assimilated to the schemata or to modify the schemata so that they can guide intelligent interactions with whatever happens to be available. One is in a state of *dis*equilibrium.

If the appropriate objects are inaccessible, the individual attempts to meet the need by accommodating the schemata to whatever is around. When the accommodation required is not too great and the equilibration process can maintain a reasonable balance between assimilation and accommodation, this results in cognitive growth, in a healthy modification of the schemata. When the amount of modification required is excessive, however, the scales may tip so strongly in the direction of accommodation that the individual resorts to pure imitation and rote learning to resolve the intellectual need.

The danger of resolving the need (or reestablishing equilibrium) in this way is that the schema may substitute quantity for quality. It's like using masking tape to repair a broken water hose in your automobile engine. You hope that the tape will last until you get to the service station a mile down the road, but when you get there, the tape will have to be removed and more permanent repair work done. Makeshift adjustments in a schema, too, may have to be totally redone in a more favorable setting. Woe to those who take the makeshift job for high-quality repair; they are likely to find themselves in a worse position than before—ten miles from the nearest service station and completely out of masking tape.

There is danger in the other direction, too. The individual may meet an intellectual need with an excess of assimilation. In order to assimilate recalcitrant objects, a schema that can see no way to make repairs on itself may distort what it comes in contact with so much that it loses touch with reality. If no objects are available to be assimilated (when one is asleep or when one is subject to extreme sensory deprivation, for example), one may resort to creating objects for the schema to assimilate. Signs of such activity are dreams and waking hallucinations.

It is not totally maladaptive to have the balance tipped toward assimilation, of course. Dreaming is a perfectly normal activity. So is make-believe and daydreaming. It may be that schemata just need more objects to assimilate than the normal environment can supply. But too much emphasis on assimilation, too often, can prevent one from learning to cope effectively with the environment. There are times for fantasy, and there are times for meeting reality head on.

When the assimilation process is directed toward objects in the *external* environment, it is a powerful force in developmental change. At all levels of development, our interests are influenced by what we are able to assimilate. So long as equilibration is doing its job, when we pursue our interests, we find ourselves making the very accommodations that allow us to extend and change those very interests. The resulting horizontal *décalages* bring the equilibration processes again into play. In reestablishing a balance among the subsystems, the equilibration process may uncover contradictions in the system as a whole. When this happens, the tendency toward organization works again through (you guessed it!) the equilibration process. In the last case, the result is a reorganization of the whole system.

So why don't we just go on reorganizing forever? Why do we stop at the formal operations stage? The answer is not a simple one. Our theory beast tells us to look at both the internal and the external factors that interact to promote developmental advances. (These are described by Piaget in a number of works—for instance, 1956 pp. 2–11; 1964; 1971b, pp. 33–47; and 1973, pp. 27–30.) The internal factors are *maturation* and, our old favorite, *equilibration*. The external factors are *social transmission* and *experience*.

If maturation were the only factor involved, we'd already have an answer of sorts. Just as any living organism reaches a stage of physical maturity, a level of maximal physiological organization, after which all organizational changes are in the direction of disintegration (and eventually death), so, by analogy, intelligence reaches its level of organizational maturity (generally fairly long-lasting) and then disintegrates. According to our theory, though, maturation alone isn't even enough to explain development up through the stage of formal operations; it can hardly be the sole reason for our stopping there. Equilibration (and its companions, organization and adaptation) brought up the question in the first place; the answer isn't there. Is it, then, just that the societies we grow up in are still so primitive that they don't teach us what we need to know in order to move to higher stages? Do we suffer from a lack of the appropriate kinds of experiences? Or do we stay at the stage of formal operations because that level of intelligence accurately reflects the nature of the world (or is the best possible way for creatures like ourselves to survive in the world)?

If you're beginning to get into the spirit of the theory, you'll be inclined to say that the answer must lie in the interaction of all four factors. The theory beast has always seemed to mumble when we posed that question to it, but as far as we can make out, you're right. Piaget seemed to feel that our cognitive structures correspond to something that actually exists in the external world—to logico-mathematical structures. Is it possible, though, that there are higher-level structures existing in the world that we have not yet constructed for ourselves, because of biological limitations and/or lack of experience? Our theory doesn't seem to deny the possibility, but, as it points out, we have no evidence for the existence of any such structures.

Piaget has claimed that mental organization at the formal operations level is stable. It is free from internal contradictions and has flexible relations established among the subsystems. Because the organization is so well suited to the environment, it is also permanent. The structure can be applied to a variety of different content areas without requiring any organizational change. Assimilation and accommodation continue to occur, of course, as do the three kinds of equilibration. Their functioning helps in the application of the organization to different content areas but does not lead to organizational change—there being, presumably, no better organization to construct (see Piaget, 1971a, p. 356; Piaget, 1950).

If a belief in the possibility of better organizations inspires you to think harder and to seek out intellectually stimulating encounters with your environment, go ahead and believe in them. If not, you needn't bother. The important thing is to recognize the interaction of the four factors in development and to realize that even at the formal operations stage, there is much for all adults to learn in applying to new content areas the cognitive structures they have.

## SUMMARY

In this chapter, you have been introduced to a theory of the origins of knowledge and the development of intelligence, a theory with evident biological leanings. We have stressed that our theory describes *qualitative* changes (or stages) in intellectual development and that it offers several basic mechanisms to explain developmental change. The three stages—sensorimotor intelligence, concrete operations, and formal operations (and the important preoperational period)—arise as each individual interacts with the environment to construct his or her own knowledge.

The construction of knowledge is perpetrated by two tendencies present throughout development. These are the tendency toward adaptation and the tendency toward organization. We distinguished three components of intelligent actions to see how these tendencies were exemplified in behavior. We said that in Piaget's theory, content refers to the actual behaviors or task being performed; function refers to the adjustment of behaviors in response to fluctuating environmental demands; and structure refers to the properties of the mental organization that is responsible for the behaviors and the kinds of adjustments made. Finally, the tendency to adapt, to make adjustments in response to environmental contingencies, and the tendency to organize one's mental procedures into coherent systems are regulated by a sort of balancing process called equilibration.

A number of new words have been introduced in this chapter. It is important to understand and be able to explain in ordinary language the following terms:

> accommodation
> adaptation
> assimilation
> content, function, and structure
> construction of knowledge
> *décalage* (horizontal and vertical)
> domains of psychological functioning—cognitive, affective, and psychomotor
> equilibration
> organization
> schema (plural: schemata)
> stage
> *structure d'ensemble*

No formal definitions of these terms have been given. In assessing your understanding, what is important is to get a grasp on the kinds of things the words refer to and how those things are related to one another.

In our description of the theory, we have tried to help you avoid some common misconceptions about its nature and have asked you, as you made its acquaintance, to think about the work you and the theory will be doing together. If you understand the terms just listed and feel comfortable with the theory so far, you are ready to tackle the Teacher Task we promised at the beginning of the chapter. Here it is.

**TEACHER TASK 2-6**

---

Suppose the theory is true—or close to the truth. What does it mean for education? To answer this question:

(1) Make a list of educational principles derived from and/or consonant with the theory as you understand it so far. Some of the principles may be ones you've adhered to all along; others may be new to you.

(2) For each of the principles in your list, describe its implications for classroom organization and for interactions with children—in the school *you presently work in* or have access to. (The aim here is to make the theory work for *you*. Hence your descriptions can be expressly tailored to *your* classroom.)

---

(3) Compare your list of principles with someone else's list. Where you disagree on general principles, try to come to some agreement about which principles should be added to or dropped from each list. Use your understanding of the theory to argue for your view. (And use your unresolved disputes to guide your further study of the theory!)

(4) Do for your descriptions of implications what you did for your list of principles. This should help clarify what the principles really mean (helping you to understand the theory more fully), and will very likely stimulate new ideas for how to implement the principles.

## REFERENCES

FLAVELL, JOHN. *The Developmental Psychology of Jean Piaget* (New York: D. Van Nostrand Company, 1963).

GINSBURG, HERBERT, and SYLVIA OPPER. *Piaget's Theory of Intellectual Development: An Introduction* (Englewood Cliffs, N.J.: Prentice-Hall, 1969).

HILGARD, ERNEST R. "A Perspective on the Relationship Between Learning Theory and Educational Practices," in *Theories of Learning and Instruction,* 63rd Yearbook of the National Society for the Study of Education, Part I, ed. Ernest R. Hilgard (Chicago: NSSE, 1964, p. 402).

INHELDER, BÄRBEL. "Criteria of The Stages of Mental Development," in *Discussions on Child Development, (Volume 1): The First Meeting of the World Health Organization Study Group on the Psychobiological Development of the Child, Geneva, 1953,* ed. James M. Tanner and Bärbel Inhelder (London: Tavistock Publications, 1956).

LANGER, JONAS. "Disequilibrium as a Source of Development," in *Trends and Issues in Developmental Psychology,* ed. Paul H. Mussen, Jonas Langer, and M. Covington (New York: Holt, Rinehart & Winston, 1969).

MODGIL, SOHAN, and CELIA MODGIL. *Piagetian Research: Compilation and Commentary, Volume 8: Cross Cultural Studies* (Windsor, England: NFER Publishing Company, Ltd., 1976).

PIAGET, JEAN. *Biology and Knowledge,* trans. Beatrix Walsh (Chicago: The University of Chicago Press, 1971(a) [first published in French, in 1967, under the title, *Biologie et Connaissance*]).

PIAGET, JEAN. *The Child and Reality: Problems of Genetic Psychology,* trans. Arnold Rosin (New York: Grossman Publishers, 1973 [first published in French, in 1972, under the title, *Problèmes de Psychologie Génétique*]).

PIAGET, JEAN. *The Development of Thought: Equilibration of Cognitive Structures,* trans. Arnold Rosin (New York: Viking Press, 1977 [first published in French, in 1975, under the title, *L'Équilibration des Structures Cognitives: Problème Central du Développement*]).

PIAGET, JEAN. "Development and Learning," in *Piaget Rediscovered,* ed. Richard E. Ripple and Verne N. Rockcastle (Ithaca, N.Y.: Cornell University Department of Education, 1964).

PIAGET, JEAN. "The General Problems of the Psychobiological Development of the Child," in *Discussions in Child Development, (Volume 4): Proceedings of the Fourth Meeting of the World Health Organization Study Group on the Psychobiological Development of the Child, Geneva, 1956,* ed. James M. Tanner and Bärbel Inhelder (London: Tavistock Publications, 1956).

PIAGET, JEAN. *Psychology and Epistemology,* trans. Arnold Rosin (New York: Grossman Publishers, 1971(b). [first published in French, in 1970, under the title, *Psychologie et Épistémologie*]).
PIAGET, JEAN. *The Psychology of Intelligence,* trans. Malcolm Piercy and D. E. Berlyne (London: Routledge and Kegan Paul, Ltd., 1950. [first published in French, in 1947, under the title, *La Psychologie de l'Intelligence*]).
PIAGET, JEAN. *Structuralism,* trans. and ed. Chaninah Maschler (New York: Basic Books, 1970 [first published in French, in 1968, under the title, *Le Structuralisme*]).
STRAUSS, SIDNEY. "Inducing Cognitive Development and Learning: A Review of Short-Term Training Experiments," *Cognition,* 1972, *1* (4), 329–357.
TURIEL, ELLIOT. "Conflict and Transition in Adolescent Moral Development," *Child Development, 45* (1974), 14–29.
TURIEL, ELLIOT. "Developmental Processes in the Child's Moral Thinking," in *Trends and Issues in Developmental Psychology,* ed. Paul H. Mussen, Jonas Langer, and M. Covington (New York: Holt, Rinehart & Winston, 1969).

# A FRAMEWORK FOR APPLYING THE THEORY
# Nine principles

**3**

## INTRODUCTION

At the end of Chapter 2 we asked you to reflect on what features of the theory were the important ones for educators to understand and apply. If you've made your list and have thought about some of the implications, then you're ready to take a look at the list we've generated. In our list we've tried to (a) maintain a cohesive structure of theoretical implications; (b) accentuate features of the theory that are most influential in applications to education, without doing an injustice to the spirit of the theory as a whole; and (c) provide a framework that can be applied in various ways, according to the needs of particular groups of children, to the demands of particular physical environments, to the taste of particular personalities of teachers and parents, to the length of the school day, and so forth.

As in the rest of the book, our aim in this chapter is to help you use and develop your understanding of theory, your knowledge of children, and your expertise in the educational system so that you can combine your skills and understandings in an intelligent way to create optimal environments for children wherever and whenever you work with them. To achieve this aim, we have explained the principles, sometimes at great length, and have occasionally introduced notions not yet brought up in our discussions of theory. We have also pointed out some of the implications of accepting each principle. In subsequent chapters we will be exploring educational implications in much greater detail; we have included a discussion of some implications here because of the light they shed on the principles themselves.

You can use the suggestions in this chapter to help you identify which principles are influencing what in the detailed discussions that follow in later chapters, but do this with caution. We have confined to this chapter our efforts to identify specific principles as leading to particular suggestions because the theory as a whole has influenced the suggestions we offer. It would be misleading to claim that one could accept certain principles, reject others, and put into practice only what followed from the principles one accepts. A theory, as was pointed out in Chapter 2, is a cohesive system in which apparently small changes may have numerous repercussions.

We have arranged our list so that the order of principles follows roughly the sequence of issues discussed in Chapter 2. As you study each principle, you may want to review relevant sections of that chapter. Also, since the discussion of the principles is meant to help *you* apply them, don't forget to think about what implications there might be for the kind of work you do (or have done, or will do) with children.

## THE PRINCIPLES

### Principle 1: Connections Among Abilities

*Growth of intelligence enhances functioning in all areas of psychological development, including affective, cognitive, and psychomotor development.*

Teachers of young children have often maintained that psychomotor development and socio-emotional (or affective) development influence a child's cognitive *performances.* They have not so often recognized that cognitive *abilities* can be influenced by these other areas of development, nor that the influence can also go from the cognitive domain to the other areas.

Our theory tells us that the three aspects of human functioning always work together. It doesn't tell us precisely how development proceeds in the noncognitive areas (as we noted in Chapter 2), but it does say that in addition to whatever stages and/or mechanisms there are that operate within each of the other domains (psychomotor and affective), there are also influences that come from the processes involved in cognitive growth. As Piaget (1962, p. 130) has put it: "First we must agree that at no level, at no stage, even in the adult, can we find a behavior or a state which is purely cognitive without affect nor a purely affective state without a cognitive element involved. There is no such thing as a purely cognitive state." We need to consider cognitive ability in relation to other aspects of a child's development.

It would be foolish to deny the importance of emotion or social skill in any problem-solving situation, or to deny the role of motor development in enabling the child to grow intellectually. After all, it is hard to systematize the results of one's actions (or, as Piaget would put it, to engage in reflective abstraction) if, when establishing the numerical equivalence between five pencils in a group and five pencils in a row, one repeatedly drops pencils—particularly if any of those that are dropped remain unnoticed. Here is "proof" to the child that changing the spatial arrangements of groups alters the number. Piaget's theory indicates, however, that it would be equally foolish to ignore the role of cognitive development for progress in the affective and psychomotor domains.

Social-emotional problems may result from cognitive deficiencies as much as from problems of self-control, hot temper, distrust, and the like. Four-year-old Emil who thinks people across from him can see exactly what he can see may become angry and frustrated when his vague descriptions are not understood. He may feel that the other person is being intentionally unsympathetic. (Think of how angry you get when you think the woman next to you knows that her foot is crushing your toe and yet fails to take any action; compare that to your feelings when you think she doesn't know she's stepping on you.)

A reluctance to participate in physical activities such as maneuvering over an obstacle course can result from limited abilities in thinking about spatial relationships. As a matter of fact, a sudden timidity about climbing activities may result from developmental advances in cognition. Five-year-old Lisa who is learning to coordinate perspectives and relative distances and who is now able to think in advance of the consequences of incorrectly positioning a hand or foot while at the top of the ladder climber may lose some of the carefree abandon with which she formerly tackled such challenges.

Our theory can help us see how cognitive abilities are influencing children's behaviors in activities that seem to call most heavily on abilities in the psychomotor or affective domains. It can also help us make use of children's interests in feelings, social relations (friendships seem to be a major concern of young children), physical activities, and so forth, in providing cognitive challenges. Children's arguments, for example, can be turned into useful problem-solving experiences rather than regarded simply as undesirable types of interaction to be smoothed over as quickly as possible.

Our first principle, then, suggests that attention to cognitive components will increase our appreciation for the demands made of children in all areas of behavior. Similarly, attention to the social-emotional, and especially to the psychomotor, components should increase our appreciation for the demands made on children in cognitive tasks. We should be able to isolate difficulties in cognition from performance factors such as high frustration, power plays, and problems in manipulating materials. *How* to do this is a problem to be taken up later. Our theory beast, though, insists that we *can* and *should* do it.

*TEACHER TASK 3-1*

Discuss with someone your answer to this question:

When adults take it upon themselves to smooth over children's arguments and quarrels, who is getting the useful problem-solving experience?

In discussing your answer, think about (1) how the psychomotor and affective demands of particular situations would affect the potential for children's participation in the intellectual component of the task; and (2) how adult intervention could be used to create cognitive challenges that the children *would* be able to handle.

### Principle 2: Cognitive Structures

*Each stage in the development of intelligence is characterized by the presence or absence of specific cognitive operations. Because children think about the world very differently than adults do, they make different interpretations and draw different conclusions from given events than do adults.*

Adherence to the second principle implies acceptance of the child as a source of information. Children do not respond the way an adult would to the same input. Given the following set of sentences: "A is a spider," "A has eight legs," and "All spiders have the same number of legs," an adult logically concludes: "All spiders have eight legs." Children, however, may see no reason to give that conclusion a different status than the conclusion: "Eight is a good number for legs." One cannot simply assume that materials or ideas presented will have the same effects on a child that they would have on adults.

For the teacher this means that it is a waste of effort to specify elaborate curriculum sequences based only on what seems to the adult to be a logical order for

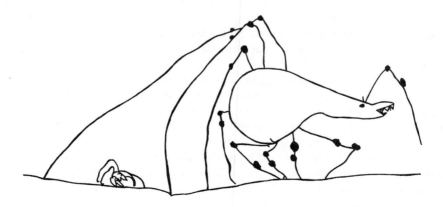

acquisition. First, one must attempt to analyze it from a child's point of view. Then one takes it to the authority—to the child. As Kamii (1970) has pointed out, by asking the right questions at the right times and listening carefully to the answers (not listening merely "for a specific answer"), the teacher can elicit from children a glimpse of their present intellectual capacities. One can uncover how they use facts as well as what facts they happen to be acquainted with. The child's "wrong" answers provide the teacher with clues for presenting situations, materials, and verbalizations that are closely matched to the child's level and that enable the teacher to test new hypotheses about the child's activities.

A child's "wrong" answers, then, show us what meaning the materials or lessons have had for the child. They do not necessarily indicate a lack of attention, a conscious refusal to cooperate, and so on. Perhaps the materials were unfamiliar, so that a large part of the child's energies were directed toward finding out about properties and attributes relevant to those objects. To maximize use of the data provided by each child (that is, by the "wrong" answers given), we can analyze the *kinds* of "wrong" answers we hear. It is the quality, and not the quantity, of these answers that generates new hypotheses about the child's ability and the appropriateness of new activities.

Piaget's theory will be helpful to us in our attempts to interpret the "wrong" answers we hear as well as in alerting us to the kinds of "wrong" answers we can expect from young children. It will help us to generate hypotheses about underlying cognitive organization and to test those hypotheses. If we use it wisely, it will help us provide experiences that elicit the kinds of behaviors we need to see in order to support, or reject, our previous hypotheses and to generate new ones. (Incidentally, those same experiences are likely to be intellectually stimulating for the children as well.)

*TEACHER TASK 3-2*

> Try asking an adult to explain to you how the water comes out of the faucet and then ask a young child the same question. What differences, if any, do you note? Analyze the kinds of differences you notice—for instance, length of explanation, accuracy, coherence, choice of words used. What factors might account for the differences? (You may want to refer back to Chapter 2 in thinking about this.)

### Principle 3: Invariant Sequence and Individual Pacing

*There is an invariant sequence of development through the major periods of cognitive growth (sensorimotor, preoperational, concrete operational, and formal operational) and the within-stage subsequences associated with the various concept domains. Each individual moves through the sequence at his or her own pace.*

Principle 3 refers us to the general guideline offered by the theory as a starting point in the hypothesis–observation–new-hypothesis cycle we hinted at in our discussion of Principle 2. A knowledge of stage-related abilities enables us to estimate the range of children's capacities—to estimate the upper and lower levels of their functioning. Since every child moves through the sequence at his or her own pace, however, this estimation is only the entryway into the cycle. Provision must be made for a variety of responses to any activity, and judgments about the success of the activity should take into account the quality of the responses given by each individual child.

An activity perfectly suited to the intellectual needs of one child will be less than ideal for another (though it may still be beneficial). One cannot avoid this situation by grouping children according to age or intellectual level. Two children of the same age may be at different intellectual levels; two children at the same overall level of organization (stage) may be experiencing different kinds of horizontal *décalage*; and two children who are at the same developmental level in September may not be at the same level by November. A difference in pace, remember, can include differences in how many periods of fast and slow change there are and differences in when these changes occur, as well as differences in the overall speed of developmental progress through the stages.

An acceptance of Piaget's stage construct has several additional consequences relevant here. First of all, a child moving from the sensorimotor stage to the concrete operations stage would not exhibit any formal operational abilities. Any behaviors that seem to imply the higher level of organization are either the result of chance or, upon closer examination, are seen to be memorized phrases rather than reflections of complex thought processes. Secondly, there will be some similarity in all of the child's cognitive performances (keeping in mind the horizontal *décalages,* of course). This similarity is an effect of the child's mental organization. A third consequence is that in periods of transition between stages, as in the preoperational period, children's responses will be highly erratic. What they think about today at the concrete operational level they may well respond to at the sensorimotor level tomorrow. According to Piaget's theory, regression is an almost inevitable component of progression.

Together these three consequences seem to have paradoxical implications for a teacher's process of hypothesis testing. The second consequence suggests that observing a few behaviors ought to give one information about all of the child's behaviors. The first and third consequences, however, point out that the limited number of observations may well be misleading. This puzzle is resolved when observations are of the type used by the Genevans in what is called the *méthode clinique.* These involve probing the child's responses, obtaining the child's reactions to the adult's countersuggestions, requesting explanations for procedures, removing or introducing misleading perceptual cues, and introducing new strategies. When observation is combined with timely interaction, then chance behaviors, transitional behaviors, and memorized responses can be distinguished from those that reflect the internal organization, the *"structure d'ensemble."*

But why, you may ask, is it so important to know what stage a child is in? Psychologists may be interested in that, but how does it affect education? Read on: the discussion of the rest of the principles should give you a basis for constructing your own answers to these questions.

### Principle 4: Organized Responses and Adaptation

*More than the mere accumulation of facts, intelligence is the incorporation of the given data of experiences into an organized framework. It involves the individual's ability to organize and adapt, through the reciprocal processes of assimilation and accommodation, to various aspects of the environment.*

The fourth principle emphasizes the need to consider children's abilities to organize information rather than to concentrate on their ability to recite lists of facts. It is not the mere accumulation of vast amounts of information that leads to increases in intellectual functioning, as learning theorists have argued (for instance, see Gagné, 1968), but the changing arrangement of those bits and the incorporation of them into an organized whole (or structure).

From the Piagetian perspective, the accumulation of information is a necessary condition for intellectual growth, but it is not a sufficient one. Thus, although a certain level of organization implies that the child has indeed accumulated bits of information (that the child has had certain kinds of experiences), the reverse is not true. Children act upon the information they receive; they fit it into an informational framework so that it acquires a broader meaning. To use an example from Fodor (1968), "camshaft" has a very different meaning when it is seen as a valve lifter in relation to other parts of an automobile engine than it does when seen as an oddly shaped piece of metal lying on the ground—especially if the viewer in the latter case knows nothing of cars or their engines.

For the teacher, this means that educational goals ought to include changes in intellectual organization as well as the acquisition of specific facts. It is not enough for children to count to twenty; they must also begin to construct for themselves an understanding of the number system. This means that we won't always be looking for the most efficient ways for children to learn facts. Sometimes the *inefficient* way to learn a particular set of facts may be what helps children to reorganize (or to see the need to reorganize) their ways of thinking.

> *The goal of intellectual education is not to know how to repeat or retain ready-made truths (a truth that is parroted is only a half-truth). It is in learning to master the truth by oneself at the risk of losing a lot of time and going through all the roundabout ways that are inherent in real activity.*
>
> *Piaget, 1973, p. 106*

The choice of curriculum material to be presented, then, would be influenced by its possible effects on mental reorganization and by the level of organization it demands of the children who are to understand it. In terms of the theory, material would be examined for the understandings it presupposes in the areas of classification, seriation, number, and spatiotemporal reasoning. These are areas we'll be discussing in detail in Chapter 6. It is important to remember here that the organization referred to is in the children and not in the materials. Ordered materials such as those characteristic of the Montessori approach will not necessarily lead to the order the children invent (or reconstruct) as they develop logical reasoning. Order in the environment (for instance, seriated cylinders) may give the children a perceptual model, but it is the ability to *reconstruct* the perceptual model that is of interest in the Piagetian approach.

Organized materials can be helpful to children, but their usefulness is limited by the child's ability to recognize the organization. A child who imitates the teacher's motions in lining up a set of nested blocks from largest to smallest may or may not understand the basis on which the decision is made to place each block where it belongs. To imitate the *organizational* aspect of the task (the arrangement of blocks according to size) rather than the specific behaviors used in the task, the child has to be able to reconstruct the organization. The ability to mentally reconstruct a particular object, arrangement of objects, event, behavior, or whatever, is a necessary part of any imitation process.

Our ability to learn through observation, and to copy what we've observed, is limited by what we already know how to do (Piaget, 1951). An infant, for example, can imitate sucking motions and gurgling or cooing sounds, but it cannot imitate cross-country running or vocal renditions of "Oh, Susannah." It can reconstruct the former, but its present level of intelligence (as well as its physical limitations) precludes its reconstruction of the latter. Young children do not become able to classify animals into hierarchical groups such as "birds," "birds that fly," and "birds that can't fly," merely by watching an adult sort pictures of animals into groups. In order to benefit from such an experience, they have to be able to understand which features of the performance are relevant. Neither the speed at which the sorting is done, for example, nor the precise way in which each card is placed with its group are relevant to the *classification* task being performed.

The moral of all this is that although learning through observation (either by observing arrangements of materials or by using other people as models for one's behavior) plays an important role in the intellectual development of a child, the role it plays is strongly influenced by the child's developmental level. To make demonstrations effective in presenting new material, we have to match the material we hope to teach to children's present levels of organization.

### TEACHER TASK 3-3

Think of an activity you have found enjoyable to do with children. Describe how you would modify that activity to make it appropriate for and interesting to older children and/or adults. (If you haven't worked with children, think of an activity you like to do with other adults. Then describe the ways you'd change the activity for children.)

### Principle 5: Timing and Quality of Interactions

*Intelligence is developed through interaction between the environment and the individual. Timing and quality in the environment are important factors for an evolving intellect.*

Keeping in mind the educational possibilities for optimizing development, Principle 5 suggests a highly active teacher role. The adult has a vital role in the choice and arrangement of materials, the arrangement of the room, and the quality of social interactions. Teacher input here has the potential either to encourage or to discourage interactions between each child and the environment. Piaget's theory offers the view that, so long as appropriate timing and quality can be maintained in such interactions, the more the better.

It is true that children seem to arrive at particular levels of cognitive ability, notably the level of concrete operations, with a great variety of normal adult interventions. Writings by Almy, Chittenden, and Miller (1966) and by Kamii and DeVries (1977) suggest, however, that advances beyond this level depend on *optimal* development during the preoperational period. Optimal, in this sense, refers to the rate of development as well as to the scope. And the fastest rate is not necessarily the best! We might think in terms of degrees of conviction; the organizations used at the preoperational and concrete operational levels may be more or less firmly grounded in experience for children. The more firmly they are grounded, the more willing children are to use (and thereby develop) their reasoning abilities, and the more likely they are to avoid resorting to the formulas and recipes concocted by others. Getting the necessary experience takes time! It is essential for the teacher to observe carefully, to plan appropriately, and to maximize the reciprocal nature of the interactions between children and their environment (social as well as physical).

As you know from reading Chapter 2, the word "interaction" is crucial to understanding the implications of Principle 5. The environment is not *the cause* of cognitive development. It is necessary for development, and it can influence the course of development within a limited range of possibilities set by human nature, but it is not sufficient for the initiation of, or for the pattern or sequence of, cognitive development. Piaget's theory acknowledges the notion of optimal environments, in which development proceeds in a fashion close to the ideal (whatever that may look like); suboptimal environments, in which development proceeds within a normal range but not with maximal quality or efficiency; and detrimental environments, which lead to abnormal development in terms of quality or quantity or both. In all of these cases, it is the *interaction* between the individual and the environment that is responsible for the course of development. The better we are acquainted with our theory, the more likely we are to be able to create and recognize optimal environments for cognitive development.

In applying Principle 5, we need to find ways to maximize appropriate interactions between each child and the environment. We already know from Chapter 2 that we need to provide challenges that require some accommodation (but not too much) and that we must help children apply whatever levels of organization they have to new content areas (so as to help them even out horizontal *décalages*). A knowledge of the developmental stages is an invaluable help to us in deciding what to do and when to do it. When we know what levels of organization a child is using, we can plan activities that are neither too easy nor too difficult.

On a general level, J. McV. Hunt (1961) has pointed out, this means that the match between levels of activities for children and their developmental levels should be close, but not exact. A puzzle that has ten pieces is not usually a challenge for a four-year-old, and hence it is of little interest. The child hardly has to think at all in putting the pieces in place. A puzzle with forty-five pieces may be too difficult for the same child; it may lead to frustration and, again, loss of interest. In this case, the child has no idea of how to think about such a complexity of variables. However, a puzzle with twenty-five pieces may provide just enough challenge.

Presenting children with problems they can recognize (if not immediately resolve) is important for both motivational and intellectual reasons. As a result of a series of carefully designed studies on the effects of adult intervention on the acquisition of levels of organization, some of Piaget's associates, Inhelder, Sinclair, and Bovet (1974), have concluded that the interactions that promote cognitive growth are those in which children are helped to integrate their experiences through the resolution of problems. Children who are asked to use their previous understandings in order to make a prediction and then find their prediction falsified, experience a conflict or contradiction as their mental processes are thrown into disequilibrium. They express surprise and amazement and attempt to resolve the conflicts. The result is that there are interactions among their schemata, or subsystems, and a compromise solution is reached to restore a level of equilibrium.

This can lead to developmental progress only when two conditions are met. First of all, Inhelder, Sinclair, and Bovet (1974, p. 267) have said that surprising results are stimulants to development only when the child has "the cognitive equipment which enables him to fit the unforeseen phenomena into a deductive or inferential framework." The child must have a level of organization that enables him or her to make use of the surprising information. Secondly, the child must be familiar enough with the content area to be able to generate predictions he or she actually believes in. Otherwise, the surprising results are no surprise. It would be as though someone required that you place a bet on one of the two unknown horses in a two-horse race. If your horse doesn't win, you may be dismayed, but you're not surprised. You are unlikely to make much use of the information you acquire unless you are already interested in and know something about horses or racing or both. Furthermore, even if you did have previous knowledge of related matters, you may not have applied that knowledge to the forced choice you made. The combination of time and exposure to different content areas does not suffice for the integration of knowledge. The right questions, suggestions, and comments from people around us help us to see the connections between different areas of our knowledge.

### Principle 6: Social Interaction

*Intellectual growth is fostered by social interaction with peers and adults as well as by interaction with the physical environment.*

Principle 6 emphasizes that the social environment must not be disregarded in attempts to create active involvement with the physical environment. In fact, the two are mutually supportive. Social interaction forces children to look again and to observe more carefully their actions and the physical and social consequences of their actions. Likewise, interactions with the physical environment create situations for social interaction—for discussion of what is happening, for disputes over property, for decisions about who will help carry the juice table over to the corner, and so forth.

An application of this principle requires provision of high-quality interactions with both peers and adults. Interactions in which various opinions are expressed or arguments ensue can help children to recognize differences in perspective and to consider the need to reassess their own points of view. This is important because one of the characteristics of young children's thinking is the inability to understand that other people may see things differently or may feel differently than the child does. Children tend to believe, even when told otherwise, that all people think and feel as they do; that when they talk, other people know what they are talking about; and that when they are talked to, they understand what the other person means. Adults, of course, may exhibit some of the same tendencies—think of those infuriating times when people sweetly insist that they "understand just how you feel," when you're pretty sure they don't—but adults recognize the possibility of misunderstandings and can interpret the subtle nuances in behaviors that indicate they are not communicating clearly or are not understanding what is being said.

Each kind of social interaction, with adults and with peers, has its own advantages and its own problems. Adults can guide children's investigations of the social and physical environments in ways that point out promising leads, focus attention on important questions, encourage thorough analyses of actions and their results, and minimize needless explorations of intellectual dead ends. Interactions with peers can provide opportunities for children to expound their own viewpoints, to confront and deal with vociferous claims contradicting their own, to discover and imitate new actions just slightly different from their own, and to incorporate the wishes and ideas of others into plans for complicated sequences of activity (as in dramatic play episodes). Social encounters of both kinds are essential for optimal cognitive development. Piaget (1973, p. 52) has claimed:

> . . . that the individual would not know how to acquire his most basic mental structures without some external influences, demanding a certain forma-

tive social milieu, and that on all levels (from the most elementary to the most developed), the social or educational factor constitutes a condition of development.

It takes considerable skill and sensitivity to create the high-quality social milieu that optimizes intellectual development. In addition to knowing strategies for listening *to children* (rather than listening *for the answer*), for providing intellectually challenging comments and questions, and for using group dynamics to foster high-quality peer interactions, one must be careful to avoid certain pitfalls. Although we'll be discussing some of the dangers as well as some positive suggestions in Chapters 4 and 7, there are two dangers worth bringing out right away.

The troublesome aspect of adult-child interactions is the danger that a child will take the adult's remarks as indications of the child's error or as nothing more than appropriate social behaviors. For example, after a discussion of the lengths of various blocks, Doug may come to the conclusion that "in situations like this, one is supposed to say that the red one is longer." Doug hasn't come to any new understanding about relative lengths. Instead, he has made a conclusion about socially appropriate behavior. This is not a farfetched example, as an anecdote from the authors' experience can testify. Shortly after what had been regarded as a very successful activity, in which a teacher worked with children in arranging paper dolls from largest to smallest, one of the children was asked by another teacher about what she had been doing. Since this was a child who had seemed very interested in the activity and who had managed to do much of the arranging herself, her answer came as a surprise. She said that she had been doing something with dolls (and she held up the tangible evidence of her participation—a sheet of paper with paper dolls pasted on it) and that although she had enjoyed working with the teacher (as she tactfully hastened to assure us), she hadn't really understood (this said very apologetically) what she was being asked to do or why. It was an important lesson for all! As Piaget's theory reminds us, children tend to view adults as absolute authorities on all topics. Unless we take steps to disabuse them of this view, adult-child interactions run the risk of demanding too much accommodation—and that, as you'll recall from Chapter 2, can hinder true understanding.

One way of avoiding this problem is to promote peer interactions in which the discussants view one another as equals. Note that not just any old peer interaction will do. Nor is this the "Each one teach one" kind of peer interaction, in which a child who already knows a skill teaches one who doesn't. The latter kind of peer teaching has many advantages, but it is *not* what we are talking about here. We want interactions that provide the kinds of conflicts that children interpret as having resolutions they can discover. The danger in peer interactions is that children may "get in over their heads." They may become involved in heated arguments that don't lead to constructive thinking. For example, they may become so emotionally involved that a verbal disagreement becomes a fistfight, or, in order to win the argument, they may resort to claims of physical superiority ("I'm right 'cause I'm stronger") or to indirect appeals to authority ("I know 'cause my mom said so").

It takes tact and expertise in well-timed interventions to channel interpersonal conflicts into beneficial intellectual experiences.

**TEACHER TASK 3-4**

> This teacher task requires some data gathering as well as some analysis.
>
> (1) Find an opportunity to observe groups of children—in a classroom, on a playground, in your neighborhood. Watch for arguments between children. Observe at least five separate arguments, and make a record of the exchanges in as much detail as you can (including nonverbal behaviors where appropriate).
> (2) Now analyze each of the arguments in terms of
>     (a) the cognitive value of the argument for each child involved,
>     (b) places where affective factors interfered with the cognitive value,
>     (c) places where affective factors enhanced the cognitive value (for instance, by prolonging the discussion or stimulating a child to give a stronger defense of his position),
>     (d) places where adult intervention would have enhanced the cognitive value (describe the kinds of intervention you think would be valuable, and explain how and why they would be helpful).
> (3) If you noticed any relationships between the kinds of arguments you saw and the kinds of analyses you gave, record them. Think about the implications these relationships might have for teaching strategies.
>
> (It would be helpful to do the observations with one or more other people, each person making his or her own records and doing separate analyses. Then both the descriptions of the arguments and the analyses can be shared and discussed.)

### Principle 7: The Role of Language

*Language helps one to focus on concepts and to retrieve them. It does not in itself build concepts.*

A de-emphasis on language as the major teaching channel in early childhood education is the message in Principle 7. As Kamii (1970) maintains, teaching a word does not guarantee the acquisition of the concept. Preoperational children who are just beginning to represent mentally what they can already represent with actions are as yet unable to make full use of their language ability. Not only are they still somewhat short on vocabulary; they are particularly deficient in knowledge of the variety of situations to which their words may be applied. According to Piaget, children cannot fully understand the meaning of a word until they have had sufficient experiences in which that word is used. This doesn't necessarily mean that children cannot use a word appropriately, but it does suggest that a full understanding of the extension of a word only comes with a variety of experiences. For this reason, words should not be relied upon as a measure of a young child's intellectual ability.

We mentioned earlier (Principle 2) that children do not interpret events or questions in the same way that adults do. Even when seemingly appropriate words are used, the young child may have a different understanding of the words than we do. It is all too easy to assume that if children talk like us, they also think like us. Often, a child's words do not truly express to us what the child is really thinking. For instance, it is typical for preschoolers to equate size with age. The bigger someone is, the older that person is assumed to be. Obviously, this way of thinking will be appropriate only part of the time. There can be a tremendous contrast between the child's outward show of language use and the inward reality of the actual level of organization and cohesion of the child's thoughts (Isaacs, 1974).

For teachers, this calls for a careful evaluation of when and how they teach language in the classroom. Kamii (1970) has pointed out that at the preschool level, there is an incredible preoccupation with the teaching of language, without coming to grips with how the preoperational child really thinks. Our theory tells us that without concrete experiences, a large amount of language teaching is wasted. In addition, there is the risk of equipping children with a verbal façade behind which they can hide (from themselves as well as from their teachers) their lack of real understanding.

Language teaching per se is valuable when new situations call for new vocabulary, and when words and sentences are used to describe actions, thoughts, and feelings obviously within the child's immediate experience. It can be detrimental when used to correct the language of a child whose mistakes reveal a particular level of misunderstanding. In this case, the child's misuse of language is an indicator of the unique way the child thinks about the world. What's needed is a change in cognitive structure, not a simple statement of what linguistic conventions are acceptable.

Language teaching is seldom effective, for example, in promoting changes in cognitive structure. Furth (1970) and Furth and Wachs (1974) stress the need to teach *thinking* rather than to teach empty words. Although language enables children to communicate the results of their thinking, the language system is not the source of thinking abilities. Actions and coordinations of actions (through the process of reflective abstraction) are the sources of operational thinking. Piaget leaves open the question of whether or not language becomes necessary for development after operational thinking has begun. After all, language can be viewed as a form of action and a way of having an effect upon one's environment, particularly when it is used in dealing with other people. But it is important to remember that language is an *instrument* of knowledge and is not knowledge itself.

As an instrument, language can provide short ways to represent long and complicated bits of knowledge. Because of this, it helps children to focus on particular features of situations, to recover from memory events and experiences no longer present, and to simplify complicated thoughts in such a way that several can be put together. Language teaching certainly *has* a place in classrooms for young children, but it must be kept *in* its place.

### Principle 8: Mental and Physical Activity

*Learning is an active process, subordinate to development, which involves manipulative and exploratory interaction with the environment in the search for alternative actions and properties applicable to objects and events. This involves both mental and physical activity.*

There are two key words in Principle 8. The first is "activity." As we mentioned in the discussion of Principle 7, actions and active coordinations of actions provide the source for increasing levels of intellectual organization. The second key word is "learning." Although we have spoken at length about developmental changes, mechanisms of developmental change, and the impetus to developmental change, we have not yet made explicit where learning fits into the picture. In Piaget's theory, activity and learning both play important roles in intellectual development.

Those who make a distinction between learning and development are faced with the question of the relation between them. Are they independent? If they are not independent, does one cause changes in the other? Just how do they interact, anyway? The answers to these questions will depend on what one takes learning to be. We can all agree that a child can *learn* to count to ten, but what kind of process has gone on in the learning? How, if at all, is it different from development? Piaget's theory gives us one way to answer such questions. We can think of learning as the change that takes place when the individual assimilates some feature of the environment. No developmental change in the level of intellectual organization is involved, either at the level of stage changes or at the level of interactions among subsystems. Intellectual activity, however, *is* involved.

There are two aspects of intellectual activity that are important to educators. First, as you remember from Chapter 2, there is no assimilation without accommodation. And accommodation is not a passive reaction! We are not always conscious of the accommodations we make, but this doesn't make them comparable to our propensity to bleed when cut or to blink when a puff of air is directed toward our eyes. To assimilate a piece of information, we have to act upon it intellectually. We have to adjust our previous understanding so that it can include the new information. Second, when we assimilate information, the equilibration process works to restore a balance between the two processes of assimilation and accommodation.

Why are these aspects relevant to educators? Here are three reasons:

(1) The balancing will take varying amounts of time—some things are harder for a particular individual to learn than are others (that is, some things require more drastic accommodation if they are to be assimilated).

(2) In some cases, the only way for a child to bring the processes into balance will be to grossly distort the input. This is detrimental when teachers are fooled into thinking that the distortion is less than it is. (Remember how deceptive a child's facility with words can be!) We run the risk of failing to provide the appropriate experiences for a solid understanding.

(3) Teachers can help children to minimize both the amount of time required for accommodation and the amount of objectionable distortions.

We can be of most help when we recognize the relation between the organizational level of a child's thinking and what is to be learned (or assimilated and accommodated). At any given level of organization, some information will be easily accommodated with a minimum of distortion. Other information won't make any sense; it won't fit in. To consider it as information at all, the person will have to alter its meaning. When we provide appropriate activities with plenty of time and the right kinds of encouragement for thoughtful exploration, we are providing opportunities for active learning. We are helping children to actively adjust their thinking as they incorporate new information with a minimum of distortion. Thus, we facilitate learning by adjusting our notions of what should be learned to children's developmental levels; we facilitate development by providing learning experiences that encourage organizational change.

The kind of classroom most acceptable to our theory is one that contains many potentially interesting materials, which children are encouraged to look at, manipulate, and talk about. Particularly valuable are objects that react in interesting ways to the child's actions upon them. The more possibilities there are for subtle differences in the child's actions to create differences in observable effects, the better the materials. A set of wooden blocks, for example, provides more valuable learning experiences than a windup toy. Appropriate teacher behaviors are also a part of the ideal classroom. Our theory suggests that teachers should ask questions that help children focus on the effects of their actions, suggest and encourage a variety of actions (both actions on objects and interactions with other people), and stimulate mental actions (such as figuring out why Red Riding Hood thought the wolf was friendly). To get the most mileage out of such teacher behaviors, the behaviors must reflect an understanding of children's developmental levels. (Chapter 6 is designed to help with this.)

The teacher's role, then, is to ensure and enhance the child's own construction of knowledge through interactions with the environment. Teachers must provide opportunities for trying out new actions on familiar objects and familiar actions on new objects. Not only must such activity be possible, however; it must be probable. Providing familiar or unfamiliar objects is only a possible first step in providing opportunity for action. Children must also know they may and can manipulate such objects. Fears of the unfamiliar (and other emotional factors that may prevent cognitive activity and, therefore, cognitive growth) must be overcome. In many cases, the teacher may have to suggest ways to test the effects of actions or to point to attributes that might be considered for their relevance to particular operations. It is important in such suggestions to encourage those that will not work as well as those that will. The child can determine which are which through experimentation.

It is no easy task to make sure that every child is actively involved in the right sort of way. Children standing on the sidelines may be actively (mentally) accommodating to the data generated by other children involved with materials—and, again, they may not. Children manipulating objects may be acting absentmindedly, so that their overt actions have little effect on their mental processes—and they may not. The teacher's questions and comments are essential for determining both the existence of mental and/or physical activity and whether or not either will soon occur. It is the teacher's job to ensure that both types of action do occur. Passive children may need encouragement to interact with their environment, and active children may need encouragement to observe carefully and to think about the effects of their "experiments." The teacher guides the interaction of thought and appropriate action that leads to intellectual development.

To effectively guide this interaction, teachers must facilitate physical and psychological risk taking. First of all, children's options for decision making must be bounded by reasonable limitations set by the adult. Secondly, negative results of inappropriate choices must be shown to children but must not be allowed to overwhelm them (and thereby effectively prevent them from further choice making, or risk taking).

It is here that the notion of intellectual honesty comes into play. Unless children are willing to risk making predictions that are incompatible with certain possible results of observation (and compatible with others), they will not progress in their construction of knowledge. Intellectual honesty refers to the willingness to make such predictions, to be found wrong, and to learn from one's mistakes in the construction of newer, more adequate but equally vulnerable, predictions. In some situations, the child can sense from our tone of voice or the formation of our statements or questions that we want a particular response. Children recognize quite early the value of pleasing adults, and in this type of situation are likely to give the desired response whether or not it is what they truly feel or believe. This is unfortunate, because the response thus reflects the adult's knowledge and not the child's. The child has been unable to be intellectually honest.

Teachers face a difficult task in creating an emotional and intellectual atmosphere that encourages intellectual honesty (and thereby maximizes children's active involvement with the environment). One of the most important things to remember is that to create this atmosphere, teachers will have to be intellectually honest too.

*TEACHER TASK 3-5*

In discussing the maintenance of a stimulating intellectual atmosphere for scientists, W. I. B. Beveridge has said: "Conscious ignorance and intellectual honesty are important attributes for the research man. Free discussion requires an atmosphere unembarrassed by any suggestion of authority or even respect" (1950, p. 86). Discuss with someone the relevance of this for the education of young children. Think about (a) when and where the free discussions referred to in the quote might be used in a classroom, and (b) what, if any, restraints might be put on such a discussion when young children are the participants.

### Principle 9: Autonomy with Cooperation

*Autonomy with cooperation, rather than simple obedience to authority, contributes to intellectual and moral development.*

The final principle stresses the need for consistency in the values for intellectual and moral growth. As Piaget (1973, p. 107) puts it, if the child:

> . . . is intellectually passive, he will not know how to be free ethically. Conversely, if his ethics consist exclusively in submission to adult authority, and if the only social exchanges that make up the life of the class are those that bind each student individually to a master holding all power, he will not know how to be intellectually active.

The need for autonomy with cooperation is not simply a value judgment in the creation of individuals suited to a democratic society. It is a necessary component in the development of the unified structure of intelligence. Rigid adherence to authority on moral questions is as much a reflection of the preoperational level of mental organization as is the inability to perform certain intellectual feats. If children are willing to accept social and/or moral rules without questioning the rationale or examining possible alternatives, they are likely to accept authorities on nonmoral matters as well. But, as we have seen, real knowledge requires that the individual do his or her *own thinking.* Experiences in making moral judgments, like experiences in acting on the physical environment, force developing individuals to restructure their intellectual frameworks.

In the classroom, this points to the need to include children's views in the resolution of conflicts and in policy decisions. Children must have opportunities to plan, to decide, to reason, and to act on their own in situations where their actions have an impact on others. The responses of other people in their environments then give them the information they need to rethink their decisions and to coordinate a variety of behaviors and consequences. In this process, children learn more than facts about how people behave—they learn more than the rudiments of psychology and sociology. They also learn how to coordinate a variety of viewpoints and reach a conclusion that does justice to the merits of each.

Each encounter with a person results in an alteration of children's previous conceptions of that person and usually also results in some change in the way children interact with that person in the future. It requires many interactions with other people for children to realize that other people have thoughts, feelings, perceptions, and desires different from their own. Only when they realize this difference can they interact with true empathy and cooperation. Autonomy and cooperation are both important here, for, as Piaget (1932, pp. 393–394) has put it:

> In order to discover oneself as a particular individual, what is needed is a continuous comparison, the outcome of opposition, of discussion, and of mutual control . . . It is only by knowing our individual nature with its limitations as

well as its resources that we grow capable of coming out of ourselves and collaborating with other individual natures. Consciousness of self is therefore both a product and a condition of cooperation.

An awareness of children's abilities enables teachers to limit alternatives so that risks involved in decision making will not be beyond children's capacities to cope emotionally, physically, or intellectually. Decision-making opportunities must be planned like any other classroom activities. They must be designed so that children are made aware of the conflicts and are challenged by them to restructure their reasoning processes. Teachers can help clarify problems so that children can devise solutions.

Situations or experiences in which children can work and be together increase the probability that children will see a need to reconsider their own viewpoints. For instance, if Sammy can't see the book held up at a group story reading, he is very likely to make his discontent apparent to Cynthia, who is standing in his way. His complaint, "I can't see the picture," accompanied by a shove, evokes a response from Cynthia. She is likely to maintain that he *must* be able to see the book, since she herself can see it. His refusal to accept her assertion forces Cynthia to reconsider the situation. After thinking it through, she may retain her original view, in which case she is likely to return Sammy's shove with one of her own. She is also likely to decide that there is something to Sammy's complaint and so respond by sitting down or stepping aside. The adequacy of her attempts to get out of Sammy's way will depend on her ability to construct what Sammy can actually see from where he is.

The teacher role in the area of moral and social decisions includes behaviors that emphasize the need to consider consequences (and thus help children get away from a focus solely on the present), that point out particular features of consequences (so that children have a basis for their decisions), and that help children relate consequences to their previous decisions. It is difficult to imagine how this could be effectively accomplished without respect for children's decisions—without a willingness by teachers to abide by decisions they have allowed children to make.

It is a ticklish business to maintain the proper balance between adult guidance for group-management purposes and the provision of opportunities for children to make and follow through on decisions. There are no clear-cut boundaries between *undesirably rigid* rules and *desirably firm* rules, which are needed in a group setting in order that children may concentrate on the varied learning experiences available. It is also difficult to draw a clear line between the *apparently disorganized* classroom situations, in which children are learning as they struggle to participate in the social organization of the classroom, and a *truly chaotic* classroom, where the lack of organization is actually preventing children from learning. Fortunately, our theory, which tells us that children need to practice social and moral responsibility, also gives us guidelines for deciding what kinds of decisions we can allow them to make. It accomplishes this by describing the kinds of intellectual organizations available to children. We can make use of that information in interpreting the various abilities and personalities of the children we work with. Then we can provide challenges that can be successfully met by the particular children we teach.


## SUMMARY

In this chapter, we have identified and described nine basic principles that provide a framework for applying Piagetian theory to educational practice. In identifying the nine principles, we have tried to capture the spirit of the theory as a whole and to highlight features of the theory most relevant to education.

Three of the principles (Principles 1, 8, and 9) emphasize the intimate connections among the different areas of psychological development. Two of the principles (Principles 2 and 3) clarify the consequences of accepting a stage theory of cognitive development. Principle 4 directs attention to the internal organization inherent in any *response* to the environment, while features of the environment itself are highlighted in Principles 5 and 6. Principle 5 points to timing and quality as crucial environmental features; Principle 6 stresses the social aspects of the environment. Finally, Principle 7 (and, to some extent, Principle 9 as well) cautions us not to mistake facility in the use of words and rules for depth of understanding.

In our discussions of each of the nine principles, we have suggested some ways in which an acceptance of the principle would influence classroom practices. Even from the rather sketchy discussion of applications we have given so far, you can probably see how adherence to the principles might help us realize what Piaget sees as the major aim of education. In one of his most often-cited statements (1964, p. 5), he says:

> The principle goal of education is to create men who are capable of doing new things, not simply of repeating what other generations have done—men who are creative, inventive, and discoverers. The second goal of education is to form minds which can be critical, can verify, and not accept everything they are offered. The great danger today is of slogans, collective opinions, ready-made trends of thought. We have to be able to resist individually, to criticize, to distinguish between what is proven and what is not. So we need pupils who are active, who learn early to find out by themselves, partly by their own spontaneous activity and partly through material we set up for them; who learn early to tell what is verifiable and what is simply the first idea to come to them.

In subsequent chapters we will be discussing the goals and practices that follow from an acceptance of these nine principles and the theory they stand for. Although few explicit references to the principles are made, their influence is clearly present. A solid understanding of the principles will be helpful in your reading of later chapters and in your own innovative attempts to apply the theory to your own situation.

## REFERENCES

ALMY, MILLIE, EDWARD CHITTENDEN, and P. MILLER. *Young Children's Thinking* (New York: Teacher's College Press, Columbia University, 1966).

BEVERIDGE, WILLIAM I. B. *The Art of Scientific Investigation* (New York: W. W. Norton), 1950.

FODOR, JERRY A. *Psychological Explanation* (New York: Random House, 1968).

FURTH, HANS G. *Piaget for Teachers* (Englewood Cliffs, N.J.: Prentice-Hall, 1970).

FURTH, HANS G., and HARRY WACHS. *Thinking Goes to School* (New York: Oxford University Press, 1974).

GAGNÉ, ROBERT M. "Contributions of Learning to Human Development," *Psychological Review, 75*, no. 3 (1968), 177–191.

HUNT, JOSEPH McVICKER. *Intelligence and Experience* (New York: Ronald Press, 1961).

INHELDER, BÄRBEL, HERMINE SINCLAIR, and MAGALI BOVET. *Learning and the Development of Cognition*, trans. Susan Wedgwood (Cambridge, Mass.: Harvard University Press, 1974 [first published in French, in 1974, under the title, *Apprentissage et Structures de la Connaissance*]).

ISAACS, NATHAN. *Children's Ways of Knowing: Nathan Isaacs on Education, Psychology, and Piaget*, ed. Mildred Hardeman (New York: Teacher's College Press, 1974).

KAMII, CONSTANCE. "Pedagogical Implications of Piaget's Theory: Differences from Other Theories and Current Practices." Paper presented at the conference, Application of Piagetian Theory to Education: An Inquiry Beyond the Theory, Rutgers University, July 20–22, 1970.

KAMII, CONSTANCE, and RHETA DeVRIES. "Piaget for Early Education," in *The Preschool in Action: Exploring Early Childhood Programs*, ed. M. C. Day and Ronald K. Parker (Boston: Allyn & Bacon, 1977).

PIAGET, JEAN. Comment made at the Conference on Cognitive Studies and Curriculum Development at Cornell University, March 1964, quoted by Eleanor Duckworth in "Piaget Rediscovered," in *Piaget Rediscovered*, ed. Richard E. Ripple and Verne N. Rockcastle (Ithaca, N.Y.: Cornell University Department of Education, 1964).

PIAGET, JEAN. *The Moral Judgment of the Child*, trans. Marjorie Gabain (New York: Harcourt Brace Jovanovich, 1932 [first published in French, in 1932, under the title, *Le Jugement Moral chez l'Enfant*]).

PIAGET, JEAN. *Play, Dreams, and Imitation in Childhood*, trans. C. Gattegno and F. M. Hodgson (London: Heinemann, 1951 [first published in French, in 1945, under the title, *La Formation du Symbole chez l'Enfant; Imitation, Jeu, et Rêve, Image et Représentation*]).

PIAGET, JEAN. "The Relation of Affectivity to Intelligence in the Mental Development of the Child," *Bulletin of the Menninger Clinic, 26* (1962), 129–137.

PIAGET, JEAN. *To Understand Is to Invent*, trans. George-Anne Roberts (New York: Grossman Publishers, 1973 [first published as two works, by UNESCO, in 1948, under the titles, "Le Droit à l'Éducation dans le Monde Actuel" and "Où Va l'Éducation?"]).

# 4

# VALUES AND GOALS

## CONCEPTUALIZATION OF GOALS

Now that we've examined our theory, let's put it to work. Since goals and values are intricately tied up with the application of theory, its first job will be to help us with a determination of appropriate goals for preschool education. It won't be able to specify all the goals, of course. It is only a theory, after all—*Intellectus developmentii* var. *Piagetiana*. Here, as in every other place where we put it to work, we'll have to be careful about when and how to use it.

One thing is certain: this kind of theory of the development of knowledge is not likely, except by some amazing coincidence, to provide us with an exhaustive list of goals for fine-motor coordination, large-motor skills, overall physical development, personality or character development, "facts" needed before entrance to kindergarten or first grade, and so on. A little of its influence will certainly rub off when we consider the cognitive aspects involved in each of these areas—and there *are* cognitive aspects, as Kohlberg (1968) has pointed out. So much the better. But the contribution remains one of influence, not an exhaustive list of goals.

Our particular theory does no better in setting specific and appropriate goals for children with learning disabilities, visual problems, physical handicaps, or emotional disturbances. It can help, but a huge portion of the work is yet to be done.

Some people have made use of the theory in these areas by examining, modifying, and testing the insights concerning normal development as they apply to special populations. For example, Stephens (1971), Wolinsky (1962), and Woodward and Stern (1963) have suggested ways of applying Piagetian theory to the mentally retarded. Furth (1966) and Bisno (1974) have made a similar effort concerning deaf children. Anthony (1956) and Pimm (1974) have applied the theory to emotional problems. The theory has been used to good advantage in these areas, but a major theoretical effort has been needed in each case to see how it might be useful and to integrate it into knowledge from other sources. The theory does not provide The Answer. Rather, it can help us find answers.

Remember, even in the area where it can contribute the most, the area of intellectual development, the theory beast stubbornly refuses to go beyond outlining some general guidelines for the kinds of changes we are likely to see. The theory cannot provide specific behavioral objectives. The changes the theory knows about are changes in the organization of thought, not changes in specific behaviors or frequencies of behaviors for individual children. A behavior can certainly give us a clue to the underlying system of thought, but we must never mistake the one for the other.

How can this be, when the theory tells us that all children go through the same stages in the same sequence and that it is their behaviors that tell us this? Behaviors are certainly valuable indicators of developmental progress; the problem is that the behaviors that tell us that children have not yet reached a particular stage are a mixed bag. A variety of wrong answers appear instead of the single correct answer (along with its variants). At each level of development there is a new mixed bag of wrong answers—not a single new wrong answer, but a new group of wrong answers. The new group may be definable by a certain set of characteristics, but there is a great deal of variability within the set. For this reason, behavioral objectives as they are usually expressed are of little use with this approach. Our theory tells us what kind of thing to look for rather than what specific thing to look for.

As the preceding discussion suggests, it is extremely important to remember the individual differences in development as well as the universals whenever we try to apply theory to real human beings. Children develop at different speeds, depending on an extremely complex network of factors, such as maturation rate, personality traits, and specific experiences. This network influences not only the rate of developmental progression, but also the expression of developmental levels. Different children think of different wrong answers. The theory tells us the kind of wrong answer that represents developmental progress. It does not tell us which specific wrong answer ought to appear.

So far, we've been doing a pretty thorough job on what the theory cannot do. We've examined some of its limitations, and it is pretty clear that this chapter will not include a definitive list of content areas and facts to be memorized, a set of clear, operationally defined behavioral outcomes, or an ideal pace for acquiring levels of understanding. What is left?

The theory is particularly useful in defining thought processes to watch for and to encourage as they appear. It also designates developmental markers that help teachers plan appropriate activities to enhance processes in development. Because motor development and emotions are so much a part of any cognitive activity (and vice versa), the theory also helps us analyze levels of intellectual development as they are expressed in socio-emotional interactions and feats of physical prowess. The theory will not give us the developmental sequences for these areas. It will show how intellectual ability is related to aspects of developmental sequences as they have been clarified for us by such workers as Freud (1949), Erikson (1950), and the social learning theorists (for instance, Bandura and Walters, 1963) in the area of social-emotional and personality development, and by Gesell (1940), Espenshade (1974), and Tanner (1971) in the area of physical and motor development. For this reason, we will not include a list of guidelines in the areas of motor development or socio-emotional growth. Affective goals will be mentioned primarily as descriptors of the climate within which intellectual abilities flourish.

Valuable contributions are made by our theory in setting goals and in clarifying values in three general areas: the physical and social environment of the classroom itself, the people in the classroom, and the developmental progression of the children in the classroom. We'll look at these contributions in this chapter and in Chapters 6 and 7.

Before we go on to a closer examination of what the theory has to offer, though, let's stop a minute and see where we are. What do you bring to the theory? The following Teacher Task is designed to help you become aware of what you bring. It is not easy to know exactly where we stand. Unless we have made a conscious effort to analyze our own beliefs and expectations, they may go unverbalized, unrecognized, and undefined—even to ourselves. Resist the temptation to skip over the exercise. To do so is to run the risk of chasing after a phantom theory. It is hard to see clearly through the tangle of misleading connotations and intricate, crisscrossing pathways in which both the true beast and the phantoms hide. Your only protection against the beguilements of the phantoms is to know yourself and to maintain a sympathetic, but critical, approach. Are you ready? Then, get out paper and pencil and do some soul searching.

*TEACHER TASK 4-1*

(1) List the major goals of the program you are teaching in (or whatever program you know most about).

(2) What do you expect of the children when they enter the program in the fall? Sort your expectations into three lists: (a) social-emotional expectations (how children relate to other people—children and adults—and how they cope with feelings), (b) intellectual or cognitive abilities, and (c) motor development (fine-motor coordination and large-motor skills).

(3) Make the same three lists for your expectations of how children should be functioning at the *end* of the school year.

(4) Now take a good look at your lists. Which one is longest? Is it the one you value most? the one you know most about? the easiest to see pro-

gress in? These are important considerations, because your answers to questions such as these will influence where and how you can make best use of the theory.

Do you have a good notion of how things stand so far? If you found the lists of expectations hard to make, try thinking of the days you've walked out of the classroom wishing that the day could have gone on forever. List the features you remember from those beautiful days. Now try to remember what the children were doing (sharing the fire trucks, solving problems by themselves, snuggling close to you to hear Sendak's *Where the Wild Things Are*). How about you? Were you doing something you particularly liked or that was particularly effective? What about the other adults in the room? Don't forget the classroom environment. Think hard. Were there special activities, arrangements of materials, social groupings, or routines?

Keep your descriptions of those great days and, now that you're some distance away from them, think about those perfectly awful days, such as the one when Eleanor managed to get play dough stuck in her nose, Paolo hit every child in the classroom at least once and was starting to make a second round, the last can of juice spilled all over Robert's painting, Kristen climbed to the roof of the playhouse again, and for some strange reason, you were so hoarse, you could barely whisper. List features of what the children were doing, what you and other staff were doing, and what the general classroom environment was like.

A comparison of your lists should help you assess what you value in a preschool program. Once you've had a chance to think about how you feel about things now, you're ready to take a critical look at what Piaget's theory has to offer. You are in a position to think actively about what the theory can contribute to your ideas of the classroom environment, to your own knowledge and skill, and to your views about what intellectual progress means for young children.

Incidentally, if you now try to analyze what each kind of day may have contributed to your own development and to the development of the children you work with, you may be pleasantly surprised. Even hard times can be valuable learning experiences.

Now that you've got a pretty good idea of where you are, let's take a look at the roads pointed out by the theory.

## GOALS FOR THE PHYSICAL
## AND SOCIAL ENVIRONMENT
## OF THE CLASSROOM

When guided by our theory, what will we value in the classroom environment? What we want is a classroom that fosters each child's natural propensities to reach out for the world and to adapt to its demands, a classroom that nurtures children's developing abilities to generate hypotheses, to test them, to carefully observe the outcomes, and to incorporate the results into their understanding of the world (into their plans, if you will, for the remodeled structure of their minds, from which they will look out on the world with new perspectives).

With this general orientation, there will be some kinds of environments we prefer to others. Some are automatically out of the running. (There may be advantages to two hours of rote drill or to complete absence of structure, for example, but our theory doesn't see them.) Others are conditional. We will think, "If children are really involved in their activities, as they seem to be, perhaps the noise is okay" or "If that quietness comes from concentration and not from submission, I guess that classroom might be a candidate." Our values refer to whatever combinations of materials, physical arrangements, social groupings, and teacher strategies foster the development of each individual in the classroom. This gives us a range of environments to work with, subject to certain constraints imposed by our theory. These constraints point out goals we can set ourselves in creating the kind of classroom we value.

In general, the classroom we value must encourage active involvement with the physical and social environment, must continually change so as to make appropriate demands on the changing individuals who use it, must have an atmosphere of intellectual honesty, and must be able to meet the needs of diverse interests, experiences, and developmental levels. Key words for the kind of classroom we'll look for (or try to create) are: (1) activity, (2) change, (3) intellectual honesty, and (4) diversity. Why are these so important?

### Activity

First of all, we have required that the classroom foster active exploration of the physical and social environment. Our theory enters here to remind us that development proceeds because of interaction with the environment. One adapts by finding out what the world is like (remember assimilation?) and adjusting oneself (accommodation) in accordance with both the physical aspects (Principle 5, Chapter 3) and the social aspects (Principle 6, Chapter 3). This alone might not seem to require active exploration. Couldn't one simply tell children how things are and how they ought to change so as to reflect more accurately the reality around them? *Nyet,* nope, *nein,* no! Chapters 1, 2, and 3 establish the case against this option. Some of the arguments presented there bear repeating.

Let's look at three major reasons for choosing to include classrooms that foster activity. The first two reasons follow specifically from Piaget's theory. The last is much more general (though it, too, is included in the theory).

(1)   According to Piaget, thought processes evolve out of action. Initially, actions are internalized into a sort of mental counterpart. (As you will recall, Piaget calls this transformation process "interiorization.") Later, the mental structures so produced are able to abstract relations between actions and thus to transform themselves into more elaborate structures. At both levels action is crucial.

(2) Children in a preschool classroom are moving toward the concrete operational stage, characterized by the use of mental operations on present experiences and on memories of specific previous experiences. Active exploration provides the content on which concrete operations do their operating.

(3) Finally, "practice makes perfect." It is one thing to discuss how quickly one's fingers must move to play Rimsky-Korsakov's "Flight of the Bumble Bee," for example, and it is quite another thing to get one's fingers to do it. The same goes for thinking. It takes practice—not just random motions, practice!

Many of these reasons apply to social interactions as well. One has to experience successful attempts to influence others, friendships that don't work out, being the only one who forgot to bring a permission slip, and the like, in order to think about such possibilities at the level of concrete operations. As with the physical world, one can generate and test hypotheses in the social realm. In this case, though, hypotheses might be of this nature: "I can get my way by talking loud and fast" or "People generally don't like it when they get hit" or "If I want Lisa to let me use her new Lego blocks, I'll have to let her be the mom when we play house." Social experiences are a part of the reality around us, part of the reality to which we must adapt. (This does not preclude the possibility of social change any more than does adapting to the physical environment preclude the changes involved in technological advance. Adapting to the environment can mean capitalizing on its potentials for change!)

In addition, social exploration involves working with others who do not always agree. Disagreements and arguments can generate thinking when the disputants are equals or near-equals. Unless we are to furnish classrooms with childlike adults, this will mean that children of similar abilities are an important part of the classroom environment—a part to be actively engaged in social interactions. Although Piaget's theory has much in common with Montessori's approach (as Elkind pointed out back in 1967), this is a point on which it differs. The peer interaction advocated by Piaget is more than the adultlike help given a younger child by an older one. It includes arguments and heated disputes. A well-timed intervention can often turn a fight into a valuable learning experience rather than an emotional catastrophe. Such intervention does not quickly dismiss the situation. It acknowledges the dispute (it may even bring it into greater prominence) and helps children work their way through it. This takes time, but it is valuable learning time.

### Change

Our second requirement for the preschool classroom was that it must change in accordance with the needs of those who use it. As we discussed in Chapter 2, the impetus for developmental change comes partly from changing demands in the environment. The kind of change we are talking about here is the kind that results in continued exploration such that previous ideas are built upon and/or incorporated into new ideas. This can mean new elements of danger to be met and conquered, new responsibilities, new complexities introduced into familiar contents, or new ideas opened up for comparison and contrast. All of these changes, of course, can refer to both physical and social aspects of the classroom. Children can be given higher ladders to climb, smaller beads to string, more choices to make in how to do activities or how to choose partners to work with, less help in dealing with emotional interactions, and so forth. Both areas include a kind of danger as well as new challenges. It is emotionally dangerous, for example, to be the one to decide what song to sing at group time (What if everybody says it is a stupid song?), and it is physically dangerous to try walking across the top of the jungle gym for the first time.

Change is important because a static environment gets boring after a while. One habituates to it and fails to notice what might have been intriguing anomalies, had they not been around for so long. It is not for nothing that most preschool teachers notice what materials get used each day and that they replace those that have fallen out of favor. It is no accident that teachers notice the effects of a humdrum routine and seek to introduce variety into the daily schedule. Our theory can do more than point out the importance of these behaviors, however. It can tell us something about how to make consistent, appropriate changes so that they contribute to an upward spiral of development and are neither erratic and chancy nor a closed circle. (There's nothing wrong with chance, of course, so long as the luck is with you.)

Novelty can be highly motivating for exploratory behavior, as Butler (1957) and Haude and Ray (1967) have shown in work with monkeys and as Harris (1965) and Berlyne and Frommer (1966) have shown with children. If the novelty is too great, however, exploration ceases. The cessation of exploration may be due to real or imagined fears, but it can also be due (our theory hastens to point out) to the size of the gap between what one knows and the thing out there. When the discrepancy is too great, the novel aspect is simply assimilated into the old structures. It is misinterpreted. We have had three-year-old children, for example, predict the outcomes of mixing a small amount of flour in a glass of water. The hoped-for outcome ("It'll make lemonade!") agreed with the visual properties of the mixture, so that the discrepancy provided by the taste test was totally overlooked. The tasters were convinced that it was lemonade and joyfully pronounced it so.

### Intellectual Honesty

We have pointed to an atmosphere of intellectual honesty as our third requirement for the kind of classroom we value. We are using this term to refer to a number of extremely important variables in the construction of knowledge. Primarily it refers to the willingness to make mistakes, but we mean it to include the *ability* to learn from mistakes as well as the willingness to do so and the *ability* to recognize error as well as the willingness to do so. If Piaget is right about why each of us has to do our own construction, our own remodeling of the building from which we look out on new views of the world (see Chapters 1 and 2), then we are each responsible for recognizing the need for remodeling as well as for tackling the project and assessing the result. We have to be intellectually honest. To foster intellectual honesty, a classroom environment must (a) provide opportunity, (b) provide security, and (c) provide aid in all areas of development: psychomotor, affective, and cognitive.

A classroom provides opportunity when people in it use materials and discussion to provoke and elicit the kinds of predictions that can be tested, when time and materials are provided for observing the actual consequences, and when the kinds of predictions tested are interesting ones to the children involved. Thus, the classroom should reflect what the adults in it know about interesting possibilities and intriguing outcomes as well as what is particularly interesting to the children in the group. Since children's experiences are limited, much of the burden falls on the adults to help children become aware of areas for investigation and ways to explore. Adults lay the table, provide the menu, bring in samples to be tasted, and (when requested) may even add a new dish or two. Children ask about the menu (perhaps requesting that a new dish be added), do the tasting, and choose a dish.

Opportunities for hypothesis testing must always be accompanied by security. Numerous researchers and theorists (such as Bowlby, Robertson, and Rosenbluth, 1952; Erikson, 1950; Harlow, 1962; Harlow and Suomi, 1970; and Maslow, 1968) have pointed out the importance of first satisfying needs for trust and security if one wishes to enhance intellectual exploration. Children's options for testing predictions must be bounded by reasonable limitations set by the adult if intellectual exploration is to occur and if catastrophes are to be avoided. Catastrophes come in all shapes and sizes, from excessive shame, embarrassment, or fright, to pain and physical danger. A child needn't be allowed to lose a best friend in order to test a prediction about people's reactions to being imitated. Nor do children have to jump in front of a speeding car to form a reasonable belief about the consequences of such action. Not every hypothesis has to be tested in its original form. For that matter, not every hypothesis has to be tested! Some can be verified by testing related hypotheses and drawing conclusions.

Protection from catastrophes comes from setting limits on what can be tested, helping children to set their own limits, and stepping in to spare them the full brunt of the consequences when they have made a mistake in setting their own limits. Negative results of inappropriate choices must be shown to children but not allowed to overwhelm them (lest they learn to avoid further hypothesis testing). A properly arranged environment will not have too many dangerous and inappropriate choices available.

Many opportunities for learning from hypothesis testing are lost without proper guidance. The teacher's aid comes in several forms. It includes both emotional and cognitive components and refers to help given in noticing relevant aspects of consequences, in connecting consequences to their cause (or relating them to predictions), and in accepting the facts of the case. Sometimes this aid is needed for cognitive reasons. In our previous example, because children didn't take account of the taste of the "lemonade," they failed to recognize the inadequacy of their prediction. At other times, aid is needed for emotional reasons. Young Meg who thought she had worked out a way to climb up a rope ladder, called her friends over, and then failed in her attempt, may need reassurance. The failure can hardly be denied—even if she tries to deny it, her friends will insist on the contrary. The teacher can help her accept the failure, find out what went wrong, and use the knowledge to modify the next attempt.

### Diversity

So far, we've discussed three of the four characteristics to look for in the kind of classroom we value. We have said, in effect, that the classroom should have objects and children (plural!), that it should encourage active exploration, and that it should change in response to developmental needs. The last characteristic is that the classroom environment be one that lends itself to a diversity of developmental levels, experiences, and interests.

We have already discussed why any classroom, no matter how homogeneous the group of children at the start of the year, must provide for a variety of developmental levels. We may be able to determine fairly accurately a child's developmental level at a particular time, but this is not an infallible guide to the pace at which he or she will move over the next couple of months. Some researchers have found that transitional periods can be detected and that subsequent acquisition of certain abilities can be predicted with some accuracy (for example, Inhelder, Sinclair, and Bovet, 1974; Parker, Rieff, and Sperr, 1971; and Wohlwill, Devoe, and Fusaro, 1971). However, even when predictions work in general (that is, for most of the children in a group), they do not hold for each individual—and it is each unique individual to whom we as teachers are responsible!

It is part of our responsibility to the children we teach to consider the previous experiences they have had. Like experience in playing scales on the piano, experience with particular situations, objects, and ways of thinking will affect the amount of time needed for acquiring new, but related, skills. Children with a minimum of experience in generating ideas will take longer to become proficient at guessing games or imagination exercises than those in the habit of it. Likewise, the understanding that volume remains constant when changes of shape are made may come faster to children who have spent hours pouring water from container to container with an eye to the effects than to those without that experience. A classroom that reflects these legitimate differences will be one in which time and activities are so arranged that children are supported in their desires to continue an activity after others have left. Group activities will include a variety of challenges—some for the "old hands," some for the "greenhorns." Such a classroom requires a teacher who can sense when repetition reflects needed practice and when it reflects boredom, the reluctance to face a new challenge, or uncertainty about how to extend the activity.

The consideration of previous experiences is also important for its contribution to finding out particular interests of children. It is important to incorporate children's interests into the classroom because of the high levels of motivation involved in pursuing one's own interests. So long as children are also shown the potentials of other areas of interest, there is nothing to lose and everything to gain.

What's that? Our theory beast is nodding its head vigorously and muttering something that sounds like "transfer." It must be a theoretical term. Ah, yes. Of course. According to Piaget's theory, structures of thought are developed in the context of specific content but are not bound to that content. What this means is that cognitive structures that are developed through interactions in one area of interest can be transferred to other areas. (Before the transfer is accomplished, we notice horizontal *décalages.* Check back to Chapter 2 if you're not clear about this.) The transfer is not immediate and automatic—a little teacher help or an extra effort on the part of the child can do wonders—but it happens. It's sort of like practicing the piano and learning to type. Practicing Beethoven's *Emperor Concerto* won't tell you which fingers to use to type the letters *l, a,* or *p,* but it will build up your finger strength and control, so that once you learn where the letters are on the typewriter, you'll improve rapidly in speed and accuracy.

A classroom which provides for diversity, then, will have a combination of activities that reflect individual children's particular interests and activities that are chosen and invitingly set out by adults. In addition, there will be evidence of relationships between activities. Different activities may share certain objects, arrangements, and so on, and there will be teacher time spent in helping children see relationships between the activities.

## THE PEOPLE
## IN THE CLASSROOM

It is difficult to examine the classroom environment without dwelling on the teacher. As others have emphasized (for instance, Klein, 1973), the teacher can make or break the program. A classroom environment is only as good as the teacher. It does little good to have objects out for exploration, for example, if the teacher forbids their being touched. In the role of teacher, we are only as good as our knowledge about the children in our classrooms, our creativity and expertise in preparing the physical and social classroom environment, and our ability to engage in high-quality interactions. We need to integrate theoretical knowledge, practical knowledge, and specific skills into our own personal styles. Competencies in these areas will be discussed in more depth in Chapter 7. For now, let's look at some of the characteristics we'd like to develop so that we can combine our knowledge of theory with our own thinking abilities in becoming the kind of teachers we'd like to be.

The following characteristics are those we value in ourselves, because of the contributions they make to our ability to help children learn to think. They are also characteristics we value in anyone, because they demonstrate a reconciliation between two opposing beliefs: (1) the belief that all individuals have the right to arrive at their own beliefs rather than to depend on someone else to tell them what and how to think, and (2) the belief that the powerful influence of one's social inheritance on one's ideas and values is not only unavoidable, but beneficial. These are the characteristics we value for the same reason that we spend millions of dollars on scientific research and next to nothing on crystal balls and modern-day Merlins. Rigid thinking and a heavy dependence on tradition may be very adaptive in static, tradition-bound cultures. In modern Western society, however, the facts and skills one learns in childhood may well be falsehoods and obsolete techniques in one's adult life. It is not specific facts we want from our elders. It is the fruitful methods we want—ways to think and grow.

Each item in this list represents a trait we value in human beings, a goal toward which we, as adults, strive, and a long-term goal for the children we work with. For human reasoning at its best, says our theory, these six characteristics are essential:

(1) Self-confidence. We need to be aware of our own self-worth in all areas of growth (emotional, social, motor, and cognitive), regardless of our present level of ability. We also need to have confidence in our ability to grow in these areas. Our first attempts to understand and apply theory, for example, may leave us frustrated and confused. We know that with patient effort, however, theoretical notions will begin to make sense and our own skill in applying them will improve.

(2) Empathy. We use "empathy" here to refer both to the intellectual ability and to the willingness to place oneself in the position of someone else. This can be in terms of the other's visual field, intellectual understanding, previous experience, and/or emotional orientation. When we have this characteristic, we can engage in appropriate interactions with peers and those in other age groups.

(3) Ability and tendency to take the responsibility for initiating one's own learning experiences. This includes exploring, experimenting, and asking questions of oneself, one's peers, and those in other age groups. We must be *willing* to take the plunge, and we must *have some ideas* about how to get started.

(4) Interest in alternative ways of solving problems. This is as important as having the solutions. As Piaget has put it, ". . . repeating correct ideas, even if

one believes that they originate from oneself, is not the same as reasoning correctly" (Piaget, 1950, p. 162). The ability to find alternate ways of solving problems is especially important when some routes are blocked. We may not have certain pieces of information, for example, or we may not have the time to take our customary, circuitous route.

(5) Habits of critical thinking. We need to have the reasoning strategies necessary for verifying conclusions, and we have to use those strategies. This means that we will not accept the first answer we come to without checking it out. In Piaget's terms, these reasoning strategies refer to logico-mathematical and infra-logical operations.

(6) Flexibility. We need to relate intelligently and creatively to our environment. Briefly, this means that we will tend to
   a) pick out the critical variables that are relevant to the problem we set for ourselves,
   b) find possibilities beyond the immediate situation (that is, we will generate hypotheses and look for alternatives), and
   c) make decisions and come to conclusions on the basis of the variables we have considered and the possible solutions we have hypothesized.

This is certainly not an exhaustive list of every valuable human characteristic. Rather, this list reflects the values that led the authors to call upon the theory in the first place. Once we began to work with the theory, we were able to clarify and refine our original values, based on our increased knowledge of how we human beings function. Other people can (and have) drawn up somewhat similar lists. In fact, our list has many elements in common with most other lists people draw up.

What is particularly important is how we use this list. Our theory tells us that these are characteristics we can develop through thoughtful interactions with a favorable environment. That is why so many of the items stress both willingness and ability. If we fall short in one of these areas, we are not evil; we are not weak in character. We are people with room to develop.

There is another important aspect of our use of this list that our theory absolutely insists upon. We must take the list seriously. If these values represent our priorities, then values such as quiet, orderly children, rapt attention focused on the teacher, and aesthetically pleasing classrooms (from an adult's perspective) will have to be assessed according to their contributions to the characteristics on this list. Even sacred goals for children, goals such as taking turns, will come under scrutiny. A child who has to wait too long before asking a burning question at group time may stop generating questions—at least in that particular setting.

Every one of us has to weigh priorities and examine our own value systems for potential contradictions in the means-ends relationship. We value certain means, and we value certain ends. Will the one lead to the other? This is where we whistle for our theory beast. Theoretical insights into developmental processes help us generate some hypotheses. Then we use all the reasoning we can muster, coupled with some careful observations of children (as unbiased as we can make them), and we decide on a course of action. We either reassess our values or we accept our system as it stands, pending further information.

## THE CLASSROOM ENVIRONMENT
## REVISITED

What has been left out of our discussion of classroom goals is as important as what has been left in. Notice that none of the goals mentioned specific numbers of children, noise levels, materials, or amounts of teacher-structured time. These are important variables, but they are context-specific. They must be assessed according to how they contribute (or fail to contribute) to the goals for the total classroom environment. Thus, a program in which a teacher holds a group together for long periods of time can be good or bad, depending on how the group time is handled—on how much opportunity there is within that setting for each individual child to explore features of the physical and social environment at his or her own level.

The theory beast closes its eyes and calmly waits for us to sort this out. However, it does have a trick or two behind its ear. "The key," it proclaims in a deep resonant voice, "is to make predictions, observe the outcomes, and modify one's views accordingly." "What," it inquires solemnly, "is happening to the *children* involved?"

We will have to assess classroom environments according to their effects on children. This is a point we will come back to again and again, for its importance cannot be overestimated. For this reason, the charts on the following pages are designed only as a guide for looking at classrooms, not as a simple checklist. The examples are illustrative, not prescriptive. The real test of what works and what doesn't is how your children react. How does your classroom (or one you know) fare under your careful scrutiny? (Don't forget to let the theory help you scrutinize; that's what it's for.)

### Another Look at Activity

Our first key word was activity. How do we see that in the classroom? We will look for both teachers and children being mentally and physically active. This means that we will want to see them

(1)  tending to rely on their own abilities to solve problems, to settle disputes, to master motor tasks, to seek information, to verify answers, to initiate activities, and to motivate themselves and others;

(2)  actively seeking explanations, testing hypotheses, and using all of their senses to find out about the world;

(3) acting upon the world—manipulating objects, exploring materials and spaces, trying new behaviors, and engaging in social interactions;

(4) making use of a variety of resources, including other children, teachers, equipment, and space;

(5) thinking about the effects of their actions (potential effects as well as actual ones), the effects of variations on their actions, the properties they have discovered through their interactions with objects and people, and possible consequences of various behaviors and activities; and

(6) transforming the information they get from the world—figuring out what an object must look like that they have explored only by touch (for instance, while wearing a blindfold), analyzing what it is they are doing when they crawl, or identifying objects by the sounds they make when used in their customary manner.

We can make sure that these types of activity characterize our classroom, by providing thinking space, by making materials accessible, and by making our classroom one that changes in a predictable way. The charts on the following pages suggest goals for a classroom that promotes activity. They do not provide an exhaustive list, nor is everything suggested there necessary. The charts are intended to help you get the idea of what we mean by promoting activity so that you can do your own thinking about goals to set for your own classroom.

*TEACHER TASK 4-2*

---

Pick a classroom and observe it for at least one session. Describe and compare the instances in which children get their own equipment to those in which teachers get the equipment for them.

(1) What factors contributed to the similarities and differences you saw? Were there differences in accessibility, time constraints, the size and complexity of the equipment, or other factors?

(2) Evaluate the consequences of each instance in terms of social, emotional, and cognitive effects. (For example, did children play longer with materials supplied by the teacher or with ones they gathered? Was there more elaborate play in one case than in the other?)

(3) Based on your observations and the evaluations you made in (2), list some advantages and some disadvantages of giving children more responsibility for gathering and caring for equipment.

(4) Pick an activity that required extensive teacher guidance in setting out materials. What are some possible ways to arrange materials, to adjust schedules, or to modify teacher behaviors (giving instructions, for instance), so that children in the particular classroom you observed could take more responsibility for the activity? (Try to think of ways that do not alter the basic nature and value of the activity.)

**CHART 1: To Promote ACTIVITY, the Classroom Provides THINKING SPACE**

| DAILY SCHEDULE | PHYSICAL ENVIRONMENT (INCLUDING MATERIALS, EQUIPMENT, AND THEIR ARRANGEMENT) | TEACHER BEHAVIORS |
|---|---|---|
| *Transition times are long enough* for teachers to help children finish what they're doing, think about the next activity, and prepare for it. An adult may make a smooth transition in 5 minutes, but it is unlikely that a teacher can help 10 4-year-olds make smooth transitions in that amount of time. (This all depends on the situation, of course. Only careful observation and experiment can tell you how much time to allow in various kinds of transitions and with the particular children in your classroom.) | *There is plenty of space* for working with available materials. When actual space is limited, this can be accomplished by flexibility in where activities are set up and where materials are allowed. | *Teachers warn children* of upcoming changes and follow through by helping children make the transition. (Warnings may be in the form of verbal reminders, signals such as a 2-minute warning bell, notes on a piano, written signals, timers). |
| | *Enough materials are available,* so that, when appropriate, a child can follow a line of inquiry without stopping every five minutes to give someone else a turn. | *Teachers clarify the boundaries* of the thinking spaces while leaving the spaces intact. Thus, teachers provide limits that prevent destruction of materials, dangerous consequences of exploration, or unnecessary confusion, but they allow the child to actually solve problems within those constraints. Rules are clear and simple, and *exceptions are allowed!* |
| *The schedule includes times for children to reflect on what they've done.* Times might be set aside for children to evaluate problems and accomplishments and for them to plan follow-up activities or to set rules. Thus, times would be set aside for discussions about whether or not to continue the pirate game when everyone goes outside, what materials would be needed outside, and whether any new rules would have to be introduced in the new area. | *Materials are arranged* in a way conducive to thinking:<br>(1) They are stored in a *systematic* way, with plenty of space between items, so that children can get an item from the shelves without taking six other things with it.<br>(2) *distinct areas* are provided, so that materials commonly used together are grouped together—art materials, materials commonly used in block play, and so forth. (However, children are allowed, and encouraged, to take materials wherever they are needed.) | *Teachers respond readily to requests for help but do not take over the problem.* They help the child solve it. (Think of times when a child asks for help in painting a picture and is entirely satisfied by your approving presence—without any intervention in the actual painting.) |

*The schedule allows time for teachers to help children resolve their own problems,* button their own coats, clean up the water they spilled, and so forth. As any harried teacher or parent knows all too well, "helping children help themselves" takes more time than simply helping children.

(3) *A limited number of materials* is available at any one time, so that the materials do not take over the activity. Rather, the activity should be allowed to guide the choice of materials. Remember, too many choices equals no choice at all.

*Teachers suggest that children ask others for help,* and facilitate such communications among children. They help children use one another as resources. Teachers say, "Find someone to read this with us," rather than, "Peter, come read this with me and Karen."

In conversations with children, teachers *wait for children's responses and really listen to them.* Really listening means changing your expectations and your own thinking as a result of the interchange.

*Teachers use activities in which children have to mentally construct or reconstruct* an idea—a game in which blindfolded children have to guess what object they're holding, for example.

**CHART 2: To Promote ACTIVITY, the Classroom Provides for the ACCESSIBILITY OF MATERIALS**

| DAILY SCHEDULE | PHYSICAL ENVIRONMENT (INCLUDING MATERIALS, EQUIPMENT, AND THEIR ARRANGEMENT) | TEACHER BEHAVIORS |
|---|---|---|
| *Plenty of time is allowed for the care of equipment.* This takes longer for children than it does for an adult, so extra time is set aside for clean-up periods and for explaining the uses of materials. Because children will be helped to use their own judgment about what constitutes a novel, yet acceptable, use of equipment, they will need times set aside for presentations, demonstrations, and discussions of how to use equipment—and *why* certain ways are or are not acceptable. | *Materials are safe and durable,* so that children are not afraid to use them. | The *teacher has ideas for materials that might enhance a particular activity* for various interests and developmental levels of children in the classroom. The teacher also *knows where to get the materials* and may even have them readily available on a nearby counter. |
| | *Storage is easy and convenient for children.* Children may have different systems for organizing materials than adults do. Also, what is easy for a child to reach may not be so for a teacher and vice versa. In such cases, the children's organization is generally preferred. | Teachers *discuss with children the care of equipment and the range of acceptable uses.* Teachers help children see constraints in the use of materials and help them decide whether each use meets the constraints. |
| *Clean-up times* may involve *individual responsibility;* they may involve *cooperative efforts;* or they may involve responsibility for all and only the things one has actually used during the day. Whichever option is taken, ample time is set aside for doing it and for discussions of what is to be done and why. | *Materials are available that allow children to try out a variety of actions* without having to worry about breaking or misusing materials. | *Teachers help children figure out where items are kept* rather than simply telling them (for instance, "What is it usually used for?" or "Where do we usually keep things used for that?"). Teachers help the child figure it out before they tell, and they tell before they get. |
| | | *Teachers model the use of a material in a variety of areas.* They help children construct guidelines for what kinds of variables to consider—for example, traffic flow or noisy activities versus quiet ones. |
| | | *Teachers help children understand the need to care for equipment* and then help children decide how to do it. |

**CHART 3: To Promote ACTIVITY, the Classroom Provides for PREDICTABILITY**

| DAILY SCHEDULE | PHYSICAL ENVIRONMENT (INCLUDING MATERIALS, EQUIPMENT, AND THEIR ARRANGEMENT) | TEACHER BEHAVIORS |
|---|---|---|
| *Routines follow a usual pattern. Flexibility is built into the pattern,* as are signals for which of the possible changes is the one put into practice today. For example, if children start the day with a free-play period either indoors or outdoors, pictures on the door of the classroom can be used to indicate where they will play on any particular day—outside, inside, or free choice. If group times are used for singing, storytelling, and movement activities, children might be warned at clean-up time about which activity was up for today—or other signals may be devised. | *The available materials encourage children to make predictions and to test them.* This means that at least some of the materials must have clearly defined changes under the transformations likely to be tested by preschool-aged children. A sandbox or table with sifters, funnels, and leak-proof containers is an example of an appropriate material.<br><br>*Available materials are the kind that respond differently as actions on them vary.* A pendulum is a good example of this (as are ramps that can be raised and lowered, rather than being of fixed height and length). Many good ideas for this type of equipment can be found in Forman and Hill (1980) and in Kamii and DeVries (1978).<br><br>*Materials are kept in a predictable place and in predictable condition.* Children share with teachers the responsibility to care for equipment and to return it to its proper place. | *Teachers encourage children to make predictions and to clarify exactly what they expect to happen;* for instance, "What does it mean to melt? Will there be changes in weight? in stickiness? in color?"<br><br>*Teachers are consistent in their demands on children*—they know what they value in their program, and communicate this to children. When they change their minds, they let the children in on the reasons. They often involve children in the decision-making process itself. |

### Another Look at Change

To see change in the environment, we'll have to look at the classroom over a prolonged period of time. During the course of the school year, we'll look for evidence that children are provided with opportunities and encouragement for

(1) taking increased social responsibility, mastering more difficult motor tasks, and solving more difficult problems;

(2) trying out their systems of thought on a variety of activities and situations that increase in complexity, require the incorporation of new ideas, or simply demand a greater number of ideas used at once;

(3) being constantly challenged, since there is no predetermined upper limit on challenges to be offered in any particular grade;

(4) reconstructing on the plane of thought what they already can master on the sensorimotor level (After children have already spent a considerable amount of time with ramps, bridges, and toy cars, for example, they are drawn into more and more elaborate discussions of what is responsible for the way things work. We already mentioned some of the features of this transition from sensorimotor intelligence to operational thinking, in Chapter 2. The examples in the charts that follow and discussions in later chapters will make this even clearer);

(5) identifying and pursuing their own changing interests, whether this be the elaboration of old themes or complete changes of topic.

As in the classroom designed to enhance activity, the provision of accessible materials, thinking space, and predictability helps to make sure the appropriate kinds of change are provided for. Charts 4, 5, and 6 suggest various kinds of evidence to look for in assessing appropriate kinds of change.

As you read through the charts, think about an environment you know—a classroom, a supervised playground, your home, or wherever adults work with children. How might change be seen in the schedules, the arrangements of the physical environment, and the behaviors of adults in that environment?

The next Teacher Task is designed to focus your attention on ways to create appropriate change.

*TEACHER TASK 4-3*

---

Imagine that you are planning an obstacle course for a group of young children. List materials you'd use and describe the kinds of obstacles you'd construct for each of the following: a group of three-year-olds; a group of four-year-olds.

In each case, what changes would you make in materials, constructions, or teacher behavior if the children were totally unfamiliar with the idea of an obstacle course? if they were very familiar with obstacle courses?

(Doing this exercise will be greatly enhanced if you think about a classroom you have access to, so that you can try out your ideas.)

---

**CHART 4: To Promote CHANGE, the Classroom Provides for the ACCESSIBILITY OF MATERIALS**

| DAILY SCHEDULE | PHYSICAL ENVIRONMENT (INCLUDING MATERIALS, EQUIPMENT, AND THEIR ARRANGEMENT) | TEACHER BEHAVIORS |
|---|---|---|
| *Transition times may become longer* as children take more responsibility for equipment—for mixing paint, preparing snack trays, making tape roadways, and the like. | *Materials previously on shelves are stored away, with their locations indicated* by photographs, drawings, (including maps), words, and so on. | *Teachers remind children of the availability of old materials* and help them learn how to find them in their new storage areas. |
| *Planning and evaluation times are introduced into the schedule* as children take a more active role in decisions about activities and materials. | *New, more complex materials are introduced* as the year progresses. | *Teachers help children learn how to adjust equipment to their needs*—to choose appropriate kinds of scissors, to thin or thicken paint, to find the light-weight blocks, for example. |
| *Some parts of the schedule may be eliminated or replaced* as children become able to manage the available resources. Snack time, for example, may be replaced by "open snack," which allows each child to have snack whenever he or she decides to. | *Extra tools and materials for finding out how things work* are introduced after equipment has been available for a while. For example, after using play dough for several weeks, children may be shown how to make it. Or extra wheels and axles may be provided for repairing toy cars. | As the year progresses, *teachers encourage children to take a larger role in deciding what materials and activities should be available* each day. Teachers may arrange planning meetings in which children participate, for example, or they may put up a suggestion board. |
| | *Old materials appear in new locations for new uses.* Play dough may be moved from the art area to the housekeeping area; books may be moved to secluded story areas outside; kernels from corn cobs used for decoration may be removed and used like sand. | |

# CHART 5: To Promote CHANGE, the Classroom Provides THINKING SPACE

## DAILY SCHEDULE

The *times allowed for free play, group activities, clean-up, and so forth, vary* as children develop longer attention spans and the ability to guide themselves in intricate dramatic-play episodes, in elaborate constructions with blocks and art materials, and so on. Juice times will be longer when children participate in the preparation and serving of food. Group times will be longer when children are taking turns in contributing to a story they make up on the spot. They will be shorter when individual activities during free play are particularly absorbing and the gathering time is used for announcements and a song or two.

## PHYSICAL ENVIRONMENT (INCLUDING MATERIALS, EQUIPMENT, AND THEIR ARRANGEMENT)

*The amount and arrangement of space* allotted to various activities changes as needs of children change. Dramatic play may be expanded into the block corner, for example, as children's play becomes more sophisticated and as their ability to build sturdy structures with a specific purpose increases.

*Activities that involve greater use of words and pictures* are introduced as the year progresses—whenever children have a grasp on the objects and actions the symbols stand for. Pictures or words can be used to demonstrate procedures for cooking, putting away materials, going on trips, and so forth.

## TEACHER BEHAVIORS

*Teachers help children make decisions* about the kinds of help they need. Teachers do this by asking about and commenting on possible outcomes of various choices.

Teachers *enter play situations to stimulate activity,* to suggest new problems to resolve, and to provide moral support when difficulties arise. They withdraw from the activity without having completely solved the problem and without having taken over the activity. The amount of involvement required changes over time and according to the activity.

Teachers *judge the needs according to the situation,* and not according to whether or not a child should know how to handle the situation.

As children learn to pace themselves and have experienced alterations in schedule, they can help decide such things as when to end the free play and whether to have juice before group time or after.

As more words and pictures are used for one aspect of an activity, direct action and manipulation of concrete objects for other aspects are encouraged by the materials available.

Materials are used for different purposes as the year progresses. Wooden beads may be used for fine-motor-control exercises early in the year. Later, they may be set up with intricate patterns to imitate—patterns that require sophisticated spatial thinking to reproduce.

Teachers give instructions that make use of understandings children already have. Children who already know how to make play dough may be guided in making red dough with instructions such as these: "Make play dough the way you did before, and then add this much red paint." An even more challenging approach is to ask the child to explain how to make the dough and then ask, "How do you think you could make it red?"

More complicated instructions are given and new kinds of questions are asked as children's memory develops and as their familiarity with the classroom grows. Early questions of the "What is it?" sort are replaced with "Why?" "How does it work?" and "What will happen if . . . ?"

Teachers ask questions that are challenging to children at their level of understanding. Different teacher behaviors are used for similar activities with the same child over time.

# CHART 6:  To Promote CHANGE, the Classroom Provides PREDICTABILITY

| DAILY SCHEDULE | PHYSICAL ENVIRONMENT (INCLUDING MATERIALS, EQUIPMENT, AND THEIR ARRANGEMENT) | TEACHER BEHAVIORS |
|---|---|---|
| As the school year progresses, *original routines learned by the children are modified in predictable ways*—that is, in ways that meet the new interests of children. Children develop the expectation that their changing needs, interests, and desires will be met; they will not be permanently classified according to the interests and abilities they showed at the beginning of the school year. | *Changes in materials and room arrangement are made for reasons children can understand* —for instance, to provide more space for an emerging interest, to make things more efficient. | *Teachers help children see similarities and differences* between established procedures and new ideas. |
| The schedule is flexible enough to allow *extra time and repeated exposure to new activities and changes in schedule.* Children are told about upcoming schedule changes days in advance and are given practice in comparing the present schedule with the one to come. | *New demands are made and new materials are introduced* in the context of familiar procedures. | Teachers *explain changes in schedule* before they occur. They remind children frequently of how things will be different and of what will be expected of them. Reminders may be in the form of demonstrations, pictures, or verbal descriptions. |
| Classroom *schedules are adjusted to seasonal changes,* with, for example, more activities outside in nice weather, some boisterous "outside" activities set up inside during long winter months, nature-study field trips in the spring and fall. | *A variety of materials that allow for similar transformations* are introduced throughout the year, with pictures, demonstrations, and verbal discussions used to help children apply what they know to predictions of how the materials will react. | Teachers *help children make and test predictions of increasing complexity.* For example, as children become more proficient in building block structures they can get in and on, teachers help them test for sturdiness and stability. |
| | The environment provides for *different ways of predicting.* Clocks can be useful if the schedule follows rigid time limits. Such cues as bells, particular songs, seeing the teacher sitting on the rug holding a flannel board, or the arrival of the delivery man can also be used in predicting the beginning of group time. | |
| | *Materials of increasing difficulty* are introduced throughout the year, so that children expect to be challenged but are not overawed by the intellectual and physical requirements. | |

### Another Look at Intellectual Honesty

In an environment that fosters intellectual honesty, we will see children

(1) expressing what they really think and feel, rather than what they suppose they are expected to think and feel;

(2) submitting their own ideas to a variety of rigorous tests;

(3) asking challenging questions of one another and actually testing for themselves what others claim is true;

(4) pursuing their own lines of inquiry, even if they seem silly to others; and

(5) taking controlled risks in the use of materials and in handling social-emotional situations.

Appropriately accessible materials, adequate thinking space, and certain kinds of predictability are vital to an atmosphere of intellectual honesty. Charts 7, 8, and 9 (pages 87–90) give a clue about how to spot these vital features.

*TEACHER TASK 4-4*

Consider the following guidelines for doing science experiments on the nature of various processes of change. Answer the questions under each guideline to test your understanding of how applications of the guideline enhance intellectual honesty.

(1) Choose an activity in which the rate of change is *relatively fast.* For example, to illustrate the effects of water on the rigidity of plants, use a droopy Coleus plant, which perks up within half an hour of being put in water, rather than a plant that takes a day or two to respond.

   (a) How would this guideline influence your decisions about what plants to grow? about the kinds of experiments you'll do with children?

   (b) List some experiments that meet this criterion and some that don't.

(2) Use some examples in which the changes *can be reversed*, so that children can repeat the experiment with the same object. (This helps them recognize that one and the same object undergoes the changes and that clearly defined procedures lead to the result.) For example, flowers such as tulips and morning glories close in the dark and open in the sunlight. They can be placed in the sunlight, then in a dark cabinet, then in sunlight.

   (a) List some examples of reversible changes for both living and nonliving things; list some examples of irreversible changes.

   (b) Now discuss with someone activities you might do with children to help them understand the items in both lists. (i) Which of the changes can readily be seen by young children? Which are difficult to see? (ii) Try doing some of the activities you thought would be easy and some you thought would be hard. As you do each, concentrate on finding out what a child really thinks is happening. (iii) Which activities enable you to enhance intellectual honesty? Why?

(3) Use examples in which the process of change is *visible*. For example, although an egg changes from a raw to a cooked state when it is hard-boiled in the shell, we cannot actually see the change occurring. Why should we believe that a particular egg has changed rather than that some eggs are runny and some are firm? On the other hand, one can watch colored water rising in a celery stalk or in a capillary tube, and one can see the change in root growth on a sweet potato grown in water.

    (a) Take any book on science experiments for young children. Find several experiments in which the process of change is visible to young children and several in which it is not.

    (b) For each experiment, write down some questions you might ask children so that they focus on relevant variables and are honest with you and with themselves about what they see. (Keep in mind the responses of children to the "lemonade" experiment earlier in this chapter.)

(4) *Limit the number of factors* responsible for the effects observed.

    (a) Discuss with someone why this is important. Choose sides on the question of whether it influences intellectual honesty and then try to show your opponent why and how it does (or doesn't).

    (b) Choose an experiment you like to do with children. List as many plausible hypotheses as you can about what is happening and why. Now ask some children about the experiment and find out what they really think—keep asking them questions and trying out parallel cases with them until you think you have discovered what they really think is going on.

### Another Look at Diversity

The last of our four key words for the classroom environment was diversity. As we observe the classroom, we want to see

(1) different children spending different amounts of time in different areas, doing *different* things with the *same* materials, and doing the *same* things with *different* materials;

(2) children rethinking previous solutions and solving old problems in new ways;

(3) children sharing experiences they alone have had, making use of what they've learned elsewhere in their classroom activities;

(4) children suggesting activities, materials, and ways of doing things;

(5) the same childen trying out a new material or in a new area what they've done with other materials in other places; and

(6) children actively manipulating materials, and children watching, thinking, and finding ways to make sense of the experiences they have had.

Goals for the classroom will touch on accessibility of materials, thinking space, and predictability. As in the charts for the other key words, charts 10, 11, and 12 (pages 91-93) give *suggestions,* not requirements.

**CHART 7: To Promote INTELLECTUAL HONESTY, the Classroom Provides for the ACCESSIBILITY OF MATERIALS**

| DAILY SCHEDULE | PHYSICAL ENVIRONMENT (INCLUDING MATERIALS, EQUIPMENT, AND THEIR ARRANGEMENT) | TEACHER BEHAVIORS |
|---|---|---|
| The *schedule provides time for error.* This is not treated as an unfortunate delay in the program; it is built in as a desirable feature. Activities are repeated over the course of the year; the same concepts are discussed in a variety of situations throughout the day; materials that may help a child understand a problem are available—at least to the teacher—even when they are not part of the planned activities. | The classroom has spaces provided for old materials to stay available when new ones are brought out. This enables children to reexamine old solutions, to relate previous uses of materials to new ideas, and to broaden their understanding of the materials and their potentials. | Teachers provide additional materials and ask searching questions if doing so will help children question predictions they have made. For example, lightweight pie tins might be given to a child who has concluded that all metal things sink. |
| During the day *children have time to "mess about"*—to explore materials and to just enjoy the feel, smell, taste of them—before the children are asked to think about whys, wherefores, and what ifs. | Spaces are provided for individual projects to be stored overnight, so that children can tackle problems too big to be solved during one school day. | Teachers model problem-solving behaviors and encourage imitation. Children are encouraged to imitate one another's solutions, but they are also encouraged to vary those solutions. |
| The schedule is flexible enough that individuals who need longer exploration time or more rapid transitions into thoughtful discussions can *move at their own pace without being singled out* as "special" or "different." Children who grasp a concept faster than their peers are not pointed out as models either by verbal comments or by extra materials blatantly presented to them while other children sit quietly. | Any rules for using materials are made explicit. Guidelines for what materials are acceptable for which activities are established, but exceptions are made—especially if they are suggested and plausibly argued for by children. | Teachers suggest experimentation with concrete objects by providing materials and by suggesting, either verbally or by modeling, ways to explore the objects and their relations to other objects. A teacher might try using a magnet as a boat, as a hairpin, as a paper holder on a refrigerator door, or as a way to pull a metal car. |
| | Materials are on low, uncrowded shelves so that children can find what they need and can detect and correct errors in replacing materials. | |
| | The range of materials available allows children to make decisions about what things are too difficult. Children can try very difficult puzzles and give up without concluding that they were bad or stupid to have tried them. | Teachers point children to the kinds of materials that will help them work through solutions. Teachers recognize, for example, that building a 3-dimensional model will help children become aware of features of an object they have been ignoring, when a return from drawings or verbal discussions to the concrete object itself is needed, or when role playing can be enhanced by props of a certain type. |

**CHART 8:  To Promote INTELLECTUAL HONESTY, the Classroom Provides THINKING SPACE**

| DAILY SCHEDULE | PHYSICAL ENVIRONMENT (INCLUDING MATERIALS, EQUIPMENT, AND THEIR ARRANGEMENT) | TEACHER BEHAVIORS |
|---|---|---|
| *Timing is adjusted to what children actually understand,* not to what they "should know by this point in the curriculum." The schedule is flexible enough to accommodate the need to spend 3 times as much time as anticipated on a task children see as vital. | *There is preparation for accidents.* Paper towels or drop cloths are under the easel; washing water is near the mud hole; bandages and tweezers are near the woodworking area; mops are near water-play areas. | *Teachers give help without taking away the challenge,* by (a) being near potential trouble spots without intervening; (b) asking "What kind of help do you want?" when children seek help; (c) showing children how to help themselves—by demonstrating how to clean up instead of cleaning up for them, for example, |
| *There are times set aside for an evaluation* of how things are going; group discussions are held, during which group decisions are assessed and the effects of individuals' decisions on the group are examined. | *Materials and equipment for mopping up* after accidents are *child-sized,* are in storage areas *accessible to children* (low cabinets and counters, possibly with pictures of the contents), and have been explained to children. Hence, children see ways to reinstate themselves if something is spilled or broken. | or by showing them some ways to go about solving a problem rather than giving them the answer; and (d) by focusing children's attention on conflicting data rather than by reinforcing correct responses. |

Throughout any activity, *time is allowed for reconsideration of plans.* Small groups of children can gather during free-play times, for example, to discuss with a teacher new rules for the block area.

*There is a supply of expendable materials.* Children can try out ideas first on tin cans, egg cartons, used computer paper, and old crayons before they try them on materials of limited availability.

*There are materials not generally considered child-proof, but such materials are under more direct teacher supervision* than others. They may be stored in high cabinets or in special areas of the room.

*Teachers encourage cooperative play and help to manage disputes* (rather than quell them). In doing so, teachers are constantly assessing the children's capabilities; demanding too much cooperation or too much autonomy in settling disputes destroys the atmosphere of intellectual honesty.

Teachers find situations in which children can make decisions, and suggest that children do so. Teachers remain available to *help children see the consequences* of their decisions, to *help them live with the consequences,* and, if necessary, to *remake the decision.*

*Teachers ask children for their opinions and take the answers seriously.* They do this by (a) following up on questions to make sure they understand the child's idea and to discover the child's underlying assumptions, (b) helping other children accept differences of opinion, and (c) paying as much attention to misconceptions as to right answers.

**CHART 9: To Promote INTELLECTUAL HONESTY, the Classroom Provides for PREDICTABILITY**

| DAILY SCHEDULE | PHYSICAL EQUIPMENT (INCLUDING MATERIALS, EQUIPMENT, AND THEIR ARRANGEMENT) | TEACHER BEHAVIORS |
|---|---|---|
| *Activities are planned with teacher/child ratios in mind.* The schedule provides times when 2 or 3 children can work with a teacher in an activity that requires that teacher's full attention—either because it involves some risk or because it requires great concentration by all participants. | *Materials are the kind that show outcomes that are clear to young children.* Ramps, for example, show clear outcomes if the prediction concerns what will happen to various blocks and toy cars placed on them. They *won't* show clear outcomes about how fast objects will move. They *can* show clear outcomes about how far things will go. Evaporation experiments are less clear to children than are more immediate changes such as the effects of food coloring in water. | *Teachers discuss reasons for changes in schedule.* They point out the problems, being honest about their own reasons for dissatisfaction.

*Teachers engage children in discussions of* whether or not a schedule change is needed.

*Teachers show surprise without dismay when children's predictions or their own aren't verified.* They encourage alternate hypotheses and the testing of them. Their approach to teaching is as experimental and consciously self-evaluative as they encourage children to be in their learning. |
| *The schedule changes according to the demands of the weather, of children's needs, or special opportunities, and so on.* If the schedule isn't working, it is changed—whatever the reason for its failure (such as, not suited to the abilities and interests of available adults, wrong season, temperaments of the particular children in the group). | *Materials are designed to be used independently by children,* so that they can conduct their own experiments, really see what's going on, and test the results of their own actions and the subsequent effects (*not* watch someone else's actions and the subsequent effects).

*Materials are stored in a systematic way that* shows children which they can explore freely on their own and which require teacher assistance. | *Teachers consistently help children test predictions,* by watching results, limiting dangerous experimentation, and helping children think through possible outcomes before acting. They help children view wrong answers as a step toward understanding. |

**CHART 10: To Promote DIVERSITY, the Classroom Provides for the ACCESSIBILITY OF MATERIALS**

| DAILY SCHEDULE | PHYSICAL ENVIRONMENT (INCLUDING MATERIALS, EQUIPMENT, AND THEIR ARRANGEMENT) | TEACHER BEHAVIORS |
|---|---|---|
| *The schedule provides time for children to learn how to clean up thoroughly*—not by tossing things into boxes or putting them in the general area where they were found, but in the place they belong. This takes extra time and teacher help planned into the day at the beginning of the year and whenever new materials are introduced. Depending on the demands for the materials on a given day, it may be important for children to replace items immediately after they are through with them—even if they will be needed again shortly. | *A variety of materials are available* to children but do not create a confusing clutter. Storage space is well planned, well labeled, and made known to children. | *Teachers use a variety of ways to help children clean up, so that materials remain truly accessible* to all. Teachers help children put things away as they finish—where that won't interfere with the child's train of thought. They suggest such clean-up strategies as, "Pick up only the red things," only the drawing materials, only this space," or "Find a friend to help you clean this up," or "Think about what you're going to clean up first, second, and third." |
| *The schedule on any given day reflects consideration of the kinds of teacher help required for various activities.* Unless there are at least five adults available, it would not be a good idea to have finger painting, rearrangement of playground equipment, slicing vegetables for snack, and woodworking all available at once to a group of 4-year-olds. | *Materials include those that emphasize smell, taste, touch, sound, and visual perception.* Some of the materials show obvious contrasts; some are more subtle.

*Available materials are suited to a variety of abilities.* Heavy blocks, for example, can be moved by two smaller children or one big child. Thick paints are available for novices, but water is available so that more experienced painters can adjust the thickness. Some materials are clearly for initial exploration (such as boxes of plumbing parts or of various textiles); others are for systematic use (for example, battery boards or sandpaper letters). | *Teachers are flexible about what can be used where,* but they remind children to notice where they are getting the materials so that they can return them later.

*Teachers make children aware of the diversity of materials available,* by asking children about other materials to look for materials; by suggesting places to look for materials; and by taking special times to explore materials with children, spending time explaining and demonstrating. |
| *The schedule provides time* for various large-motor activities; refined small-motor tasks; quiet thinking times; verbal exchanges; use of films, pictures, and other representational devices; access to music—both listening and producing it; and access to a variety of "grown-up, job-related" materials (for instance, typewriters, hospital equipment, plants). | There are *materials for acquiring knowledge* (materials to explore and test systematically) and *materials for representing and communicating knowledge* (drawing and modeling supplies, word cards, dance equipment, tape recorders, pictures). | *Teachers help children discover new ways to use old materials and apply old techniques to new materials.* |

**CHART 11: To Promote DIVERSITY, the Classroom Provides for THINKING SPACE**

| DAILY SCHEDULE | PHYSICAL EQUIPMENT (INCLUDING MATERIALS, EQUIPMENT, AND THEIR ARRANGEMENT) | TEACHER BEHAVIORS |
|---|---|---|
| The schedule provides for *different kinds of thinking space:* | The environment includes *spaces and materials that lend themselves to* | Teachers *provide time and encouragement for individual children to set their own tasks and assess their own accomplishments.* |
| (1) *solitary thinking*—a time to be alone (quiet times are one of many ways to work this into the schedule); | (1) *individual activities*—materials such as puzzles and private places to work; | |
| (2) *thinking with other children*—a time to debate and discuss problems without the continuing guidance of an adult (free play is the usual, but not the only, time explicitly included for this purpose); | (2) *cooperative play*—activities, such as dramatic play, water tables, or sand, that cry out for several children and work places large enough for those children; | Teachers *help children learn from one another.* Group sizes are adjusted in accordance with children's personalities and their abilities to handle group interactions. Teachers point out special sources of information (for instance, the child who has a new baby brother) and actually help children cooperate (rather than telling them to "share" or "play nicely"). Different children will require different amounts of help. |
| (3) *thinking with adult guidance*—either on a one-to-one basis or in groups. | (3) *work with adults*—activities such as woodworking, which requires adult skills, and special places for the activities. | |
| The schedule provides for *flexibility about where things are done.* A juice time out of doors, for example, requires time and work to get set up but provides new ways of thinking about food—it highlights different features. To allow a story to be read in a tree house, there must be activities going on that are not likely to require the teacher's immediate presence in order to avoid catastrophe. | *Materials of varying degrees of difficulty are available to children.* Time, space, and materials allow for a variety of outcomes in an activity. For example, a water table is set up with mops and towels for children likely to spill water, with intricate tubes and containers for those ready to experiment, and with a separate area available for the child who needs some time just to feel the water running through the fingers. | Teachers *plan activities by thinking of a variety of questions, helpful hints, and alternative directions for follow-up activities,* so that they can adjust the activity to the needs of the particular children involved. |
| | | Teachers *consciously help children notice a variety of ways to be wrong and to be right.* They may summarize the variety of suggestions made during a group discussion, for example, and they ask children to explain in their own words (perhaps to inform another child) what others have said. |

**CHART 12: To Promote DIVERSITY, the Classroom Provides for PREDICTABILITY**

| DAILY SCHEDULE | PHYSICAL ENVIRONMENT (INCLUDING MATERIALS, EQUIPMENT, AND THEIR ARRANGEMENT) | TEACHER BEHAVIOR |
|---|---|---|
| *Children help to plan the schedule and/or help record plans,* through using some sort of calendar, tape-recorded messages, pictures, or the like. Then they know what to expect —and if they forget, they know where to find out. | *Available materials encourage children to distinguish* between things that always react in a particular way (for instance, liquid water always goes through a sieve), things that sometimes react in a particular way (for example, sand goes through a sieve when dry but not when wet), and things that never react in that way (large stones never go through the sieve). | Teachers *encourage and support diverse interests* by making time and materials available and by helping other children accept the special interests or abilities of each child. Teachers discuss different interests and abilities with children. |
| *The schedule provides special times for distinct activities.* Challenging motor tasks might usually be in the early part of the school day, for example, and one-to-one work with a teacher might come during the end of a free-play period for a particular child. Small-group acitvities might have a regular time, just as juice time typically does. | *Changes in materials and room arrangement are made in a predictable way.* The dramatic-play area might be moved next to the large blocks, for example, after children have been transporting dress-up clothes to the block area or after teachers and children have discussed the change. | Teachers work conscientiously on *maintaining an open mind about children's interests and abilities.* They try to avoid deciding what a child likes to do and then unconsciously steering the child to what they have come to expect him or her to like. |
| *"Surprises" are usually announced beforehand,* so that children are part of the secret and don't have the feeling of being duped. | *Materials that react in slightly unusual ways are available for testing predictions* after other standard materials have been explored. Silly Putty, for example, might be stored in a teachers-only area, for introduction at opportune moments. | Teachers observe carefully, in order to *maintain the right amount of diversity.* Too much leads to chaos; too little leads to decreases in learning potential. They explain to children the reasons for limited availability of materials on a particular day when they see a need for reduced diversity. |
| | *Equipment-storage areas are clearly marked,* in such a way that children know which equipment they must use only with teacher help and which is to be used at their own discretion. | |

> Imagine yourself with unlimited resources. How would you *schedule* room for solitary thinking and for adult-guided thinking into a school day? How would you arrange the *environment* to compliment the schedule you propose?
>
> Now think about a program you know of. How could you adjust its schedule, environment, and/or teacher behaviors to enhance provision of all three kinds of thinking space (solitary, with other children, and with adults)? Discuss your suggestions with the staff members of that program. Find out what they think of the feasibility and general desirability of your ideas.

## SUMMARY

Theoretical concepts, from Chapter 2, and principles for applying those concepts to an educational program, from Chapter 3, have been used in this chapter to identify some general, cognitively oriented goals for the classroom environment and the people in it. The goals we suggested for the people in the classroom were

(1)  self-confidence,
(2)  empathy,
(3)  ability and tendency to take the responsibility for initiating one's own learning experiences,
(4)  interest in alternative ways of solving problems,
(5)  habits of critical thinking, and
(6)  flexibility.

We looked at four key words designating desirable features of the classroom environment. *Activity* was important because of children's need to construct their own knowledge, or, in the words of Chapter 1, to do their own remodeling of the structure from which they view the world. *Intellectual honesty* was important for the same reason; to take responsibility for one's own learning, one has to admit errors and make changes in the way one thinks. *Change* and *diversity* were key words because of the nature of development (as described by the theory). They are important because each child remodels in his or her own way and at a unique pace; an environment that is optimal for a variety of children must have diverse opportunities and must change over time.

As in previous chapters, we have asked you to test hypotheses as you read. We have asked you not to simply take our word for it. To show how important we think this is, we have given you some guidance in how to test hypotheses: where to start looking, what questions to ask of yourself and of what you see, and how to assess your initial attitudes. The Teacher Tasks are difficult and time-consuming, but they are important. They should be taken seriously if maximum benefit is to be gained from this chapter. In addition, the twelve charts were included to help get you started on your own, more specific lists of goals for your classroom. Chapters 5 and 6 will help you augment your lists.

## REFERENCES

ANTHONY, E. "The significance of Jean Piaget for Child Psychiatry," *British Journal of Medical Psychology, 29* (1956), 20–34.

BANDURA, ALBERT, and RICHARD H. WALTERS. *Social Learning and Personality Development* (New York: Holt, Rinehart and Winston, 1963).

BERLYNE, DANIEL E., and F. D. FROMMER. "Some Determinants of the Incidence and Content of Children's Questions, *Child Development, 37,* no. 1 (1966), 175–190.

BISNO, ANN. "An Application of the Piaget Model to a Curriculum for Deaf-Blind Children," in *Piagetian Theory and the Helping Professions,* ed. Gerald I. Lubin, James F. Magary, and Marie K. Poulsen (Los Angeles: University of Southern California, 1975).

BOWLBY, J., J. ROBERTSON, and D. ROSENBLUTH. "A Two-Year-Old Goes to the Hospital," in *The Psychoanalytic Study of the Child,* Vol. 7, ed. R. S. Eissler et al. (New York: International Universities Press, 1952).

BUTLER, R. A. "The Effect of Deprivation of Visual Incentives on Visual Exploration Motivation in Monkeys," *Journal of Comparative and Physiological Psychology, 50* (1957), 177–179.

ELKIND, DAVID. "Piaget and Montessori: Three Ideas They Have in Common," *Harvard Educational Review, 37,* (1967), 535–545.

ERIKSON, ERIK. *Childhood and Society* (New York: W. W. Norton, 1950).

ESPENSHADE, ANNA, and HELEN ECKERT. "Motor Development," in *Science and Medicine of Exercise and Sports,* 2nd ed., ed. Warren R. Johnson and Elsworth R. Buskirk (New York: Harper & Row, 1974).

FORMAN, GEORGE E., and FLEET HILL. *Constructive Play: Applying Piaget in the Preschool* (Monterey, Cal.: Brooks/Cole Publishing Company, 1980).

FREUD, SIGMUND. *An Outline of Psychoanalysis* (New York: W. W. Norton, 1949).

FURTH, HANS G. *Thinking Without Language: Psychological Implications of Deafness* (New York: Free Press, 1966).

GESELL, ARNOLD L. et al. *The First Five Years of Life: A Guide to the Study of the Preschool Child* (New York: Harper & Row, 1940).

HARLOW, HARRY. "The Development of Learning in the Rhesus Monkey," in *Science in Progress: Twelfth Series,* ed. W. R. Brode (New Haven: Yale University Press, 1962).

HARLOW, HARRY, and SUOMI, S. J. "Nature of Love—Simplified," *American Psychologist, 25* (1970), 161–168.

HARRIS, L. "The Effects of Relative Novelty on Children's Choice Behavior," *Journal of Experimental Child Psychology, 2* (1965), 297–305.

HAUDE, R. H., and O. S. RAY. "Visual Exploration in Monkeys as a Function of Visual Incentive Duration and Sensory Deprivation," *Journal of Comparative and Physiological Psychology, 64* (1967), 332–336.

INHELDER, BÄRBEL, HERMINE SINCLAIR, and MAGALI BOVET. *Learning and The Development of Cognition,* trans. Susan Wedgwood (Cambridge,

Mass.: Harvard University Press, 1974 [first published in French, in 1974, under the title, *Apprentissage et Structures de la Connaissance*]).

KAMII, CONSTANCE, and RHETA DeVRIES. *Physical Knowledge in Preschool Education: Implications of Piaget's Theory* (Englewood Cliffs, N.J.: Prentice-Hall, Inc., 1978).

KLEIN, JENNY W. "Making or Breaking It: The Teacher's Role in Model (Curriculum) Implementation," *Young Children, 28,* no. 6 (1973), 359–366.

KOHLBERG, LAWRENCE. "Early Education: A Cognitive-Development View," *Child Development, 39,* no. 4 (1968), 1013–63.

MASLOW, ABRAHAM H. *Toward a Psychology of Being,* 2nd ed. (New York: D. Van Nostrand Company, 1968).

PARKER, RONALD K., MARJERY L. RIEFF, and SHELBY J. SPERR. "Teaching Multiple Classification to Young Children," *Child Development, 42,* no. 6 (1971), 1179–1789.

PIAGET, JEAN. *The Psychology of Intelligence,* trans. Malcolm Piercy and Daniel E. Berlyne (London: Routledge and Kegan Paul, 1950 [first published in French, in 1947, under the title, *La Psychologie de l'Intelligence*]).

PIMM, JUNE B. "The Clinical Use of Piagetian Tasks with Emotionally Disturbed Children," In *Piagetian Theory and The Helping Professions,* ed. Gerald I. Lubin, James F. Magary, and Marie K. Poulsen (Los Angeles: University of Southern California, 1975).

SENDAK, MAURICE. *Where The Wild Things Are,* story and pictures by Maurice Sendak (New York: Harper & Row, 1963).

STEPHENS, WILL BETH, ed. *Training The Developmentally Young* (New York: John Day, 1971).

TANNER, JAMES M. *Education and Physical Growth* (New York: International Universities Press, 1971).

WOHLWILL, JOACHIM F., V. DEVOE, and L. FUSARO. "Research on the Development of Concepts in Early Childhood." Final Report, National Science Foundation Grant G5855. Pennsylvania State University, January 1971.

WOLINSKY, G. "Piaget and the Psychology of Thought: Some Implications for Teaching the Retardate," *American Journal of Mental Deficiency, 67,* no. 2 (1962), 250–255.

WOODWARD, M. and D. STERN. "Developmental Patterns of Severely Subnormal Children," *British Journal of Educational Psychology, 33* (1963), 10–21.

# 5

# THE
# PREOPERATIONAL
# CHILD

## BEFORE AND AFTER

In the preceding chapters, we emphasized the need to adjust the environment (social as well as physical) to the developmental level of the child. In the process, we pointed out some general characteristics of young children. In this chapter, we'll take a look at what our theory tells us specifically about children in the preoperational period, which is the transitional period between the sensorimotor stage and the stage of concrete operations. In most cases, this means we are interested in children between the ages of roughly two and seven years. (For a large majority of children, as you'll recall from Chapter 2, the sensorimotor stage is fully attained around the age of two years, and the concrete operational stage is clearly recognizable somewhere around the ages of seven to eleven years.)

As you read and think about the material presented in this chapter, it would be a good idea to keep in mind children you know who are in this age range. Or, better yet, find some new children to observe and talk to. This will facilitate your attempt to avoid preconceptions about what a child knows, and it will sharpen your skills in finding out how and what children think.

As usual, we'll make use of the theory where it has the most to say—in the cognitive domain. As we noted in Chapter 2, Piaget's theory is about what we hu-

mans in different stages of development do to gain knowledge and what we do with
the knowledge we have gained. In reading this chapter, think about what specific
experiences young children are likely to have had, how this influences what they do
to gain knowledge, and how both of these things interact with the way they make
use of the knowledge they have. Right now, you probably have the most to say
about the first issue. That's as it should be; we'll use our theory to help us examine
the other issues as we go along. Since young children, being in the preoperational
period, are in the transition from one level of organization to another, their intellectual activities are best understood if one has some idea of the stages that immediately precede and follow this period. After reminding ourselves of the relations
among content, structure, and function, we'll take a closer look at the sensorimotor
and concrete-operational stages. Then we'll concentrate on the preoperational
period.

### Content, Function, and Structure

In the context of our theory, you'll remember, *content* is what children do
and what they think. To describe the content of intelligence at a particular developmental level, we describe the kinds of things children at that level enjoy doing, the
kinds of things they say, and the kinds of things they know about. Very young infants know how to suck; they enjoy looking about and waving their arms and legs;
they cry. One-and-a-half-year-old children know how to crawl and walk; they enjoy
imitating adult words; they can build towers with blocks. Five-year-old children
talk about friends, taking turns, who makes the moon light up, and why anything
and everything is the way it is or does what it does; they can run, climb, hop, and
draw pictures; they know their way about the house, how to cross streets carefully,
and how to write their names. Fifteen-year-old children talk about clothes, politics,
the opposite sex, and how to solve complicated mathematical problems; they know
how to talk their parents into letting them stay out later than usual, how to ride a
ten-speed bicycle and a skateboard, and how to dissect a frog.

Have you got the idea? To get your observational skills tuned up for the job
ahead in helping you teach young children, put some of your past observations to
use in Teacher Task 5-1.

*TEACHER TASK 5-1*

(1) Remember the three areas of human functioning we discussed in Chapter 2—the psychomotor, affective, and cognitive domains? Under each
domain make a list of behaviors and thoughts characteristic of (a) infants aged one to two years; (b) preschool-aged children, say, two to
five years old; (c) grade-school children, aged six to eleven; and (d) high-
school-aged children.

(2) Now sort your list into behaviors that are unique to a particular age (developmental level) and those that run across groups. If all of your behaviors are age-specific, try some more general descriptions to see if
you can find some behaviors common to all the groups. If all the behav-

iors on your list run across groups, be more specific in your descriptions. For example, infants and teenagers both cry, but do they cry in the same way? at the same cues?

(3) Examine your list for any patterns you see. In which domain are the between-group differences greatest on *your* list? Is your list longer for one domain than for another? Are there some age groups you have little to say about? Find some children to observe so that you can fill in the gaps on your list.

(4) Save your lists. They will be useful to you later in providing examples to analyze in terms of the theory.

The *functioning* of intelligence is its constant adjustment of behavior in response to the environment. The adjustments made depend in part on the content: newborn infants don't adjust their sentence structure to the formality of the occasion, because their behavior doesn't include speech; grade-school children don't constantly adjust their mouths to every new object they pick up, because sucking has become only a small part of their behavioral repertoire. The adjustments also depend, however, on the way each individual interprets the environment. If I don't see the chuckhole ahead of me, I don't swerve to avoid it. Similarly, three-year-old Beth, who isn't bothered by the contradiction in saying, "There are more daisies than there are flowers" in a bouquet of flowers, will not adjust her thinking to account for comparisons of part of the group to the whole.

In short, the particular adjustments made depend both on a variety of situational features and on the developmental level of the individual. My failure to notice the chuckhole ahead of me is because of where my attention is directed—my momentary preoccupation with the book I am writing, perhaps. I would easily perceive the chuckhole and adjust my behavior to avoid it, were my train of thought to be broken by the warning nudge of my companion. On the other hand, Beth fails to notice that there is a contradiction in the statement about daisies and flowers because of the way her thinking is organized. The oversight is a result of her developmental level. Attempts to focus her attention on the problem are likely to be utter failures. She won't recognize the contradiction because she doesn't have the mental structure required to compare a part to the whole that includes it (rather than simply to compare one part to another). No subtle nudges, broad hints, or patient explanations are sufficient for bringing her the understanding she presently lacks.

Although the specific adjustments made vary from one developmental level to another, from one individual to another, and from one situation to another, the basic adjustment mechanisms—assimilation, accommodation, and equilibration—remain the same. To see these mechanisms at work so that we can facilitate their contributions to the development of intelligence, we need to see both how they are revealed in specific behaviors and what limitations are placed upon them by different organizational levels, or mental structures. Since Piaget has tended to organize his discussions of intelligence around changes in structure (the stages of intellectual development), we'll do the same when we look at the preoperational child and the organizations from which and to which the child is making the transition.

### The Surrounding Stages: Sensorimotor
### and Concrete Operations

*The sensorimotor stage*

The sensorimotor stage is characterized by intelligence consisting of well-integrated and -coordinated action schemes. Think of a scheme as a pattern or type of action (such as sucking, grasping, reaching, dropping) that can be applied to different objects in a variety of ways (fast or slow, precisely or imprecisely, in combination with other actions or alone). This is not entirely accurate as an account of what Piaget means by "scheme" or "schema," but it won't lead you too far astray.

When the sensorimotor stage is fully attained, each of the child's action schemes is well organized and is adjusted to the objects to which it is applied. For instance, one-and-a-half-year-olds tend to adjust their actions to specific objects: they put necklaces around their necks, stack blocks on top of one another, and hug stuffed toys. Previously they had used their whole repertoire of actions, such as holding, banging, dropping, and popping into their mouths, on every object that came their way. Now they are more discriminating. They can also adjust their actions to the demands of the situation before they begin the action. The ability to coordinate what they are presently perceiving with the action schemes they are going to use allows them to anticipate needed variations on the pattern. Instead of simply reaching out their hand until it bumps into the object they want (or stretching their hand too far and having to pull it back in order to grasp the object), as they did as very young infants, they move their hands quickly and surely, right to the object. All of this sophisticated action goes on apparently without the benefit of what we could ordinarily call conscious thought. Nonetheless, it is well coordinated with perception and is sensitive to changes in the environment. For this reason, it is intelligent action—not random groping or mere trial and error.

This is not the limit of sensorimotor intelligence, however. Different action schemes can also be put together into sequences of gamelike and goal-directed activities. As researchers have pointed out (see Uzgiris, 1976), when infants fully attain the sensorimotor stage, they can combine action schemes such as crumpling a piece of paper and then straightening it out, putting objects in a container and then taking them out, or dropping objects and then picking them up. (What a relief when they finally take over the second part of that last sequence!) As is the case with individual action schemes, the coordinated schemes are also adjustable. Human infants are not like robots that pick up an object, turn 87.3 degrees, release the object, and then return to the original position. If an object sticks to the child's finger in the dropping/picking up sequence, the child interrupts the sequence to remedy the situation (calling upon one or more new action schemes in trying to pull it off). Nothing less than a whole network of coordinations between schemes can allow the child to do this.

The sensorimotor period might be viewed as the culmination of achievements needed for intelligent *physical actions*. We acquire new skills as we grow older, but the basic ways for integrating action are already formed. What is left is the arduous task of applying those ways to new and complex situations.

The sensorimotor period is not only the completion of one phase of development; it is also the beginning of the next stage. This is particularly evident in the area of representation. Children at the end of the sensorimotor stage show rudimentary symbolic activities. They can watch another child's temper tantrum and then put on their own opening performance of it a day or so later. (In the language of our theory, this is called deferred imitation.) They repeat words spoken by adults and often use the words to show recognition of familiar objects. We mustn't be too hasty in attributing adult understandings of these words, however, or even adult understandings of what words are. As Baldwin (1967) describes it, words to the very young toddler are more like a tune one hums than like labels. The capacity to mentally represent information has *appeared*—and Piaget treats this appearance as strictly maturational in the way that the blue of every infant's eyes changes over time to the color the adult will have—but it has not yet *developed*. A look at the concrete operations stage will show us some of the remarkable accomplishments in this area that occur over a five-year period.

### The concrete operations stage

The concrete operations stage is characterized by intelligence on the level of thought. The coordinations between well-developed action schemes have been transformed (interiorized) and elaborated into the operations of thought. Such transformations are examples of the vertical *décalages* we discussed in Chapter 2. The transformations lead to some remarkable changes, but the underlying similarities can be detected. To make the similarities clearer, here are three examples of the content of sensorimotor intelligence and the corresponding content of operational intelligence.

| SENSORIMOTOR INTELLIGENCE IS CHARACTERIZED BY | CONCRETE OPERATIONAL INTELLIGENCE IS CHARACTERIZED BY |
|---|---|
| (1) The *combining of action schemes* into a single coordinated sequence such as reaching, grasping, and bringing an object to the mouth. | (1) The *combining of classes* (say, daisies and poppies) into a more inclusive class (flowers), so that hierarchical relations are understood. This involves the *recognition* that when two actions are combined, the result can be a more complex action and not merely a sequence of two single actions. |

**SENSORIMOTOR (Cont'd)**

(2) The ability to *act so as to compensate for changes* required by various environmental contingencies. This allows the same goal to be achieved in different ways. This can be seen in the use of detours and in the use of alternate patterns of action (as in the earlier example where the child stopped to pull a sticky object off the finger before continuing a game).

(3) The systematic *reversal of actions,* such as putting things into containers and taking them out, or moving one's arm away from the body and then back.

**CONCRETE OPERATIONAL (Cont'd)**

(2) The *recognition that one change may compensate* for another, so that the status quo is maintained. A number of dimensions are taken into account, so that one realizes that a taller, but thinner, container may hold exactly as much sand as a short fat one. (The focus on several dimensions simultaneously is called *decentration*; the recognition of compensatory changes is called *reciprocity*).

(3) The *recognition* that for every action, one can conceive of the situation that would occur if the action had not been taken. For example, the grouping of boys and girls into a room and calling them the class of children does not destroy the class of boys or the class of girls. One can mentally compare the class of children to the class of boys. This simultaneous recognition of the consequences of an action and the absence of that action is called *reversibility*.

The similarities in the content of intelligence at the two stages lie in the schemes or patterns that are first exhibited in overt physical actions and then in the nature of thought. The use of the word "scheme," which allows both *physical actions* and thinking processes, or *mental actions,* to be instances of the same scheme, is what made our earlier characterization of scheme (in our discussion of sensorimotor intelligence) somewhat inaccurate. As Piaget points out in *Biology and Knowledge* (1971), an action scheme is whatever it is about an action that can be transposed, generalized, or differentiated from one situation to another. The basic scheme of reuniting, for example, is found in an infant who piles up blocks and in an eight-year-old child who classifies both mammals and fish as vertebrates.

As you can see from the three examples we have given, there are dramatic changes as well as striking similarities in the shift from sensorimotor to concrete operational intelligence. For one thing, thought is considerably more flexible than physical action. Instead of merely coordinating their actions with what they presently perceive, children in the concrete operational stage can mentally compare previous perceptions and actions to the situations at hand. They can evaluate alternate sequences of action and their consequences. They can explain why certain results are to be expected and can solve relatively difficult intellectual problems when the subject matter is familiar.

Thought is also applicable to a wider variety of subject matter than is action. We can think about combining numbers, though we can't act on them physically; we can use words, with all their subtleties of use and shades of meaning, to communicate ideas, instead of relying on more limited physical demonstrations (it is not a simple matter to demonstrate through actions the theory that the earth is about 4.5 billion years old); we can think about purely logical relations, such as what kinds of inferences hold across a variety of subjects, including both tangible and intangible things; and we can think about past or future states of affairs, which we certainly can't act on at the moment.

We have already mentioned *decentration* and *reversibility* as important features of thought in the stage of concrete operations. A third important feature is the *tendency to focus on the processes of change,* rather than to focus on the final results of a change. Concrete operational children tend to pay attention to processes such as the gradual thickening of scrambled eggs in a hot skillet, the way water looks in a jar as the jar is slowly tilted, or the continuously changing shape of clay as it is molded in a sausage shape. These three features reveal much about the mental organization characteristic of this stage and are largely responsible for the stage-specific content. In contrast to infants and toddlers, children in the concrete operational stage are proficient at verbal communication; can agree with other children on a set of rules and then follow them; can imagine and predict processes of change as well as the end result; can understand that not only does the *object* remain (as they realized in the sensorimotor stage), but various of its *attributes* are unchanged when certain dramatic perceptual alterations are made; and they can engage in logical reasoning about familiar objects.

The abilities just listed are not mere refinements of the abilities of infants. Many of the problems grade-school children can solve could not even have been recognized as problems by children in the sensorimotor stage. Infants don't even ask themselves whether changes in the shape of a ball of clay affect its weight, much less decide that the weight remains constant. Infants don't concern themselves with how many fingers they have and certainly don't wonder whether the number changes when they spread their fingers out. These examples of questions to which infants are oblivious are precisely the questions that children in the concrete operational stage grapple with and successfully answer. The answers don't come immediately after the questions are posed, obvious as they may seem to us adults. The lengthy transitional period between the sensorimotor stage and the concrete operational stage is one in which such questions are raised in a vague sort of way, partially answered, refined, answered in a new way, turned topsy-turvy, answered again, rejected as irrelevant, reintroduced as crucial, and so on, until the relatively stable concrete operations provide the mental organization that puts them in their place.

Although there is much more to be said about the stage of concrete operations, further descriptions are likely to take us away from our main task, which is to examine the transitional period that culminates in that stage. We now have enough of an idea of where preoperational children are headed, developmentally, so that we can appreciate the difficulties they face in transforming the intelligence of actions into the intelligence of thought. Before turning to the preoperational child proper, it will be helpful to try the next teacher task.

*TEACHER TASK 5-2*

(1) Return to the lists you generated in Teacher Task 5-1. Refine and augment your lists to include some of the kinds of behavior discussed in
this section.
(In order to understand the contributions our theory can make, it
will be particularly profitable to look at the kinds of behaviors children at different stages tend to imitate, and the kinds of actions,
words, or questions they tend to repeat. What children are able to
imitate is a good sign of what kinds of things interest them, what
features they attend to, and how their mental organization affects
the way they interpret their environment. A hard look at what they
repeat can show you what they regard as difficult and/or important
problems to solve.)

(2) If you find yourself intrigued by some of the changes we've discussed
and you want to find out more about either stage, there is a tremendous number of helpful references available. Here are a few to start you
off. On the sensorimotor stage:

BOWER, THOMAS G. R. *Development in Infancy* (San Francisco:
W. H. Freeman, 1974).
PIAGET, JEAN. *The Construction of Reality in the Child,* trans.
Margaret Cook (New York: Basic Books, 1954).
PIAGET, JEAN. *The Origins of Intelligence in Children,* trans. Mar-
garet Cook (New York: International Universities Press, 1952).

On the concrete operational stage:

BOWER, THOMAS G. R. *Human Development* (San Francisco: W. H.
Freeman, 1979).
FLAVELL, JOHN H. "Concept Development," in *Carmichael's Manual
of Child Psychology,* Vol. 1, 3rd ed., ed. Paul H. Mussen (New
York: John Wiley & Sons, Inc., 1970).
PIAGET, JEAN, and BÄRBEL INHELDER. *The Psychology of the
Child,* trans. Helen Weaver (New York: Basic Books, 1969).

As guides to your own observations, these works are probably best used
if you browse through them, stopping to read carefully those observations that catch your interest. These will give you ideas on what behaviors to look for and how to elicit them. Pay particular attention to the
kind of detail the authors include in their descriptions of behavior.

## THE PREOPERATIONAL PERIOD:
## SOME GENERAL CHARACTERISTICS

Now that we have some general idea of the developmental tasks facing children in the approximate age range of two to seven years, lets look at how children go about accomplishing those tasks. Because the developmental changes are far-reaching and because they depend so heavily on what experiences one has and how one manages to make use of those experiences, we can expect the transitional period to be filled with hesitant first steps, overconfident solutions that dissolve as new problems are encountered, wavering opinions on the hows and whys of the world, a plethora of new questions to be asked and answered, and initial attempts to solve problems mentally—attempts that slip easily into the familiar action schemes of the sensorimotor stage as soon as obstacles are encountered. Understandably, reliance on untried systems of thought is somewhat erratic. Unlike the stages that flank it, preoperational intelligence lacks structural properties; it is not a unified system.

We don't need our theory to tell us that many of the labels commonly applied to preoperational children (two to seven years old) are well founded. By contrast with older children and adults, young children seem to be particularly curious, impulsive, unselfconscious, physically active, and overtly affectionate. They are continually asking, "Why?" but then forgetting to listen to the answer. They would rather act on objects to see the effects than to think about what the effects might be; they are fascinated by their physical and social world and want to *do* things to it. Friends of their own age are becoming increasingly important to them, although they are still wrapped up in themselves and their own experiences. A likely response to a discussion of how many legs a cat has, for example, is: "My cat sleeps on my bed." They are just beginning to find out that there are life-styles other than their own—that their teacher may not only live away from school, but he or she may not live with a mommy and a daddy.

A look at any good child-development-oriented program for young children will show that these characteristics are reflected in room arrangements, materials, schedules, and teaching strategies. A good classroom can also show you what interests young children tend to have. They like to read stories—especially ones with pictures; construction activities are a favorite (it's hard to find a program for young children without blocks of some kind or other); sensory materials are a must (witness the universality of clay and play dough, sand, water tables, and finger paint); singing and movement games are always popular; climbing, running, riding tricycles, and rough-and-tumble play occupy a sizable portion of the day; drawing and painting are in constant demand; and dramatic play (pretending to be a mommy or a daddy, a firefighter or a superhero) run through most of the children's activities.

Piaget's theory adds to this description. The detailed observations that led Piaget to his theory of cognitive development help explain why children have these interests and suggest additional characteristics for us to look for as children pursue

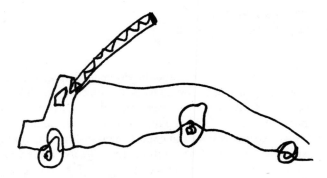

their interests. Many characteristics of young children's thinking had simply gone unnoticed (or at least were not explicitly noticed) until Piaget found ways to elicit their expression. In particular, Piaget has pointed to three very general characteristics of the young child's newly emerging thought. The thinking of children in the preoperational period lacks the three important features we mentioned as being central to concrete operational thought: (1) reversibility, (2) a tendency to focus on the processes of change, and (3) decentration. Instead, it is characterized by *egocentrism, intuitive solutions* (rather than reflective thought), and *centration.* Although these latter are rather vaguely defined descriptive terms, they are useful in summarizing, and showing the connections among, a wide variety of behaviors. We'll look at each of them in turn.

### Egocentrism

Egocentrism refers to children's inability—not their reluctance— to consider viewpoints other than their own. They don't see a need to consider an alternative viewpoint because it doesn't even occur to them that there is one. Furthermore, the existence of alternative views cannot simply be pointed out to them. Because young children frequently fail to distinguish between their own ideas and the ideas of others, between what they've said and what others have said, a single example of a conflicting opinion may not be recognized by children as a distinct view. They may interpret it simply as another idea of their own. A statement such as, "Different people have different ideas," will not be very convincing, nor will it make much sense, to a child who isn't yet tuned in to the fact that different viewpoints exist— or who doesn't even compare ideas to one another to see whether or not they are different.

If you've been around young children, you'll have seen many instances of how egocentrism is displayed in overt behaviors. The three-year-old who gleefully proclaims, "I was right," after seeing another child's prediction confirmed is showing signs of egocentrism. So is the child who gets irritated when a stranger professes ignorance of the reference for some idiosyncratic name such as "Bubba" to refer to a favorite blanket or teddy bear.

### Egocentrism in language

Egocentrism shows up in a wide variety of content areas, though its effects are perhaps most pronounced in language. Although most two-, three-, and four-year-olds can use language for communication—to express wants, to get what they need, to share anecdotes, and so forth—they tend to believe, when they stop to think about it, that other people know and understand everything they know. Speaking is a pleasurable activity that accompanies actions and is enjoyed in the company of other people, but it is not consistently viewed by children as a device for communicating *new* information to another person about what one knows or thinks. For this reason, children in the early preoperational period tend to give jumbled and abbreviated accounts of stories, with little attempt to help the listener see the real order of episodes. There are few expressions like, "Oh, that came before she saw the wolf" or "I forgot to tell you that . . ." By the end of the preoperational period, such expressions are beginning to find their way into the telling of stories, which themselves are already in less disarray.

### Egocentrism in the social-emotional domain

Egocentrism also characterizes the social interactions and emotional responses of children. For example, children's failures to recognize another's intellectual point of view can lead to behaviors frequently mislabeled by those unacquainted with Piagetian theory as stubborn, selfish, rude, inconsiderate, and even disobedient. It is perhaps because of these symptoms that egocentrism is sometimes confused with egotism. The difference between the two may be subtle, but it is important. When we say of people that they are *egotists,* we attribute to them both intellectual and emotional capacities. We are suggesting that these people see a clear difference between themselves and others but that they have distorted the significance of that difference. They think that a consequence of the difference is that their needs are the more important, that their views are the more correct (or the more insightful), and that they are generally better than others. This is in marked contrast to the *egocentrism* of the child, a characteristic that reflects a failure to see a clear difference rather than a distorted interpretation of the significance of the difference.

The behaviors of a young child, especially behaviors labeled selfish, rude, and the like, may seem similar to the behaviors of the egotistical adult, but there are important differences. The young child has no clear consciousness of self and of one's own experience as distinct from the experience of others. Children may have some awareness that others haven't shared all of their experiences, but they have great difficulty in figuring out what others have shared and what they haven't. The result is a very uneven mixture of "selfish" behavior and idiosyncratic explanations with acts of generosity and conscious attempts to make others understand. Rules are obeyed because they come from prestigious persons, but they are easily forgotten and are not seen as ways to balance one's own interests and the needs of others.

The lack of a clear distinction between self and others also shows up in children's views about nature, their inability to consider or describe what other people might be seeing, and their failure to give justifications for claims they make. It's not easy to construct a system of thought!

### Egocentrism and views of nature

Piaget has described many of the beliefs children hold about natural phenomena in *The Child's Conception of the World* (1929). He refers there to a variety of beliefs that most of us can remember holding as children. For example, in failing to fully differentiate themselves from their surroundings, children often believe that nature (trees, rocks, the moon) is alive, conscious, and shares their outlook. They may believe that the moon follows them and that it does so because it wants to go wherever they want to go. Or children may believe that they can make rain come and go by chanting special words. The first kind of belief is often cited as an example of *animism*; the second is sometimes called a feeling of magical *omnipotence*. These labels can be a little misleading, especially if they are taken to suggest the belief in a clear distinction between oneself and others with the additional belief that inanimate objects are conscious beings or that the individual has special powers. To hold specific beliefs such as those mentioned about the moon or the rain, however, young children needn't have such well-defined general beliefs. As our theory tells the story, they simply do not distinguish things in nature as being distinct from themselves (and so out of their immediate sphere of influence). To exaggerate a bit, it is as though children see trees and rocks as being extensions of themselves—like fingers, toes, and the hair on their head.

### Egocentrism and spatial perspectives

When asked to describe how things look to a person sitting across from them, children may think the question absurd, interpret the question as being about what they themselves can see, or faintly understand the legitimacy of the request but show great difficulty in answering it. They try to describe a perspective different from their own but wind up describing the people, chairs, and windows that they are seeing.

### Egocentrism and justifications

When asked how they know that something is the case, children are likely to answer, "Because I just know." When pressed, they may go so far as to appeal to authority: "My mother told me twelve years ago," or "I know 'cause I'm big." Some of these answers seem to be made up in order to satisfy adults who seem to be pressing for answers where none are needed. But another factor is also important here. Young children very frequently have no idea of how they know what they know. The last two of the three characteristics we mentioned earlier (that is, intuitive solutions and centration) help explain this.

Although a variety of cognitive characteristics are responsible for the difficulty children have in describing how people at different physical vantage points see things and for their obliviousness to the need to justify their claims, much of the problem comes from egocentrism. Children fail to see a need to describe a thing in any way other than how it appears at the moment, and they see no reason to establish a conviction when they are already convinced. And failing to fully differentiate themselves from others, they act as though others were also convinced.

## Intuitive Solutions

Intuitive solutions, rather than conscious processes of problem solving, are the rule for children in the preoperational period. Young children are in the process of constructing on the plane of thought what they already know on the plane of action. Because their structure of thought is not well developed, they tend to rely on unconscious procedures, many of which are not yet logical in the adult sense of the word, for solving problems. Children who know perfectly well how to crawl, for example, and who can use language easily for communication, often are at a loss to explain the pattern of leg and arm movements involved in crawling.

*TEACHER TASK 5-3*

Stop for a moment to think about the pattern of crawling. Is it left arm, left leg, right leg, right arm? or, perhaps, left arm, right leg, right arm, left leg? (No fair doing any crawling until you've tried to figure it out!)

If you have any doubts about your answer after you've given the problem some thought, go ahead and watch someone crawl—or do it yourself. Notice how you think about the problem and what you do with the chance to test your description against an example. Your awareness of how you solve the problem will help you to help children solve it.

If you found this problem so easy to solve that you couldn't focus on your thought processes, you might check one of Piaget's later works, *The Grasp of Consciousness* (1976), for more difficult problems of the same sort.

If you had difficulties with Teacher Task 5-3 (either with the example of crawling or with others you found in *The Grasp of Consciousness*), don't worry. It doesn't mean your thought is preoperational. There is an important difference between your resolution of the problem and a young child's resolution. The difference lies in the use you make of the actual crawling. You are able to compare your description to an example of the motion and make corrections. Three-year-old Ricky is likely to generate an erroneous description, "test" it against an example of the movement, and conclude that his description was adequate. His system of thought is not rich enough, relative to his action schemes, for him to note the discrepancy between the results of using one to characterize the other.

In many cases, intuitively generated solutions are far better than any the conscious self-reflection of young children could uncover. However, since the solutions are generated through unconscious processes, and since children have not yet learned to infer what procedures are being used, they have no way to correct for any errors, oversights, or hasty conclusions in the procedure. Children can often feel their way through a problem and arrive at a correct answer without having a clear conceptual representation (a conscious and generalizable notion) of precisely what the problem is, how they got the answer they did, or why (and whether) the answer is a good one. They may solve problems for a few familiar cases without ever formulating a rule that will work for other cases as well.

A result of this feature of children's thinking is that we can easily mistake children's resolutions of problems as indications that their systems of thought are the same as ours. We are particularly prone to this error if we look in only a general way at children's success in dealing with their environment. Apparently, they can easily solve a myriad of everyday problems: they make successful predictions about causes and effects, they quickly acquire practical knowledge such as how to let the water out of the sink and how to keep it in, they have a variety of techniques for getting other children to let them join ongoing play, and they can do hundreds of other amazing things that you already know about if you've had even a slight acquaintance with young children.

If we look more closely at what children say and do—especially if we ask them questions about why the answers they give are the correct ones and if we give them unfamiliar problems of the same type to solve—we get a very different picture. The correct predictions in cause-effect sequences are seen to be limited to, first, sequences that occur frequently in the child's usual environment, and, second, to predictions of end results rather than to processes. Furthermore, if you listen very carefully, you'll hear children give explanations such as, "The egg fell because it broke" (which we adults frequently mis-hear as, "The egg broke because it fell"). You might be tempted to explain away this confusion by saying the child meant to say something about how he or she *knew* the egg fell—something like, "I *know* the egg fell because I can see that it is broken." That may be a good explanation for the child's sentence structure in some cases, but it is not plausible in every one. The common-sense notion of cause is still unclear to preoperational children.

Our closer look at children's attributions of cause and effect show us two consequences of intuitive thinking in young children. First, children can apply intuitive solutions only to the familiar problems for which the solutions were originally designed. Second, just as children are oblivious to the fact that a *process* of thinking has given them their answer, they are oblivious to the external *processes* to which their thought might be directed. Instead, they focus on states—initial states and end states. Unlike the child in the stage of concrete operations, the preoperational child focuses on the look and feel of raw eggs, and later, the cooked scrambled eggs, rather than on the gradual thickening of the eggs as they cook. This has its advantages, of course; transformations make more sense when one understands and remembers the initial state and when one has some reasonable expectations concerning the result than when the whole thing is mysterious. Any attempts to help the child acquire the concrete operational characteristic of a focus on processes of change ought to be tempered by efforts to make sure the child has a good grasp of the initial state and some idea of what the end state will be like. This is the reason for our advice on plant-growing experiments, back in Teacher Task 4-4: make sure the child expects two similar plants in similar growing conditions to follow the same pattern of growth before you do experiments testing the effects of different growth conditions.

Like the concept of egocentrism, which we were at pains to distinguish from egotism, the intuitive character of young children's thinking must be distinguished from adult intuitions. In this case, however, the difference is a little more subtle. Adults may generate good solutions through some sort of intuitive process of the mind, but they do so when they have applied their conscious attention to the nature of the problem (see, for example, Jacques Hadamard's [1945] discussion of mathematical intuition). Furthermore, they see the need for the use of their logical reasoning capacities in a conscientious evaluation of the proposed solution. Children's intuitive processes may be as good (and as well developed) as those of an adult, but children don't apply the processes to clearly defined problems and don't verify the outcome.

As is the case for egocentric behaviors, the need to modify the behaviors, in this case to test the products of intuitive thinking, cannot simply be pointed out to young children. The need is not visible from their windows. Children will need many opportunities and lots of encouragement for testing the solutions they think of—and for doing so in a wide variety of contexts—before they see a need to re-model their intellectual structures. They'll need practice in assessing carefully the nature of the problem they solve and in determining exactly how their proposed solutions are able to resolve the problems. The process is long and slow. Unfortunately, centration, the next preoperational characteristic we'll discuss, doesn't make things any easier.

### Centration

Centration refers to the tendency to focus on single variables rather than to compare the effects of different variables or to examine the interactions among variables. Consider the question of whether the amount of milk remains unchanged when a pitcher of milk is emptied into ten glasses. Preoperational children are likely to believe that because there are more separate containers of milk, there must be more milk in the ten glasses than there was in the pitcher. They neglect to take into account both the smaller amount of milk in each glass and the remarkable property of substances their belief leads them to: if their belief were true, there should be no starving people in the world! We could keep dividing food into smaller and smaller bits, until we had enough to feed everyone. Concrete operational children, on the other hand, are able to coordinate the change in number of containers with the change in size of the containers. By taking into account both of the relevant variables, they are able to conclude that the amount of milk has not changed. They cannot yet systematically test the relations among a large number of interacting variables, but they are aware of interactions and make judgments with the possibility of an interaction in mind.

We are speaking here, of course, of a tendency of thought. It is not that young children don't have the perceptual experience of ten small glasses and one large pitcher. They simply fail to take the size into account when they think about what they see. Although what they experience perceptually is, in this case, comparable to what an adult experiences, preoperational children have an impoverished way of representing the situation to themselves; they have a limited way of thinking about it. The limitations on their way of thinking about what they experience show up in the way they reason about perceptual phenomena, their views about right and wrong, and their adoption of social stereotypes.

### Reasoning about perceptual phenomena

As we have emphasized before, preoperational children are just beginning to reconstruct on the plane of thought what they already know on the plane of action. Toddlers adjust their behaviors to the distances of things from them. They act as though a person who looks small in the distance actually has remained full-sized. But preoperational children, because they are now coordinating perceptual information with their new questions about what causes what, are likely to ask a previously unasked question: do objects actually change size as they move toward or away from a person?

Perhaps you remember having fears like the one a friend had. She remembered being afraid, as a child, to go down into Royal Gorge because she noticed how tiny the people looked down below. Not distinguishing between the way things appear and the way they are, she feared that she would become very small if she went down into the gorge and that she might not regain her full size when she came back up. Not all preoperational children hold such beliefs very long. One child we know, for example, came to us one day, charmingly, but egocentrically, trying to help us come to understand the remarkable fact she had just discovered. "Those trucks that look very small when you've driven away from them don't *really* change size; they just *look* that way."

A way of resolving such issues that lies intermediate between the two solutions given in the foregoing examples is what Piaget calls *renversabilité.* In size/distance relations, an example of *renversabilité* is the belief that objects systematically shrink as they recede into the distance and grow as they move closer. The example our theory beast usually gives us is the belief that the number of objects in a row changes as the objects are spread out, making the row longer, but that bringing the objects back into their original position restores the number.

In general, preoperational children are likely to represent single objects, events, or actions and to associate them with particular experiences they have had, but they do not tend to represent whole sequences or true classes. They have what we might call preconcepts, but they do not yet have real concepts. The fear of remaining small after going down into Royal Gorge shows inattention to the fact that all the people who purportedly diminished in actual size were full-sized when they returned to the top. The systematic relation between apparent size and how far people had gone down into the gorge was not represented as being systematic. On the other hand, the child with the discovery about the actual size of the truck had been able to coordinate and reconcile successive perceptions—at least for that specific case. The Royal Gorge example is a case of *centration*; the truck example is a case of *decentration*.

**TEACHER TASK 5-4**

(1) Kamii (1973) has suggested that exploring objects by touch alone is of more use in helping children decenter than is pure visual exploration of objects. Why might this be so?

(2) Would exploration by smelling objects or by listening to the sounds they make also be helpful in helping children decenter? Why or why not?

(3) Describe in detail how you would conduct a nonvisual perceptual exploration activity in which your main goal is to help children decenter. Include an explanation of why you would do it that way. (Remember, you want children to do more than to simply label the object; you want them to explore it fully, to ask themselves questions about it, and to think about the connections between the different sensations they get.) In describing the activity, think about the following:

What questions would you ask?
Would you use familiar objects, unfamiliar ones, or both?
Would you switch from one sense to another (for instance, from touch to taste) or would you stay with one?
Would you encourage visual exploration afterward? If so, how? (For example, would you allow children to touch, taste, and so on, the objects while they look at them?)

### Views about right and wrong

Centration characterizes young children's moral behavior and attitudes as well as their attempts to understand what they see. (Remember our claim in Principle 9, in Chapter 3, that a sense of morality develops at pace with intelligence and that it requires practice in order to develop.) The inability to coordinate variables shows up initially in young children's inability to follow rules, even though they use the rules as their guides to right and wrong. To apply rules, one has to ignore some of the specific features of a situation and to categorize the situation according to its similarity to others in which the rule applies. Young children's inability to represent classes and their idiosyncratic associations of events makes their adherence to rules erratic at best.

Later in the preoperational period, children tend to take enough variables into account to recognize and follow rules, but they apply the rules rigidly; there are no extenuating circumstances. They may change the rules, but when they do, they don't realize they've made a change; they are just as rigid about the changed rules as they were about the original ones. Initial beliefs that rules are handed down by people with authority, coupled with preoperational children's lack of concern for how they know what they think they know, lead to changes in rules (as children rationally or irrationally acquire a new belief about what the rules are) and rigid adherence to whatever they now think the rules are (because they assume they are given by an authority). This would lead to many more disputes than it does if young children decentered enough to notice, and try to resolve, the discrepancies between the rules they are following and the rules other children are following— often in the same game!

Does this give you some ideas about what to watch for in the children you work with and how to intervene? It should. It should also help you understand why some children get so terribly upset at the injustice done them by an infraction of some relatively unimportant—as we adults see it—rule. Think about how you'd deal with children's feelings in such cases.

### Adoption of social stereotypes

A surprising consequence of centration is children's tendency to adhere to stereotypes, even in the face of obviously contradictory evidence. You have probably seen or heard about children's insistence that "Daddies don't cook dinner" or that "Girls can't climb very well." If you've talked to parents, or are one yourself, you know that such stoutly defended claims are as likely as not to come from children whose fathers do most of the cooking or whose sisters are expert climbers. If children's logic were as systematic as ours, the claim, "No girl can climb very well," would be rejected in the face of Susie's obvious expertise. It doesn't work that way with young children. Preoperational children can accept the claim and can acknowledge the expertise without ever bothering to coordinate or reconcile the two.

This is a frustrating state of affairs for anyone with an ounce of liberal tendencies. On the one hand, the onset of stereotyping is a developmental advance: children are beginning to make generalizations that depend on the coordination of several attributes, one of which is not visible (climbing ability is not visible when a child isn't climbing). On the other hand, it is hard not to cringe when Adrian sweetly remarks to Juanita, "We won't play with Chicanos, will we? because they're lazy," or when Stevie says to Henry that all white boys are sissies. It won't help for us to point to an obvious counterexample and expect children to change their generalizations. Nor will it help much if we simply deny that all Chicanos are lazy or that all white boys are sissies. Doing so simply gives children another disconnected statement, another piece of information that remains uncoordinated and unreconciled with the other information the child has. We have to bring the contradiction into focus for the particular child involved. This will require careful attention to the child's thoughts, careful inquiry strategies, and patience.

### Interpretations of Experience

We hope you are convinced by now that children do not view the world the way we adults do. The experiences they have in a given situation are not likely to be the same as those an adult would have. They often see different problems than adults do—even when they respond appropriately to a question posed by an adult—and they resolve problems in their own ways.

We do not adequately describe a child's experience when we say, for example, that Seth has had a trip to the zoo and has found out where the different animals come from. Seth may have no idea of what a country is, what a jungle is, or how far away India is. Instead, the particular experience he has had might be something like the discovery that a camel can nuzzle your hand without hurting you, the pleasant visual sensation of watching the motion of a giraffe, the test of his hypothesis that loud screams make the lions roar, or the fun of repeating adult exclamations with strange-sounding words such as "Australia" and "wallaby" and finding the adult enthusiasm contagious.

When we ask questions of children, we can expect them to give answers to what they see as the problem—and this may not coincide with the problem we intended for them to think about. When we ask about the result of pouring milk into ten glasses, as in our earlier example, we may think the problem is to coordinate the number of containers with their sizes in order to reconcile the perceptual information with the fact that the amount of milk is not altered by mere changes in size, shape, or number of containers that hold it. A preoperational child might think the problem is to count the number of containers before and after the pouring and then to compare the two numbers. If the numbers are unequal, then there is more milk in one case than in the other. Or perhaps the child thinks the problem is to compare the height of the pitcher to the height of one of the glasses. The pitcher then has more milk in it, because it is taller.

We need to know how children interpret our questions and the experiences we provide if we are going to help them resolve the problems they're working on, facilitate their view of new problems, and avoid needless misunderstandings that hinder good teacher-child relationships. Attention to the three characteristics of preoperational thinking—egocentrism, intuitive solutions, and centration—can help us make good inferences about which of our questions and comments children are likely to misinterpret and what kinds of interpretations children will make.

We will gain additional insight into how we can help children resolve the problems they set themselves if we pay attention to the transitional nature of the preoperational period. But before we go on, make sure you've had a crack at Teacher Task 5-5.

*TEACHER TASK 5-5*

---

Psychologists have noticed that a number of two- and three-year-old children correctly say that the amount of water stays the same when water from a tall thin container is poured into a short wide one. Many four- and five-year-old children, on the other hand, say that there is more water in one case than in the other, adding that one container is very thin and the other is very wide or pointing to the relative tallness of one container. Nearly all ten-year-olds give the same answer (the correct one) as the two- and three-year-olds.

Offer an account of this phenomenon using what you now know about the sensorimotor stage, the concrete operational stage, and the preoperational characteristics of egocentrism, intuitive solutions, and centration.

---

## THE PREOPERATIONAL PERIOD: A TRANSITION BETWEEN STAGES

The preoperational characteristics we've been describing in this chapter result from children's struggles to construct a fairly sophisticated system of thought (concrete operations) by integrating the coordinated action schemes of the sensorimotor stage into their rapidly developing ability to symbolize. The struggle is long and hard. Children have to give up their reliance on sensorimotor organization—the only successful way they've had of making sense of the world—before they have constructed a new organization that they can rely on. Not only do they have to construct new ways of thinking, but they have to become skilled in using them. It is not surprising that children frequently slip back into the old familiar ways, even when they have begun to develop new, more efficient ways; we all tend to opt for what comes most easily. Because it is relatively easy for adults to represent things mentally, we adults often prefer to think about problems rather than to physically try one solution after another. With young children, the situation is reversed. Preoperational children tend to try actions first; they resort to thought only when action schemes and trial-and-error approaches fail. Thinking through a problem with newly developing systems of representation is a difficult task, and one they understandably reserve for problems they recognize as being unresponsive to sensorimotor solutions.

To fully appreciate the difficulties children face in constructing and using adult systems of thought, we'll have to look a little more closely at the task they face and the mechanisms of development. We'll turn first to a description of two ways of mentally acting on information, two ways of knowing. These two ways, called *figurative* and *operative* knowing, are fully developed and coordinated in adult thought but are no more than rough sketches in early preoperational thinking. Then we'll examine the kinds of action involved in the factors that help children to successfully build the structures for which they have the rough sketches.

### Figurative and Operative Ways of Knowing

Piaget has taken great pains to distinguish the descriptive aspect of knowledge, our internal copies of particular states and transformations in the world, from operational knowledge, the "know-how" that enables us to reproduce and alter the transformations that occur in the world and to make generalizations about our environment. The first aspect of knowledge is called *figurative knowing,* because it is what gives us acquaintance with the configurations of the world—shapes, melodies, patterns of movement, tastes, smells, and so forth. The second aspect is called *operative knowing,* because it consists of the operations we have for manipulating the descriptions we get via the figurative aspect. The operative aspect of knowledge consists of our coordinated systems of physical and mental actions. (Mental actions, you recall, are interiorized physical actions and coordinations of them.)

In Piaget's theory, the distinction between these two aspects of knowledge is coupled with the claim that neither one is the developmental source of the other. Although these two aspects of knowledge interact in important ways, they have separate developmental histories. Figurative knowing arises through refinements of the ability to symbolize, an ability that emerges during the second year of life. The exercise of this way of knowing is often referred to as the *semiotic function.* Operative knowing arises from action. Initially, the action is overt physical motion—the organized kind of activity seen in the sensorimotor stage. Later, the actions are interiorized and modified, so as to become the full-fledged logical operations of adult thought.

You may wonder why we are making so much of this distinction. After all, it's nothing new; everyone knows that being able to ride a bicycle is very different from recognizing that the particular pattern of activity someone else is demonstrating is in fact bicycle riding. There are two important reasons for stressing this distinction and for clarifying it. First, although it may be true that we are all aware of the distinction, somehow the distinction is often ignored in both psychological research and educational practice. Secondly, attention to the distinction raises some very important questions about cognitive development. If the distinction is genuine, as it seems to be, then how are the two aspects of knowledge related to each other? Does the development of one aspect enhance development of the other? Is one aspect of knowledge developmentally ahead of the other? Does an environment that aids development of one also aid development of the other? What are the special contributions and limitations of each kind of knowing? Is either aspect particularly amenable to instruction? If so, to what kind of instruction? Should subject matter be presented so as to appeal to one rather than the other?

These and similar questions can only be answered by more information on the nature of figurative and operative knowing. We'll look at some examples of each and then see what Piaget's theory has to say about their interaction.

### Figurative knowing

The figurative aspect of knowledge shows up in the ability to *recognize* an object or event; the ability to physically *reconstruct,* or imitate, someone else's behavior; and the ability to mentally *reproduce,* or represent to oneself, what one has experienced. The infant who smiles as the face of his or her father appears over the edge of the crib is showing the beginnings of figurative knowledge. Perception (and perceptual recognition) is the earliest form of figurative knowing. The three-year-old children who love to sing imitative action songs such as "Did you ever see a lassie?" and who can be found repeating nursery rhymes to themselves at odd moments are showing a somewhat more sophisticated form of figurative knowing. The ability to store perceptual information about a sequence of motions (including vocalizations), each of which is already in one's repertoire, and to enact that sequence at a later time emerges only toward the end of the sensorimotor period. It takes even longer for the well-developed representational mechanism (sophisticated semiotic functioning) to show itself. Children who can represent to themselves how a simple puzzle is to be assembled, without actually moving any of the pieces, are showing the ability to mentally reproduce a previous state of affairs—the completed puzzle—by transforming their representation of the present state of affairs, the scattered puzzle pieces.

As the semiotic function develops, children begin to invent their own personal symbols to use in the construction of fantasies, dreams, and dramatic-play episodes. The egocentric language we mentioned earlier occurs only after the child has become able to use mental symbols (rather than overt physical actions) to represent the environment. Young children's passion for drawing, painting, block building, songs, rhymes, stories, and dramatic play (playing house, playing hospital, or being superheroes) are all indications of the rapid development of the semiotic function during early childhood. All of these activities require the ability to use an object, image, or action to stand for something else—a two-dimensional line drawing stands for a three-dimensional house; words such as "you dummy" stand for complicated feelings of anger, frustration, and defiance; a hand-to-ear motion stands for a telephone; a three-dimensional clay object stands for the excitement of a recent trip to the circus.

As facility in the use of symbols develops—and as operational thinking becomes more sophisticated—private and idiosyncratic symbols make way for words, gestures, and other symbols that conform to social rules and customs. Have you noticed the passion many kindergarten children have for stereotyped drawings? You may even remember your own use of symbols such as ⌂ for house, ☼ for the sun, or ⚧ for a person. Maybe you make use of such symbols even now. The adoption of such conventions indicates an awareness of the communicative function of symbols and at least a partial coordination of the figurative and operative aspects of knowledge.

### Operative knowing

As children acquire the ability to represent things mentally, they acquire a totally new kind of object, mental representations, to which their previously developed, sensorimotor action schemes can be applied. (Action schemes, remember, are whatever it is about an action that is applicable to a wide variety of different objects.) Without any help from us and without conscious attention to their mental activity, children begin to bring together a few specific images on the basis of their similarity, to compare two objects that exist only in their thoughts, and to wonder about the discrepancies they find. The sporadic first applications of action schemes to static mental representations are enough to begin the mutual modification processes that eventually result in sophisticated figurative ways of knowing and the structure of operations characteristic of operative ways of knowing in adults.

When fully developed, operative knowing is an organized system of reversible interiorized actions (see, for example, Piaget, 1977). Operations are the actions that have been interiorized, made reversible, and organized into a totality. In case the foregoing is just a string of meaningless words to you, let's briefly review the notions of interiorization, reversibility, and organization. (You might also want to take another look at the end of Chapter 2.)

Interiorization is a process in which overt physical action schemes (such as pulling, or putting objects together) are transformed into the mental procedures we use in thinking. The interiorization of the action scheme involved in putting all the different-colored blocks into one box, for example, is the mental activity of considering the whole group of blocks.

Because thoughts are free of some of the limitations of physical objects, interiorization allows an action scheme to be extended and elaborated. One of the most important changes the action scheme undergoes is that of becoming reversible. A reversible action is one that allows both the effects of the action and the consequences of not performing the action to be held in mind simultaneously. To return to our example of colored blocks, when the interiorized action becomes reversible, one can consider the whole group of blocks without ignoring the subgroups. One can compare the group of blue blocks to the group of all blocks even when the blocks themselves—blue ones, red ones, yellow ones—are all jumbled together in a single box. Reversibility plays a key role in nearly every facet of logical thinking. And it is only just beginning to appear during the preoperational period!

Because the characteristics and development of operative knowing have been a major concern of our theory throughout its life, a good portion of the next chapter is devoted to examples of operative knowing in the making. Here's a brief rundown of what we'll be talking about. The operative aspect of knowledge, usually referred to as logico-mathematical knowledge, is divided into three areas: (a) classification abilities—the understanding of what constitutes a genuine class and of how classes are related to one another; (b) seriation abilities—the understanding of relations such as "less than" or "darker than" and the ability to systematically arrange things (mentally or physically) according to increases or decreases in some characteristic; and (c) number abilities—the synthesis of classification and seriation abilities that allows one to understand the relations among numbers, to see the universality in the applications of numbers, and to distinguish between such things as the number that represents your age and the number spoken when someone points to you as they count the people in a group. (Many three-year-old children become quite upset when they are pointed to and some number other than three is named. "No, I'm *three*," they insist.)

Logico-mathematical knowledge is often considered to include another large area of knowledge called *infra-logical knowledge*. Infra-logical knowledge is the understanding of temporal and spatial relationships. It includes the realization that, contrary to appearances, certain transformations do not alter length, area, volume, duration, and the like. Young children often confuse the rate of activity with the amount of time that has elapsed, for example, and confuse distance with the number of objects. In the first case, they are likely to believe that if one does the morning's activities faster, then it will be time for lunch sooner than usual. They confuse the way it seems with the way it is. An example of a confusion of the second type is children's belief that putting objects between two tables shortens the distance between the tables. Again, their reliance on perception leads them astray. Infra-logical knowledge allows them to ignore deceptive appearances in cases such as these and to draw correct conclusions.

Unlike the figurative aspect of knowledge, which captures properties that are specific to a particular event, the operative aspect focuses on properties that are common to a wide variety of events. The image one has of one's own father is an example of figurative knowing; the tendency to call all men of a certain size "daddy" reveals the operative aspect, primitive though it may be, at work.

### The interaction of the two ways of knowing

The operative and figurative aspects of knowledge work together in most acts of knowing throughout development. The interaction can be seen in the sensorimotor period, when children coordinate their goal-seeking strategies, such as a reaching and grasping sequence, with their recognition of a desired object, such as a bottle. The action sequence is rudimentary operative knowing; the perceptual recognition is rudimentary figurative knowing; their coordination is an organized, adaptive way of dealing with the world. In the preoperational period, children are constantly (but unconsciously) trying to reconcile their new figurative ability to imagine combinations of objects and events with their perceptual awareness of how things actually are and to modify their previous operative knowing so that action schemes become applicable to mental events. The ability to remember the original configuration of a piece of string and to compare that memory to the altered shape may lead them to wonder whether the size of the string has actually changed. Reflections on their action schemes show them that they can at least restore the original configuration, but this alone does not show that the length of the string remains the same. Who knows what kind of magic there is in the world?

The string they act on physically is in only one configuration at a time. Their mental imagery allows them to simultaneously consider (or mentally act on) two different configurations of the same string. It is no longer a question of changing a present configuration back to a previous one. Rather, the mental act is such that it allows them to infer that the length of the string is the same in the two configurations.

Although our theory hasn't spelled out the process in great detail, the action seems to be something like hypothesis choice or theory building. To show what a difficult task the child faces in the transition from sensorimotor intelligence to logical thought, let's look at the example in more detail. During the sensorimotor period, the child has already correctly determined that alterations in shape don't affect the *identity* of the string; it's the same string whether you move it, hide it, bend it, or whatever. Now the question is, what happens to the *length* of the string? The child sees that many different configurations can be made in which the length seems to differ, but in every case the string can be returned to its original configuration and its original length. What can account for the generality of this phenomenon?

One might trust perceptual information; in this case, if it looks like the length changes, then the length does change. If this is correct, then one has new questions to answer. How much longer is the string in one case than it is in the other? What is it about the change in shape that causes a change in length? If you paid attention to the sections on egocentrism, intuitive solutions, and centration, you're probably thinking that it will take awhile before children answer—or even pose—these questions. You're absolutely right. That's what makes you and other people in the child's environment so important. You can suggest questions yourself, or you can arrange materials in such a way that children's attention is focused on the features that lead to the questions.

Before we look at an alternative hypothesis, try Teacher Task 5-6.

*TEACHER TASK 5-6*

Imagine that you are planning to ask some three- or four-year-old children about the effects of shape changes on the length of a piece of string—or some other flexible (but nonelastic!) material.

(1)  What questions would you ask? (Be specific; say exactly what words you'd use and what you'd be doing with the material, if anything.)

(2)  If the children think the length changes when the shape of the string is altered, what will you do or say to help them focus on appropriate variables—the variables that will lead them *in the long run* to the appropriate conclusions? (Remember, you're not trying to get children to give you the right answer; you're trying to get them to think about the problem.)

(3)  What are the important variables to think about anyway?

A second hypothesis one might offer for the generality of returning altered configurations to their original shape and length is that perception does not coincide with the facts. It looks as though the length of the string changes (or as though objects get smaller as they move away, or as though there is more milk in the pitcher than in the glasses), but, in fact, the length stays the same. If one already understands enough about numbers to know that ten cookies in a row are just as many as ten cookies in a stack, then one could verify this hypothesis by measuring the string in each configuration. But young children have to construct the notion of number as well as their theory about constancy of string length. They can't rely on well-established facts about numbers to support their hypothesis until they realize what the facts about numbers are. They have a tremendous number of hypotheses to put to the test all at once.

(The preceding paragraph should give you some ideas about what questions to ask children in order to help them think about problems such as the one in Teacher Task 5-6. If you find out what claims they already believe in, you can help them see discrepancies between their analysis of a particular situation and their other beliefs. You can also help them bring together relevant information so that they can choose the hypothesis that best fits everything they know so far.)

As the foregoing example has been designed to show, advances in figurative knowing trigger the recognition of problems whose resolution leads to more sophisticated operative knowing. However, these problems are only recognized as problems because of the kind of operative knowing already available. Figurative knowing doesn't itself generate operative knowing; rather, it provides developmental opportunities and challenges for the operative knowing that is already present. Similarly, operative knowing isn't responsible for the onset of figurative knowing. However, it plays a major role in determining what configurations, patterns, sequences, shapes, and so forth, we can recognize and remember. Young children who have little understanding of seriation, for example, may recognize a staircase made of blocks, but they are likely to have great difficulty in reconstructing one; the mental representations they have are not rich enough to enable them to decide where to place each block.

The interaction between figurative and operative ways of knowing, then, is one in which operative knowing plays the major role (see Piaget, 1973). And operative knowing originates in children's own action! This is why we have continuously stressed the need for children's action, for their own construction of knowledge. This is also the reason that activity, diversity, change, and intellectual honesty are so important in the classroom environment.

### The Importance of Action

We have been insisting on the importance of each child's own activity in the construction of knowledge, and we have emphasized that the activity we have in mind includes mental activity as well as physical activity. Attention to both kinds of activity is particularly important for teachers of children in the preoperational period. There are two reasons for this—reasons that show us something about the kind of attention needed. The first reason concerns the nature of sensorimotor intelligence; the second concerns general factors enhancing development.

#### *Sensorimotor origins*

Sensorimotor intelligence, consisting of systems of action, is modified as actions are applied to new objects. Earlier, we stressed the importance of applying systems of action to mental representations. There are also many new physical objects to which the systems can be applied. Many two-and-a-half- and three-year-olds, for example, have never put on roller skates, pushed a wheelbarrow, walked on a balance beam, felt the consistency of bread dough, or swung a pendulum. Because symbolic abilities are just emerging, the best way for young children to learn about such things is to apply their sensorimotor schemes; they must take action— overt physical action.

Common-sense experience and research studies both support the claim that children learn much better when they do the experiments, manipulate objects, and go through the motions than when they watch someone else. Piaget's theory offers an explanation for this observation: when children are allowed to act on objects—to touch, push, turn, and shake them—they can make use of their well-developed sensorimotor schemes. Teaching young children in a "don't touch" environment is like teaching reading to people with normal vision by first turning out all the lights. Even if one could think up ways to accomplish the objective, what a waste of effort it would be! One fails utterly to take advantage of the remarkable capabilities of the learner, capabilities that would allow the task to be accomplished much more efficiently and pleasantly if only one could make use of them.

It is true that most preschool programs try to emphasize children's active involvement with materials, but how often are teacher demonstrations neither followed nor preceded by opportunities for children to do the procedure themselves. (Incidentally, this is also a problem when children teach others of the same age. They are often more interested in doing the activity before an appreciative audience than in helping another child do it.) Some very important learning occurs through observation, of course. If this were not so, few of us would survive to adulthood. But learning through observation alone is generally more effective for learning *what not to do* than for learning *how to do* something.

### TEACHER TASK 5-7

We have been discussing the nature of sensorimotor intelligence because of the light it can shed on how to help children in the preoperational period. What light does it shed?

Make a list of recommendations for teaching young children, and explain how each is related to sensorimotor intelligence. Here are three suggestions to get you started. First explain how each of them follows from the nature of sensorimotor intelligence; then add your own suggestions to the list.

(1) Provide situations in which the child is physically active, either moving just his or her own body or manipulating objects.

(2) Use activities in which the child's action is the direct cause of some interesting event.

(3) Help children pay attention to their actions and the effects of their actions. Talk to them about what they're doing, and surprise them occasionally by making objects behave in unusual ways (by using a magnet to move a toy car, for example).

### General factors enhancing development

So much for our first reason for attending to activity. What about the second? Children in the preoperational period are in the process of constructing new systems of thought as they incorporate sensorimotor schemes and symbolic abilities into a higher level of organization. The four mechanisms of developmental change (maturation, equilibration, experience, and social transmission) are in full gear. Though it may not be obvious, all of these are closely tied to the child's activity. To see what kinds of activity are important, we'll look first at maturation and equilibration. Then we'll make use of a tripartite division of knowledge to see how different kinds of activity influence what knowledge is acquired through experience and through social transmission.

*Maturation and equilibration.* Like many other psychological theories (for instance, see White, 1959; Berlyne, 1965), Piaget's theory ascribes a powerful motivating force to the mere possession of an ability. Living creatures seem to have an intrinsic desire to exercise their capabilites, especially when the ability is newly acquired. As soon as infants learn to crawl, for example, there's no peace in the house; they explore every nook and cranny, crawling on bare floors, over rugs, on couches—anywhere there's a surface. When children learn to run (somewhere between the ages of two and three years), they want to run whenever possible. The exercise of emerging capacities is vital to their becoming an established part of one's behavioral repertoire. Walking becomes second nature to us only after considerable practice. The same is true of intellectual abilities, such as the representational abilities that develop after the onset of the semiotic function.

If we are to help maturation play its role in development, we have to watch for signs of emerging abilities, and we have to provide opportunities for children to use those abilities. That's why change is such an important part of the classroom (see Chapter 4). Infants don't need space for running and jumping; preschool children do. Three-month-old infants don't profit much from storybooks, paints, and clay; three-year-old children do. One of the important contributions Piaget's theory can make to people in the business of helping children develop is to specify some of the less obvious, but equally important, developmental steps that are not so much a part of everyday knowledge as those in the examples cited here.

We have already mentioned the major maturational advance in intelligence—namely, the onset of the semiotic function. We know, then, that preschool-aged children will want representational activities: imitative movement games, simplified versions of charades, words, pictures, paints, films. We also know that they are expanding and refining their physical skills. To decide which and how much of each kind of activity to provide and when to provide them, we have to know what the child does with the new ability. We have to know more about *mental* activity and equilibration.

When we first made our acquaintance with the theory, back in Chapter 2, we discussed three kinds of equilibration. The first was the constant balancing of assimilation and accommodation. This is an activity that characterizes all intelligent activity; it is not peculiar to the construction of a new level of mental organization. The second kind was the balancing of subsystems within a particular organizational level—the kind that eventually smooths out horizontal *décalages* at a given stage of development. It is the third kind, however, that is the most striking feature of the preoperational period. To move from one stage to another, old connections between subsystems (or schemata) have to be broken and new ones established. This is the process of reflective abstraction. Our theory tells us three important things about this process: (1) it takes time, (2) it can't be imposed from the outside—individuals each have to do their own constructions, and (3) there is a strong element of chance in the process—sometimes we're lucky and we find the right connections straightaway; other times we're not.

These features of the process show us that we have to find ways to help each child engage in activities that are likely (not guaranteed) to lead him or her to make the right connections, and that we have to be patient. We can focus attention on the right kinds of variables if we take the time to find out what children think the problem is, why they think it is a problem, and what they think about similar situations. We can help children test their proposed solutions and then ask about connections between the new solutions and their other views. In short, we can help children keep their attention focused on the connections between different problems and their solutions. We can also present interesting and relevant problems —problems that are likely to help them see new connections or to see why old ones have to be broken. The developmental guideposts in Chapter 6 are designed expressly for this purpose: to help you see what kinds of problems are likely to be fruitful for children.

In thinking about what experiences to provide and how to maximize their benefit, we have found it helpful to think of three kinds of knowledge: physical knowledge, logico-mathematical knowledge, and conventional knowledge. These are closely tied to the third and fourth mechanisms of development, experience and social transmission.

*Experience and social transmission: three kinds of knowledge.* As we interact with the world, we have many different kinds of experience. Piaget has grouped these experiences into two very broad categories, according to their role in development. Physical experience is the kind in which we find out about the physical characteristics of the world—about weight, shape, types of motion, what causes what, which things will dissolve in water, and so on. In acting on objects, we use simple abstraction, the coordination of our actions, to discover general principles about the world. Logico-mathematical experience is the kind that enables us to construct logical principles using the process of reflective abstraction. It is the kind in which we construct the basic logical, mathematical, spatial, and temporal relations that characterize our world.

The different kinds of experience give rise to two distinct kinds of knowledge: physical knowledge and logico-mathematical knowledge. My knowledge that a stone will fall to the ground if I drop it is physical knowledge. My knowledge that half of anything is always less than all of it is an example of logico-mathematical knowledge.

What about my knowledge that people in the same family often share the same last name, that running in the halls is against the rules in my school, or that many stores are closed on Sunday? Although Piaget's theory doesn't pay much attention to this kind of knowledge (because it is less directly connected to inner mechanisms of development than are the first two), it is important for education. We call it conventional knowledge because it is a knowledge of the conventions in one's society. This is the kind of knowledge that can be effectively learned through social transmission. We can be told what the rules are (though this won't guarantee that we know how to obey them), and we can be told how family names work in our culture. This knowledge of facts helps us adjust to society's demands, and it may lead us to challenge those demands as we question the whys and wherefores (thus stimulating our use of logico-mathematical knowledge), but it does not by itself lead to developmental progress.

The division of knowledge into these three distinct areas is not without its problems. If you try to apply the distinction to every activity, you'll find places where the borders are a bit fuzzy. However, there are cases where the differences are dramatic and important. You can make use of the division in cases where the boundaries are clear if you remember that conventional knowledge is acquired largely through social transmission (through being told or shown); that physical knowledge is acquired through acting on a variety of similar objects and observing the outcomes; and that logico-mathematical knowledge is acquired through the lengthy process of reflective abstraction, which comes into play when similar actions are applied to radically different objects and when conflicting views are reconciled.

## SUMMARY

In this chapter, we have examined a number of characteristics of children in the preoperational period of intellectual development. Because this period is the transition between two stages, we began our investigation with a look at the preceding (sensorimotor stage) and following (concrete operational stage) stages. The result of our preliminary investigation was an appreciation of the task facing young children. Preoperational children are in the process of constructing a system of thought out of the raw materials of sensorimotor action schemes and the newly emerging *semiotic function* (or representational ability). They are reconstructing on the level of thought what they already know on the level of action.

The struggle to accomplish this task shows up in the characteristics of *egocentrism* (the inability to take another's perspective), *intuitive solutions* (the almost exclusive reliance on unconscious and unanalyzed heuristic procedures), and *centration* (the tendency to focus on one or two features at the expense of others). The appearance of these three characteristics in numerous contexts reminds us that children's experiences are quite different from those of an adult. To help children develop, we will first need to find out how they are interpreting their experiences. Only then can we stimulate the appropriate mechanisms of development.

The key discovery of our investigation was the importance of action. Coordinated overt physical *action* schemes constitute sensorimotor intelligence. Coordinated interiorized *actions* (mental actions) constitute concrete operational intelligence. And the transition from one stage to the other requires the child's own *activity*.

A predominant part of the transition-making activity in preoperational children is their internal coordination of two independent ways of knowing: *operative knowing* and *figurative knowing*. The first of these consists of interiorized actions; the second is the mental representation of configurations in the world—the material on which the interiorized actions operate. Insofar as we are guided by Piaget's theory, our primary task as teachers of young children is to stimulate and direct the child's own activity.

For guidelines on how and when to stimulate and direct, we considered a division of knowledge into three types: *conventional* knowledge (gained through social transmission), *physical knowledge* (gained through actions on objects), and *logico-mathematical* knowledge (gained through coordination of actions and reflection upon them). In Chapter 6, we'll put this division to work.

## REFERENCES

BALDWIN, ALFRED L. *Theories of Child Development* (New York: John Wiley & Sons, Inc., 1967).

BERLYNE, DANIEL E. *Structure and Direction in Thinking* (New York: John Wiley & Sons, Inc., 1965).

HADAMARD, JACQUES. *The Psychology of Invention in the Mathematical Field* (Princeton: Princeton University Press, 1945).

KAMII, CONSTANCE. "Pedagogical Principles Derived from Piaget's Theory: Relevance for Educational Practice," in *Piaget in The Classroom*, ed. Milton Schwebel and Jane Raph (New York: Basic Books, 1973).

PIAGET, JEAN. *Biology and Knowledge,* trans. Beatrix Walsh (Chicago: The University of Chicago Press, 1971 [first published in French, in 1967, under the title, *Biologie et Connaissance*]).

PIAGET, JEAN. *The Child and Reality: Problems of Genetic Psychology,* trans. Arnold Rosin (New York: Grossman Publishers, 1973 [first published in French, in 1972, under the title, *Problèmes de Psychologie Génétique*]).

PIAGET, JEAN. *The Child's Conception of the World,* trans. Joan and Andrew Tomlinson (London: Routledge and Kegan Paul, 1929 [first published in French, in 1926, under the title, *La Représentation du Monde chez l'Enfant*]).

PIAGET, JEAN. *The Grasp of Consciousness: Action and Concept in the Young Child,* trans. Susan Wedgwood (Cambridge, Mass.: Harvard University Press, 1976 [first published in French, in 1974, under the title, *La Prise de Conscience*]).

PIAGET, JEAN. "The Role of Action in the Development of Thinking," trans. Hans Furth, in *Knowledge and Development, Volume 1: Advances in Research and Theory,* ed. Willis F. Overton and Jeanette McCarthy Gallagher (New York: Plenum Press, 1977).

UZGIRIS, INA C. "Organization of Sensorimotor Intelligence," in *Origins of Intelligence,* ed. Michael Lewis (New York: Plenum Press, 1976).

WHITE, ROBERT W. "Motivation Reconsidered: The Concept of Competence," *Psychological Review, 66,* no. 5 (1959), 297–333.

# 6        DEVELOPMENTAL GUIDEPOSTS

## WARNING

The lists in this chapter designate characteristics and abilities likely to appear during the preoperational period. Some of these abilities may be seen more often than others, but all will concern us to some degree in work with three- to seven-year-old children. In general, they are indicators of developmental progress. They are also the characteristics and abilities teachers strive to enhance in their role as environmental engineers. The lists can be helpful to us, but they must be used with caution. Before turning to the actual lists, let's see what precautions we must take. There are three important caveats to consider.

### Caveat Number 1

As mentioned in Chapters 2 and 4, Piaget's theory doesn't tell us everything we need to know about how children develop. It says nothing, for example, about physical growth and the development of motor skills. Nor does it tell us much about a child's abilities to cope with grief or anger. The lists in this chapter are confined to characteristics specifically pointed out by the theory. Thus, they are deficient in the areas of general psychomotor development, the growth of self-confidence and a positive concept of self, specific motor skills such as jumping or cutting, aesthetic development, and specific content appropriate for early childhood education. *Don't replace your store of information with these lists. Add to your store!*

### Caveat Number 2

The behaviors and tendencies described in the lists are not meant to be interpreted as behavioral objectives. Neither are they meant to be used as criterion-referenced items of assessment. Why not? There are three major reasons, each of which is already familiar to us from Chapter 1 through 5. First of all, the theory claims that development occurs with periods of reorganization. This means that old abilities and "correct answers" may be lost as a new system for interpreting the world is constructed by the child. True, such abilities are generally regained, but inabilities by themselves are not indicators of failure. They may even be indicators of definite progress. A child may progress from the right answer for the wrong reason, through the wrong answer for the right kind of reason, and finally to the right answer for the right reason. The overt behavior by itself does not tell us all we need to know about the underlying structure of a child's thought.

The second reason is that while the child's new systems are in the process of construction, "correct answers" may disappear and reappear, seemingly at random. Children adjust their belief to account for discrepant information in one situation, but they may not see a parallel problem in another. They may decide that they shouldn't make the adjustment for just one case. Later on, they may become aware of the problems in related areas and so readopt their initial adjustment—but with greater generality than they had originally foreseen. For example, six-year-old Gary may think that the amount of orange juice wouldn't change when you pour the juice from a cup into a glass, but that the amount of sand under similar circumstances would change. If he ponders the reason for the difference, he may temporarily give up his "correct" conserving response with the orange juice in order to maintain a coherent notion of what can and cannot change when relatively continuous quantities are transferred from one container to another. Should we say he has made no developmental progress? Certainly the recognition of the problem and the attempts to maintain coherence count for something.

Together, these two reasons tell us that development will not occur in a neat linear fashion, with clear behavioral indicators of each step. There won't even be a well-ordered series of wrong answers! This is our third reason for refusing to use these lists as behavioral objectives. Children's construction of any particular solution to the problems they see will depend on how they conceive of the problem, their present mental organization, the environment in which they find themselves, their motivation to solve the problem, and the chance occurrence of hitting on a particular solution. Our knowledge is limited, and we simply cannot predict with accuracy what particular solution a child will put forth in response to a problem.

Lest it seem from the foregoing discussion that we needn't even bother to look at caveat number 3, since our use of these lists is so restricted, let's hasten to look at what they *can* do for us. They can help us in two ways. First of all, they help us to assess each child's intellectual characteristics, so that we can adjust our questions and activities appropriately. Remember the house remodeling metaphor from Chapter 1? The questions and activities we provide are the "enticing bit of driftwood," the "wheelbarrow full of bricks over by the sagging porch support," the people on the footpath munching apples. We have to know what building materials to provide, and we also have to know where and when to display them. Unless children already know something about where apples come from, for example, they are not likely to arrange their windows so as to see the apple tree that they infer must be just out of sight. The lists of characteristics and abilities of pre-operational children give us ideas about what kinds of materials are likely to be noticed and incorporated into the remodeled structures. They can help us to figure out what questions to ask and what kinds of activities to provide so that we can tempt children to undertake the remodeling task. They also give us clues about the view seen from the child's windows and so can help us "tune in" to each child's developmental level.

If we present materials that cannot be perceived (seen, heard, smelled) from the windows of the child's present structure, there is little chance of their being noticed. We either have to find a way to make them perceptible or, if that is not possible (and many times it isn't), we have to find materials that can be seen by the child. We can reserve the other materials until the child's remodeling has given him or her new windows from which such materials are visible. A good question, for example, is only good when it is appropriately matched to the child's intellectual structure. We want to provide activities and questions that are related to the content areas that interest the child, but they must also be appropriate for the child's developmental level. A two-year-old looking at a picture book may be challenged by questions such as, "What is that?" or "Where is the doggie's eye?" A three- or four-year-old child is more likely to be stimulated by such questions as, "What's happening in this picture?" "What do you think will happen next?" or "Why do you think he's crying in this picture?"

The first way these lists can help us, then, is in providing guidelines for assessing and responding to each child in day-to-day interactions. The second way is in providing goals against which to assess the potentials of the environment we create. We can use them before children even enter the classroom, to evaluate our plans, our proposed teaching strategies, and our room arrangement according to how likely they are to foster the behaviors indicated in the lists.

Our key words for the classroom environment (active, changing, intellectually honest, and diverse—see Chapter 4) must be interpreted according to the range of abilities for the particular children in it. The lists give us guidelines for assessing characteristics of children so that we can make the environment entice the children we have—with their own particular abilities and interests—to act on objects, vary their actions, and take note of the effects. The lists can help us make judgments about what mistakes are to be accepted as legitimate indicators of thought and growth for the children we work with and which mistakes represent inattention, disinterest, or childish jokes. In the jargon of modern educators, the list can help us "individualize instruction."

### Caveat Number 3

Like the first two caveats, this one is intended to give advice about how best to make use of the lists, rather than to send us fleeing hastily on to Chapter 7. It is a warning about the organization used in listing characteristics and abilities. We have divided items in the list into three major categories according to the three kinds of knowledge discussed in Chapter 5: physical knowledge, conventional knowledge, and logico-mathematical knowledge (in its broad sense). Logico-mathematical knowledge has been further divided, into infra-logical knowledge and logico-mathematical knowledge proper, the former being more closely tied to properties of the physical world.

At the risk of belaboring the point, it is important to remind ourselves that the divisions are somewhat arbitrary. It is nearly impossible for one kind of knowledge to exist without the other two. In addition, some examples of knowledge don't seem to fall neatly into one category or another, even when we are willing to grant that they only exist given the existence of abilities in other areas of knowledge. Representation abilities are of this type. They have been grouped in the conventional knowledge category because the use of specific words, pictures, gestures, and so forth is arbitrary and culturally determined. However, the ability to use words or gestures to represent things and the understanding of relationships among words or among the linguistic, pictorial, and gestural systems for representing things are *not* simple matters of convention and of learning specific facts. Other cases of overlap can be seen in number understandings (which appear both under infra-logical knowledge and under logico-mathematical knowledge proper) and in understandings of the physical and social environment. The recognition of *principles* underlying regularities in the environment (for instance, basic principles of psychology, sociology, biology, or physics) is listed under infra-logical knowledge. The ability (and tendency) to make accurate predictions or generalizations about the environment, but *without* recognition of underlying principles, is listed under physical knowledge.

In spite of problems in drawing clear-cut category lines, the division of knowledge into these areas has some important advantages. First and foremost, it reminds us that not everything we know is acquired (or verified, for that matter) through the same process. Different kinds of knowledge (whether or not the categories used by Piaget ultimately turn out to be the true ones—or even the most useful ones) are the results of different kinds of interaction with the environment. This tells us that we need to adjust activities and teaching strategies to the kinds of understandings we hope to instill. More will be said on this in Chapter 7.

A second benefit in distinguishing among these different areas of knowledge comes in assessment. Different techniques for finding out what someone "really knows" or "really thinks" become prominent, depending on what kind of understanding we are trying to uncover. If we want to know whether a child is aware of certain regularities in the environment, for example, we might ask him or her to predict the outcome of continuing to pour juice into a cup after the cup is full. (Try asking your three-year-olds this question. We were amazed at how many of ours held their hands high above the cup, indicating that the level of the juice would be higher than the lip of the cup.) If we want to assess a child's knowledge of *why* things are the way they are, more extensive probing and the use of counter-suggestions are often needed. Chapter 9 explores in more detail the relationships between techniques and the three kinds of knowledge.

A final advantage to the division of knowledge—and an advantage that accrues from this particular way of dividing it—is the clarification of the role of our good friend, the theory. Piaget's theory deals most specifically with the development of logico-mathematical knowledge, somewhat less with physical knowledge, and even less with conventional knowledge. The heart of the theory, the notion of structurally distinct stages with mechanisms of stage transition and functional invariants, lies in the area of logico-mathematical knowledge. This is where we rely most heavily on our theory for guidance. The theory has strong implications for the other areas as well, however, and especially for the relationships among areas. Progress in logico-mathematical reasoning, after all, is partly dependent upon direct experience with the world—upon conventional and physical knowledge. It is the nature of the dependence that is crucial in educational planning. An over-emphasis on conventional knowledge without the appropriate base in physical and logico-mathematical knowledge, for example, can actually inhibit progress in the development and expression of abilities in the other areas. It can lead to a reliance on pseudo-knowledge, or, as Hardeman (1974) poetically calls it, "verbal twilight learning."

With these three caveats in mind, let's turn to the lists. (Don't neglect to do the Teacher Task at the end of each list.)


## PHYSICAL KNOWLEDGE*


Physical knowledge refers both to a knowledge of the attributes and dispositional properties of the physical environment and to a knowledge of how to interact with the environment so as to discover those features. Such knowledge involves the

---

*The rest of this chapter is a revised and expanded version of an unpublished paper written in 1975 by Ruth Saunders, Joan Ershler, and Ann McAllister.

discovery of regularities in the environment—that ice melts when brought into a warm house, for example, or that objects thrown into the air tend to come down again. Children construct this kind of knowledge as they actively manipulate objects and discover the effects of their actions. Abilities and characteristics to watch for in this area are

(1) The tendency to make predictions or hypotheses and to test them out —that is, to experiment. This includes asking questions such as, "What can I do with this? What else could I do with it? What would happen if . . . ?" and the systematic observation of answers to those questions. Don't forget that many of the questions may be posed nonverbally. A child who looks thoughtfully at an object, does something with it or to it, then stops for a moment before trying something else, is giving nonverbal evidence of this tendency.

(2) The conscious observation of objects and the effects of actions on objects. Here we must look closely at nonverbal responses. Children's verbalizations can tell us that they have noticed particular features, but verbal expression requires conventional knowledge in addition to the ability to observe. Thus, we must not assume that children have failed to notice particular features simply because they have not verbalized them. We will have to watch for nonverbal indicators of observation skills. Looks of astonishment, for example, indicate that children have observed something—something they were not expecting.

(3) A knowledge of the physical attributes of objects in the environment and of the self (for instance, color, shape, size, weight, texture, smell, taste, sound). Children can show us that they are aware of these properties and their relationships as they match two objects of the same color or texture, as they react with surprise to the lightness of a large box filled with styrofoam, or as they reject a new food that looks similar to one whose taste they abhor.

(4) A repertoire of actions that enable one to explore the properties of unfamiliar objects (actions such as squeezing, pinching, dropping, heating, cooling, blowing, turning). Watch for the variety of spontaneous actions used in exploration as well as for the ability to try actions that have been suggested (verbally or nonverbally) by someone else.

(5) A knowledge of how objects react when acted upon in various ways. In particular, watch for generalizations such as, "Clear things are likely to be breakable," regardless of how accurate they are. Even inaccurate generalizations are important, because they can be refined, tested, and revised.

(6) Specific knowledge about the physical world in line with each child's own interests and experiences. Here, we are referring to nonverbal knowledge of physical properties and of the effects of performing certain kinds of actions on various kinds of objects. Verbal expression of this knowledge comes *after* the knowl-

edge has been constructed. The choice of topics used in any particular year will depend on current events (a tornado in the area, a new space mission), on the interests of specific children (dinosaurs, death), and on teacher interests and abilities. The following topics are ones we have consistently found intriguing to preschool children.

(a) Properties of gases, liquids, solids, and intermediaries (such as Silly Putty or baker's clay) in terms of the results of actions performed on them.

(i) Differences and similarities in actions one can perform on each (for instance, float objects, break and bend, pour, weigh, put into a variety of containers, melt, freeze, break).

(ii) Actions of combining liquids and gases (for instance, bubbles), liquids and solids (such as sugar and water, sand and water), different kinds of liquids (for example, oil and water, dishwashing liquid and water), different kinds of solids (mixing sand and mud, flour and butter).

(b) Properties of plants and animals (including people) and actions useful for finding out about

(i) Growth and reproduction.

(ii) Food ingestion (animals versus plants).

(iii) Survival (food, water, shelter).

(iv) Movement (ways animals and people move).

(c) Weather and seasonal changes (including the effects of wind and rain, what happens in the winter—snow, frozen lakes, hibernation, and so on).

(d) Actions related to the properties of light and color (such as the effects of a prism, how things look through colored cellophane, how to make shadows, how objects look through a magnifying glass).

(e) Effects of using tools and machines (for instance, a lever such as a teeter-totter, simple pulleys, screws, gears, woodworking materials—including varying effects due to densities of wood, size and length of nails, force of pounding).

(f) Effects due to the physical forces of gravity, magnetism, inertia—including centrifugal force and centripetal force (for example, experimenting with what objects are attracted to magnets, ease in running down hill versus uphill, pushing and pulling objects, making streams of water flow downhill, balancing blocks and making stable towers, experimenting with weight-and-size relationships, working with swings and swinging objects, twirling objects on a string).

It is important not to be misled by the technical terms used in this list. Preschool children do not need to know such terms as "inertia" or "centrifugal force" in order to understand the different phenomena. The knowledge we are describing here is the kind that would lead children to predict that if they let go of the string they are twirling, the string and the object on the end of it will fly off in a straight line. Only after children have some feel for the phenomenon are they ready to attach the term "centrifugal force" to it. Then they can go on to find new examples of the same force and refine their understanding of the term. Physical knowledge requires considerable "messing about," as David Hawkins (1965) says.

**TEACHER TASK 6-1**

(1) List some behaviors that would convince you that a child is testing a hypothesis.
(2) Suppose you are given a rubber toy with something inside of it. List at least ten things you could do to get clues about what's inside. (Really let your mind go. You'll come up with more than you think.)

For more on Piaget's views about physical knowledge, we recommend

PIAGET, JEAN. *The Child's Conception of Physical Causality,* trans. Marjorie Gabain (London: Routledge and Kegan Paul, 1930 [first published in French, in 1927, under the title, *La Causalité Physique chez l'Enfant*]).
PIAGET, JEAN. *The Grasp of Consciousness: Action and Concept in the Young Child,* trans. Susan Wedgwood (Cambridge, Mass.: Harvard University Press, 1976 [first published in French, in 1974, under the title, *La Prise de Conscience*]).
PIAGET, JEAN. *Success and Understanding,* trans. Arnold J. Pomerans (Cambridge, Mass.: Harvard University Press, 1978 [first published in French, in 1974, under the title, *Réussir et Comprendre*]).

## CONVENTIONAL KNOWLEDGE

Conventional knowledge is the knowledge of specific rules and conventions used in one's culture. It can only be acquired through social interactions—interactions with *people,* not as warm (23° C), moving objects, but as social beings. In acquiring this kind of knowledge, one must adapt the abilities discussed in the section on physical knowledge so that they are effective in eliciting social conventions. For example, children need a repertoire of behaviors that elicit labels, statements of social rules, and the like, if they are to find out how to express things in their culture. However, before this type of activity is maximally useful to them they must be able to understand that sounds and actions can be used to stand for objects and events, and they must have some understanding of social relationships (for instance, what sorts of things rules are). The onset of the semiotic function somewhere around one and a half to two years of age is a major step. It allows the child to move from physical experiences in a social milieu to a representation of those experiences in ways that can be communicated to others through a variety of media.

Because conventional knowledge is only useful to children when they have an understanding of its nature (that it is established by agreement among people in the society, for example, and that it does not influence the laws of nature, though it may refer to them), we have included in this section some general characteristics and abilities of representation ability per se. Without this ability, conventional knowledge would remain at the level of turn-taking and imitation games in infant-parent interactions.

Characteristics to look for in representation ability, and in knowledge of specific rules and conventions, are listed next.

### Representation Ability

(1) The ability to use three-dimensional objects to stand for other objects when (1) both objects are very similar (substituting a toy iron for a real iron), (2) the objects are dissimilar (using a wooden block to represent a telephone), and (3) a variety of objects are used to construct a model of the real object (using wood, glue, construction paper, and styrofoam pieces to make an airplane).

(2) The ability to recognize and use two-dimensional representations of real objects (for instance, using a picture of a doctor's office to create the atmosphere for a dramatic play episode).

(3) The ability to represent objects by the use of actions typically performed on them or with them (making a pounding motion to stand for a hammer or a dribbling motion to stand for a basketball).

(4) The ability to represent animate beings by imitating behaviors associated with them (using phrases such as "Yes, dear" to indicate that one is the mommy in a dramatic-play situation, or illustrating an elephant by moving one's arms like an elephant's trunk).

(5) The ability to use shortened versions of an action or action sequence to stand for the real event (for example, in a dramatic-play situation, the child brings a spoon to the mouth three times to stand for eating breakfast).

(6) The recognition that the same idea can be represented in a variety of different ways. Sigel (1976) calls this ability "conservation of meaning."

### Knowledge of Specific Rules and Conventions

(1) A knowledge of classroom rules, routines, and socially desirable behaviors.

(2) A knowledge about the society, culture, and so on, within the child's milieu (such as community workers, types of homes, different kinds of music and art).

(3) An acquaintance with culturally defined systems of language and representation and the ability to use conventional forms of representation unrelated to the object or action itself. (Piaget refers to these as "signs.")

(a) An ability to recognize and use socially defined gestures such as waving a hand to indicate "goodbye" or frowning to indicate displeasure.

(b) An ability to use common onomatopoetic expressions to refer to domestic animals and a limited number of wild animals; to refer to sounds of the man-made environment (car horns, bells, machinery); and to refer to sounds of the natural environment (wind blowing, rain falling).

(c) An ability to use and recognize verbal speech to focus on and retrieve concepts the child already has, to aid memory, and to clarify experiences for others.

(i) The use of verbalizations in expressing concepts, actions, feelings, and thoughts.

(ii) The use of increasingly socialized, nonegocentric speech that reflects the increasing ability to take into consideration another's point of view.

(iii) Knowledge of words that describe concepts the child already has. For example, a child who has topological concepts would learn words such as "between," "on," and "next to."

(d) Ability to recognize simple graphic signs used to indicate rules of the classroom (for instance, a frowning face used to show areas that are off limits) or routines (a picture of a garbage can that is displayed at clean-up time); or signs chosen by society to indicate such things as traffic rules (for example, pedestrian-crossing signs) or safety precautions (such as the "Mr. Yuk" logo on poisons).

(e) An ability to recognize a number of letters and words that are meaningful in each child's experience. For example, children might recognize the letters in their name and in words referring to favorite foods (such as Pepsi) or to favorite toys (for instance, kaleidoscope).

(f) An ability to copy (i) figures such as circles, squares, and triangles, (ii) simple drawings such as houses, trees, clouds, stick men, (iii) individual letters of the alphabet, and (iv) short sequences of letters or words. Such ability presupposes spatial knowledge as well as competence in psychomotor ability.

*TEACHER TASK 6-2*

---

(1) How many different ways can you convey the message, "I love you" to a child? to a pet? to another adult?

Think of some ways that won't work for at least one of these cases. Why won't they work?

(2) What rules and socially acceptable behaviors do you think preschool children should know? Justify your choices.

---

For more on Piaget's views about conventional knowledge, we recommend

PIAGET, JEAN. *The Language and Thought of the Child,* 3rd ed., trans. Marjorie and Ruth Gabain (London: Routledge and Kegan Paul, 1959 [first published in French, in 1923, under the title, *Études sur la Logique de l'Enfant*]).
PIAGET, JEAN. *Play, Dreams, and Imitation in Childhood,* trans. C. Gattegno and F. M. Hodgson (London: Heineman, 1951 [first published in French, in 1945, under the title, *La Formation du Symbole chez l'Enfant; Imitation, Jeu, et Rêve, Image et Représentation*]).

## LOGICO-MATHEMATICAL KNOWLEDGE

In its broad sense, logico-mathematical knowledge includes logical concepts that are closely tied to the physical world we live in as well as concepts of pure logic. Both of these types of concepts can be distinguished from the concepts of physical knowledge by the way they are developed. Although physical knowledge can be *discovered,* logico-mathematical knowledge must be *invented.* Thus, a child may discover through repeated experiences that the weight of clay doesn't change when the shape is altered. This is an example of physical knowledge. The child's invention or construction of the rule that changes in shape *never* alter the weight of substances like clay (or *could not possibly* alter the weight of such substances) is an example of logico-mathematical knowledge—in this case, infra-logical knowledge. An example of a concept of logico-mathematical knowledge in its narrow sense (what we are calling logico-mathematical knowledge proper) is the child's construction of the notion of groups and subgroups. When children not only know specific facts such as that there are more people in their family than there are children, but also realize that, in general, there are a number of categories in which to place an object, some of these completely encompassing others, children have made an advance in logico-mathematical knowledge proper.

Notice that in both of these examples, the child had to have had experiences with the real world and a knowledge of specific pieces of information. Encounters with the real world of objects and facts lead the child to construct the rules and relationships that make up logico-mathematical knowledge. Likewise, the rules and relations the child has constructed provide new windows to use as that child looks out on the world. The more logical relationships the child has constructed, the more sense will be derived from physical phenomena. The more physical experiences the child has encountered, the more his or her logical knowledge is likely to be enhanced.

We will look at the two kinds of logico-mathematical knowledge separately. First, let's see what characteristics we might look for in children's constructions of infra-logical knowledge. Then we will delve into logico-mathematical knowledge proper.

### Infra-logical Knowledge

Infra-logical knowledge refers to the knowledge of relationships among properties and physical objects in the real world. It requires an understanding of logical concepts such as "all," "and," "or," "always," "never"—though the child needn't be able to express these verbally—and it requires a knowledge of the particular world we live in. In short, it combines what we have called physical knowledge with what we have called logico-mathematical knowledge proper. In our division of knowledge into different areas, infra-logical knowledge refers primarily to understandings of spatial relationships, temporal relationships, and the relationships between certain properties and potential transformations of objects having these properties. The last type of understanding, the recognition that certain properties of objects *always* remain unchanged under specified transformations, is referred to as the ability to conserve.

Characteristics to look for in the area of spatial relationships have been divided into two sections, the first dealing with understandings of topological space, and the second with the transition to projective and Euclidean space. Characteristics to look for in the areas of temporal relationships and conservation abilities follow the sections on spatial understandings.

### Spatial relations—topological space

Topology is the study of the kinds of relationships between points, lines, and regions that are not altered by compression, expansion, or tilting. Imagine, for example, a group of drawings made on a balloon. When the balloon is blown up, the lines get longer and acquire greater degrees of curvature, squares may begin to look like circles, and spaces get larger as lines move farther apart from one another. Lines that did not previously intersect remain separated, however; continuous lines remain continuous; and the order of drawings remains unchanged. Any properties of space that do not change when the balloon is stretched, twisted, or compressed are topological properties. Piaget and his coworkers have found that although topology is a highly sophisticated and recently developed area of mathematical study, rudimentary topological concepts develop in advance of rudimentary concepts of Euclidean and projective space (the concepts we deal with, for example, in distinguishing triangles from squares, straight lines from curved lines, and right angles from acute angles). Here are some things to watch for in a child's developing ability to understand topological space:

(1) Enclosure: the ability to distinguish completely closed spaces from partially closed spaces in two and in three dimensions. For example, in constructing buildings and deciding whether or not to include entrances, a child is applying this ability to three-dimensional space. A two-dimensional problem might involve distinguishing a "C" from an "O." (This includes an understanding of relationships generally expressed verbally as "inside," "outside," "edge," "open," "closed," "in.")

(2) Separation: the ability to deal with part-whole relationships, including figure-ground distinctions.

(a) The ability to divide and reconstruct wholes in their original arrangement (for example, work puzzles).

(b) The ability to use comparable parts to make different wholes (such as re-using the same fifteen Lego blocks to build four different structures).

(c) The ability to use different parts to make comparable wholes (for instance, using five large blocks to make the same-sized fence as one made with fifteen small blocks).

(d) Recognition that the choice of what is to be considered the whole is arbitrary and depends on immediate demands. For example, the classroom could be viewed as the whole, with a table as a part of that classroom; or the table could be considered as a whole and one leg viewed as a part.

(3) Proximity: the ability to make judgments of distance. (This includes an understanding of relationships expressed verbally as "near," "far," "next to," "beside," "on.")

(a) Skill in moving one's own body through space.

(b) Good judgment in moving objects in relation to one another in space (for instance, placing upright blocks at the correct distance to form a bridge).

(4) Order (spatial succession): the ability to maintain direction and consistent sequence in reproducing a linear arrangement of five or more objects using an identical set of objects. (This includes an understanding of relationships expressed

verbally as "next to" and "between.") Watch for children's ability to reproduce the display when they must arrange their objects in the following ways:

    (a)  in exact linear arrangement,

    (b)  spread out or squeezed together,

    (c)  in reverse order of the original, and

    (d)  from a different orientation.

(5)  Continuity: the ability to view space as continuous, so that several paths can lead to the same point.

    (a)  Recognition that a circuitous route may lead to the same end point as a straight line. This includes the recognition that roads, for example, can curve and turn sharp corners and remain the same road. One can take detours around obstacles in the process of reaching a goal even though they require movements in the "wrong" direction. Solutions to mazes require this understanding.

    (b)  Development and use of alternate routes for oneself or for objects. For example, one could go around a table in order to get to an activity.

### Spatial relations—euclidean and projective space

Concepts of Euclidean space include absolute length, degree of angularity, amount of curvature, and direction in a coordinate system. Unlike concepts in topology, these properties are changed when a surface is stretched or compressed. To get an idea of the difference between a focus on topological concepts and a focus on Euclidean concepts, imagine three figures: a circle with a hole in its center (such as a doughnut), a solid circle, and a square. A child focusing on topological concepts might say the two figures most like each other were the square and the solid circle. One can be transformed into the other by simply stretching, in the appropriate places, the surface on which they are drawn. Someone focusing on Euclidean concepts would very likely claim that the circle and the doughnut shape were most alike. After all, the boundaries of each are curved and without angles. Both answers are right, of course. It all depends on which properties one uses as the basis for comparison.

Concepts of projective space overlap to some extent with the concepts of Euclidean space. The former include those properties that are the same for an object and for the shadow it casts. The shadow of a straight object such as a pencil is always straight, although the absolute length will vary as the pencil is tilted. The shadow of a circular disc retains the curved boundaries of the disc, though the shadow becomes elliptical as the disc is tilted. There are limits, of course. When the pencil is pointed at right angles to the screen on which its shadow is projected, the shadow becomes a mere point. When the disc is held horizontally, its shadow looks like a straight line. Though an understanding of projective space has much in common with an understanding of Euclidean space, the two are not the same.

Characteristics to watch for in the child's construction of these concepts of space include

(1) Quantifying distance: the ability to measure through repeated use of a unit of measurement—this implies an understanding that the length of a standard is conserved (that is, remains the same) even when it is moved in a variety of directions (horizontally, vertically, diagonally). For example, a block standing upright on a table is the same size as it would be placed upright on the floor.

(2) Quantifying direction: the ability to focus on degrees of change in direction (for instance, angles versus curves) and degrees of similarity in direction (such as parallel lines versus divergent lines). For example, a child would be able to use blocks to construct parallel roads and would be aware of the options for making curved roads and/or roads with sharp angular turns to get to the same destination.

(3) Noting differences in viewpoints from different positions in space. This involves a coordination of abilities to quantify distance and direction. For example, two children building "houses" might find that to get from Peter's house to Freddie's one has to go straight out Peter's door a distance of five blocks, turn left, and go three blocks. To get from Freddie's house to Peter's, however, one would walk three blocks straight, turn right, and walk five blocks. Incidentally, if children recognize that both Peter and Freddie have the same distance to travel to get to the other's house, they are on the way to number conservation and basic mathematical skills. (See why it's so hard to draw clear distinctions between the areas of knowledge?)

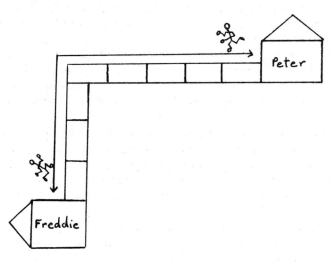

(1)  Try some work in topology: find or make a necklace of different-colored beads and twist it so that it looks like this ∞ ; not like this ∞ . Now make a list of the beads in order. Is it the same order that you get when you untwist the string?

(2)  Here's a problem in Euclidean and projective geometry. Imagine a hollow cube. You are going to unfold the cube so that you get a flat surface. What will it look like? Describe variations in what the flat surface would look like if you unfolded the cube in different ways. Think hard! You may discover more than you expect.

### Temporal relations

The development of a system for making sense of temporal relations involves the gradual dissociation of time from activities that go on at various speeds and from motions that occupy various amounts of space. Before children construct a clear notion of time, they tend to confuse temporal order with spatial order and duration with the distance covered. Living in time, where some things necessarily happen before others, is not the same as having a conscious awareness of the relationship between time and motion (or lack of motion) through space. Children have to be able to recall sequences of temporal and spatial events before they can distinguish the two, but the ability to recall a temporal sequence is just the beginning of their construction of temporal relations. Here are some developmental steps to look for in the evolution of their understanding:

(1)  The ability to recall the temporal order of a sequence of three to five events. This requires that events be remembered in a particular order rather than haphazardly. The main thing this characteristic demonstrates is that the child is aware of time as a relevant dimension along which to order events. Time and space may still be confused, however.

(2)  An understanding of efficient causality—that is, that the cause must precede the effect. For example, the child can understand "because" in the following situation: "I scraped my elbow because I fell off my trike." The child would not maintain, "I fell off my trike because I scraped my elbow."

(3)  The recognition of the distinction between events that *cause* other events and those that merely precede others. Snack time may come before large-group time, for example, but one doesn't cause the other.

(4)  An understanding that present activities may serve as a means for attaining a future goal. Included in this understanding are planning abilities and the abil-

ity to keep the end in mind even when one is sidetracked by interesting aspects of the process itself. Watch for such statements as, "I'm going to make a block house for the guinea pig," followed by careful construction of the house and by an attempt to place the guinea pig in the house. (If you've ever wondered about a child who suddenly broke into angry tears at the signal for clean-up time, this may give you a clue as to the reason. A child who has just acquired this ability and who has spent all morning keeping the end in mind while getting sidetracked with details of the house-building is bound to be frustrated in finding that external time constraints prevent enjoyment of the fruits of the new intellectual skill.)

(5) The ability to reconstruct a temporal order of three to five events by using a knowledge of the logical connection between events. In telling a story, for example, the child would indicate that in a sensible sequence of events, Hansel and Gretel would have dropped the bread crumbs *before* their parents left them; that *after* the children realized they were lost, they would have searched for signs of the trail of crumbs they had left; and that the old witch would have told them of her plans to eat them *before* they pushed her into the oven.

(6) An understanding of duration without a clear separation of duration from distance. Children may recognize, for example, that it will take longer to walk all the way across the room than it will to walk three quarters of the way. They will still deny that someone going as fast as a speeding car could reach the end of the room before they themselves had reached the three-quarter mark, however, since space and time are still confused. Since the end of the room is farther away, they reason, it will take longer to get there—and that's all there is to it.

(7) A recognition of velocity with an erroneous understanding of how it relates to duration and space. A child may identify the amount of time elapsed with the velocity, for example, and claim that the faster you put sand into a bucket, the more time it takes you to fill it, and, therefore, the more sand it can hold relative to a bucket filled more slowly.

It takes a good number of years before the child has a clear, sophisticated theory of temporal relations—ten to fifteen years, in fact! If we take a close look at how young children deal with time, we gain an understanding of why they are frustrated by events that seem perfectly understandable to us. Think of children who have told you after a field trip that it can't be time to go home, because "we haven't had group time." Have you ever seen children arguing over who won a race? Their insistence that the winner started too soon, when this is clearly not the case, may not be a ploy for winning an argument, after all. It may be an appeal to what the child sees as a logical necessity. A child who doesn't focus on differences in velocity may think that the only way to win a race is to start earlier than your competition. (In that case, is it cheating to start ahead of the signal? Or does that simply demonstrate the only possible way to win?)

*TEACHER TASK 6-4*

---

(1)   A child is carefully filling cups of various sizes with dried corn. You ask her which one has the most corn in it. She points to the smallest one. What's going on?

(2)   Suppose a child tells you the story of Snow White and the Seven Dwarfs from beginning to end, not missing a single episode. What, if anything, can you infer about his understanding of temporal relations? What can you do to test your inferences?

---

### Conservation

In Piaget's system, conservation ability refers to the realization that certain properties (such as number, weight, length, volume, area) remain the same when particular, and often perceptually misleading, changes are made (changes such as rearrangement or bending). This requires the knowledge that some changes are reversible. For example, a string can be bent and then straightened again or tied and then untied, and the final length will equal the initial length. True conservation ability requires even more than this, though. A true conserver has constructed the theory that even when the string is tied in a knot—when it looks considerably shorter than it did before—the length is really the same. Not only can the change be reversed so that the string is once again as long as it was at the beginning, but, in fact, the child's theory says, the real length never changes! Appearances can be deceptive.

The ability to conserve properties such as weight and volume is generally taken as an indication of concrete operational ability. Since few preschool-aged children have constructed this level of infra-logical knowledge, indicators that children are at this level are not included in this list. One is quite likely to find four- and five-year-old children who conserve length and number, however, and characteristics of these abilities have been included. Characteristics to look for in this area are

(1)   An awareness (physical knowledge) of which actions lead to reversible changes and which do not. For example, the effects of pouring lemonade from a pitcher to a cup can be reversed, but the effects of dissolving sugar to make the lemonade can not.

(2)   The recognition of which properties change (for instance, the granular *texture* of sugar) and which properties remain the same (the amount of sugar) when various actions are performed.

(3)   The knowledge that number remains the same when objects are rearranged or counted in a new order (see the guideposts given under "Number" in the section on logico-mathematical knowledge proper).

(4)   The knowledge that length remains the same when various changes are made. For example, a shoelace itself does not change in length when it is tied in a knot, laced in a shoe, or strung with beads.

(5) The knowledge that the distance between two objects is not affected by objects placed between them. The distance "as the crow flies" remains the same regardless of how many trees, houses, or roads spring up between two airports.
(6) The knowledge that the passage of time is independent of the activities that go on. Three hours spent at a circus may seem shorter than the fifteen minutes at the doctor's office, but, in reality, the former is much longer than the latter.

**TEACHER TASK 6-5**

> (1) Does a metal ruler *always* stay the same length, no matter what you're measuring? (What if you measure a hot furnace?)
> (2) Find out whether a preschool child you know conserves distance. (You might try racing games and put a piece of colored tape in the middle of one of the tracks.)

For more on Piaget's views about infra-logical knowledge, we recommend

PIAGET, JEAN. *The Child's Conception of Movement and Speed,* trans. G. E. T. Holloway and M. J. MacKenzie (London: Routledge and Kegan Paul, 1970 [first published in French, in 1946, under the title, *Les Notions de Mouvement et de Vitesse chez l'Enfant*]).
PIAGET, JEAN. *The Child's Conception of Time,* trans. Arnold J. Pomerans (London: Routledge and Kegan Paul, 1969 [first published in French, in 1946, under the title, *Le Développement de la Notion de Temps chez l'Enfant*]).
PIAGET, JEAN, and BÄRBEL INHELDER. *The Child's Conception of Space,* trans. F. J. Langdon and J. L. Lunzer (London: Routledge and Kegan Paul, 1956 [first published in French, in 1948, under the title, *La Représentation de l'Espace chez l'Enfant*]).

### Logico-mathematical Knowledge Proper

As with infra-logical knowledge, the construction of logico-mathematical knowledge proper is stimulated by experiences with the physical and social environment. Unlike infra-logical knowledge, however, it is not tied to the way things are in our world. Rather, as philosophers would say, truths in the logico-mathematical realm are true in all possible worlds—even in imaginary worlds where there is no gravity or where changes in shape do influence the weight or mass of substances. Since our world is a possible world, logic works here. To be fully adapted to our world is to have constructed for oneself the system of logical and mathematical truths.

One of Piaget's most controversial and most radical contributions to the study of cognitive development has been his claim that children have to invent this system of logical thought. They are not born with the system of logic we adults call upon so frequently in our thinking. All of us manage to construct the same logical system because we have human abilities and limitations, and because we live in a world where logic works. We can facilitate children's construction of the system by watching to see what kind of a system they are presently using, by asking questions that provoke the invention of relationships, and by providing plenty of physical experiences that reflect the way the real world operates—not some artificial world constructed through an adult-centered analysis of the logical steps in learning a task.

The characteristics in the following list are important because they demonstrate how much invention and construction goes into the logical notions we take for granted. In keeping with Piaget's discussions of logico-mathematical knowledge, they have been grouped into three areas: the construction of the notion of classes, the construction of an understanding of relations, and the synthesis of these understandings in the construction of number concepts.

### Classification (the notion of classes)

(1) A recognition of similarities and differences among objects. For example, a child might comment, "Your shoes are red like mine, but yours have buckles and mine don't." (When looking for evidence of this characteristic, notice whether or not a child has seen more than one similarity or difference.)

(2) The ability to *match identical objects and to make small groups* of similar objects (for example, red things, broken things, things you can squeeze) without necessarily including all of the objects that belong in each group. A child might successfully pick out three or four pennies from a group of objects on a tray, for instance, and then find it perfectly acceptable to add bottle tops and bits of aluminum foil to the group of pennies. Such groups are not true classes, and are called collections in Piaget's terms.

(3) The ability to *choose criteria* for making groups before objects are gathered and to list the criterion (or the criteria) by which a grouping was made. This kind of ability includes the discrimination of various possible criteria and the selection of appropriate criteria for sorting.

(4) The ability to *sort consistently* according to some criterion. Watch for the ability to make a number of small groups (red cars and trucks, green cars and trucks, blue cars and trucks) as well as for the ability to make dichotomies. Dichotomous sorts are those in which only two groups are made, and every object is placed into one or the other. An example would be the division of all the cars and trucks into a group of cars (of all colors) and a group of trucks (of all colors). This is a more difficult task than sorting the objects into a group of red trucks and a group of everything else—the kind of sorting described in characteristic number 2.)

(6) The ability to *shift criteria* in forming new groups after an initial sort

has been made. (This is called horizontal reclassification.) For example, after Nora has separated cars from trucks, she might reconsider her groupings in the light of a new purpose and re-sort them into a group of broken vehicles and a group of intact vehicles.

(7) The ability to *construct hierarchical classification systems* and to understand the relationships among the levels (subordinate and superordinate classes). For example, children would distinguish the total class of vehicles (superordinate class) from the cars and from the trucks (each of these being a subordinate class). They would also know that there must be more vehicles than there are trucks or than there are cars. The crucial point is that children will not be misled by disproportionate numbers of cars and trucks (say, ten and two) so that they compare cars to trucks instead of comparing vehicles (both cars and trucks) to trucks alone or to cars alone.

As children construct more sophisticated systems of classification, they expand their total repertoire of problem-solving techniques. Competence with true classification systems (including the ability to re-sort and to construct class hierarchies) enables children to choose from a full range of sorting techniques (including collections as well as true classes), depending on their immediate purposes. Thus it allows them to be creative and flexible in their use of materials and in their view of the world. If a child's purpose in sorting a group of cars and trucks is to put all the broken ones in a box to be thrown away, it is an advantage to sort consistently; that is, to put *all* the broken ones and *only* the broken ones into the box. Thus, although not every situation profits from the use of true classification ability, some situations are best approached in this way.

### TEACHER TASK 6-6

> (1)   Gather about ten objects and find a way to sort them into two groups. (It's no fair to use groups such as "red spoons" and "everything that's not a red spoon.") Now re-sort them as many different ways as you can, making sure each time that every object belongs to one group or the other. When you run out of ideas, let someone else try.
>
> (2)   Danny is playing with a set of parquetry blocks. He has just put three green diamonds into one pile and has placed all the squares, of various colors, into another. What could you do and/or say to find out his abilities in the area of classification?

### Relations (seriation)

(1) The ability to *recognize relative differences* among two or more objects. The child would be able, for example, to find something bigger than, or smaller than, a plastic spoon.

(2) The ability to sort dichotomously a set of objects according to a *relational criterion*. In this case, the child would find or name *everything* on the table that is bigger than the plastic spoon, or two children would resolve their dispute over blocks by having one child get all the blocks that are shorter than the chair leg.

(3) The ability to use *transitive reasoning*. An example is a child's statement such as "I am too older than Aldo. I know 'cause Mary's older than him, and she's only three and a half. And I'm older than Mary, so there." The example here is given in the way a child might respond to a challenge. Children's arguments provide wonderful situations for detecting characteristics of their reasoning processes.

(4) The ability to *serially order* five to ten objects through a process of trial and error. The exact number of objects is arbitrary. The point is that the child is able to solve the problem on a conceptual level rather than on a perceptual level only. When children consistently arrange three or four objects on some basis (height, for example), one cannot be sure that they have actually constructed an understanding of the relations involved. They may simply be making an arrangement that has perceptual appeal. When they have arranged a larger number of objects in a serial order, it is more likely that they used a conceptual basis for the arrangement.

(5) The ability to order five to ten objects in sequence and then *insert two to five more objects appropriately* into the original sequence. To do this, the child has to realize that an object can simultaneously be greater in a given dimension than one object and lesser in that same dimension than another object. This is not a simple concept. "Bigger" and "smaller" are opposites, after all. How can they both be applied to the same object? We have seen a child on the verge of tears because she couldn't fit a block into a previously constructed staircase. She found a place where the new stair was higher than the step on one side—that much she knew was required—but somehow the staircase didn't look right. (The new stair was also higher than the step on the other side.) She could not resolve the problem because she did not grasp that her stair could be—and *had* to be—simultaneously *higher* than the step on one side and *lower* than the step on the other side.

(6) The ability to *construct a one-to-one correspondence between two ordered sequences* of five to ten objects. Again, the exact number of objects is not crucial, so long as there is a conceptual basis for the arrangement. The knowledge we're looking for here is the recognition that when two groups of objects are arranged serially, the fourth item in one sequence will correspond to the fourth item in the other, the fifth with the fifth, and so on. This understanding enables one to easily solve problems such as finding the shoes that fit a particular doll. If you know you have the doll with the third largest feet, then all you have to do is find the third largest pair of shoes.

> (1) Suppose Michael has successfully worked a seriation puzzle—the kind where there are four or five pieces, each one smaller than the last. What, if anything, has he shown you about his understanding of relations? What other information would you like to have before making a judgment?
>
> (2) Try asking a four-year-old you know to think of something that is "smaller than a tree but bigger than a dandelion." Pay careful attention to the kind of answer you get. What does it say about the child's cognitive development?

### Number

(1) The ability to make quantitative comparisons between two groups of objects.

(a) Make gross comparisons: a lot compared to a little compared to the same amount.

(b) Make exact comparisons by placing two groups of five to ten objects in *provoked* one-to-one correspondence. The child would be able to determine, for example, whether or not there is the same number of socks as sneakers by placing one sock with each sneaker. In this case, pairs of objects (one from each group) clearly belong together.

(c) Make exact comparisons by placing two groups of five to ten objects in *unprovoked* (or spontaneous) one-to-one correspondence. In this case, the groups of objects do not necessarily "go together." To see whether two easels each had the same number of paint brushes, a child might establish equivalence by pairing off brushes, one from each easel.

(2) A global understanding of the effects of adding objects to a group or of removing objects from that group.

(a) Understand that adding objects to a group increases the number ("makes more"), so that if one were to count the objects, one would have to count a higher number—or so that if objects in the group were to be paired off with objects in another group that had previously been equivalent, there would be some unpaired objects left over.

(b) Understand that removing objects from a group decreases the number ("makes less").

(3) The ability to distinguish number from attributes such as arrangement, color, and size. This enables the child to conserve number—that is, to realize that

number remains the same in spite of various perceptual changes. This applies both to identity conditions (involving changes within a single group) and to equivalence conditions (involving changes in one group when there were several equivalent groups to begin with).

(a) Identity I (*renversabilité*): Realize that the number of objects in a single group that has been altered (that is, different configuration, color, and so on) can be reestablished when the objects are put back into the original form. A child who realizes this does not necessarily realize that the number has remained the same all along.

(b) Identity II (reversibility): Realize that the number of objects remains the same even when the original arrangement is altered and has not been reestablished (for instance, five chairs in a stack is just as many as those same five chairs in a row).

(c) Equivalence I (*renversabilité*): Realize that the number of objects in equivalent groups remains the same when the destroyed correspondence is reconstructed. (For example, if the pairs of paint brushes for two art tables are placed in a jar on each table, a child might think there is no longer an equal number of brushes. The child would believe that if they were put back together in pairs, however, equivalency of the groups would be reestablished.)

(d) Equivalence II (reversibility): Realize that the number of objects in equivalent groups remains the same when one-to-one correspondence no longer exists. The child has no need to physically reconstruct the correspondence.

(4) An understanding of the way the number system works.

(a) Know how to count in sequence from one to twenty.

(b) Realize that adding one to any number gives the next number in that counting sequence.

(c) Realize that all numbers smaller than a particular number are included in that number. Thus, four includes three, which, in turn, includes two. If you have four raisins, then it must also be true that you have three raisins. To fully realize this property, children must know that when they point to an object and say "Seven," they are identifying a whole group of objects. This particular object is just the seventh one they have counted.

*TEACHER TASK 6-8*

(1) Two children are pretending to be pirates and are stashing away "gold." How could you find out something about their understanding of number without detracting from their play? Be creative!

(2) Remember the old joke about people getting on and off a bus at various stops? You think the final question will be "How many people are

left on the bus?," but instead you are asked how many stops were made. Why is it hard to give the right answer? How is this related to the responses children give to your questions about number?

For more on Piaget's views about logico-mathematical knowledge, we recommend

PIAGET, JEAN. *The Child's Conception of Number,* trans. C. Gattegno and F. M. Hodgson (London: Routledge and Kegan Paul, 1952 [first published in French, in 1941, under the title, *La Genèse du Nombre chez l'Enfant*]).

INHELDER, BÄRBEL, and JEAN PIAGET. *The Early Growth of Logic in the Child,* trans. E. A. Lunzer and D. Papert (London: Routledge and Kegan Paul, 1964 [first published in French, in 1959, under the title, *La Genèse des Structures Logiques Elémentaire*]).

## SUMMARY

In this chapter we have looked at developmental guideposts for physical, conventional, and logico-mathematical knowledge. Although these guideposts will play a significant role in our attempts to put the theory beast to work, they must be used with caution, because (1) our lists are not exhaustive—there are other sorts of developmental steps taken by children; (2) they are not behaviors we'll try to teach—rather, they help us to understand children's thought and to find strategies that might stimulate their thinking; and (3) the division of knowledge into three types is not sacred—the division merely provides us with rules of thumb to be applied with good sense.

The guides for physical and conventional knowledge provided outlines of children's progress in the knowledge of attributes in their environment and in their ability to systematically find out more about the environment. In the case of physical knowledge, children come to know more physical facts, and they also progress in their ability to think and act scientifically. In the case of conventional knowledge, children learn specific rules and conventions, but they also develop representational abilities.

We looked at two kinds of logico-mathematical knowledge: infra-logical knowledge and logico-mathematical knowledge proper. The first of these includes the emerging understanding of spatial relations, of temporal relations, and of conservation (the recognition of an invariance in the face of change). Logico-mathematical knowledge proper was divided into the notion of classes, the notion of relations (or seriation), and the synthesis of these notions in the understanding of number.

Our guideposts have introduced us to new complexities in the personality of our theory beast. As usual, teacher tasks have been included to enhance the deepening relationship we hope is evolving between you and the theory.

## REFERENCES

HARDEMAN, MILDRED.  "Introduction," in Isaacs, Nathan, *Children's Ways of Knowing: Nathan Isaacs on Education, Psychology, and Piaget,* ed. Mildred Hardeman (New York: Teachers College Press, 1974).

HAWKINS, DAVID.  "Messing About in Science," *Science and Children, 2,* no. 5 (1965), 5–9.

SIGEL, IRVING E.  "The Development of Pictorial Comprehension." Paper presented at the Visual Scholars' Program Invitational Conference, The University of Iowa, Iowa City, October 1976.

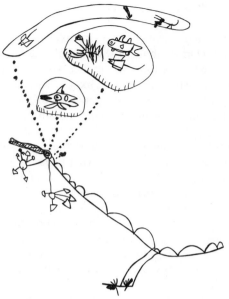

# THE THINKING TEACHER

# 7

## WHAT IS A THINKING TEACHER?

A teacher's role has many facets—far too many to be adequately explored in this book. We will confine ourselves, then, to what Piaget's theory adds to that role. In applying Piagetian theory, the teacher acts as a facilitator whose most fundamental goal is to stimulate and encourage the child's own construction and reconstruction of systems of thought. This means that the teacher must be a coworker with the child—a cothinker who helps to clarify, focus, and communicate. It means that the teacher must be an assessor who knows how to discover a child's interests and understandings. And it means that the teacher must be a human-relations expert who understands group dynamics and can motivate children and fellow teachers to give their best to the thinking process. The teacher must be all of these in addition to being someone who meets the numerous other demands of the teacher role, demands that are not specified by the theory. In short, the teacher applying Piagetian theory must be a *thinking teacher*.

Thinking teachers are people who think hard while helping others to think well. They help children understand thinking (just as science teachers help children understand science and music teachers help children understand music), and they also do a lot of thinking themselves in their continual efforts to develop their own thinking about teaching and learning. They are excited by the thinking process itself and are eager to know more about how children's thinking develops.

It's not hard to recognize a thinking teacher when you see one. It's someone who tries hard to figure out what each child is like—how each child thinks and what each child's interests are. It's someone who ponders how best to help children become good thinkers. This means spending hours in planning activities with a variety of options, so that the right one can be pursued when children point it out. It's someone who constantly makes hypotheses, tests them out, and makes new hypotheses in order to find out what works and what doesn't. It's someone who uses every resource available in order to find out more about thinking in general and about the way children in his or her classroom think. It's someone who respects children, respects parents, respects other teachers, and works with all of them to facilitate children's intellectual growth. It's someone who is *still growing.*

A thinking teacher is always developing—becoming. Each thinking teacher develops at his or her own pace, moving from one wrong answer to the next. A thinking teacher must be an active agent in self-development. Growth comes with conscious efforts to cultivate habits of careful observation, of constant assessment of children's abilities, of thorough analyses of classroom interactions, of careful planning, of continuous self-evaluation, of evaluating goals in terms of observations and theoretical insight, and of active participation in children's intellectual activities. Growth comes from the willingness to make mistakes and to correct them.

> *Give me a good fruitful error anytime, full of seeds, bursting with its own corrections. You can keep your sterile truth for yourself.*
>
> *Pareto, 1962, p. 59*

As they grow, thinking teachers keep three major questions in mind:

(1)  What are my children like?
(2)  What will help them become better thinkers?
(3)  How can I, with whatever talents and limitations I have, help them develop?

Piaget's theory can help us answer these questions. If we use it thoughtfully, the theory can help us find out how children are thinking, make extensive plans for learning activities, implement those plans flexibly so as to maximize children's participation in classroom activities and classroom decisions, evaluate activities before and after implementation, and integrate logico-mathematical and infra-logical content areas into all aspects of curriculum planning. It is flexible enough to help us regardless of considerations such as class size, length of class day, type of program (nursery school, parent co-op, day care, public school), amount of money and materials, number of teachers, urban or rural setting, and so forth.

In this chapter, we'll explore ways to make the theory useful in addressing the first two questions listed earlier. First we'll look at how the theory influences our observations of children and the inferences we draw. (A more detailed look at observation techniques is reserved for Chapter 9.) Then we'll examine some of the ways in which the theory influences how we set up the classroom, how we schedule the day, how we plan specific activities, and how we interact with children to help them become better thinkers. Although our discussion here is certainly relevant to the more personal third question, there are more specific things to be said, which we will reserve for Chapter 10. In the last section of this chapter, we use the example of blocks to see how a single material can supply a variety of potentials for learning (by teachers as well as by children). As usual, you'll have to do plenty of thinking as you go. What we offer are hints, promising directions, and potentials— not specific *must's* and *never do's.*

## OBSERVATION AND INFERENCE (FINDING OUT HOW CHILDREN THINK AND WHAT THEY KNOW)

If we are to really know the children we work with, skills in observing and in making sound and useful inferences are crucial. We have divided these skills into four abilities: (1) the ability to distinguish between observation and inference (granted that the boundary between them is somewhat fuzzy), (2) the ability to focus on those elements of a child's behavior that have relevance to Piagetian theory, (3) the tendency and ability to act on the basis of accurate observation and reasonable inference, and (4) the tendency to test hypotheses (to observe, make inferences based on those observations, and observe again to test the inferences). The theory can be useful in our development of each of these abilities. Let's see how.

### Distinguishing Between Observation and Inference

First of all, we have to distinguish between what we observe and the inferences we make. This is often a difficult task, but it is important. We often tend to assume, for example, that a child who tells us that there are six beads on each of two strings understands numbers the way we do. It would be a big mistake simply to make a mental note: "Paul understands numbers, at least up to six." By doing this, we might miss some crucial elements in his understanding of numbers. Paul may well have been able to count six beads on each string without realizing that the two strings each had the same number of beads. Furthermore, he may have "counted" by pointing to each bead as he said each number, or he may have just gotten the same number by chance or by some vague perceptual intuition of how many "six" would look like.

A thinking teacher must constantly ask questions about observations. When you watch Louise put red trucks in one box and yellow cars in another, ask yourself, "Did she put *all* the red trucks in one box? Did she put *only* the red trucks in one box? Were the trucks identical in respects other than color? How many vehicles were there?" These must be answered through observation before you can make useful inferences about Louise's classification ability.

Making a clear distinction between observation and inference is not always possible. We cannot directly see a child's thought process. All we can see is behavior. But just what counts as behavior? Can we "observe" the anger in an expression—or is it only inferred? Can we accurately recognize (observe) a thoughtful expression? Can we distinguish facial expressions that are accompanied by thought from those that are not? What does it mean to say that Paul counted the beads? If he says the names for the numbers from one to six in order, has he really counted them—even if he has never before come up with the correct number for a group of objects and did not point to individual beads as he said the numbers?

Piagetian theory does not solve this problem for us. It does, however, give us guidelines for evaluating some candidates for observational terms. The theory tells us that words such as "sorted," "counted," and "compared" are terms of inference, not observation. What we need to know is what specific behaviors were involved in the sorting, counting, and comparing. Such words as "sorting" need to be carefully analyzed so that we know what specific observations justify our use of them in describing a particular event. The lists of developmental characteristics in Chapter 6 can be a big help in telling us what to look for and how to analyze such terms.

The theory is very useful in making certain distinctions between observation terms and inference terms. It does this primarily by specifying the differences in the mental organization of children and adults. This sort of distinction helps us focus on elements of behavior that are related to logical thought processes. These behaviors are the ones that can help us determine the adequacy of various parts of the theory. If we have an idea of the kinds of behaviors to look for, we can make the observations we need for testing our hypotheses about what a particular child is capable of doing or about what level of ability he or she tends to use in various kinds of situations.

So far, we have found that we need some guideline (some frame of reference) to help us clarify the border area between observation and inference. We also need a basis for deciding what kinds of behaviors to look for and how long to continue an observation.

### Focusing on Relevant Behaviors

The ability to focus on relevant behaviors is vital for the thinking teacher who applies Piagetian theory. People seldom get a chance to replay their observations. Even those lucky enough to have the use of video-tape equipment have to choose what incidents to tape, how long to tape a particular child, and so on. Since we cannot even notice every aspect of a situation, much less record it, we need some basis for deciding what we will attend to. Piaget's theory helps us make this decision a rational one. Unfortunately, any choice of focus in observation will necessarily exclude other legitimate choices. In the teaching situation, we often have to observe on several levels simultaneously, or, because this is often impossible, to fluctuate rapidly from a focus on cognitive abilities to a focus on emotional behaviors, physical abilities, or conventional knowledge. While the Piagetian framework is of immense help in all areas of development, it makes its greatest contribution in the cognitive-developmental area.

There are cognitive components in nearly every interaction the child has with the environment, and the theory can help us sort out these components from other crucial aspects. For example, the reason Kirsten consistently fails to "Stop at the red line!" in a large-motor exercise may be that she does not realize the meaning of the spatial preposition "at." She could also be having difficulty in motor coordination. A theory of cognitive development does not tell us which is the problem, nor does it help us pinpoint the motor problem (if there is one). What it does is to give us another angle to explore—a cognitive angle. Knowledge of Piaget's theory helps us become aware of what our choices for observation are and makes it possible for observations of intellectual development to be as useful as those we make in other areas traditionally associated with early education.

Using the Piagetian framework, we can focus on aspects of behavior relevant to particular abilities instead of simply letting the most prominent stimuli (for example, the loudest noise, the closest movement, the fastest action) capture our attention. Suppose Adam has lined up six toy cars of various colors in a row and is just beginning to line up another row. Have we enough of an observation to yield useful information about his ability? What might we watch for if we continue to observe him? One possibility is to look for evidence of the infra-logical ability to recognize and reconstruct linear orders. In this case, we should be careful to notice first whether the new line had the same number, sizes, and colors of cars. If so, we definitely want to know if the sequence of color and/or size is identical for the two rows. Even if the sequences are the same, this is not enough for us to safely infer that Adam understands spatial ordering relationships. If the two rows are quite close together, it is likely that Adam's strategy has been to match identical objects —a large red sports car with an identical one in the first row, a small green one with its mate in the first row, and so on. This tells us something about Adam's perception (and perhaps something about his topological notions of proximity), but very little about his understanding of order relations.

What if the second row is on the floor and the first one is on the table and the rows have identical objects in identical sequences? Then can we infer that Adam has a mastery of linear ordering relationships? It would certainly seem so, but we must limit our inference to relationships that do not undergo certain types of transformations. We cannot be certain from this observation that Adam can deal with the order relationships involved in constructing the sequence of objects as they would look in a mirror, for example.

If this description has left you somewhat frustrated and you can't wait to interact with Adam—to try giving him a circular arrangement to replicate, to ask him how he figured out how to make the second row, and so forth—then you are a thinking teacher. If you feel something is missing and want to know what Adam has done in other similar situations—whether he can write his name with the letters in the proper sequence, and so on—then, again, you are a thinking teacher.

Much of what we are able to observe depends on us—on what materials we provide, how we structure the classroom, and what kinds of questions we ask. We have to be able to act on the basis of what we know so far. This is the third important ability we need in finding out how children think and what they know. Teacher Task 7-1 should help you get started on cultivating this ability.

*TEACHER TASK 7-1*

---

(1) Pick two children with very different personalities or at very different developmental levels.

(2) Describe three situations that are likely to elicit behaviors relevant to a particular area, of your own choosing, within the domain of infra-logical knowledge. (A look back at Chapter 6 may help you choose an appropriate area.)

(3) Consider one of the situations you described in number 2. With the specific characteristics of each child in mind, think through what you might say or do to elicit more of the kinds of behaviors you are interested in.

(4) Create the situation you've described and find out about the understandings of each of the children you picked.

(5) Evaluate what you've learned. You may find it helpful to address yourself to these three questions: (1) What did you learn about each child's understandings? (2) What might you have done, if anything, to learn more? (3) How did the individual differences in the children affect what you did and what you learned?

---

### Acting on the Basis of Observation and Inference

To extend our knowledge of children's mental abilities, we have to elicit some behaviors. We have to arrange the classroom so that it encourages certain behaviors (in the hopes that they may be in the child's repertoire). We have to create an environment that evokes certain levels of mental organization (on the chance that they are there to be evoked). We also have to know when and how to interact in order to increase the value of the observation. We have to think beyond the immediate situation we are confronting, let our imaginations go, and pose all kinds of possible questions to extend the situation at hand. In addition, we need evidence from a wide variety of situations before we make definitive claims about cognitive structures. If we are careful, we can combine continuous observation and timely interactions to help in distinguishing chance behaviors, transitional behaviors, and memorized responses from those that reflect the internal organization, the *structure d'ensemble.*

Let's look at an example. Suppose we observe Monica placing lotto cards on a lotto board. She finishes the task and announces that there is just the right number of cards for the pictures on the board. What inference do we draw? Or shall we suspend judgment for a while? Choosing the latter, we're still left with two options: we can either store this incident away somewhere in the back of our minds and wait for other examples of Monica's understanding of numerical equivalences or we can find a way to elicit more of what we want to know right now. What kinds of things can we try? We might look for Monica's reaction to countersuggestions, we might ask her how she knows she is right or how she figured it out, we might introduce a misleading perceptual cue (introducing tiny lotto cards that don't cover the pictures, for example, or rearranging the cards), we might introduce new strategies for finding out whether or not the amounts are equivalent, or we might try combinations of these.

Since we know that preoperational children are easily misled by spatial arrangements, let's see how resistant Monica's number concept is to distortions of the spatial configuration she produced. First we ask her if there would still be just as many cards as pictures if we took the cards off. "Yes," she says, "Ah, ha!" we think. "Maybe we have a conserver here." But we try a harder question to make sure. We actually remove the cards from the pictures and stack them up in a nice neat pile. She falls for our trick. "Now there are more pictures," she says, indicating the marked contrast in how much space is taken up by the cards and by the pictures.

Shall we stop here? Remembering how complex the development of number concepts can be, we decide to go on. We know Monica does not yet conserve number, but we do not know how far she has progressed toward this understanding. We ask Monica if there is anything she can do so that there will once again be the same number of cards as pictures. From her response, we infer that she has constructed a notion of *renversabilité.* Can you now infer what her response was? (If you're unsure, look at the characteristics listed under "Number" in Chapter 6.)

In this example, we used our knowledge of theory to generate plausible inferences about Monica's knowledge. We also used each of her responses as an observation on which to base future interactions. Finding the time for in-depth questioning like this when one has a whole classful of children is no easy matter. Sometimes we simply have to suspend judgment. That means that we must plan materials and activities to use later in the day (or week, or month)—plans that will elicit clues about Monica's understanding of number relationships. We base our plans on what we have observed to be Monica's interests and on any hunches we have about her level of understanding. We are continually making guesses and testing them against observation. As thinking teachers, we want to cultivate this tendency.

### Making and Testing
### Inferences and Hypotheses

The tendency to make predictions and to test them is the fourth ability necessary for an adequate understanding of the children we work with. We need to continually make inferences, observe and interact with children to test the accuracy of our inferences, and then revise our inferences in the light of our experience so that we may test the revised versions. There is no official starting point and no certified stopping point, but somehow we have to break into the spiral of observation-inference-more careful observation-refined inference. The description of stage-related abilities provided by Piagetian theory can be very helpful in our attempt to focus on relevant behaviors. It enables us to estimate the likely range of a child's capacities, so that we do not have to start at the very base of the spiral. We know something in advance, we have some inferences in hand, before we start our observations. This is a great help, because it gives us an idea of what to look for.

If we accept Piaget's notion of stages, then we will not expect to see any formal operational abilities in a preschool-aged child, who in all probability is in the preoperational stage. We would guess that any behaviors that seem to imply the higher level of mental organization are either the result of chance or, upon closer examination, prove to be memorized behaviors rather than reflections of the advanced operational abilities. We would not rule out the possibility of formal operations entirely, but we would be wary of the evidence. We would take a bit of convincing.

Using the stage concept, we will also expect some similarity in all of the child's cognitive performances. For example, since centration and egocentrism are dominant characteristics of the mental organization in the preoperational child, we would expect to detect these characteristics in a variety of contexts. To complicate matters, the preoperational stage is not really a proper stage at all; it is a lengthy period of transition from the sensorimotor stage to the stage of concrete operations. One of the characteristics of transitions, in Piaget's theory, is that responses are highly erratic. Sometimes the child may think like someone in the concrete operational period; sometimes the child will fall back to sensorimotor schemata for help in solving problems; and sometimes the two types of thinking may even follow each other in the same activity. We have an idea of the child's possible level of mental organization, but we must be very careful about jumping to conclusions.

Limited numbers of observations may be especially misleading during this period of development, but we have our thoughtful and timely interactions with the children to help us avoid totally erroneous inferences. We must constantly be on the lookout for chances to test our hypotheses and for ways to revise them. We can never be certain about our inferences, but we can know what to look for in putting them to the test. We can seldom formulate hypotheses that will stay valid very long (since the children are constantly developing), but we can know what revisions are likely to be needed next. This is the kind of information we use in helping children become better thinkers.

*TEACHER TASK 7-2*

---

This exercise will be especially helpful if you do it with one or two other people. Each person should write down five hypotheses concerning the reasons for each of the following behaviors:

(1) One of the children in your small group smiles at you during group time and then runs into the other room.
(2) Outside with climbing equipment, a child says, "I can't do it."
(3) A child stops crying when her cookie is broken and one piece is placed in each of her hands.

When everyone has finished, discuss your hypotheses with one another. Consider what assumptions each person made about the age and abilities of the child, why you thought of the particular hypotheses you did (for instance, because of previous experiences similar to those described), what you might want to know to test various of the hypotheses, and which hypotheses seem most plausible to the group as a whole.

---

## HELPING CHILDREN BECOME BETTER THINKERS

Now that we have an idea of how to get to know about children's thinking abilities, let's find out how that knowledge can be put to work. We'll need to combine our knowledge of theory (Chapters 2 and 3), our values and goals for the classroom (Chapter 4), and our knowledge about children (Chapters 5 and 6) if we are to make the most effective use of our ability to find out about the particular children we work with. We'll call upon all of these resources when we prepare the environment before children enter the classroom, when we plan thinking activities, and when we interact with children.

### Preparing the Environment

#### Equipment, materials, and activities

So far we have only hinted at the enormous amount of work that goes on behind the scenes before children even enter the classroom each day. Let us look a little closer at the teacher's job here. Setting the stage for thinking involves three major tasks, all requiring the choice and arrangement of activities and materials.

*Task 1:* Provide for *change* and *diversity* as one supplies cognitive challenges appropriate to children's abilities, previous experiences, and current interests. The latter can be

    (a)  sparked by teacher-initiated ideas,

    (b)  generated in parent-teacher conversations,

    (c)  inferred from children's responses to classroom activities, or

    (d)  directly requested by children.

*Task 2:* Provide for *activity* by encouraging the following:

    (a)  autonomous problem-solving,

    (b)  group interactions in the use of materials (adding cooperation to autonomy as well as encouraging awareness of different points of view), and

    (c)  application of generalizations derived from one activity to others.

*Task 3:* Bring about self-confidence and *intellectual honesty* (for example, by using child-sized equipment, a minimum of "adults only" materials, and activities that guarantee a reasonable amount of success in the child's eyes—although various responses may be "wrong" from the adult's logical perspective).

A review of the charts in Chapter 4 will remind you of the many ways these tasks can be accomplished. To get you back into the spirit, we'll look briefly at each of the tasks here. Don't hesitate to turn back to Chapter 4, though, and to think through those suggestions, using the knowledge you've gained from the intervening chapters.

*Task 1:* A teacher who knows children and who knows Piaget's theory of cognitive development is in a good position to implement the first task area. A particular child's concern with hospitals and illnesses can generate a wealth of challenging and interesting activities. The possibilities are enhanced or restricted by the materials made available and by the way they are introduced. A teacher can set up the "hospital," for example, with equal numbers of beds, splints, and doctor's coats. This sets the stage for one-to-one correspondence between doctors and patients. The teacher could also seriate various pieces of equipment, the largest bandage first, followed by the next largest, and so on. Then, when children enter the play, the teacher is able to observe for evidence of serial correspondence—that is, matching each item in one series with the appropriate item in another.

Equipment might also be arranged so that children construct the hospital. In this case, a variety of materials could be made available to children, their task being to organize and arrange them. A more demanding way to present materials is to include some "misfits"—items such as tickets, engineer hats, or toy ironing boards—that are not usually associated with hospitals but that might be worked into the play by an ingenious four- or five-year-old. (Remember, though, that what is an intellectual challenge at one level of development may be an irrelevant complication at another. Very young children may not even recognize the inappropriateness of these materials.)

A strategy that can be used at a variety of levels is to set up the hospital in some stage of completion, leaving out additional materials and equipment for children to choose from. For very young children, the choice could be as simple as: "You can have either the stethoscopes or the splints today. Which would you like?" Older children could make more complicated choices. Arranging materials this way asks children to plan ahead—to imagine ahead of time what they're going to do and what they'll need to do it with. If your goal is to stimulate planning and forethought, however, don't forget to remove the unchosen materials *before* the play begins!

*Task 2:* The hospital play can also be adapted to help in accomplishing the teacher's second task in setting the stage. Autonomous problem-solving can be encouraged in "isolation wards," where "patients" can be allowed to work puzzles, read books, work with pegs, and so on, while they recuperate. Social interaction is encouraged when the hospital is set up near the block area, so that an ambulance service could be constructed nearby. A few hospital signs made with crayons and construction paper provide the impetus for combining work in the art area with dramatic play. And if your children enjoy body painting, there's no reason why the hospital staff can't "heal" black-and-blue paint spots or clean the "wounds" of children streaked with red body paint.

> Recipe for body paint:
> Mix small quantities of cold cream and powdered paint until you get the color you want. (It wipes off easily with tissues.)

As long as the children are constructing the hospital, why not include some equipment too big or too heavy for one child to handle alone? This requires social interaction in problem solving and in coordinating several points of view—"When your end goes that way, my end bumps me in the nose!" Generalizations that arise in moving heavy equipment to make a "hospital" can easily be transferred to the block area—especially if the area is large enough so that several children can work simultaneously. Such generalizations can also be used and tested in the outdoor play area.

**TEACHER TASK 7-3**

(1) Take a look at a classroom you know. What opportunities are there for autonomous problem-solving? Are there nooks and crannies created out of cardboard boxes, tables, and blankets, or even large cupboards with shelves and doors removed—places where children can retreat with such things as a basket of beads, a lotto game, or a set of toy horses and riders varying in size?

    (a) List the private places you see.

    (b) Spend one day observing children in the classroom and make note of what spaces they use for playing alone.

    (c) What in the classroom, if anything, would you change as a result of your observations?

(2)   Take a look at the same classroom, and this time look for arrangements of materials and equipment that encourage joint problem-solving. Are there easels placed side by side, large sheets of paper for making murals (so that children have to work together to decide how the space is to be used), or work areas large enough for several children? List the places you see, watch children using the space, and think through any changes you would make if it were your classroom.

An important thing to remember in setting the stage for thinking activities is to have materials accessible to children—accessible from the *children's* point of view. This is vital for both individual and group problem-solving. A number of art supplies (such as scissors, staplers, paper punches, crayons, and even paints) can be kept on low shelves. Demonstrations in the early part of the year will help children feel competent in using these materials. Teachers, throughout the year, can remind children of their options by suggesting that they look for possibilities "in the art bins" or "in the doll cupboard."

For children, accessible means more than within one's physical capacities to obtain. Accessible materials are those that may be used wherever they're needed. Small manipulative toys, for example, can be taken to a favorite private space— under a table or behind the bookshelf. So long as the use of the materials in those spaces doesn't interfere with the rest of the classroom activities, there is much to be said for such flexibility. With a little help, children can figure out how to tell when they've picked an inappropriate place and how to find the best spots. Flexibility about where materials are used fosters the integration of activities, creative thinking about how materials can be used (without destroying their potential for more conventional uses), and the testing of hypotheses in a variety of situations. As teachers, we can model such flexibility. We can carry materials from one area to another, we can consciously put the village set in the small-manipulative area one day and in the large-block area the next. Easels can be set up outside in good weather; old tires and ropes can be brought inside when the weather is inclement.

When materials are made truly accessible to children, this does more than increase their sense of the classroom as their own; it also does more than remove the need for the teacher to run back and forth for supplies. Accessibility of materials actively encourages creative problem-solving, particularly when it is combined with appropriate teacher interaction styles and when it includes free-flowing exchanges of materials from area to area.

*Task 3:*   The final task in the teacher's behind-the-scenes preparation of the physical environment is to provide for an atmosphere of intellectual honesty. If children are to think creatively in the classroom, they must be willing to make mistakes. They must have confidence that they can eventually correct their errors and find a solution to a problem they are working on. They must also feel that their environment provides them with the means for doing so. And *we* must share their confidence!

> *If we distrust the human being, then we must cram him with information of our own choosing, lest he go his own mistaken way. But if we trust the capacity of the human individual for developing his own potentiality, then we can permit him the opportunity to choose his own way in his learning.*
>
> Rogers, 1963, p. 280

We must create an environment that says to the child, "I am predictable, and I can be changed by you to fit your needs."

Child-sized equipment that children can manipulate themselves enables them to work on solutions to problems through overt actions. To determine whether there are exactly enough chairs for everyone at the snack table, a child can physically add or remove chairs. For a young child, counting people and chairs may be meaningless, and the problems of keeping track in one's head of extra or missing chairs may be too great a task. What stimulates thinking in this case is the opportunity for physical action, for altering the actual situation rather than thinking hypothetically about it. For the same reason, unbreakable materials are preferable to breakable ones. Clear plastic containers, for example, can be used for plants (for sprouting seeds, and so on) instead of glass containers. Small plastic pitchers enable children to work directly with alterations in quantity and with changes in appearance when a liquid is transferred from one container to another of a different shape.

> *Maybe many of these suggestions sound like descriptions of how you have arranged things all along. Terrific! Keep doing more of what you are doing— and the theory can help you decide how and when to do more of it.*

### Schedules and areas

In preparing the environment for thinking, we have to consider all areas of the classroom and all parts of the class schedule. We must implement our three tasks for setting the stage at Clean-Up Time, Snack Time, Small-Group Time, Large-Group Time, Free-Play Time, and Outdoor-Play Time.

*Clean-up time.* Clean-up time, which is so often seen merely as a necessary hassle for the teacher, is rich in thinking potential. Storage areas for materials can be arranged to encourage matching objects to their pictures; to foster grouping objects together by shape, color, function, or size, to give practice in arranging objects in order from largest to smallest, and to allow the placement of sets of items in one-to-one correspondence (for instance, providing a peg for each hat and coat in the dress-up area, with space for shoes underneath each peg). When children enter the picture, they can help decide how to divide the labor so that each person picks up a certain number of objects or so that each picks up a particular kind of object. This can range from tasks involving gathering identical objects (such as all the large red pegs) to tasks such as picking up everything that can be used to make a mark on a piece of paper, everything that can stand on end, or everything that has a metal part. The teacher helps this happen by allowing plenty of time for clean-up in the daily routine and by preparing an environment where each item has its place.

*Snack time.* Setting the stage for thinking at snack time involves the use of child-sized tables and chairs (so that children can arrange the furniture); the storage of cups, napkins, and other supplies within children's reach (so that children can count out appropriate amounts); the choice of foods that lend themselves to making comparisons (texture, taste, color, size), to looking at number (as in comparing amounts of different-sized foods or in passing out portions), or to examining part-whole relations (for example, fruits and vegetables that are cut apart at the table); and the provision of ample time for lengthy discussions.

The kind of program you have will influence when you serve snacks, of course, but in general it is wise to have snacks when children are hungry. If children come to school without breakfast (or without lunch), serve snacks early. Otherwise, regular snacks can be served as a midmorning (or midafternoon) break, or snacks can be made available as a sort of self-service cafeteria throughout the school day. Regular snack times provide structure to the school day that is helpful to many children, and they allow for a variety of group interactions, depending on what procedures are used. Cafeteria-style service allows children to pace themselves (to judge for themselves when they are hungry and/or need a break) but it requires a good distribution system and extra teacher time to ensure that all children who would profit from it do get a snack.

Because of the feedback a teacher can get in interactions with a small number of children, and because of the opportunity for guided interactions and serious discussions among children when they are sharing a relaxing activity, our favorite option for routine snack-time procedures has been to have a designated snack time, in which groups of one adult and four or five children eat together. If we had to rate snack-time procedures according to how likely it is that they will take full advantage of the cognitive potentials uniquely present in snack-time experiences, the ordering would be: most likely—small groups of children with an adult; next most likely—cafeteria-style self-service available throughout the school day; and least likely—a snack time in which everyone eats together. A small group of children with a teacher has the advantage that children can be helped to serve themselves without having an excessive wait before food and juice pitchers (small ones, so that they can be handled easily) get passed. In facilitating children's efforts to serve themselves, you can take advantage of some great opportunities for thinking about preconservation notions, one-to-one correspondence, spatial continuity, classification, and seriation. We'll look at some more specific suggestions in Chapter 8.

If there's a shortage of adults who are regularly in the classroom, you might invite guests for snack time (older brothers and sisters, for example, or grand-parents, or janitors who work in the building); or you might want to stagger the snack time so that only one or two groups of children are eating at a time. Which-ever way you work it out, the important thing is to take advantage of the cognitive potentials in the arrangement you use.

When a lengthy snack time is scheduled in the day's activities, it can be a time of quiet conversation and of thought that is not directly tied to materials and on-going activities. It is then an ideal time for teachers to find out how children are thinking. Imagination games such as "What Could This (cup, napkin, invisible object) Be If I Were A Cricket?" get interesting results that invite the teacher to look at developing logical thought processes as well as at free-flowing associations. Games involving decentration in dealing with spatial relationships are also well suited to this time of the class day. Questions such as "Whom is Betsy between?" or "Who is between Kathryn and me?" are fascinating and challenging to three-year-olds. Older children are often challenged by trying to describe what the child across the table can see.

This is also a good time for work on continuity as children name the people at the table in order or as they pass a basket of crackers or a pitcher of juice around the table. It takes practice to continue in the same direction you started and to avoid skipping anyone. Children who understand this aspect of continuity know that with this method their turn will come eventually. This knowledge is often all that is lacking when we see children apparently unwilling to wait their turn. They have no basis for believing that their patience will be rewarded. This is one of many examples in which what seems at first glance to be a purely emotional prob-lem (learning to be patient) is actually highly influenced by the child's level of cognitive development. The thinking teacher is alert to these possibilities and plans conversation starters that deal with such interesting problems and misunderstand-ings. He or she can also think ahead of ways to pick up on children's comments so that they, too, can become thinking games for the group.

*Small-group time.* Thinking games with a small group of children need not be limited to snack times. Special small-group times can be scheduled as part of the daily routine. Groups of three to five children might be assigned to work with a teacher at certain times on topics of particular interest. These periods can be a very special part of the day for both teachers and children. They provide an oppor-tunity for teachers to remain with the activity to its completion, and they provide a unique situation for watching children's thinking in action. Social interactions can be directly encouraged in such groups as a teacher clarifies differences in view-points and asks directly what various children think about a situation. For children, small-group time is a time for concentrated group effort on intriguing problems, a time when others really pay attention to what you think, a time for cohesiveness with no fear that outsiders will interrupt your activity. It is a time when teachers and children may establish close relationships with one another.

Teachers have found various ways to incorporate small groups into typical classroom schedules. For the teachers we've worked with, the popular way of handling small groups has been to have relatively permanent groups of four or five children, each assigned to a particular adult. The groups would meet at regular times and in fairly regular places. One group might meet behind the kitchen door, for example, another in the book corner, and another in a large cardboard refrigerator box. If you have space that can be set aside for use only at small-group time, so much the better.

We have seen a variety of successful alternatives to this procedure, all of which adhered to the important maxim, "No surprises!" However groups were chosen, however frequently small groups were used, and wherever the groups met, all of the successful variations involved ways of letting children know what was coming. For example, in one program, only one or two small groups were conducted each day. A group of two or three children met with one of the teachers during each free-play time. Teachers made a schedule of who would be doing a small-group activity for each free-play period during the week and then used large-group times and arrival times to explain to each child how to make sense of the schedule and how to figure out when his or her turn would come. As you can see from this example, not every child has to do a small-group activity every day. More important than the frequency of small groups is the children's advance knowledge of what is to be expected of them.

There are three advantages of letting children in on your plans: one advantage for you, two for children. The advantage for you is that when children know where to go, when to go, and how they are expected to behave, they can take the initiative for making the transition. You don't have to plead and cajole; they will help get the group together. The advantages for children are both cognitive and emotional. On the emotional side, children feel a real part of the program if they are let in on the secrets—if they know what the small-group activity will be, as well as when and where it will be. The feelings of belonging and self-worth, and of having some control over one's life, are not helped when one's activity is likely to be interrupted at any moment (as far as one can tell) by the request to join a small-group activity. If this isn't obvious to you, think of situations in which you've felt helpless—in a hospital, for example, when you'd like to ask the doctor a question but you have no idea when she'll make the rounds again. Or think of the frustrations of waiting for the dishwasher-repair person when you need to get groceries for the party you're having this evening, but you don't dare step out for fear you'll miss the repair person and will have to wait until Monday to even make another appointment, much less get the dishwasher fixed.

Knowing what to expect has the cognitive advantage of enabling one to plan one's activities and to judge when one can allow oneself to become deeply involved in various problems without fear of an interruption that can't be brushed aside. Since estimations of temporal duration and the learning of temporal sequences are new and exciting activities for young children, as our theory has pointed out, discussions of when things will happen (often stated in terms of what events will precede the event) and how much time there is before it will happen (often understood in terms of what activity one can complete—for instance, "You have time to build the road to your castle, but not enough time to build all the turrets") are valuable experiences.

This brings us to a sensitive issue that troubles every person new to teaching and many experienced teachers as well. The issue is one of how much teacher structure should be imposed on the child. Is it good or bad for teachers to require children to participate in a small-group activity (or, for that matter, a large-group activity)—an activity "forced" upon the child? How can we demand that children come when we say, "Come!" and still expect them to do their own thinking? There is no simple answer to such questions, but there are some considerations that teachers should take into account as they begin to formulate their own positions on the issue.

As the discussion above shows, scheduled events provide opportunities for children to develop a sense of temporal sequence and duration. But do the children have to come to the scheduled events? In most programs, since there is a dearth of extra adults to supervise children, safety considerations require that the answer be yes. There are some other reasons for giving an affirmative answer, though. First, when groups are formed for the purpose of teaching reading or arithmetic, most teachers have no qualms about insisting that children participate in the groups. If you have carefully planned a thinking activity, the advantages for participation are just as great. It is as important to think well as it is to read well. In fact, it is hard to see how the second could be accomplished without the first. Second, the child is unlikely to realize the full potentials of the small-group activities until long after the experience. Although we will stick with our admonition in Chapter 3 (among other places) that children should be helped to make their own decisions, the decision whether or not to come to small groups is not one that they're in a position to make—unless, of course, your small groups are consistently poorly planned, badly executed, and boring to you and the children. (But if that's the case, you shouldn't have to do them either. It's a waste of your time as well as of the children's.) Finally, if one never tackles the hard work of thinking about a problem and becoming confused about it, one is never exposed to the marvelous sense of accomplishment when the problem is solved.

> *Those who do not know the torment of the unknown cannot have the joy of discovery.*
>
> *Bernard, 1927, p. 222*

As you gain confidence with Piagetian theory and your use of it in the classroom, you will find yourself viewing teacher-structured activities as both enjoyable

and worthwhile for children. You will see ways of directing the activity and keeping the discussion to the predetermined focus without taking over the activity—
without telling children what and how to think.

*TEACHER TASK 7-4*

> (1)  Give a rough description of as many alternate small-group schedules as
>      you can, remembering to consider variations in programs (half-day
>      versus full-day programs, programs with volunteer help versus those
>      without, and so on).
> (2)  Describe in detail several variations in small-group scheduling that
>      would work for a program you know well. Be sure to specify what
>      each teacher would be doing and how provisions would be made for
>      any children who are not in small groups. List some of the advantages
>      and disadvantages of each schedule you propose.

*Large-group activities.*   Large group activities can also provide special thinking opportunities. But each child must be an active participant, mentally and/or
physically. Remember, Piaget's theory tells us that the origins of intelligence are
in *action.* Imitation games, movement experiences, group storytelling, and songs
all help to make the child an active participant. Sometimes very subtle techniques
will turn a story session into a thinking activity. The teacher who pauses after
rhetorical questions such as, "And what do you suppose Br'er Rabbit did then?"
gives children an opportunity to think of potential behaviors for Br'er Rabbit and
to weigh their possibilities against alternatives. A variety of stories can be created
that explicitly involve seriation or classification. Use your imagination. You might
make up a story about a giant looking for a home—first trying a mouse's house,
then a doghouse, then a children's playhouse. The story can go on through as
many houses as you can think of, each bigger than the last. The children can help
determine whether each proposed house is big enough. If you use a flannel board
or pictures that can be displayed simultaneously, the children see houses seriated
by size as the story progresses. If allowed to work individually with the materials
after the large group, they can either use the series to help them recall the story or
they can use their memory of the story sequence to help them in reconstructing the
series.

Like small-group activities, large groups are usually best when they're short.
It is a good idea to keep the whole group session to twenty minutes or so. This
includes time for conversation, songs, or whatever, with children who arrive first
at the designated meeting spot; announcements and organizational activities; and
the focal activity itself. When planning the time into the whole day's schedule,
however, don't forget to add some extra time for making the transition into and
out of large group.

The kind of program you have, the time when children arrive and depart,
and the role you want your large group to play, all enter into the decision about

when to have the large group. A large-group activity can provide an opening experience (in a program where most of the children arrive at once), a break in the day's routine (provided the large group isn't sandwiched between other teacher-centered activities), or a closing experience to end the school day with a group feeling. You might want to experiment with when to have the large-group time, but if you do, don't forget to (1) allow a week or more of the new schedule so that both you and the children can investigate its unique potentials, and (2) prepare children by describing the change in procedures repeatedly, and as concretely as you can. Instead of simply stating the change in procedures with an announcement such as, "Next week, large-group time will be *after* juice," have the children help you describe the whole sequence of new daily routines. You'll undoubtedly have to do considerable prompting by asking questions about the present schedule, by repeating the sequences of events told you by the child, and by making comparisons between the two schedules. (For example, you might say, "The way things are now, we have large group right after free play, but next week it will be different. What will happen after free play next week?")

**TEACHER TASK 7-5**

---

(1) Why is it important to go over the whole sequence of routines when only a small part of the schedule is to be changed? (To answer this, make use of what Piaget's theory tells you about preoperational thinking.)

(2) The discussion of schedule changes provides you with an opportunity both to stimulate children's thinking and to find out about their concepts of temporal sequence and duration. What would you do (and, in particular, what questions would you ask) to take maximum advantage of both opportunities?

---

With the exception of our comments on the number of children involved, our recommendations for large-group procedures are the same as those for small-group times. The maxim, "No surprises" is particularly important here. Management problems at large-group time are minimal if children have a clear idea of what is expected of them—including some idea of the length and sequence of events in the activity. If you've ever listened to an after-dinner speech without set time constraints, you know how important it is to have an idea of what's coming next. Are you hearing a lengthy warm-up for a longer talk, or is the speech about to end? No matter how interesting the talk, we like to be able to pace our attention, to prepare for asking questions we may wish to raise, or to prepare ourselves for adjustments we'll have to make in our later activities because of the time we've committed ourselves to in attending the dinner.

What we want to be able to do as we listen is to exercise our intellectual abilities for rationally guiding our actions. When we fail to provide children with time estimates, we deprive them of an opportunity to exercise and develop cognitive abilities.

The large number of children involved in large-group activities (usually from ten to twenty in preschool programs) poses a transition problem; it takes awhile for the group to gather. This being the case, how can one make waiting a valuable activity for the first children ready for the activity without excluding others? "Valuable" waiting time need not be spent in cognitively oriented activities, though it may be. The time is equally valuable if spent in sharing *familiar* songs or finger plays, chatting amiably, or even exercising. So long as such activities are recognized by children as distinct from the group activity per se and have approximate time limits indicated by your comments or by some tradition you've established (a certain number of songs, for example), the transition activities help to establish the group feeling without excluding those who are the last to join the group.

Similar problems arise at the end of the large-group activity. If your schedule makes it advisable to dismiss the group one, two, or five children at a time, you'll want to avoid wasting the time of children who are the last to leave. Guessing games in which you describe features of the child or children who will be the first to be dismissed are both fun and intellectually stimulating. For variation on this idea, you might try using initials, favorite activities, descriptions of family members, or the day's accomplishments as clues. (Make sure you explain the nature of this game, though. One child we know tearfully begged her mother to buy her some red shoes after a group dismissal in which children wearing red shoes were dismissed first.) Good-bye songs can also be enjoyable and can be cognitively beneficial if there is a particular order to the sequence of *good-bye's* (as we suggested in earlier comments on children's need to construct notions of linear order).

There are many good transition activities; the important consideration is to avoid the competition in phrases such as, "The one who guesses it first gets to leave." The message there is that large group is so unpleasant that it is a privilege (to be earned by those who can read the teacher's mind) to leave. Of course, if you really meant that, you wouldn't have large-group activities in the first place!

*Free-play time—indoors.*   One of the longest parts of typical preschool schedules is the free-play time. In kindergarten, this is often called a time for work in interest centers. In open classrooms for older children, it is often simply referred to as the work period. Regardless of the label, this time is probably the most important part of the day so far as potentials for cognitive development are concerned. Not surprisingly, then, much of the planning we discuss later is for this part of the day.

The special opportunities free-play time can supply for cognitive growth are only available if the time allowed is long enough for children to get deeply involved in an activity (and many children will need your help in this). You can be somewhat flexible on the time limits in accordance with the nature of the activities on a particular day and the mood of the group. Like the rest of us, children need time to get into their work, but they also need breaks and diversions. Two hours of uninterrupted time is probably too long. A general guide is to keep the free-play period between forty-five minutes and an hour and fifteen minutes at a stretch.

    In half-day programs, there may be only one long indoor free-play period (or perhaps two shorter ones). In longer programs, one would expect correspondingly more free-play periods. When these periods occur will depend on your classroom situation. If you have relatively few external constraints, you might experiment with the free-play schedule, in order to determine when the children in your class work best—or when you and your staff are best able to cope with the demands of free play. That will be your preferred slot for free-play activities.

    Free-play time is the part of the day in which teachers' obligations to provide balanced variety is most pronounced. Ideally, this is the time when children have the opportunity to practice how to pace themselves, how to make decisions about activities, how to integrate their discoveries and inventions, and how to encourage others to share their ideas and activities. To set the stage here, the thinking teacher has to be aware of potentials in a wide variety of materials, spaces, and potential groupings of children.

    Free-play time is also the part of the day that provides the best opportunity for certain kinds of teacher interactions with children. Children's freedom to choose their own activities provides teachers with the chance to discover children's interests and to talk with them about *what* they're interested in *when* they're interested in it. The high level of motivation in such situations can reveal a depth and persistence in thinking that is not otherwise exhibited. Teachers can ask a question or suggest a new approach to a problem, then leave and return to the activity half an hour later to see what the child has been able to do alone. Or they can have continuous interactions with children, following their leads in what problems to look at and how to work them out.

    Teacher interactions during free-play periods range from prolonged intensive interactions with a single child to "butterfly contacts"—a quick word to Timmy, a little more play dough for Anita, a little redirection for Jim, smiling recognition of Naomi's proudly held picture, a stern look at Jennie's limit-testing behavior, then a little help to Stevie in joining the block play. In between are interactions of varying degree and quality with tremendous potential for developmental impact. Meeting the socio-emotional, physical, and intellectual needs of a whole group of children engaged in diverse activities is one of the most exhausting tasks the teacher faces—and, from the Piagetian perspective, one of the most important.

To handle the task at all, teachers have to plan carefully, weighing learning potentials of various activities, the need for variety in the classroom, and the interests and abilities of the children in the group against demands on teacher time and energy. Planning for thinking in the free-play time is largely a management problem. One has to estimate how much teacher help should be given to various activities, how much energy and patience teachers will be able to allot to various activities (considering what else has been planned), how long various activities are likely to take, and how to make on-the-spot adjustments for children's unexpected fascination with an activity that was expected to be only a minor part of the day's activities. It might be nice to allow each child the choice of whether to be inside or outside, but this won't be possible if there is only one teacher—or even two, but one is back in the kitchen helping children bake cookies, and the other cannot get a clear view of the yard from the classroom. Provision for children's decision making does not have to be given up in this circumstance; it just has to be incorporated somewhere else in the day's plans.

Because there are so many different opportunities for stimulating intellectual development in free-play times, and because these opportunities incorporate features that show up in other parts of the schedule, we have limited our comments in this section to the importance of "getting it all together." Many of the techniques that our theory advocates for free-play times are part of good teaching anywhere. Whatever the theoretical orientation, if there's free-play in the program, good teachers practice at least the following six guidelines:

(1)  Never (well, hardly ever) sit with a child or small group of children in such a way that you lose your sense of what else is going on in the classroom.
(2)  Be alert to potential trouble spots and get there before the going gets rough.
(3)  Enter children's activities in ways that enhance what they're already doing and withdraw as soon as your task is accomplished (don't hang around to press *your* point, make sure they follow *your* idea, and so forth).
(4)  Communicate with your fellow teachers—before, during, and at the end of the day.
(5)  Follow up on promises such as, "I'll be with you in a minute" or "I can help you as soon as Susie and I finish painting."
(6)  Grow eyes in the back of your head; sprout seven extra pairs of hands; and take a nap after children leave.

Good teamwork by teachers is particularly noticeable during the free-play periods. We have found it especially useful to have one teacher play the role of manager during the free-play times. The manager's job may standardly be given to the lead teacher in the classroom, or it may be a rotating position (held by the teacher who conducts the large group on a particular day, perhaps). In the latter case, some means of communicating the role will have to be devised. This could be done with verbal announcements, a picture of the teacher in charge posted on the wall or door, and/or teacher reminders during the day (such comments as, "Pete's in charge this week; we'd better check with him before we get the play dough out").

Although all adults in the classroom attend to the needs of children, the manager has the ultimate responsibility for (1) making sure there are adults where adults are needed, (2) adjusting the quality and quantity of available materials so that things run smoothly, (3) making decisions about whether and when to bring out additional equipment, (4) helping children make transitions from one activity to another (helping them think before choosing and helping them pace themselves), (5) deciding whether to extend or shorten free-play-time and reminding everyone of the upcoming clean-up period, and (6) keeping the peace. With this kind of responsibility, it is rare for the manager to have time to observe an activity from beginning to end or to engage in any prolonged interactions with children. (This is one reason that so many of the teachers we know favor a rotating manager's position. Another reason is that the rotating scheme allows children to see shared responsibility and teamwork in action—a good model for their own behaviors.) Other adults can fill in the gap left by the manager's responsibilities by taking charge of particular activities, of certain areas, or of children with special needs (social, emotional, physical, or whatever). Freed of managerial duties, the other adults can get deeply involved in activities. Good communication among the adults involved is obviously essential to the success of this arrangement.

Perhaps the most significant task of the manager (or head teacher, lead teacher, "boss," chief—whatever title you and your kids prefer) is to keep the peace. We are not talking about resolving a dispute here and there; in such cases whichever adult is closest or has seen the precursors would step in. If there are an excessive number of arguments and tears, however, there may be a mismatch between the environment and the needs of the people in it. If children and teachers are tired (because lots of colds are going around, there was a big storm the night before, or whatever), sharing may be difficult, and efforts could be made to reduce the need. More duplications of equipment could be brought out, activities to be done alone could be introduced, play dough could replace the glue and popsicle stick construction activity, and story reading could replace some of the dramatic play.

Maybe the problem is not the social mood on a particular day, but a general mismatch. In this case, a staff consultation may be called for. One would want to look closely at classroom rules (too many? too few? not enforced? unenforceable?), amounts of space and arrangement of equipment, how disputes are generally handled, and ways for detecting and avoiding potential troubles before they begin. The manager's job here is first just to make it through the day, spending a good deal of time trouble shooting, no doubt. Then it would be wise to call a staff meeting. As you'll have already guessed from previous chapters, we recommend that the staff meeting be devoted to generating plausible hypotheses about causes and cures (where plausibility is determined with the help of previous observations and anec-dotes about the classroom), and then to deciding on ways to gather evidence. A fruitful solution, not blame, is the aim of such a meeting.

If tension among adults and/or differences in values concerning rules is caus-ing the problem, there's a big job ahead. We'll address ourselves more directly to that issue in Chapter 10. For now, we'll leave the problem with this general advice. Instead of thinking about some ideal situation, think about the present needs of *this* classroom, *these* children, *these* adults with their interests and strong points.

### TEACHER TASK 7-6

If you are not already teaching, find a preschool or kindergarten program to visit on two consecutive days. (If you are already teaching, you can use your own classroom and plans. Just adjust the following directions accord-ingly.) On the first day you have two major tasks: (1) get a feel for the size of the room, the arrangement of furniture, the visibility of one area from another, and the number of children present; and (2) ask the teacher to explain to you what activities are specifically planned for the free-play period on the following day and what other materials and activities are available for spontaneous use.

After gathering this information, spend about thirty minutes imagining yourself in the role of the teacher you talked to. Think about where you'd be in the room and when. List potential trouble spots and consider how you'd make sure you keep an eye on them. Think through the issues of where you'd like to spend most of your teaching time, why you'd like to spend it there, and what you'd do.

On the second day, visit the classroom during free-play time and observe how the teacher you imagined yourself to be arranges time and energy. (If you are the teacher you were imagining, you may be able to get someone else to observe you. Otherwise, try to make quick notes about your behavior as soon as possible after free-play time and before looking at any notes you made during the imaginings of the previous day.) After the observation, think through, and, if possible, discuss with the teacher, why he or she did what was done.

*Free-play time—outdoors.*   The problems and potentials of free play are basi-cally the same, whether indoors or outdoors. Worth special mention, however is the particular opportunity outdoor play can provide for developing spatial concepts. Construction work, where cooperative planning is clearly needed, is a popular and beneficial outdoor activity. This can range from the building of pirate ships out of A-frames, old boards, and large boxes, to the construction of walls and sophisti-cated obstacle courses (for toy cars or real tricycles as well as for children). Body painting and water play can focus on spatial concepts when done outside, where it doesn't matter so much if a container overflows, a trough tips, or the soles of the feet leave red footprints. Free exploration outside can be followed by more con-trolled experiences inside.

Though weather is a limiting factor in many parts of the country, it needn't preclude taking full advantage of outdoor play. Large-muscle activities, such as climbing an obstacle course or taking walks, can be done even in inclement weather; flexible use of equipment and plans will enable you to make use of warm, sunny days whenever they appear. In very cold or very hot weather, fifteen minutes of outdoor activity may be your limit. In snowy or rainy weather, it is wise to schedule outdoor activity at the beginning or end of the school day. This minimizes the number of times boots, mittens, and snowsuits have to be struggled with. In good weather, outdoor free play can last as long as indoor free play—with no loss of cognitive benefits if careful planning is done. Don't forget that other activities (including snacks, large groups, small groups) can be done out of doors, too, though, unless you live in a predictable climate, you may find yourself spending hours carrying equipment back and forth from the building to the yard.

Setting the stage for thinking during outdoor free-play times is similar to the task for the indoor equivalent, with a little extra attention given to climate and safety. In providing equipment suitable for a variety of abilities, some potential risks will be introduced and will bear careful watching. It is easier to get hurt falling off a trike or jungle gym—especially in the excitement of a game of chase or of "I can go higher than you"—than it is falling off a chair. Teachers can reduce the risks while helping children develop spatial understandings and representational ability. Helping children figure out when there's room for them in a tree house, increasing their awareness of the need to inform others of their plans (that is, overcoming egocentrism), and helping them to recognize and solve problems concerning the stability of various structures, all contribute to better safety as well as to intellectual development.

As in outdoor activities for adults, there are the usual possibilities of sunburn, frost bite, chill (especially when jackets are removed after vigorous exercise and then forgotten), wet feet, and so on. Again, as in the case of safety, teachers can help children monitor their own needs. For those days when boots have been forgotten and the ground is still wet, for sudden showers, and for inevitable slips into mud puddles, it is good to have extra dry clothing available. Many teachers find it useful to request that children bring extra socks or slippers and slacks to school during rainy or snowy seasons. Others keep a stock of miscellaneous clothing for such purposes.

### Planning for Thinking

Thinking teachers are compulsive planners, but they must also be willing to abandon plans that do not fit the needs of children. Thinking teachers *plan* on abandoning plans. (They can do this because they have numerous alternative plans up their sleeves.) For flexible implementation, teachers must anticipate a wide variety of learning potentials for any particular activity and prepare reserve materials for changes in the direction of the activity. In addition, they must keep in mind teaching strategies to enhance various potentials, know the particular interests of the children in the classroom, and have a good idea of the abilities of individual children.

A sound knowledge of developmental sequence is required if teachers are to be able to anticipate how children will be likely to view an activity. For example, what logical or prelogical operations might they apply? How might they interpret activities and results? What kinds of "wrong" answers are they likely to generate from an experiment? It is the use of theory in conjunction with observation and inference that enables the thinking teacher to be a flexible, on-the-spot curriculum developer as well as a long-range planner. Since observation, inference, and really knowing the particular children we work with are so important, it is obvious that a good curriculum cannot be planned over the summer vacation and then implemented according to schedule over the school year. Nor is this the type of curriculum that can be written out in a book. Plans must be devised—and revised—week by week, day by day, and even from moment to moment during the class day. This is one reason that the teacher in this type of program must be a thinking teacher.

### Characteristics of a thinking activity

What characterizes this curriculum the teacher plans for? Just what makes an activity a thinking activity, anyway? We can look at such questions in two ways. We can look at what an activity was designed to do; that is, we can look at it in relation to the *teacher's* thinking. We can also look at how it works, at its relation to *children's* thinking.

*The teacher's point of view.* From the teacher's focus, a thinking activity is one designed to challenge the intellectual abilities of children without presupposing understandings that are beyond their present stage of intellectual development. One would not use a class-inclusion game, for example, with children who are unable to sort consistently using one criterion. For such children, a matching game might be challenging. We could start by matching pairs of identical objects and then make groups of three or more identical objects. The theory tells us that preoperational children are particularly likely to notice properties such as "having holes" or "being inside of." If we really want children to concentrate on grouping identical objects, it would seem most helpful to choose materials with those properties. We might choose round cookies and doughnut-shaped cookies, or pictures of a cat in a house and pictures of a cat outside a house.

From the teacher's point of view, then, the activity is geared to the expected developmental level of the children; this shows up in plans for actions to be performed and in the choice of materials. Developmental appropriateness is a necessary aspect of a thinking activity, but it is not enough. A thinking activity is also designed for modification, extension, coordination with other activities, and a variety of different demands on teacher interaction. Thinking activities are often planned well in advance of their use, but the timing of their use and variations in implementation are determined by short-term (weekly, daily, or even momentary) assessments of the needs and interests of children. The thinking teacher keeps a file of activity cards, just like anyone else. What distinguishes these activities is the *basis for deciding* when and how to use them and the focus on children's *thinking processes*.

> *. . . we must not apply even the soundest doctrine too rigidly, without a day-by-day regard for the actual needs of the particular children we are dealing with, at their particular stage of growth.*
>
> *Isaacs, 1929, p. 41*

Careful observations are crucial in making the decision to use a particular kind of thinking activity. Suppose you see Terry alone in the small-manipulative-activities area. He touches with his forefinger each of five beads on a string in the following order: R, B, Y, G. P. He labels each one as he touches it, saying, "A red one, a blue one, a yellow one . . ." Then he makes a new string of beads using the same colors as on the first string but in this order: Y, B, G, R, P. Pointing to the appropriate beads, he says to himself, "A red one, a blue one, a yellow one, a green one, a purple one. Now they're just the same." Reasonable inferences would include the hypothesis that Terry has not yet mastered linear order. If further observation and interactions bear this out, then thinking activities for Terry might involve games using the concept of "between," in which sequences of three objects are matched to other sequences. Games such as "I Packed My Daddy's Suitcase," story pictures, and bead stringing would be helpful. One might also work on continuity—that is, starting in one direction and continuing without skipping objects. Many commercial games for young children require this ability. Obstacle courses on which it is very difficult to reverse directions would help here too. Road- or fence-building activities also have some built-in continuity demands.

**Notice that these activities are not designed to teach children linear order. Rather, they provide experiences that will give them the opportunity to construct it for themselves.**

Many thinking activities are specifically designed to stimulate particular mental abilities. Examples of these include sorting games, number games involving either provoked or spontaneous correspondence, spatial-relationship games involving the reconstruction of particular arrangements, and staircase building or color ranking by preference. Many other types of activities can be thinking activities, however. A bear cave in the dramatic-play area may have as one of its primary purposes the communication of specific information about bears in winter. Such an activity can be transformed into a thinking activity when the teacher makes a detailed account of the potentials for development in classification, seriation, number, and so on. Particular materials are chosen to enhance these potentials, and a specification is given for both teacher role and the kinds of child behaviors to focus on in order to make effective, on-the-spot modifications. A thinking-activity plan includes a variety of possible appropriate intervention strategies, guidelines for questions, comments, materials to add or remove, and the like. A lot of teacher thinking goes into such an activity.

*The child's point of view.* Our second way of looking at thinking activities is from the child's point of view, from what the activity looks like in the classroom. There is a thinking activity going on as Mei-Ling tries to figure out a way to divide up some play money among four of her friends. They are not about to let her egocentricity prevent them from getting their fair share. A teacher is very likely to be nearby, although he or she may take no active part in the discussion. The teacher role here is to watch carefully for signs of understanding—of number, of conservation, of differences in perspective. Mei-Ling feels free to turn to the teacher for help if the problem-solving efforts should break down. She does not expect *a solution,* though; rather, she expects *help in finding a solution* from someone who will refrain from taking over the problem.

Thinking activities can encompass a wide variety of things for a child. Sometimes they involve close work with a teacher, who maintains the focus on a particular problem. Sometimes they involve problems that seem to arise spontaneously. (Of course, they seldom actually arise with complete spontaneity. The good teacher has made certain materials available or has set a tone for a particular activity so that certain kinds of problems are very likely to arise. Occasionally, a teacher may make comments that introduce problems into an activity.) From the children's point of view, one of the chief characteristics of such activities is that they are encouraged to do their own thinking. No adult takes the problem away and magically replaces it with a solution. Such solutions may indeed work, but their origins and their rationale remain a complete mystery to the child.

Any activity in the classroom can become a thinking activity. An activity becomes a thinking activity when it is allowed (and encouraged) to extend to other activities—when it crosses the boundaries of planned areas of the classroom, when it extends into other parts of the class schedule, and when it makes use of whatever materials may aid in the solutions to problems. From the teacher's point of view, as we have noted, this often means a change in plans, a rearrangement of schedules, the addition of new materials, and new challenges for interaction skills for the child. The extent of such changes may not be obvious. What the child perceives is an environment that holds exciting challenges and the freedom to work through problems to a satisfactory end. Neither arbitrary signals to end an activity nor arbitrary restrictions on how a particular material was meant to be used by its manufacturer should completely determine the course of an activity.

Another aspect of thinking activities apparent to the child is the role played by the teacher. Since many of the questions asked are intended to uncover thought processes and to stimulate further thinking, plenty of time is allowed for answers.

The atmosphere of intellectual honesty and a real appreciation for the reasoning process means that the child can pause for thought before answering a question—and can even fail to find an answer—without fear of recrimination. The general atmosphere of acceptance extends from the emotional sphere to the cognitive one. The child gets the message, "Your way of thinking is a perfectly acceptable one, even though it will undoubtedly change with time." This can be contrasted with the emotional-acceptance message, which says, "You're a good person despite the fact that you think like a child."

**TEACHER TASK 7-7**

> This exercise is best done with an episode captured on film or videotape, but if neither of these is available to you, an audio recording of a situation you've observed would do as well.
>
> (1) Observe, or listen to, a five-minute episode between teachers and children.
> (2) Take the teacher's point of view and describe the extent to which what you observed was a thinking activity.
> (3) Now take the child's point of view and do the same. (Rerun the tape, if you like.)
> (4) Run the tape again and revise your characterizations as you see fit.
>
> As is often the case, the value of this exercise is greatly enhanced if you do it with someone else, so that you can compare reactions. It is also extremely helpful to discuss it with the teacher you observed. You might also team up with another teacher and take turns observing and being observed.

### Interacting Effectively: Enter the Children

Setting the stage for action and getting appropriate observation techniques in mind is no easy task, but when children enter the scene, the teacher must work harder than ever. There is no stepping back just to watch the performance or to let the materials take over. The teacher is an active player, with a key role in the classroom drama. A knowledge of sound interaction techniques is vital. Piagetian theory is of tremendous help here. For the development of logico-mathematical knowledge, interactions are most effective when they are based on the use of theory in making careful observations of specific situations and when they are an integral part of appropriate activities (whether these be part of long-term or of on-the-spot curriculum innovation). Likewise, effective interaction skills enable the teacher to probe the child's thought processes and thereby to create useful observation settings. Such skills also enable the teacher to see how theoretical notions get tied to the real world, and to develop new and deeper insights into the child's cognitive development.

Different situations will require different types of interactions. A determination of just which type is most useful is aided by the division of knowledge into three areas. Let us review each of these areas as we begin our specifications of the kinds of interaction most appropriate for each.

### Teacher strategies for conventional and physical knowledge

Conventional knowledge—the knowledge of the cultural use of language, social expectations, and social conventions—is knowledge of an essentially arbitrary system and is learned from people. To help a child acquire this type of knowledge, the teacher must model appropriate behaviors, describe particular social conventions, respond honestly when questioned about thoughts and feelings, and provide children with experiences involving a variety of representational media (such as words, pictures, photographs, and gestures).

Physical knowledge refers to the knowledge of properties and regularities in the physical environment. It is gained through repeated encounters with the physical environment—with rainstorms, frogs' eggs, wagons, bean plants, wind, magnets—and through active manipulations of objects. After setting up the environment (with help from the charts in Chapter 4), the teacher's role here is to (a) establish ground rules for the use of equipment (so that children can explore freely without fear of unwittingly exceeding some unspoken limit); (b) use nonverbal strategies to encourage active exploration (such as demonstrating ways of exploring, moving objects with contrasting properties next to objects children are already exploring, or testing actions on new objects); (c) use verbal strategies to help children actively explore and to observe the effects of their actions (using questions and suggestions such as; "Find a way to use your mouth to get the boat across the water," or "Say, what happened to the cracker when the juice spilled in it?"); and (d) provide ample time for experimentation (using techniques such as remaining near an activity without asking questions or otherwise taking part in it, making materials available before and after they are used in teacher-structured activities, or modeling and showing approval of varied uses and combinations of materials).

The last item on our list, "experimentation," requires a little explanation. We must not forget that the origins of experimentation lie in random exploration (seemingly idle play and pure enjoyment of the materials). Only after a period of random trial and error does the child engage in purposeful exploration or hypothesis-testing. After all, one needs experience with a particular material or type of material in order to generate hypotheses worth testing. Acquiring experience takes time.

In attempts to foster development in conventional and physical knowledge, we must be careful not to mistake one for the other. The appropriate use of such a term as "air pressure"—an example of conventional knowledge—does not guarantee a knowledge of the physical properties of air.

Consider an attempt to teach the concept of air pressure with an experiment in which a book is raised by blowing air into a blue balloon placed underneath. Unless the child is aware of the physical knowledge involved in the demonstrations (for instance, what wind feels like or what it feels like to have air in one's lungs—not to mention awareness that there is a strong connection between blowing air into a balloon placed under a book and the elevation of the book), the words "air pressure" constitute merely a synonym for "magic." For all the children know (inexperienced as they are in the ways of the world), the book may have lifted because something blue was placed under it. Or, making a more sophisticated guess, the children may think that air pressure is a term relating to balloons or to rubber. (The suggestion to try the experiment with a paper bag, then, would seem preposterous.) Or the children may demonstrate social knowledge by giving a "correct" response when asked why the book was lifted, without having any real comprehension of the concept of air pressure.

Just as one must not mistake conventional knowledge for physical knowledge, so, too, it is important to distinguish logico-mathematical knowledge from either of these. Although this type of knowledge depends upon experiences that provide conventional and physical knowledge, it is all too easy to overemphasize conventional knowledge at the expense of logico-mathematical knowledge. In fact, the premature emphasis on the former can actually inhibit progress in the development and expression of abilities in the latter. As Piaget (1973, p. 100) points out in reference to a problem dealing with velocity, when the child does not understand the logical structure of the problem, the numbers applying to lengths and distances "obscure the system of relationships." The result is that the child gropingly tries the various procedures he knows, "which has the result of blocking his reasoning powers."

It is the concern with logico-mathematical aspects of thought that differentiates a thinking teacher influenced by Piagetian theory from other teachers. Such an emphasis leads to a number of characteristic interaction skills that must be acquired by the teacher who uses Piaget's theory as a program guide. They will be adopted as prominent, though certainly not exclusive, modes of interaction in the classroom.

Our emphasis on logico-mathematical knowledge is in no way intended to minimize the importance of acquiring experience in the areas of conventional knowledge and physical knowledge during the preschool years. The latter two areas are important for three primary reasons. First, such knowledge is essential to self-sufficiency in the physical and social world we inhabit. Second, basic experiences in the preschool years provide the foundation for advanced work later. (For an excellent article making just this point, see Hawkins, 1965.) Finally, physical and conventional knowledge are necessary for the development of logico-mathematical thought. Children need experiences to think about, to apply their logico-mathematical reasoning to; experiences in these areas generate the disequilibrium that stimulates the construction of new systems of thought.

So why do we concentrate our efforts on logico-mathematical knowledge?

One reason, mentioned in earlier chapters, is that our theory beast has the most to contribute in this area. A second reason is that the dependency between logico-mathematical knowledge and the other types (physical and conventional knowledge) goes both ways. A full appreciation of the complexities of language, for example, and the ability to work in any of the physical sciences is clearly dependent on logico-mathematical abilities. An equally important reason is that there are already some excellent sources for conventional and physical knowledge. Regardless of theoretical orientations, most curriculum books emphasize conventional and physical knowledge, as you can see if you compare them to the developmental guideposts in Chapter 6. (Don't be fooled by words such as "classify" or "seriate." They only indicate logico-mathematical activities if the activity requires children to *think about the process* of classifying or seriating—not if children are simply asked to point to all the dogs, to name the colors, or to use big and little blocks.)

For curriculum source books with a Piagetian approach to physical and conventional knowledge, the following list should get you started. For conventional knowledge, look at

COPPLE, CAROL, IRVING E. SIGEL, and RUTH SAUNDERS. *Educating the Young Thinker: Classroom Strategies for Cognitive Growth* (New York: D. Van Nostrand Company, 1979).
FORMAN, GEORGE E., and DAVID S. KRUSCHNER. *The Child's Construction of Knowledge: Piaget for Teaching Children* (Monterey, Cal.: Brooks/Cole Publishing Company, 1977).

For physical knowledge, look at:

FORMAN, GEORGE E., and FLEET HILL. *Constructive Play: Applying Piaget in the Preschool* (Monterey, Cal.: Brooks/Cole Publishing Company, 1980).
KAMII, CONSTANCE, and RHETA DeVRIES. *Physical Knowledge in Preschool Education: Implications of Piaget's Theory* (Englewood Cliffs, N.J.: Prentice-Hall, Inc., 1978).

### Teacher strategies
### for logico-mathematical
### knowledge

As you recall from Chapters 5 and 6, logico-mathematical knowledge must be invented or constructed by the thinker through interaction with the environment. It is not directly teachable or demonstrable in the way that physical and social knowledge are. The physical and social environment is essential for the development of this type of knowledge, but, as Bertrand Russell (1912, p. 74) puts it, "the experience which makes us think of it does not suffice to prove it." This kind of knowledge enables children to organize their thinking so that they can see relationships and ask the kinds of questions that enable them to further their knowledge.

> *Once you have learned how to ask questions—relevant and appro-*
> *priate and substantial questions—you have learned how to learn*
> *and no one can keep you from learning whatever you want or*
> *need to know.*
>
> *Postman and Weingartner, 1969, p. 23*

Although this is the kind of knowledge Piaget has analyzed in detail, it is also the kind of knowledge most difficult for teachers to deal with. It is usually easier to teach facts and test the child's memory of them than it is to help the child learn to ask good questions. In fact, all too often, the children with an inquiring approach are viewed as an annoyance in the classroom. Such children are not satisfied with a superficial answer. They want to have things thoroughly explained; they want to try things out for themselves; they want to explore every possible angle. If we are interested in true intellectual development, however, this is the kind of attitude we will try to inculcate.

Interaction strategies that are likely to aid children in constructing this type of knowledge are those that inspire them to remodel their intellectual structure. We have grouped these strategies into three types: (1) those that require children to reassess their present mental structure, (2) those that create an atmosphere conducive to such reassessment (an atmosphere of intellectual honesty), and (3) those that make use of group dynamics and peer interactions in enhancing cognitive development.

*Type 1: Thought-provoking questions and cognitive conflict.* The first type of strategy includes both the use of thought-provoking questions and the use of cognitive conflict.

*Open-ended, thought-provoking questions.* Open-ended, thought-provoking questions are those that are consistent with the child's train of thought but that introduce particular aspects overlooked by the child in attempts to resolve a problem or explain an event. They help clarify a problem, and then they turn it back over to the child. In order to account for additional variables, children must eventually construct new levels of reasoning. Initially, they may "explain away" data that do not fit their interpretation of the world. As has been suggested in analyses of scientific theorizing, however, when enough contradictory evidence is accumulated, when the theory fails repeatedly to predict accurately, when no amount of stretching will enable the theory to explain certain events, then the old theory is abandoned, and a new one, encompassing various aspects of the first, is adopted.

Piaget's theory suggests that, given this process of "theory construction" and given certain universal factors in the physical and social environment and in the nature of human beings, the child inevitably goes through the sequence of "theories" (stages) described in the theory. Logico-mathematical reasoning in this sense is self-correcting, self-regulating. In any such system, however, extreme conditions external to the system may cause malfunctions such that the regulatory mechanisms fail. The role of education in this area of knowledge is to ensure that this process is in fact a "given" and to optimize conditions so that it occurs without undue hindrance.

There are two major implications of this discussion. First, the determination of whether any particular open-ended question is likely to be thought-provoking depends on our knowledge of the child's thought (knowledge based on observation and inference). Second, it is almost impossible to determine immediately whether or not any particular question has been thought-provoking. Notice that the use of such questions does not *lead* the child to the "correct" conclusion. It makes it possible for the child to make conclusions on a broader base, on a consideration of a larger number of appropriate variables, than might otherwise be the case. Whether or not this possibility is realized will be a function of time and the number of related experiences and thought-provoking questions the child has previously been exposed to.

Although we may not be able to tell for certain that a particular question will be thought-provoking, some questions are more likely than others to have that result. It is often helpful, for example, to clarify the situation before turning a problem over to a child. If Anna and Jimmy are struggling over the possession of a fire truck, one might explain that it is a very special truck for Anna and also for Jimmy. Two people badly want the same truck, and there are no others like it. Then the problem can be turned over to the children: "What can we do when two people want the same thing?" Perhaps there are other considerations that would enter into the resolution of the problem too. Expecting that Anna and Jimmy will both be fairly egocentric (that they will have difficulty recognizing points of view other than their own) and that they will have trouble coordinating all the factors in the situation, the thinking teacher has to do some thinking. What relevant factors are Jimmy and Anna likely to overlook? How can these factors be made apparent? How can I give the children what they need to solve the problem, without imposing one particular solution—which may not be the best solution, although it is all I can think of at the moment? *Asking thought-provoking questions is a thought-provoking activity for teachers.* (Incidentally, there are good ideas for turning social conflicts into valuable thought-provoking situations in Spivack and Shure, 1974.)

Another type of open-ended question that frequently stimulates thinking is the "what else" type. This includes such questions as, "I wonder what else this could be if I were a giant?," "What else can you chew?," "What else could we make with this string?," and "What else could we say about this block?" Some other questions might be put into this category, although they don't actually use the words "what else." One might propose that we find out everything we can about the tire swing or that we try to imagine what Henry can see from the top of the jungle gym.

Drawing children's attention to attributes, possible actions, or aspects of a situation that they have ignored often stimulates a new direction of thought, especially if the children are trying to figure out a specific problem. This can be done with "I wonder . . ." statements, such as, "I wonder if you could make that paper smaller" when a child is trying to fit a large sheet of paper into a small lunch box. Using this type of question is a little tricky. We have to be very careful not to propose only the strategy we think most efficient, and we mustn't suggest specific strategies that are beyond the child's comprehension. In such cases, the child may well treat our suggestions as directives and act on them without thinking about why they might be useful.

**TEACHER TASK 7-8**

> Imagine yourself at the water table with two children and a plastic pail filled with straws, popsicle sticks, hollow tubes, funnels, and a strainer. Joannie has just discovered that blowing through a straw into the water makes bubbles. Billy is staring intently at the effect.
> Make a list of at least five thought-provoking questions you might ask. Explain to someone why you think your questions would be thought-provoking.

*Cognitive conflict.* The use of cognitive conflict is also effective in getting children to reassess their present mental structure. This includes the introduction of specific materials, actions, or statements that challenge a child's thought. Actually performing an experiment challenges a child's predictions about certain regularities in the environment. Introducing a pencil that is half red and half blue to Bonnie, who has exhaustively sorted pencils into a group of red ones and a group of blue ones, forces her to make a decision about the class relationships involved. The use of Silly Putty may call for new interpretations of the notions of liquid, solid, or gas. A statement such as, "But Bob is a teacher too, and he's a man," challenges a classification system based on the merging of two distinct attributes— gender and professional or social role.

To provide useful cognitive conflict, the conflicting stimulus must be similar enough to children's concepts that they can recognize both that it ought to fit into their concepts and that it does not, and will not, until they modify their previous concepts. In other words, children must see the relevance of the stimulus to their ongoing thought processes. Here again, the theory can guide us, but we have to match the theoretical notions to what we have gleaned from careful observation and thoughtful inferences.

Effective use of this type of strategy presumes, of course, a self-confidence on the children's part and a positive emotional atmosphere such that they are willing to admit to themselves any error they see in their own thinking. In addition, children must be willing and able to question what seem to be errors in the thoughts of other children or of adults. This kind of atmosphere is not the result of chance, but of carefully planned experiences and a skillful arrangement of the environment. The second type of strategy helps ensure such an atmosphere, the atmosphere of intellectual honesty. Strategies of the second type enable the strategies of the first type to be effective, and they are aids to development in their own right.

*Type 2: Creating an atmosphere of intellectual honesty.* Among behaviors that fit into this category are those in which the teacher communicates: a desire to hear a variety of viewpoints; a willingness to take a stand, knowing that it might turn out to be a wrong one; obvious delight in gathering views and sorting out facts without recrimination for wrong guesses; a genuine appreciation for the child's present abilities; an empathic sharing in the child's intellectual discoveries; a genuine interest in the nonstandard criteria a child may suggest in seriation and classification games; and a willingness to make an all-out effort to work through a problem using the child's suggestions. A thinking teacher has to be really "turned on" by thinking.

The provision of verbal and behavioral models in problem solving can be very helpful in providing the atmosphere we want. A teacher playing a game of sorting dolls into two groups might model a way to deal with cognitive conflict by saying something such as, "Oh! I guess this isn't going to work. I thought I could separate the long-haired ones from the short-haired ones, but then what would I do with these three with medium-length hair? Maybe I could sort the ones who have eyes that open and close from those that don't." Other models include verbalization of search behaviors in classification and seriation tasks (for example, repetition of a criterion, as in, "I'm looking for soft things; here's one. I'm looking for more soft things . . ." or, "Now I'm looking for the next shortest one"); the use of organized approaches to a problem (for instance, "I have to find out which doll goes with which umbrella, so first I'll line up the dolls and then I'll line up the umbrellas and see if I can figure it out"); and the correction of mistakes (for instance, "I'm looking at all these cars to see if I've forgotten any yellow ones. Oh, here's one").

We as thinking teachers must recognize and take seriously the child's way of viewing things. We must avoid making corrections or laughing at "cute" mistakes. It is the thinking process we value, after all, and not simply correct answers. It is not always easy to communicate this value to children. Being right has its own rewards, and society often adds to those rewards praise for superficial accomplishments. As teachers who foster thinking, we have to be careful to reinforce the process itself. We have to look for and reinforce behaviors used in working through problems rather than behaviors that announce correct or incorrect solutions. Such comments as, "You're really working hard on this one" have to be used with care, however—not only when we notice that the child is coming up with the right answer!

It is no easy task to reinforce process rather than product. Think of how carefully we ourselves may scrutinize every aspect of a person we are trying to please. We search for cues in the tilt of the head, the lift of an eyebrow, or a trace of motion around the corners of the mouth. We notice the stiffness in various body parts, whether the person leans toward us, the direction of the gaze, any shifts in position, motions of the hands, and so on. We search for these cues because we believe them to be aspects associated with the person's real feelings, though the person is very likely to be unconscious of these behaviors. Think, then, of the cues we, in turn, may unknowingly give the children we teach! How can we avoid unconscious behaviors that children, being eager to please, will seek out and use to guide their communications with us? How are we to avoid letting children know that they have or have not gotten the accepted, adultlike answer?

Perhaps the only way out is to change a basic aspect of ourselves. We must nurture a genuine concern for thinking, so that we tend to focus on the process rather on the product. But even if we reorient our priorities, how are we to recognize sound thinking? If we cannot judge the quality of the thinking by the correctness of the outcome, how can we judge it? Piagetian theory, together with our careful observations and reasonable inferences, helps guide us in getting a good picture of the child's capacities. We must attempt to compare the way children search for solutions with what knowledge we have of their competence. In short, we must compare the performance of the moment to the underlying competence. This takes continuous assessment and perceptive interactions with each child in the classroom. There is no rest for the thinking teacher. But do not despair. With time and patience, this approach to teaching can become almost second nature. It will always be challenging work, but careful and perceptive observation can become a habit, and appropriate interaction strategies can become an established part of the repertoire, to be easily pulled out when needed.

An important way to generate an atmosphere of intellectual honesty is to act as a coworker with the child in solving problems. The teacher's job here is to help children to clarify, focus, and communicate their thoughts—not to elicit "correct" answers or to force the discovery of certain solutions. Like a Rogerian therapist, the teacher attempts to perceive and understand as the child perceives and understands (Rogers, 1951). We have to get away from our own *tendency* to be egocentric; we have to figure out what the world is like from the child's point of view. Fortunately, we have that option. Unlike the child, our egocentrism is only a tendency. We can refrain from an egocentric perspective if we so choose. A willingness to take this approach in various interactions implies a belief that intellectual development requires *intellectual activity*.

A teacher who is truly concerned about the development of thinking and about providing an atmosphere of intellectual honesty must extend the child's participation beyond the stereotyped cognitive areas. Children can even play a role in setting classroom rules once the ground rules have been established. Although there are many decisions that children have neither the experience nor the intellectual maturity to make, there are numerous other cases where children's input is extremely helpful. A thinking teacher can ask Jimmy what he thinks would help him to remember not to run, what the effects of running might be, under what conditions running might be allowed, and so forth. Although Jimmy is capable of exploring these topics, however, he may not be able to convincingly explain his answers to his peers. Here the thinking teacher can step in to help the whole group analyze the situation or to help Jimmy communicate his ideas and their rationale.

*Type 3: Using group dynamics and peer interactions.* So far the interactions discussed have been primarily between a teacher and an individual child. The third type of interaction strategy involves the teacher's knowledge of group dynamics (conformity effects, power structures, and so on) as they apply to young children. The teacher's goal in this type of interaction is to encourage children to listen and respond to one another's ideas. The teacher attempts to facilitate the kinds of interactions between children that he or she attempts to engage in with a child.

This is a vital aspect of the teacher's role in the development of logical thought processes, for several reasons. First, it is not always easy to avoid the child's view of the adult as an absolute authority—at best, a benevolent dictator. Because it is obvious to the child that the teacher has an intellectual advantage in all three areas of knowledge, the child is often more open to the conflicting ideas of peers than to those of an adult—no matter how well the teacher has mastered the interaction techniques just described. Second, unless there is one teacher for every one or two children in the classroom, the major portion of a child's interactions is with peers. It is certainly in the interests of the child's intellectual development, then, to optimize the quality of that interaction. As Piaget (1964, p. 4) said, "Doing things in social collaboration, in a group effort, . . . leads to a critical frame of mind, where children must communicate with each other. This is an essential factor in intellectual development."

What can we do to enhance the quantity and quality of interactions between children? There are three major strategies that are helpful. The first of these involves some *modeling* as we follow through on children's ideas without corrections, as we turn to children for advice and opinions, and as we imitate some of their activities. We might, for example, notice Brian's unique way of constructing a marble chute and attempt to replicate his basic procedures in a new construction. If we are willing to accept children's intellectual abilities, then perhaps other children will also see their peers as a source for ideas and as a source of feedback about the validity of their own ideas.

A second strategy is to actively *encourage discussion of differences in opinion.* We can make comments such as, "Sandy said the apartment house had more space inside of it; Mary said the ranch house had more space. What do you think, Susy?" or "Some people thought there were more dolls in the bed, and some people thought there were more in the toy box; how could we find out for sure?"

Finally, we can *suggest to children that they turn to their peers for advice or help.* We might suggest to Paul, who is having difficulty constructing a fort, that Mary worked on a similar problem and could probably be of help. Jenny might be set the task of finding out what three of her classmates think about what would happen to sand if it were heated. Help can be physical or mental in nature. As thinking teachers, we have to search especially hard for opportunities for children to help one another in mental tasks, since the need for help in physical tasks is often easier to see and more readily facilitated by the types of equipment used. In either case, children are developing habits of searching out a variety of viewpoints.

*TEACHER TASK 7-9*

(1) Make an audio tape or a video tape of yourself interacting with several children. (This will probably be easiest if you record yourself in a story-reading situation or in the small manipulative area.) In the interaction you record, make a conscious effort to use strategies for encouraging peer interactions.

(2) Listen to (and/or watch) the tape of the interaction, making note of which strategies you used and how often you used them. You can categorize your strategies according to the types just discussed, or you may want to devise your own scheme. The following source may be helpful in devising a way to analyze the different kinds of interactions:

SIGEL, IRVING E., and RUTH SAUNDERS. "An Inquiry into Inquiry: Question Asking as an Instructional Model," in *Current Topics in Early Childhood Education,* Vol. II, ed. Lilian G. Katz. Norwood, N.J.: Ablex Publishing Corporation, 1979.

### Blocks: An Example of Varied Potentials in an Activity

From what we have said so far, it is pretty clear that facilitating intellectual development is a complicated job that no clever kits or step-by-step teacher manuals can do for us. We have to think for ourselves about the opportunities different materials can provide and about how to help children take advantage of those opportunities. To help you get started in your own thinking, this example of blocks has been arranged according to Piaget's descriptions of logico-mathematical abilities. Clues for what to observe and suggestions for the teacher's role have been included to show how the potentials for enhancing intellectual development might be realized. Incidentally, long as it is, the list of potentials is not exhaustive. (This example was inspired and heavily influenced by handouts used in a workshop given by Dr. Mary M. Moffitt on October 10, 1970, and entitled "Play is Valid." You may also want to look at her article in *The Block Book,* 1974.)

As you can see, even simple materials can have a tremendous variety of learning potentials. As thinking teachers, we can help the materials meet present needs and interests of children. A single material can be used for classification, seriation, number, or spatial concepts, as well as to stimulate peer interactions or to provide aesthetic pleasure; a variety of materials can be used for a single type of learning. From the Piagetian perspective, knowledge is not a function purely of the materials but of the human interactions with them. We help most when we help children learn from whatever materials and activities are most appealing to them.

# Cognitive Potentials in Blocks

## SERIATION

| LEARNING POTENTIAL | WHAT TO OBSERVE FOR | TEACHER ROLE |
|---|---|---|
| 1. Simple comparisons—for instance, of height, weight, length, width, amount of space needed, number of blocks needed. <br><br>2. Construction of a series—steps, bridges, roads, houses, and so on, can be ordered along dimensions such as length, width, complexity, stability. <br><br>3. Serial correspondence—the first in one series goes with the first in the other, the second with the second, and so forth. | 1. Evidence of comparisons. <br><br>2. Which attributes the child focuses on (length, weight, shape, color). <br><br>3. Use of trial and error in building bridges, walls of equal size, steps, and the like. <br><br>4. Number of blocks seriated. When? On what basis? <br><br>5. Use of a correspondence between series—the construction of roads of different widths for trucks of different widths before use of trucks on the roads begins (or a similar procedure with buildings for dolls, toy animals, cars, and so forth). | 1. Arrange equipment. <br> a. Start with a few sizes (extremes); then add intermediate sizes and comment on additions. <br> b. Arrange blocks on shelves according to size, weight, and so on. <br> c. Occasionally, have steps, different sized bridges, and the like, built before children arrive. <br><br>2. Verbalize. <br> a. Point out the effects of what children are doing—for instance, "They're getting smaller and smaller." <br> b. Recall previous buildings in terms of size, complexity, shape, and so on. <br> c. Compare buildings with size of other objects in the room. <br><br>3. Add props of different sizes (dolls, toy animals, cars, and trucks). |

## CLASSIFICATION

| LEARNING POTENTIAL | WHAT TO OBSERVE FOR | TEACHER ROLE |
|---|---|---|
| 1. Matching—especially of size and shape. <br><br>2. Sorting (Such as *all* the long blocks, curved | 1. Matching of identical blocks—for example, by stacking identical blocks, repeating a | 1. Use suggestions such as, "Here's a block the same size as yours," or "Since you and |

blocks; *all* the houses built by me, or by my friends; *all* the children who helped build this building).

3. Multiple classification—*buildings* such as houses and hospitals made with *long blocks*, for example, rather than *things* made with *long blocks* (which could include roads as well) or *buildings* made with *blocks* (which could involve any size block).

pattern, or adding identical stories to make a "skyscraper" even higher.

2. Sorting of similar blocks—for instance, by choosing only the curved blocks or by putting blocks in consistent positions such as flat, on edge, on end.
3. Multiple Classification—verbalizations of children are the best clue here.
4. Identifiable structures (such as houses) and children's verbalizations about them.
5. Anticipation of building—by identifying what one *intends* to make rather than simply what one *has* already made. (Watch for statements of intent and for evidence that the structure is designed for use in other play.)

Johnny both need blocks, you could take all the short ones and he could take all the long ones."

2. Help children find the appropriate shelf for each kind of block at pick-up time.
3. Point out what children have done and offer such suggestions as, "Could you make another kind of house to go with that one?"
4. Ask questions about what children have done, and extend the activity with such questions as, "What else would a hospital (garage, house) have?"

## SPACE: TOPOLOGICAL PROPERTIES

### LEARNING POTENTIAL

1. Continuity—A continuous line is a series of connected points and can extend in a variety of directions. It can be straight or bent.
2. Proximity and separation—Objects and parts of objects can be distinguished from their surroundings. They can be near other objects (expressed by relations such as "next to," "beside," "on") or far from them.

### WHAT TO OBSERVE FOR

1. Use of continuity.
   a. Series of blocks end to end or in rows.
   b. Shapes or rows expanded into L-shaped, hexagonal, or curved shapes.
   c. Use of ramps or steps as access to bridges or roads.
2. Understanding of proximity and separation.
   a. Verbalizations of spatial prepositions such as "near," "far," "on top of," "beside."

### TEACHER ROLE

1. Use questions, such as, "How does the car get off the bridge?" or make tape roads with intersections and corners—encourage continuous motion around corners and over bridges.
2. Verbalize spatial prepositions (on top of, around, near) in describing where children can build in and in describing buildings.

(continued on next pages)

**Cognitive Potentials in Blocks (cont'd)**

## SPACE: TOPOLOGICAL PROPERTIES (cont'd)

| LEARNING POTENTIAL | WHAT TO OBSERVE FOR | TEACHER ROLE |
|---|---|---|
| 3. Enclosures—Space can be enclosed with a complete boundary between inside and outside space, or it can be open with a continuity between the inside and the outside. Structures can be built with doors or windows for continuity between inner and outer space. | b. Alignments of blocks. (How tightly built is the structure?)<br><br>c. Uprights placed at the correct distance for bridging.<br><br>3. Use of enclosures.<br>   a. Space left for doors or windows.<br>   b. Objects (or self) made to fit into or to go under other forms such as bridges or doors. | 3. Use questions such as, "Could someone get through that door, fit inside that house?" "Is there space inside your building?" Supply equipment, such as rubber animals or trucks, that encourage the use of enclosures. |
| 4. Space is three-dimensional—Objects may be "on top of" one another, "under" another object; one can go "around" objects, "through" doorways, and so on. | 4. Concepts of three-dimensional space.<br>   a. Care in walking around or stepping over structures.<br>   b. Movement of objects (such as cars, trucks, rubber animals) around, through, over, or under other areas.<br>   c. Use of horizontal or vertical space in constructing. (Notice height, spaciousness, orientation, complexity, and balance.) | 4. Use questions and comments emphasizing three-dimensional space. (For example, ask, "What's behind this wall?" or say, "The cars have to go up and over the bridge.")<br><br>5. Talk about alignment, balance, and the like, when child is constructing. Help child recall previous solutions to construction problems. |
| 5. Problem solving involving topological properties—constructing access to roadways and bridges; raising structures for objects to go under; determining what goes into, or fits into, a structure, and the like. | 5. Use of spatial concepts in problem solving.<br>   a. Change of direction in roads. (When does this occur? Does child anticipate a need for direction change? Do children make the road *end* when it reaches an obstruction or do they make it *turn*?)<br>   b. Response to problems of fit. (For example, when a truck is too big for a garage, does the child rebuild the garage to make it larger, temporarily remove | |

part of the building to fit the truck in, use a smaller truck, or try some other method?)

c. Kinds of access to bridges, roads, buildings, and the like.

## SPACE: EUCLIDEAN PROPERTIES

| LEARNING POTENTIAL | WHAT TO OBSERVE FOR | TEACHER ROLE |
|---|---|---|
| 1. Angularity—Carefully placed blocks make angles of varying sizes; the size of the angle can be changed by moving the blocks without losing their point of contact. | 1. Use of angles in walls, bridges, and so on. (variations in size of angle; reactions to use of curved blocks for corners or tops of bridges; alignment—so that other blocks fit well at corners). | 1. Help children make careful alignments by asking about, showing, telling, and/or suggesting reasons for the insecurity of a structure. Verbalize the use of alignment (For instance, comment, "You had to fit the blocks together carefully to make that corner.") |
| 2. Distance and Measurement—The length of a measuring instrument is not changed when it is moved to a new position; the distance between two blocks is not changed when objects are placed in the space between them. | 2. Use of distance estimation in placing uprights for bridges. (Is judgment more accurate when there are no extraneous objects under the bridge? Is there any evidence of measurement and distance judgment?). | 2. Verbalize parallelism in roads, walls, and the like. Suggest two roads for two cars going to the same place. |
| 3. Straight lines and curves—One can determine whether or not a line is straight by looking at the whole line from a suitable perspective. | 3. Use of parallel roads, walls, and so on. (Do lines of block follow lines of wall, block shelf, floor tiles? Look for two-track roads spaced so that a toy car can span the gap.) | 3. Use suggestions about where to expand buildings—"all the way to the wall," "up to the ceiling," and so forth. |
| 4. Parallels—Parallel lines are always the same distance apart; they never intersect. | | 4. Use string to measure heights of buildings, distances, and so on. Hold blocks (for instance, top of bridge) while child judges distance for uprights. (This involves use of parallel blocks as well as distance estimation.) |
| 5. Coordinate system of reference—concepts of left and right, above and below, in front of and behind. | | 5. Make sure straight blocks are not warped (and so nonparallel). |
| | | 6. Verbalize child's measurement ("You measured to see if the car would fit in the . . ."). |

**Cognitive Potentials in Blocks (cont'd)**

## SPACE: PART-WHOLE RELATIONSHIPS

| LEARNING POTENTIAL | WHAT TO OBSERVE FOR | TEACHER ROLE |
|---|---|---|
| 1. Recognition of subunits—doorways, windows, walls, as parts of buildings. <br> 2. Relation between individual blocks and a whole structure made up of them. <br> 3. Destruction of a whole (say, a building) into its parts (blocks) and construction of a new whole (for example, by making a new building or by returning blocks to the block shelf). <br> 4. Recognition of smaller patterns within a construction. | 1. Construction of specific parts of buildings (such as, "That's a door"). <br> 2. Elaboration of structure (addition of thresholds, window ledges, shutters). <br> 3. Repetition of a pattern within a structure. <br> 4. Combination of structures or addition of new parts to expand a building. <br> 5. Cooperative building with group accomplishment verbalized. ("We built it, and I did this part.") | 1. Discuss parts of the building with children (noticing windows, patterns, and the like). <br> 2. Ask questions such as, "Did you use any blocks like this one? Point to them for me." <br> 3. Suggest the possibility of combining buildings or making additions. <br> 4. Emphasize parts at pick-up time. ("Let's break the road into parts. How many parts can we get? How small do the parts get? Are all the parts the same?") |

## TIME

| LEARNING POTENTIAL | WHAT TO OBSERVE FOR | TEACHER ROLE |
|---|---|---|
| 1. Action sequences in construction—what comes first in construction or in carrying out ideas. <br> 2. Sequence of turns in using blocks. <br> 3. Estimation of time intervals—for instance, how long it takes to build a small tower or an elaborate building using all the blocks. | 1. Anticipation of cause and effect as shown by correction for possible mistakes ahead of time—for example, two uprights placed before top of bridge is put on, aligning tower before adding height. <br> 2. Verbalizations about taking turns, who'll use what next, and so on. <br> 3. Expressions of time needed for large projects. | 1. Reinforce verbalization of first, next, last. <br> 2. Help children plan verbally before acting. Help them stop and think through what needs to be done to solve a problem. <br> 3. Give children warning before pick-up time ("It's time to start putting the blocks away, because we'll be having juice in five minutes.") <br> 4. Use time estimates yourself. ("I'll bet it would take a long time to make a tower as high as the block shelf, but I think we could finish it in one day.") |

# NUMBER

| LEARNING POTENTIAL | WHAT TO OBSERVE FOR | TEACHER ROLE |
|---|---|---|
| 1. Equivalence<br>  a. Ratios of one size to another—recognition of "how many of those make one of these" through perceptual impressions of space occupied.<br>  b. Provoked correspondence—such as one car for each house.<br>  c. Spontaneous correspondence—for instance, Peter and John have the same number of blocks. | 1. Equivalence<br>  a. Use of different sizes of blocks to make equal lines; comparison of different-sized blocks; picking up or using blocks in groups of one, two, three, or four, and so on.<br>  b. Set-ups with provoked correspondence (one man by each car, one tree by each house, six blocks for support under each end of a bridge).<br>  c. Use of spontaneous correspondence such as repetition of a pattern or matching rows of equal numbers of blocks. | 1. Verbalize child's actions of equivalence and correspondence. Ask such questions as "How many?," "Are there enough . . . ?," "Will there still be as many if you lay them all out end to end?" |
| 2. Grouping—one can add one more and one more and one more; blocks can be arranged, disarranged, and then rearranged (this leads to *renversabilité* and then to reversibility). | 2. Grouping<br>  a. Adding blocks one at a time (or two at a time) to a building, tower, or whatever.<br>  b. Using the same number of blocks to make a building, knock it down, and build another structure. | 2. Help child build by adding one block at a time, bringing piles of twos, and so on. Offer suggestions for rebuilding with the same blocks, grouping and regrouping. Let children do the actual manipulation to encourage *renversabilité*. |
| 3. Linear ordering—as in sequences or patterns. | 3. Linear ordering<br>  a. Repetition of pattern (vertical, horizontal).<br>  b. Blocks in one or more rows.<br>  c. Symmetry of design, balance in design. | 3. Have patterns set out before children arrive. Copy a child's pattern; point out where a pattern has been repeated. |
| 4. Quantitative comparisons—a lot versus a little; more versus less. | 4. Use of comparisons of number<br>  a. A lot versus a little (as in estimation of amount of blocks needed).<br>  b. Small and large buildings or piles of blocks.<br>  c. Use of words "more" and "less." | 4. Verbalize "a lot" versus "a little." If a child requests blocks, ask how many are wanted and give what is desired. One day, remove a lot of blocks or bring out a few more from the storeroom. |

**Cognitive Potentials in Blocks (cont'd)**

## NUMBER (cont'd)

| LEARNING POTENTIAL | WHAT TO OBSERVE FOR | TEACHER ROLE |
|---|---|---|
| 5. Measurement—perimeter, height, length, volume, area. | 5. Measurement—by eye, with instruments, through movements, and so on.<br>a. Notice what is measured, why, and when.<br>b. Watch for repeated use of a short measure to find the length of a longer one and the use of one long measure to compare others to. | 5. Encourage measurement verbally. Ask questions such as, "How could you find out if it's high enough for . . . ?" Supply equipment for measuring—string, ruler, large blocks. Suggest comparisons of buildings to children, to the ceiling, to other objects in the room. "Could you make a house big enough to hold this truck but not big enough to hold you?" |

*TEACHER TASK 7-10*

> Pick a material (such as play dough, the sand table, pegboards, beads, tricycles) and analyze its potentials, using the example of blocks as a guide. As you do your analysis, try out some of the teacher behaviors you suggest, to see whether or not they help actualize the potentials.

## SUMMARY

We began our look at teacher role with an impassioned description of the ideal thinking teacher and the skills, abilities, and personality traits we mortals try to cultivate in approximating the ideal. We made heavy use of Piaget's theory in characterizing our aims in the areas of observation and inference, preparing the environment, planning for thinking, and interacting effectively.

Using a combination of examples and guidelines, we noted the value of integrating into our teaching the generation and testing of hypotheses. We used our theory to help us focus on relevant behaviors. Then we put it to work in preparing an environment that fosters thinking—an environment characterized by change, diversity, activity, and intellectual honesty. We found that all parts of the school day could benefit by a visit from the theory.

We then turned to plans for specific thinking activities. We found two perspectives from which to assess an activity as a thinking one. From the teacher's point of view, a thinking activity is one that is geared to the expected developmental level of the child and that is designed for modification, extension, coordination with other activities, and a variety of different demands on teacher interaction. From the child's point of view, the activity is one in which children do their own thinking and have the freedom and encouragement to work through a problem to what they consider a satisfactory end.

Next, we tackled interaction strategies. After a quick review of the three kinds of knowledge and a summary of the interaction strategies appropriate for each, we concentrated on interaction strategies for enhancing development in logico-mathematical knowledge. We grouped the strategies into three types: thought-provoking questions and cognitive conflict, creating an atmosphere of intellectual honesty, and using group dynamics and peer interactions.

Finally, we used blocks to illustrate the enormous number of potentials in ordinary classroom materials for enhancing logico-mathematical development. Each of us was left with the task of analyzing the potentials in other common classroom materials—and, of course, with the task of using the materials in our own classrooms in ways that actualize those potentials.

# REFERENCES

BERNARD, CLAUDE. *An Introduction to the Study of Experimental Medicine,* trans. Henry Copely Greene (New York: Macmillan & Company, 1927 [first published in French in 1865, under the title, *Introduction à l'Étude de la Médicine Expérimentale*]).

HAWKINS, DAVID. "Messing About in Science," *Science and Children, 2,* no. 5 (1965), 5–9.

ISAACS, SUSAN. *The Nursery Years: The Mind of the Child from Birth to Six Years* (New York: Schocken Books, 1929).

MOFFITT, MARY W. "Children Learn About Science Through Block Building," Chapter 3 in *The Block Book,* ed. Elizabeth S. Hirsch (Washington, D.C.: National Association for the Education of Young Children, 1974).

PARETO, VILFREDO. A quotation from *The Practical Cogitator,* 3rd ed., ed. Charles P. Curtis, Jr. and Ferris Greenslet (Boston: Houghton Mifflin Company, 1962).

PIAGET, JEAN. Comment made at the Conference on Cognitive Studies and Curriculum Development at Cornell University, March 1964, quoted by Eleanor Duckworth in "Piaget Rediscovered," in *Piaget Rediscovered,* ed. Richard E. Ripple and Verne N. Rockcastle (Ithaca, N.Y.: Cornell University Department of Education, 1964).

PIAGET, JEAN. *To Understand Is to Invent,* trans. George-Anne Roberts (New York: Grossman Publishers, 1973 [first published as two works, by UNESCO, in 1948, entitled, "Le Droit à l'Éducation dans le Monde Actuel" and "Où Va l'Éducation?"]).

POSTMAN, NEIL, and CHARLES WEINGARTNER. *Teaching as a Subversive Activity* (New York: Delacorte Press, 1969).

ROGERS, CARL R. *Client-Centered Therapy* (Boston: Houghton Mifflin Company, 1951).

ROGERS, CARL R. "Learning to Be Free," in *Man and Civilization: Control of The Mind, Part 2: Conflict and Creativity,* ed. Seymour M. Farber and Roger H. L. Wilson (New York: McGraw-Hill, 1963).

RUSSELL, BERTRAND. *The Problems of Philosophy* (London: Oxford University Press, 1912).

SPIVACK, GEORGE, and MYRNA B. SHURE. *Social Adjustment of Young Children: A Cognitive Approach to Solving Real-Life Problems* (San Francisco: Jossey-Bass Publishers, 1974).

# 8

# THINKING ACTIVITIES

## SOME THOUGHTS
## ABOUT THINKING ACTIVITIES

So far in this book, we've talked a lot about theory and have seen numerous scattered examples of the theory in action. In this chapter, we'll concentrate on more thorough descriptions of a few selected activity ideas, in order to help you apply what you've learned so far. Our aim is to offer some ideas for you to work with while you are in the process of generating your own activity ideas and finding ways to integrate Piaget's theory into your own teaching style—or, if you have never taught before, while you are developing a teaching style based on Piaget's theory. Much of what we give you in this chapter are hints for turning ordinary preschool activities into thinking activities.

The activities you will find discussed in this chapter do not begin to cover the variety of important kinds of experiences a good preschool program provides. There is an obvious space limitation, which has kept us from including detailed suggestions for transition times, clean-up times, or special events such as field trips, and which has limited to a few of our favorites the number of activity ideas presented. Furthermore, the activities we've selected and the way we've described them grossly underrepresent the attention any good teacher must pay to conventional and physical knowledge. It is important for young children to learn words to songs and to acquire good table manners (examples of conventional knowledge) and to learn that water usually runs downhill (an example of physical knowledge), but for reasons we've already given in previous chapters, we will focus primarily on logico-mathematical knowledge. (We use the term here in its broad sense, to include infra-logical knowledge.)

### Thinking Activities
### and Logico-mathematical
### Knowledge

The activities discussed in this chapter become thinking activities in your classroom when they are used to help children *construct* new ways of thinking and when they stimulate your own thinking.

In the last chapter, we discussed what a thinking activity is. We mentioned that, from a teacher's point of view, such an activity makes use of materials and procedures chosen with children's developmental levels in mind and is designed for flexible implementation (so that individual interests and insights can be incorporated into the ongoing activity). From the child's point of view, such an activity is one in which there are interesting problems to tackle, help is provided in the search for solutions, but no solutions are magically imposed by the adult. An important feature of thinking activities in general was that such activities *do not teach* the child the understandings involved in logico-mathematical knowledge. The other side of this is that, in thinking activities, children *do not learn* certain developmentally advanced understandings, such as how to compare a group to its subgroups, conserve number when objects are rearranged, copy complex spatial patterns, or seriate twigs according to their flexibility.

We are making a big to-do about the learning/development issue here, because a failure to fully understand the relationship in the way our theory sees it will lead to gross distortions of the intention behind the activity plans presented in this chapter. Our activity plans are a little like recipes that give directions such as, "Add flour to make a slightly sticky dough," or "Season to taste." Unless you know something about the kind of results expected and about the nature of the ingredients, you won't get much help from such instructions (ask anyone who is trying to cook for the first time). A good cook also has to adjust procedures and ingredients in accordance with the temperature and humidity on the day the cooking is done. Similarly, our activity plans will only be useful to you if you know something about children's socio-emotional and psychomotor characteristics as well as about their intellectual development. You will have to do some thinking about the adjustments needed for the situation in your classroom—the number of children, the number of teachers or other adults, the special interests and abilities of both children and adults in the classroom, the amount of flexibility in your schedule, the amount of space and materials available, the mood of the day, and so forth.

It is absolutely crucial that, in making the inevitable adjustments, you do not lose the point of the activities. This chapter will have been an actual detriment to your teaching if it leads you to try to explain or demonstrate the understandings that children have to construct for themselves.

*TEACHER TASK 8-1*

---

From the perspective of Piagetian theory, what's wrong with the claim that the child *learns* to do certain developmentally advanced tasks (or the claim that children should be *taught* to classify, seriate, or conserve volume)? Try to make your answer convincing to someone who does not know much about child development.

Hint: You might want to look back at Chapter 2 and the first section of Chapter 6 to make sure you really understand what's at issue.

---

### Thinking Activities and Training Procedures

The mistaken notion that logico-mathematical understanding should be taught has probably arisen from misinterpretations of what is generally known as "training research." In the late 1950s, the 1960s, and, to a lesser extent, in the 1970s, psychologists interested in Piaget's theory were asking two kinds of questions. They asked, "Are the so-called developmental changes in Piaget's theory really better described as behavioral evidence of the accumulation of facts through learning?" Here they generally had in mind the stimulus-response kind of learning made so well known by B. F. Skinner (for example, Skinner, 1953). They also wanted to know answers to questions of this type: "Suppose Piaget is right about qualitative changes in development; what abilities indicate that the child is about to move on to the next stage?"

To answer the first kind of question, researchers used a variety of methods to train children to respond correctly when they were asked questions beyond their assessed developmental levels. Usually the training attempts were failures, but occasional success kept research interests going—and kept teachers wondering whether they ought to devote more energy to direct teaching of classification and other logico-mathematical abilities. After all, these are fundamental principles of rational thought, aren't they? Without a clear idea of exactly what was involved in teaching logico-mathematical knowledge, many people took the early studies to indicate that teaching could accelerate developmental processes. Surely, they thought, a really good teacher could find a way to teach children logico-mathematical knowledge. As they saw it, complicated concepts should be broken down into a series of small steps, each of which could be taught separately. If the steps were presented in the right order, children would master each of them easily, and an efficient, effective training program would have been developed. The most important things to know next were how big the steps should be and what the correct sequence was.

The second kind of question provided tentative answers to the sequence question—or so researchers thought. It was found, for example, that children who preferred games with rules based on size or number, rather than with rules based on color or shape, began to conserve number not too many months later; children with the opposite preferences were not so likely to be conserving number so soon thereafter (Wohlwill, Devoe, and Fusaro, 1971). Given the old learning-theory assumptions, the natural interpretation of such results was that children should be trained to pay attention to size and number before they were taught (or told) that the arrangement of objects did not change how many objects there were. In spite of conscientious efforts using all the latest findings, the success rate of teaching sessions remained disappointingly low. It was only after much research had been done that enough successful attempts were reported and described so that the reasons for their success could be analyzed (see Saunders, 1976, for a review of classification studies, and see Modgil and Modgil, 1976, for a summary of training studies generally).

Effective teaching turned out not to be "teaching" in its learning-theory sense at all. Children didn't *learn* the answers; they solved problems, resolved contradictions, and eventually constructed the understanding that enabled them to give the expected, adultlike answers. Basically, effective teaching strategies were the kinds of interactions we've been advocating in this book; they were not the more traditional teaching techniques, such as explanations, demonstrations, or drill (techniques that admittedly have proved their effectiveness for certain kinds of conventional knowledge). It did not help to try to teach specific behaviors that studies had shown to be correlated with future performance on specified developmental tasks in the area of logico-mathematical knowledge.

There is an important lesson here for interpreting results of psychological and educational research—and the lesson applies both to sophisticated research studies and to informal observations from "real life" (to observations made by teachers, parents, friends, or whomever). Correlation does not mean causation. The fact that two abilities are related, and even that one precedes the other, does not show that one causes the other. The earlier one may be merely an early *symptom* of a developing ability, not an *aid* to the developing ability.

The analysis of successful training studies also showed that adult intervention (of the kind mentioned earlier) accelerated children who were already very close to being at the developmental level for which they were to be tested but did relatively little for children who were not so close. For those almost over the wall, so to speak, a properly placed and well-timed push did the trick; for those who had barely begun the climb, the push was wasted. Teachers clearly have a role to play in children's development of logico-mathematical abilities, but their role is not the one that has been traditionally assigned to them.

A final important consideration addressed by training research is the problem of when and how to evaluate the effects of teaching. In general, training studies have borne out our theory's claim that successful teaching is not best measured by such things as "correct" responses at the end of a half-hour session or by a comprehension test after a week's unit of study. Such measures may be precisely what is needed for conventional knowledge, and perhaps for some limited parts of physical knowledge, but they definitely won't do in the area of logico-mathematical knowledge. We'll be making a more detailed examination of assessment and evaluation procedures in Chapter 9. For now, the important point is that traditional assessment techniques should not be blindly superimposed on the activities suggested in this chapter. That would only be misleading.

### Thinking Activities and You

#### *The need for plans*

So far, we have reminded ourselves that our concern in thinking activities is with underlying intellectual structure, not with behaviors. We have seen that developmental change is not the result of a carefully programmed, step-by-step learning sequence—though careful planning of a different nature is a must—and that traditional teaching methods are not helpful in the area of logico-mathematical knowledge. In previous chapters, we have discussed some guidelines for setting up the classroom environment (see Chapter 4), for observing signs of developmental progress (see Chapter 6), and for interacting with children (see Chapter 7). It takes thoughtful and thorough planning to implement these guidelines. Not only must specific activities be planned in great detail for all parts of the day, but the various activities must be coordinated in such a way that both teachers and children are left with room to think—to reflect on what's happened so far during the day and to adjust plans accordingly.

In applying Piaget's theory to preschool programs, we have found it helpful to plan specific thinking activities for each of the parts of the daily schedule we briefly discussed in Chapter 7—snack time, small-group time, large-group time, and free-play time (both indoors and outdoors)—and to do so on a weekly basis (with allowances for day-to-day adjustments, of course). The suggestions for thinking activities that we discuss in this chapter are arranged in categories corresponding to those parts of the schedule.

#### *How to use the suggestions*
#### *described in this chapter*

The specific activity ideas described in this chapter are included in order to help you start to think about the cognitive potentials in various activities. They are meant as a springboard for your own creative thinking about how to promote the mental and physical activity that enhances development in the children you teach, how to go about creating and maintaining an atmosphere of intellectual honesty, and how to provide for desirable amounts of change and diversity throughout the school year. Many of the activities we describe are ones you'll already be familiar with (perhaps in other versions) if you've been teaching for a year or more. We've tried to point out ways to enhance the cognitive value of many of the activities that have worked so well over the years. With an understanding of the valuable potentials in the activities, you can gain some understanding of why they continue to be so popular, and can monitor your own behavior to make them even more effective. In reading through these activities, the important thing is to look at the general kind of activity rather than at specific details of particular examples, and to get a feel for the general approach to use.

To make good use of these suggestions, you'll have to call upon everything you've read in previous chapters and the thinking you've done along the way. The suggestions cannot achieve their purpose if they are used the way one would use an instruction manual for assembling a tent. You'll be making the best use of this chapter if you take the suggestions as fuel for your own thinking about what to do with children—and why and how and when.

On that note of caution (which we hope you take as seriously as we do) and with the usual reminder to do the Teacher Tasks as you go, let's turn to the suggestions for activities.

## SUGGESTIONS FOR ACTIVITIES

### Snack-Time Activities

As we saw in Chapter 7, the activities of preparing snacks, gathering together for snack time, and conversing during the snack time are all rich in cognitive potential. A thinking teacher can take full advantage of this potential by making specific plans for each kind of activity. We'll look at some sample ideas for each.

#### Snack preparation
#### as a thinking activity

When snack preparation is made into a challenging intellectual experience for children, they will need help and plenty of time to get the job done. Unless it is feasible for you to spend plenty of time at the activity yourself, it would be better for you to do the preparation and to concentrate on good intellectual experiences for children during the serving and eating of snacks. Chaos and flared tempers are the likely result if your decision to let children prepare snacks is made only five minutes before the usual snack time. (The children will work too slowly, other children will become impatient, and you'll be tearing out your hair.)

It is often easier to incorporate children's help into the preparation process if snack materials are placed on trays well in advance of snack time and are then stored in a convenient place. Even if food is going to be prepared during free play or has to be kept in special containers, cups, napkins, and juice pitchers can be counted out and placed on trays. Depending on your schedule and the kind of snack preparation you have in mind, snack preparation can be done as a small-group activity, a free-play activity, or as a special activity for children who come early or who need some time with an adult away from other children.

Because thinking activities are not so much new activities as they are old activities done in a new way, we'll present sample ideas by contrasting them with other more traditional procedures. To get you started on connecting theory with practical procedures, we'll also make use of the Developmental Guideposts from Chapter 6 to indicate the kinds of understandings challenged and/or enhanced by the changes in procedure. It will be helpful to turn back to Chapter 6 as you go through the various suggestions, adding ideas about how to proceed and thoughts about how understandings might be further enhanced. As you think about how to elaborate and improve on the suggested procedures, remember that you are *not* trying to *teach* conservation, serial ordering, and so on; you are trying to stimulate wonder and perplexity.

The ideas in Chart 8-1 (next page) show how to connect procedures with theory via the Developmental Guideposts. Such ideas, and the other ones we hope you generate as you read through the examples, will, of course, have to be chosen and adjusted so as to challenge and intrigue children at different developmental levels. For example, more complex kinds of number correspondences are involved when the task is to get enough carrot sticks so that each person will have two. If you ask Aaron (example 5) to figure out how many cups are needed and then to stack them on a tray, you can stimulate thoughts about numerical identity—"Are there just as many cups when they're stacked up as when they're spread out? It sure doesn't look like as many."

You have probably already thought of a variety of ways to stimulate thoughts about classification. If not, remember that you can make sorting easier by using topological properties (as described in Chapter 6). You can make the task harder either by focusing on nonperceptual properties (such as the use or origin of the objects) or by including misleading perceptual cues (as was done in example 6, below when some graham crackers had to be put into the basket with the soda crackers). As you decrease the opportunity for a child to rely on obvious perceptual properties, you encourage more active thinking about the classification procedure itself. Your choice of snack foods can enhance or diminish the intellectual demands of sorting tasks. Compare the sorting opportunities with Cheerios and Kix to that with Cheerios, Kix, and Fruit Loops; or think of what adding dried pineapple to a snack of yellow and black raisins can do. And of course the kind of classification understandings being challenged will vary according to whether children choose criteria, whether you set the criteria, or whether different criteria are used to sort the same kinds of food for each tray.

**CHART 8-1  When Children Help Set the Table for Snacks**

| PROCEDURES | AREAS OF KNOWLEDGE ENHANCED BY THE CHANGE IN PROCEDURE |
|---|---|
| (1) *Instead of:* passing out cups yourself or pointing to each place where a cup should go, *Do:* ask Barney to walk around the table, putting one cup in front of each chair (with the chairs already carefully counted by you). | Infra-logical Knowledge Topological Space—Order (spatial succession) and Number—Provoked Correspondence |
| (2) *Instead of:* telling Liza where each name card goes, *Do:* give her a picture of the table with the place cards arranged and let her reproduce the arrangement. | Infra-logical Knowledge Topological Space—Order (spatial succession—reproduce linear arrangement) |
| (3) *Instead of:* simply handing Ahmed the cups to pass out, *Do:* ask him to put out just as many cups as there are chairs; ask him whether there would be the same number of cups as chairs if he were to restack the cups. | Number—Provoked Correspondence and Infra-logical Knowledge Conservation of Number—Equivalence (*renversabilité* and reversibility) |
| (4) *Instead of:* having Mara simply fill the pitcher with juice, *Do:* encourage her to fill it cupful by cupful (using one or all of the cups children will be drinking from); have her count out as many cupfuls as there will be people drinking, and encourage her speculations on whether (and why or why not) there will be juice left for second helpings. | Number—Provoked Correspondence and Infra-logical Knowledge Conservation of Amount |
| (5) *Instead of:* having Aaron count out 5 cups, 5 napkins, 5 carrots, *Do:* have him figure out how many napkins he'll need, by using the cups as a guide (or by using a list of children's names, the chairs around the table, or even some set of blocks you've chosen). | Number—Provoked Correspondence (using cups and napkins or chairs) or Number—Unprovoked Correspondence (using cups and counting blocks) |
| (6) *Instead of:* handing Carol soda crackers and graham-cracker halves to pour into a basket, *Do:* have her put the squares (which includes both graham and soda crackers) into one basket and the nonsquare rectangles (the skinny ones you get by breaking the graham crackers) into another. | Classification—Sort Consistently Note: cognitive conflict introduced with two different kinds of crackers in the same basket. |

If you've had the suspicion that these same procedures have application for preparation and clean-up activities elsewhere in the classroom, you're absolutely right. Try Teacher Task 8-2 to turn your suspicion into constructive activity ideas for your own classroom.

*TEACHER TASK 8-2*

Choose three classroom activities (such as easel painting, blocks, and outdoor play) and three areas of logico-mathematical knowledge (use the Developmental Guideposts in Chapter 6 for specific ideas). For each activity, describe how you could arrange preparation *or* clean-up procedures to exercise children's logico-mathematical understandings in each of the areas you chose. A sample format is given below.

In your description, be sure to include suggestions for teacher behavior (questions to ask, ways to induce cognitive conflict, when to interject new materials or strategic comments, and so on) as well as suggestions for the arrangements of materials and physical space. The discussion of the hospital in Chapter 7 (the section "Helping Children Become Better Thinkers") may start your ideas flowing.

**Sample Format**

| TEACHER BEHAVIOR | MATERIALS | LOGICO-MATHEMATICAL UNDERSTANDINGS ENCOURAGED |
|---|---|---|
| PREPARATION FOR PAINTING | | |
| Suggest that children set out the paint brushes. Ask them how they'll make sure that each child at the easel will have the necessary materials . . . . (*To be completed in this manner.*) | Easels already set up 12 paint containers, 12 brushes loose on the table . . . . (*To be completed in this manner.*) | Number—Provoked Correspondence, . . . (*To be completed in this manner.*) |
| CLEAN-UP IN BLOCK AREA | | |

*Eating snack—a time
for thinking*

Gathering children to the snack area is usually no problem; food is an effective attraction. As children are gathering, however, you can begin to investigate children's understandings of spatial concepts such as "next to," "across from," and "between" as seating arrangements are made. When food and/or utensils are passed around the table, with each child receiving the item from one person and passing it on to the next, children come to grips with linear orderings and may even be provoked to ponder about more complex relations like correspondence between several serial orderings.

"Well," you may be thinking, "that's a lot of fancy talk for what seems to be a fairly straightforward (and relatively common) activity. After all, many preschool teachers have children pass the basket of crackers around the table, whether or not they've even heard of Piaget's theory. Why bother to work through all the fancy terms and the connections with the Developmental Guideposts?" Here's why. Sometimes it is a challenging intellectual task to pass an item (or items) around the table, and sometimes it is merely a ritual. Consider the extra challenges you can create (not to mention what you can discover about children's understanding) when you add variations such as the following.

> As the basket of crackers is passed to each child, ask that child who will get the basket next; ask children across the table who they will get the basket from and who they will pass it to; or let each child figure out which direction to pass the basket (perhaps with hints from you and the other children).

> Pass a stack of different-colored cups to add problems in serial correspondence: ask children to notice the direction cups are being passed and the procedure of taking the *top* one; then ask questions such as, "Which color will you get?" or "Will there be any cups left over?"

> Stimulate comparisons of number with questions about the number of cups (crackers, napkins, and so on) on the table and the number left to be passed.

Attention to Piaget's theory, coupled with careful observations of your children, can help you distinguish between genuine confusion and hesitations that arise from boredom, rebellion, or simply the sudden thought of how nice it would be to have three whole cups to oneself. Clearly, the desired strategy for handling the difficulties will vary according to the source of the difficulty. Without understanding Piaget's theory it is easy to mistake children's genuine confusion for obstinacy, failure to pay attention, or other undesirable attitudes.

*Creating an atmosphere for thinking.* Although snack times have many cognitive potentials, their main purpose is to provide sustenance and friendly conversation. In taking advantage of cognitive potentials, one must be careful not to defeat the main purpose. Snack time, for example, may often be spent in discussions of the day's events so far, in casual speculation concerning the rest of the day's activities, in describing home situations, and rambling over general topics of current interest as they are initiated by children. As you practice using the theory, you'll be able to see more and more ways to enhance the cognitive potentials in such casual conversation without destroying its basic nature. (Think of the potentials for temporal reasoning, for example.) The kinds of conversation topics and activities suggested in the following pages are not meant to replace the casual, rambling conversation that arises naturally. They are meant to be used simply as conversation starters or to be slipped into the ongoing conversation unobtrusively when new directions are needed.

Conversation starters are more effective when they are coordinated with the planned menu of the day and with other activities of the school program. Peanuts, raisins, carrot slices, and crackers, for example, lend themselves to discussions related to number; jello and ice cream do not. Discussions of the relative amounts of food eaten by different-sized animals or the different kinds of food they eat might be good topics for the week or so following a trip to a farm or zoo. You may find it helpful to place a list of suggested conversation topics for the day or week on a wall near the snack area. Then, if you need an idea, it's there for the taking, and you won't be so concerned with remembering possible topics that you can't really concentrate on what children are saying.

Because snack time is used to teach manners in many programs, a word on how to accomplish that objective without destroying the atmosphere for thinking is in order. Manners belong to the area of conventional knowledge, not to logico-mathematical knowledge. If you want children to learn standard procedures, explain simply and clearly what is to be done—with demonstrations wherever they can be used. Have children practice the procedures until they get the hang of it. Any technique (such as stories or games) that makes this more fun is appropriate here.

Understanding why certain procedures are reasonable ones to use is another matter. It involves both physical and logico-mathematical knowledge. It will not be immediately obvious to children, for example, that the result of their taking half the apple slices on the plate will deprive someone else of apples. If they are helped to think about it, though, by trying passing the plate to see what happens, they are likely to gain some understanding.

*Ideas for conversation topics.* The ideas suggested next have been arranged according to the kinds of knowledge they draw upon most heavily. The divisions are not rigid; they are included just to give you an idea of the relation between various suggestions and the developmental guideposts in Chapter 6. Some of these topics can be discussed for a week or more; others are good for five minutes. To determine how long to pursue a topic, you'll have to be sensitive to the interests and abilities of the children you teach. As you read through the suggestions, work on the next Teacher Task.

*TEACHER TASK 8-3*

---

Pick five of the conversation starters suggested below. Correlate each of these with appropriate Developmental Guideposts from Chapter 6, as was done earlier for snack-preparation procedures. You will probably want to add suggestions as you go. For example:

| CONVERSATION STARTER | AREA OF KNOWLEDGE |
|---|---|
| Generating ideas—foods with holes | Classification based on topological properties |

*Suggestion:* minimize representational demands and encourage a wide variety of ideas by *displaying* foods with different kinds of holes—foods such as doughnuts, Swiss cheese, macaroni, licorice sticks.

*Or:* keep the representational demands constant but be prepared to *name* foods with different kinds of holes to stimulate ideas.

*Experiences to provoke thought
in the areas of classification,
seriation, and number*

(1) *Guessing games based on foods.* Two examples of these were given in Chapter 1, the "I spy" game and the "I'm thinking of . . ." game. When you play such games, don't forget to ask children about why particular clues were good ones, to help them think through whether or not their guesses met the conditions set by the clues, to occasionally try limiting the number of questions or clues allowed, and to keep the game fun by using some preposterous suggestions such as, "Maybe we're having liver-chip ice cream for snack today."

(2) *Generating ideas (within constraints).* Chapter 1 offers some examples of these also, but here are a few more ideas:

(a) Think of foods that you can crunch, you can sip, you can squish with your teeth so that juice comes out, or you can fit into your cup. Let your imagination go; you and the children will think of many more variations on this theme. You may want to try harder questions, such as these: think of things that are *not* crunchy or that are *not* bigger than a carrot.

(b) Think of foods that are bigger than a grape, or bigger than a grapefruit, or smaller than a watermelon. For a really difficult task, try for foods that are "bigger than a raisin but smaller than an orange." (Using the theory, can you explain why this last kind of question is so hard?)

(3) *"What if" questions.* Ask and elaborate upon questions such as this: "What if you had two mouths; how many cups would you need?" This can be followed with, "Could you eat more or less than you do now? Why do you think so? Would you need two stomachs too?" Or try, "What if this spoon belonged to a giant; what could he do with it?"

*Experiences to provoke thought
in the areas of space, time,
and conservation*

(1) Explore changes in shape, size, and amount when fruits are cut, crackers are broken, or peanut butter is spread. Investigate ways to restore the original shape or size. You might try to reconstruct an apple from the pieces, for example—provided they are not eaten first! Instead of simply cutting apples and sharing the children's delight in the discovery of the seeds inside, ask Tina to predict what the second apple will look like inside, get Tommy to speculate about whether there is more to eat before or after the apple is cut, and ask Tammie to consider whether she'd get the same amount to eat from a piece of the big apple as from a piece of the small one.

(2) Explore the kinds of designs one can make with snack and how to overcome various limitations. For example, set such problems as:

"How can we make wheels, when all our crackers have corners?"

"Can you think of some food we're *not* having today that would make a good finger for your cracker person?"

(3) Make use of children's previous experiences to stimulate thought about temporal duration, with questions such as:

"Which takes longer to chew, licorice or jello? Why?"

"Which takes longer to drink, hot chocolate or juice? Why?"

(4) Explore relative amounts, as suggested in Chapter 1. Direct children's attention to problems of checking one's judgments concerning amounts and of separating the size of items from the number of items (three oranges may look like more than twenty raisins). See what younger children do when offered a choice between two graham-cracker halves or one whole graham cracker. Have children choose one big thing and two little things from a basket of raisins, peanuts, and orange sections. Let children "buy" food with tickets (passed out before snack time), where a single ticket buys either one big food or two little ones.

*Experiences to provoke thought*
*in the area of physical knowledge*
*(with a strong component*
*of classification)*

(1) Stop and listen to sounds made at juice time. Encourage children to describe them and to try to think of other times when such sounds are made. Are any sounds heard only at juice time? Does that pet guinea pig make any of the same sounds when it has snack? (Get the idea? This kind of discussion can go on for days with excursions into the colors seen at juice time, the shapes used, the textures felt, and so forth.)

(2) Help children think of foods that make good snacks for people and of snack ideas that are silly. Discuss why some ideas are silly. (Note: here, as elsewhere, the word "discuss" means ask questions, make "I wonder" statements, and in general try to get children to think through and express their reasons for their views.)

(3) Encourage children to think of some animals that drink juice, or eat peanuts, or eat grass. Provoke thought by asking questions such as why fish don't eat grass, or whether a worm could eat peanuts (and if not, why not).

(4) Encourage wonder and discussion about how snack was made. (Where did the crackers come from? How did they get so crispy? How did the children who made the pudding do it?)

(5) Stimulate careful observation and probe representational skills by asking such questions as, "How can you tell when you're hungry? thirsty? Would one cracker fill you up?" (Variations on this suggestion include such things as, "How can you tell if your baby brother is hungry?" or "How can you tell if your pet rabbit is hungry?")

(6) Help children think about whether one could eat when upside down. Could one drink that way? Explore ways to make it easier.

(7) Encourage careful observation and hypothesis testing by introducing cognitive conflict. Try serving

cherry juice in one pitcher, water with red food coloring in another

lemonade in one pitcher, grapefruit juice in another

sugar and salt to sprinkle on tortillas

shelled nuts, some of each kind salted, some unsalted

sugar water and honey water

*Remarks on snack-time activities.* This may have seemed to be a rather lengthy discussion for what is frequently a fairly small part of the school program and may often be considered a break from the intellectual demands of the rest of the day. We've devoted so many pages to snack-time activities for two major reasons. First, snack time is naturally rich in cognitive potential (as well as vitamins and minerals), and it would be a shame to waste that potential for lack of adequate preparation. Second, the expertise you develop in the conscientious coordination of snack foods and theory-inspired conversation topics and techniques will provide you with a valuable repertoire of ideas for on-the-spot curriculum development throughout the day.

Teacher Task 8-4 will give you practice in planning an integrated snack-time activity. The coordination of menu with conversation topics will help your conversation starters flow naturally from the situation and will help you focus your thoughts. It will help you become sensitive to unobtrusive ways both to find out what children think and to stimulate their thinking. If you've made careful plans, you have the flexibility to implement them as they are, modify them to accommodate unforeseen events, or to postpone them for a later day if the situation warrants it.

As you think about snack-time activities, remember that you can plan extended themes (a week on part-whole spatial understandings, for example, or on comparisons of size and amount), themes coordinated with free-play activities or special events on a particular day, or just themes that enable you to investigate an area of understanding you are interested in. The Developmental Guideposts from Chapter 6 can help you generate ideas and a rough sequence for exploring understandings. As you work through the Teacher Task below, keep your mind open to possibilities for applying your ideas to other areas of the classroom.

*TEACHER TASK 8-4*

---

Pick an area of logico-mathematical knowledge and plan a juice-time activity that will stimulate children's thinking in that area. Be explicit about

(1)  what will be served for snack;
(2)  the arrangement of the food—any special containers, self-serve procedures, and so forth;
(3)  how children will be seated—inside, outside, at small tables;
(4)  what questions you will be prepared to ask;
(5)  what responses you especially want to notice; and
(6)  contingency plans (what you'll do if the jello hasn't set, for example).

---

## Small-Group Activities

Because the activities we're describing as small-group activities are teacher-structured activities, the gathering of materials and the organization of the activity are generally the teacher's responsibility. On occasion, you may find it beneficial to have children help gather materials—one small-group session might be the preparation for another—but, in general, you'll want to gather what you need before children come. A rough rule to follow is that children shouldn't be asked to gather materials unless you have good reason to expect that doing so will be particularly beneficial to them.

The use of a tray or basket for storing materials makes the transition to small groups easier on you. You might even like to use a particular bag or box to make the time more special. You may also like to have a set of instructions right with the materials. Then, if you are suddenly ill or are called away to mend a fractured friendship, someone else can start your activity for you. It also eases your thinking load, so that you can concentrate on what children are saying rather than on what the next step should be. A five-by-eight index card makes a good instruction card. It is easily read and is visible to children so that, if you wish, you can share in the "game" and use the card as the task master. If the area to be used for the small group is separate from the classroom, the tray (or box or basket) can be stored there. If not, a convenient shelf somewhere en route from where you'll be just before small groups start to where they will be held is a good storage place.

SAMPLE 8-1  *SAMPLE SMALL GROUP CARD*

---

AK:*  Spatial continuity and Number (one-to-one correspondence)
Rep:  match name to visible objects
SE:  visual, tactual, continuity of movement
VE:  labeling objects in sequence, providing descriptive labels

---

*Materials*

Large bag or basket with about thirty small objects in it (pegs, dolls, spoons)

Tray

*Activity*

Play "I packed my grandmother's trunk (or daddy's suitcase), and in it I put a . . ."

Teacher starts by putting one object on the tray ("suitcase") and naming it.

Children take turns choosing objects from the basket and adding them to the tray.

As each object is added, teacher lines up the items on the tray and helps children *touch each one* as they name all the items *in order*.

*Variations*

Spend time discussing attributes of each new object—let children do the talking.

Ask children to choose objects with specific features from the basket.

Use objects that vary primarily along a single dimension (color, texture, shape) and use descriptive labels—for instance, ". . . and in it I put a furry thing, a smooth thing, and a bumpy thing."

Cover tray with a cloth and ask children to list the items in order.

*Explanation of abbreviations

AK—area of knowledge

Rep—representational demands

SE—sensory experience

VE—verbal experience

Clean-up for small-group activities is usually minimal and can be a ritual part of the ending of the activity. The return of materials to the tray (or whatever) can provide the signal that the official small-group time is over. Of course, there's still the task of returning the materials on the tray to their usual storage places, but that's a teacher job, to be done after children have left.

A ten- or fifteen-minute activity is generally ample for a small-group session. A particularly interesting activity can always go on longer, but after ten or fifteen minutes, children are generally ready to go their own ways rather than to continue to meet the demands of the group interaction and the structured nature of the activity. In maintaining the thinking atmosphere you want for such groups, it is crucial to end the activity before the children get tired of it. The purpose of the group, after all, is to stimulate thought, to get children excited about a problem that they may not be able to solve immediately. The purpose is *not* to crank out adult reponses to questions about number, space, or order relations. Small-group activities serve their purpose best when they are short and sweet. If children are really interested in pursuing the activity, it can be continued during free play or tried again on another day with the children who are especially interested. Children may seem eager to go on for another half an hour, but often they will have misjudged their own stamina—thinking is hard work, and tiring! It will help children, and make things easier for you, if you temper their enthusiasm with your own judgment in such instances. One of the most common mistakes we have seen ourselves and other teachers make is to pass up an opportunity to end the activity on a high note and to push on to the point of group disintegration.

An exception to the time constraints discussed is the small-group field trip, which is likely to take longer than the recommended fifteen minutes. Even so, it should be kept relatively short.

### Creating an atmosphere
### for thinking

Small-group times are for heightened mental activity—for meeting stimulating, but nonthreatening, intellectual challenges. To make the most of these times, you'll need to apply every ounce of skill you possess. It is especially important in creating the right environment for such thinking to make sure that you yourself will have room to think during the activity. Not every event can be prepared for: you will not always get the responses you expect (even when your expectations are based on Piaget's theory), and emotional responses may catch you off guard. To handle such challenges without destroying the ongoing activity of the group, you'll have to do some fast, on-the-spot problem solving. Only if you know what you can reasonably hope to accomplish during the small-group time and if you have a theoretically sound and well-rehearsed plan for achieving it will you have the necessary mental energy to spare for resolving unexpected difficulties. Detailed planning, making full use of the theory beast, is an absolute must.

It is not only the surprises that take extra energy on your part. Finding out what someone really thinks about fundamental issues, regardless of the age or intellectual level of the person, requires thoughtful interactions. In small-group activities, you're trying to help children clarify what they really think about some very knotty problems. (Remember that it is difficult to even recognize a problem as a problem unless you're clear about what you think you already know.) Your skill in interviewing can help them clarify what they think, and, equally importantly, show them that the problems they are grappling with and the self-examination involved in dealing with those problems are both worthwhile. Spending time and effort to find out what someone else thinks gives this message loud and clear. Mere lip service to the claim does not. However—and this can make the difference between a successful small-group experience and an unsuccessful one—the message may not get through without some explanation to the group of what you're doing and why. You may have to make comments such as, "I'm having a hard time under-standing what you mean, Andy; Paula, do you think you know what he's trying to explain?" or, "Sometimes, it takes a lot of talking together before I can understand what you're thinking, and sometimes, talking together can help *you* know what you're thinking too," or even more blatantly, "This is a hard problem, and we're trying to help each other figure out what we each think about it."

Knowing that you have to think hard yourself during small-group time is one thing; knowing what to think about is another. Clearly, more is required than wrinkling your forehead and holding one hand to your chin—but what exactly is it that is required? In previous chapters, we've summed up what you need to think about by claiming that you want to do everything in your power to develop intel-lectual honesty. We've used this expression to mean both the ability and the willing-ness to recognize errors and to examine one's own thoughts. Although the creation of an atmosphere of intellectual honesty is largely an art, which each person culti-vates in a unique way in accordance with each's own personality and tastes, there are a few general pointers that may be helpful to you.

First, as you work to maintain interest and the appropriate intellectual level, you'll find yourself having to adjust the original task (using the developmental guideposts from Chapter 6 as a rough framework), or even to change it completely. When children are aware of this shift, explain it with such comments as, "Wow! This is really a hard problem. It would be a good idea to do some other kinds of thinking first; then we'll tackle this one again." It is even better if you can lead children to figure out what's so difficult about the problem: what information is missing, what strategies will be required, and so forth. Comments such as, "Oops, I guess this game is too hard for us; let's try another," seem innocuous enough, but there is some tendency for them to be interpreted as, "We can't do this task; we aren't clever enough." Without an accompanying plan of attack for future ventures into the same problem, the added message may be that the problem should be left to greater minds.

A second point to remember is that competitive games, whether they arise spontaneously or as a planned part of the activity, are likely to destroy intellectual honesty. Differences of opinion can be faced openly if the emphasis is on the rela-tion between each opinion and the facts rather than on who was right and who was wrong. In general, it is better to concentrate on a dialogue like this:

> Remember what you thought would happen, Jennifer? But look! What's different from what you thought? Why do you think it turned out like this?

or this:

> That was a good guess, Tim. You thought that maybe, because the truck had rubber wheels, it would bounce like the rubber balls did. Maybe there's some-thing else about the truck we should think about.

or even this:

> What happened to the marshmallow, Seth? That's what you thought would happen, isn't it? Why did you think it was going to turn black? If we did it again, do you think the same thing would happen?

and to avoid exchanges like this:

> Oh, look. It's different than you thought. The water turned purple. That's because the blue and red form a solution.

or this:

> Let's think about what the truck is made of. It is metal, isn't it? And what do you know about metal?

or even this:

> It turned black because it burned, didn't it?

In general you will want to avoid comments such as, "You got it right, Louisa! And Harold and Beth did, too. Now let's see who gets the next one right." Your aim is to help children become aware of the differences in answers without having that awareness make them feel inadequate.

Third, it is important to keep in mind the motivation for doing the activity as a group, rather than on a one-to-one basis. The whole group should be involved in trying to understand an idea being expressed or in trying to resolve the problem at hand. When a child directs comments or questions to you alone, try to bring the other children into the discussion by requesting their opinions, clarification of the issue, or responses to the question or comment. You will have to help children actively listen to one another. This is especially difficult for young children, as you'll recall from Chapter 5, because of their egocentrism—in this case, their assumption that they understand exactly what other people have in mind, it being no different from what they themselves are thinking.

Because active listening and cooperative intellectual efforts are complicated abilities just being acquired (rather than abilities already possessed and being applied), progress will be slow. Actual small-group sessions are not likely to be as cohesive as you may picture them in your planning. Keep in mind that your task is *not* to get the group as a whole to focus on a single problem; your task is to increase the quality and quantity of group time spent in doing so. Since you want to maintain individual thinking as well as group cooperation, you'll want to be tolerant of some divergent activities and/or topics of conversation. A little tact in acknowledging the tangential topics and then refocusing the group on the original discussion can do wonders.

## *SPECIFIC SUGGESTIONS FOR ACTIVITIES*

The two activity ideas described next represent over a month's worth of activities for children at various levels of understanding within the preoperational period. Our aim is to show how ordinary activities commonly found in preschool classrooms can be varied and refined so as to challenge children more deeply and to give teachers more understanding about their children's thinking than is usually the case. Application of Piaget's theory does not require special equipment and activities; it requires special ways of thinking about ordinary activities.

We suggest that you read through each activity once just to get the idea and then, using the remarks following the description, reread it carefully, noting the features that enhance active thinking for both teachers and children. Write down ideas for modifying the activity to suit your children's interests and developmental levels. Remember, each activity suggestion is a framework for many different specific activities.

### Squish It (a sorting game)

*General comments.* The basic idea of this activity is to provide interesting materials to explore and to devise a classification task appropriate for those materials. The example given here is just one of many variants and is particularly suited to fairly young children (two to three years old).

*Materials.* Several boxes for sorting and a tray containing a collection of items that can be squished, items that cannot be squished, and items whose status is uncertain. For example:

| ITEMS THAT CAN BE SQUISHED | ITEMS THAT CANNOT BE SQUISHED | ITEMS WHOSE STATUS IS UNCERTAIN |
| --- | --- | --- |
| sponges (moist) | metal toy cars | dry sponges |
| marshmallow (fresh) | old, dry marshmallow | shoe |
| play dough (fresh) | dried play dough | hairbrush |
| scarf | blocks | rubber ball |

*Procedures*

(1) Encourage children to explore the materials thoroughly.

(a) Asking questions will be very helpful here. For example: "What can you do with this? Can you bend this? Do you see any red things? Who can find something smooth? Is there anything else that smells like the one you picked up?"

(b) Encourage children to show others the features they've noticed.

(c) Model prediction and investigation behaviors. For instance: "Oh, here's another marshmallow; I'll bet it feels mushy too. Hey! It's hard," or, "Let me see if I can find anything else with bristles."

(d) To extend this part of the activity, you can try having children feel the objects with their eyes closed or smell objects without touching them. The aim is to have children experience the various qualities, so don't worry about identifying the objects by feel or smell.

(2) When children have had a chance to thoroughly explore the items on the tray, introduce the classification game.

(a) A story line is often fun and makes the task clear. Here's one kind of story you might use:

> Did you know that all these things on the tray once belonged to Mr. Squishit? They were given to him by his Aunt Anything for a birthday present. When Mr. Squishit opened the present, he didn't know what to do. You see, he had always made sure he only had things he could squish. The couch in his living room was so soft and squishable, you sank almost to the floor when you sat on it. Every morning, he squished his pajamas into a ball and stuffed them into the pocket of his squishable teddy bear. And he even ate soft bread he could squish before he took a bite. But his aunt didn't know that. She thought he liked anything, and now he had all these new things. What was he to do? He thought for almost a whole day. Finally he had an answer. He'd have a garage sale and let his neighbors buy the nonsquishable things. So he very carefully sorted his gifts into two boxes—the things he could squish and the things he couldn't squish. Let's see if we can figure out which things he kept and which things he sold.

(b) As children help sort the items, ask them to justify their decisions. Ask for other children's opinions about the decisions made. (The items of uncertain status are meant to provoke some disagreement here and to help focus on features as children argue for their decisions.)

(c) To extend this part of the activity you might try: (i) a re-sorting task; (ii) sorting on the basis of two attributes simultaneously (squishable *and* yellow or, for a harder task, squishable *or* yellow); (iii) asking children for suggestions about other squishable things in the classroom—you may even motivate the establishment of a Mr. Squishit corner in the classroom during free play.

For the first two kinds of extension, you might continue the story line like this:

> Mr. Squishit got very excited about his sale. He decided to sell some tomatoes from his garden and some old quilts he didn't need. He got so busy and excited with all his preparations that he didn't even notice that his carefully sorted boxes had both been put out for sale. Mrs. Rolling came by and bought both boxes. She dumped them into her shopping bag and took home to sort out. She wanted to give

things that roll to her cousin over the hill. Let's figure out what she sent to her cousin.

The third kind of extension will be facilitated if you have some tempting soft things around the room—perhaps pillows, old pieces of fur, sponge-rubber toys.

### Watch for and encourage

*Physical Knowledge*—use of predictions about squishability and the testing of them, variety of exploratory techniques used, which features are noticed, recognition of two states of a single substance (for play dough and marshmallows).

*Classification*—comments about similarities and differences between items (note which features and how many are used in making such comparisons), deviation from or adherence to the criterion of squishability (when is the criterion abandoned?), unwillingness to sort the objects in a new way, reverting back to squishability when a new criterion has been decided on, awareness that Mrs. Rolling's new sorting uses all and only Mr. Squishit's things.

*Relations*—comparisons of relative squishability, attempts to find the softest or most squishable.

*Number*—comments about the numbers of items (for example, in comparing squishable to nonsquishable things or in comparing Mr. Squishit's things to Mrs. Rolling's things), skill in counting the items.

**Remarks on Squish It.**   This activity framework includes a variety of features inspired by Piaget's theory. In particular, notice:

(1)   the deliberate inclusion of materials whose status is uncertain, rather than a careful choice of clearly distinct sorts of things.

(2)   the emphasis on features particularly salient for sensorimotor understandings, rather than on traditionally used features such as size, shape, and color. (What properties might you use for children later in the preoperational period? What properties might you use whose presence could be tested only indirectly? Hint: think of features such as making the scales tip a certain direction or magnetism.)

(3)   the encouragement of thorough exploration rather than requests for quiet attention while the teacher points out features.

(4)   the encouragement of hypothesis formation and testing, rather than a focus on features of just one object at a time.

(5)   the request for an explanation of sorting decisions and a comparison of viewpoints, rather than a simple comment such as "Good job!"

(6)   the kinds of extensions suggested by the theory—extensions that preserve the level of difficulty and extensions that require more complex levels of understanding.

When you've worked through the activity suggestion with the foregoing remarks in mind, try at least one of the next Teacher Tasks.

*TEACHER TASK 8-5*

Suggest six different sorting criteria to use in the Squish It activity format.

(1) Include at least one perceptual criterion that is complex enough to increase the representational demand and one nonperceptual criterion (such as function or a feature such as, "has a name that rhymes with 'string' " or "has a name that starts with an *s* sound").

(2) Pick one of the criteria you suggested and write up an activity plan in the format given for Squish It. Be sure to include some specific suggestions for materials and teacher behaviors. Don't forget to do a thorough job in describing what logico-mathematical understandings to watch for.

*TEACHER TASK 8-6*

(1) How would you modify the Mr. Squishit activity to emphasize understandings of relations rather than classification? What materials would you use? What questions would you ask? Hint: It may help you generate ideas if you go around your classroom, or your home, gathering odds and ends that strike you as likely to encourage a focus on relations. The materials you collect will often suggest appropriate story lines, projects, or other motivations.

(2) How would you modify the activity to emphasize spatial relations?

## Will It Fit? (a spatial relations game)

*General comments.* This is a very popular game with children we know, particularly when they discover ways to change the size of rubber animals or scarves to make them fit into the box.

### Materials

A small box (3 X 3 X 5 inches is good)

Some very small items that will fit easily into the box—pegs, small plastic animals, Tinker Toy parts.

Some fairly large items that pretty clearly won't fit—long unit blocks, a stuffed toy, a drum, a shovel.

Some middle-sized items—dollhouse furniture, toy cars and trucks, the smallest-sized unit blocks, a hard-boiled egg.

Some changeable-sized items—a scarf, a piece of paper, a sponge, a flexible rubber animal, clay, play dough.

Having plenty of items that obviously will or will not fit gives children a feeling of success before they tackle the harder items. They also can provide occasion for humor—if a puppet, for example, insists that the smallest peg is really much too big. The changeable-sized items make opportunities for extensions of the activity if children discover the trick of folding or crushing them.

*Procedure*

(1) Encourage children to explore the materials in the ways suggested for the Mr. Squishit activity.

(2) Introduce the task of predicting and testing whether each item will fit in the box.

    (a) To get things started, you might want to use a story about going on a trip; the box can serve as a suitcase or even as the vehicle (a boat, car, or whatever).

    (b) Concentrate on getting children to make predictions (they will probably want to try the objects in the box straight off). Ask the group for a variety of predictions, and, as the activity progresses, help children evaluate the plausibility of new predictions by comparing sizes of new objects to those objects already tested. Then test the new predictions.

    (c) To extend the activity: (i) Add representational demands, by either covering the items after children have had a chance to explore them, so that their spatial judgments depend on memory, or by blindfolding children, giving each an object to explore tactually and a chance to feel the box, and then asking them to make judgments about fit. (ii) Introduce a different-sized box for the same objects. (iii) Make the box into a sort of puzzle board and ask questions such as, "Find three objects that will all fit in the box together," or "Find two objects that completely fill the box so nothing else can be put in." (iv) Put the box and the objects to be tested some distance apart.

*Watch for and encourage*

*Physical Knowledge*—systematic testing of predictions, variety of efforts used to make objects fit, generalizations about flexibility.

*Infra-logical Knowledge*—accuracy of judgments (does it improve during the game? does it change when the extra demands are made?), recognition of size constancy (for instance, when the box is close but the objects are some distance away), willingness to try different arrangements of objects to get them to fit, use of some objects to measure others.

*Classification*—sorting of objects by size or crushability before making estimates.

*Relations*—attempts to try objects systematically; for example, (1) with the smallest tested first, then the next smallest, and so on (for how many objects is this done?);

and (2) by finding an object that fits and then searching for items smaller than that one.

*Number*–discussions of how many objects can fit in the box, comparisons based on number and size, recognition that number is independent of how much space is taken up when objects are of different sizes.

*Remarks on Will It Fit?* Although this activity idea could be used to emphasize classification understandings (in finding *all* the things that could fit in the box, for example), that is not the focus we are intending to illustrate. We have included this activity suggestion to provide a framework for activities in the area of infralogical knowledge. One might appropriately extend the activity idea to estimations of duration, for example. Would there be enough time to sing "Mary Had a Little Lamb" during free-play time? Would there be enough time to eat a whole cracker before someone else finishes the first verse of the song? Could you skip across the room before the song is finished?

Noteworthy features of this activity as guided by our acquaintance with Piaget's theory include

(1) the inclusion both of items that obviously will or will not fit and of items that require some testing;

(2) the inclusion of changeable items to stimulate thinking about the respects in which changes in momentary spatial features leave other spatial features unchanged (a sort of conservation of spatial features);

(3) the emphasis on representation abilities (mental activity) as children are asked to make predictions before actually trying to fit an object into the box;

(4) the encouragement of the use of previous results in making new predictions to help children tackle the problem more systematically;

(5) the solicitation of a variety of predictions from the group and the request for a reason to think any given answer is right or wrong.

Variations on the theme should come thick and fast as you work through the next Teacher Task.

*TEACHER TASK 8-7*

Modify the "Will It Fit?" activity so that it combines large-motor challenges with the spatial judgments involved. You might consider an activity with larger boxes that requires children to make judgments about their own body size. Or try an activity that makes use of spatial images and measuring devices, however primitive they may be. For the second kind of modification, you might have children look at the box, climb through an obstacle course to a table of objects, and bring back something that will fit in the box. If you want to try an even harder activity, have one child tell another how big the box is (with the aid of measuring devices, perhaps) and have the second child choose an item to fit in the box. Then the first child can go back to the box and try it out.

In devising your activity, be as specific as you can about procedures and what to watch for. If possible, get someone else to use your activity in the classroom.

### Large-Group Activities

Since large-group time is a teacher-directed activity, preparation and clean-up are largely the teacher's responsibility. It is a good idea to gather any materials you will need for the group time well before the activity is to begin, preferably before children come to school. That way, if a crucial piece of equipment is missing, you have time to find a substitute and/or rethink your plans for the activity. There's more to preparation than gathering materials, of course; your mind has to be in gear, too. You will want to have thought carefully about both the main group activity and strategies for the transition times before and after. Spontaneity in large-group activities is more likely to be successful if you've already thought carefully about what you want to do and why. Then, with the security of a good plan to fall back on, you can engage in controlled improvisation. (Remember our discussion of insight back in Chapter 2? This is just the same advice in a new context.)

Careful planning is crucial because of the demands on your time and energy during large groups. One of your most important and difficult tasks in conducting large groups is to be sensitive to the individual members of your audience without losing the cohesion of the group. You can't meet this challenge if your mind is preoccupied with trying to remember the story line, wondering what finger play will hold the attention of the children beginning to gather on the rug, or thinking up ways to get children to be active participants. You will need all the mental energy you can spare for handling accidents (wet pants or an elbow jammed in someone's stomach), excited announcements children want to share with the group, and last-minute changes in plans made in order to take advantage of unexpected events (a first snowfall, a lizard discovered on the window sill). As with snack time and small-group time, you may find it helpful to post notes to yourself near the large-group area.

### Creating an atmosphere for thinking

Ideally, each child will leave the large group time feeling good about her*self* or him*self* as a competent, thinking person; good about the *group* of which she or he is a member; and good about the *time* spent in an enjoyable, and cognitively stimulating, activity. You stand the greatest chance of achieving this ideal if you've done some hard thinking about what activities are particularly well suited to large groups of children and what strategies will best actualize the potentials in those activities. Our experience has been that group settings are invaluable for generating a variety of different ideas (for "brainstorming"), for songs, for movement activities, and for imitation games. At least for children four years of age and younger, group settings are *not* helpful for resolving a problem in great detail, settling a personal dispute among several members of the group, or encouraging children to explain or demonstrate their views to one another (as is often done with older children in "Show and Tell" times). For egocentric young children, who have difficulty in expressing their thoughts, the process of struggling to listen to each of twenty children puts excessive strain on the patience of the group. Small groups and free-play settings are a better place for the activities we don't recommend for large-group time. Such activities certainly can occur in large-group settings, of course —and are sometimes successfully done—but the success is usually in spite of the group setting rather than because of it.

The major task in large-group settings is to keep each child mentally active while maintaining the cohesion of the group. Pacing is crucial. We have found that asking individual children to respond to questions or to suggest ideas tends to stifle thinking in large groups. The tension involved in speaking before the whole class and the long waits before one gets a chance to speak all put a damper on thinking— why bother to think of a good idea if you'll have forgotten it (or someone else will have already said it) before your turn comes around, anyway? We've discovered three fairly effective solutions to the problem of maintaining individual activity without losing group cohesion; maybe you will find more.

Our first solution is to use large-group times for songs, movement activities, and the teacher's presentations. Although one would not want every large-group time to be spent in one or more of these activities, they are valuable parts of one's repertoire. In doing such activities, particularly in presenting stories, one must be careful not to identify the stereotyped model of good teaching (a silent group of children, all eyes focused on the dramatic efforts of the teacher) with a valuable learning experience. Even television commercials can command children's undivided attention. While so engrossed, children may sometimes be mentally active, but they are often not. You have more to offer than an unresponsive television screen does. You can pose rhetorical questions and then listen to, and respond to, some of the answers. You can revise your account when you see puzzled expressions. You can encourage a variety of suggestions. And you can help children recognize good thinking whether or not the result is the standard correct answer.

Our second solution is to develop the art of responding to a variety of comments made simultaneously. Effective use of this solution requires the ability to encourage open discussion for brief periods, followed by your summaries of the ideas presented. You'll find yourself using expressions such as this: "Some people think he'll get free. Let's see what happens"; and this: "We've had lots of ideas— some people said he'd get stuck, some people said he'd cry, and some people said he'd wriggle free. Are there any other ideas?" Although you'll often want to know who gave which ideas, you needn't worry about keeping track. Your aim, after all, is to compare a variety of ideas, *not* to see who is right and who is wrong.

Our third solution is to divide the group. For many activities, two not-so-large groups may serve your purposes better than one very large one. A group of ten children, for example, has many of the advantages of a larger group (for enjoying songs, stimulating the flow of ideas, and so forth) but decreases the frustratingly large amount of the time wasted in waiting for turns in circle games (such as "Duck, Duck, Goose"), group storytelling efforts (in which each child contributes to the story line), and discussions in which children are called on one at a time.

*TEACHER TASK 8-8*

---

Suppose Mark refuses to come to large group. What would you do?

(1) Explain what he'll be missing, but say it's okay not to come.
(2) Insist that he come (even if you have to carry him), but don't force him to participate.
(3) Ask him why he doesn't want to come.
(4) Hand him over to another teacher or aide.

Explain your choice(s) and add the details (qualifications, kinds of situations, and so on) that show when your choice(s) would be the best. Compare your decisions with those of someone else.

---

*Specific suggestions
for activities*

Like the suggestions for small-group activities, these activity frameworks admit of innumerable variations and reveal the way theory can be used to increase the value of the "tried and true."

**Story Construction**

*General comments.* This activity is best when preceded by activities in which children have contributed by offering a variety of answers to rhetorical questions, by suggesting as many ways as they can think of for accomplishing some task, and by discussing suggestions with one another in the large-group setting. The idea is for the story to evolve in the group time and as a result of the contributions different members of the group make to it. (How much is determined by the teacher and how much is constructed by children will vary as the group becomes more adept at this sort of thing.) The activity is presented here in the way you'd do it the first or second time. As you and children become more comfortable with this kind of activity, and as children develop understandings of temporal sequences and cause/ effect relations, the group can take over more and more of the responsibility for the structure of the story—even to the point at which a child starts it off by saying, "Let's do a story about dragons; I'll start."

*Materials.* Paper and felt pens (a large easel with ten to twenty sheets of paper on it would make things easier) *or* a blackboard with chalk *or* a felt board with a box of felt pieces appropriate for the story you've planned.

*Procedure*

(1) Decide on an outline for a story. The first couple of times you do a story like this, you may want to use versions of stories you are already familiar with—even "Little Red Riding Hood" will do.

(2) Sketch pictures, or make felt pieces, to go with the main themes in the story, but omit various details such as the color of the flowers and the kinds of cookies Little Red Riding Hood was taking to her grandmother.

(3) When you plan the story, make sure you leave out enough details so that each child can fill one in. Also, make sure that the main story line will not be affected no matter how the child fills in the detail.

(4) Decide on a procedure for soliciting children's contributions to the story. If children sit in a circle, you can simply go around the circle, giving each child a turn. This helps with children's understanding of continuity and between-ness while giving you a handy system for making sure no one is left out. You might also preassign names for each missing detail.

(5) When children have gathered and other group-time routines and announcements are out of the way, explain to children that this is a story they are going to help tell. Be explicit about the procedures for who gives what details, and enforce the rule that the detail is decided on by the child whose turn it is.

(6) Some children may need help in deciding on details. If there is no response to such questions as, "What color was her shirt?" or "How many houses could she see?" you can rephrase them as, "Was her shirt the color of your favorite one?" and "Maybe she didn't see any houses; what do you think?" If a child doesn't have an answer and seems to want to bow out, you can accept that fact and leave the detail out, as in, "Well, we really don't know what color her shirt was, but she did have her shirt on and she went out the door with her new baseball bat."

(7) This activity can be extended in ways that emphasize particular concepts or particular kinds of knowledge and in ways that demand more group contribution to the story line itself.

  (a) You can choose details that require cause/effect analyses—so long as you are willing to tolerate some strange causes (but it *is* a story, after all, not real life)—by asking such questions as how the flower got in the garden or why her shoes kept slipping off. If you decide ahead of time which child will be asked to fill in which detail, you can tailor the difficulty of the question to each child's abilities and interests. Physical knowledge, logico-mathematical knowledge, and infra-logical knowledge can all be worked into the story by the kinds of questions you ask and the details you pick. It is your attention to such details—your growing expertise in devising questions to stimulate hard thinking (mental *activity*) without excessive risk (so as to promote intellectual honesty)—that turns an ordinary activity into a Piagetian one. However you assign questions, and whatever kinds of knowledge you focus on, be prepared for some arguments. What seems perfectly okay to you may not seem so to children. (We were surprised that children allowed a dinosaur to talk, sleep in a bed, and eat at a table, but not to wear clothes. "Dinosaurs don't wear clothes," they insisted.)

(b) Contributions to changes in plot can be initiated with limited options. "It was the day Henry had been waiting for," you might begin, "and he wanted it to be a good one. Should he take his friend Tom to the zoo or to the circus? he wondered." Children can decide which he chose. Later on, the choices may be completely open. When the plot line is developed by the group, you'll have to do a lot of reviewing and summarizing. If the story line begins to lose cohesiveness, you can tie it back together before asking for the next contribution. In general, we have found that for plot construction, a group of ten children or so is better than one of twenty; it helps to divide the group if you can find another adult willing to do the story telling (or some other activity) with half the group.

*Watch for and encourage*

*Representational Ability*—use of elaborate or abbreviated actions and gestures to represent details of the story (such as how the main character felt, what she used to rescue the armadillo), use of onomatopoeia, use of appropriate descriptive words, arguments over the plausibility of various suggestions (note reasons for disagreement and the kinds of rationale given in defense of a suggestion), attention to others' suggestions, so that the new details are compatible with the old. (Don't be surprised if initial attempts at group plot construction have a disconnected, dreamlike quality. This will change as you work on summarizing and as children develop understandings of temporal and causal relations.)

*Infra-logical Knowledge (Temporal Relations)*—recall of sequences of events in the story (How many events are remembered? What kinds of mistakes are made?), reconstruction of the story line based on logical connections among events (for instance, "No, she asked him *before* she started the hike; otherwise she wouldn't have known how to find the fairy ring"), awareness of the difference between causal connections and mere temporal precedence or simultaneity, characterizations of a cause as following its effects.

*Infra-logical Knowledge (Conservation)*—consistency of characters throughout the story; comments that indicate lack of conservation of number, distance, time, and so on, as in, "How come she only has a little rope now?" after the main character has coiled the rope.

*Remarks on Story Construction.* First, a non-Piagetian reminder; we have tried to choose examples of story lines with girls as well as boys playing major roles and to avoid emphasizing stereotyped sex roles. You have a better chance of having all children (boys *and* girls) leave the group with good feelings about themselves if you do the same.

Now for some theory-inspired remarks. Things to notice include

(1) the promotion of activity in the variety of procedures suggested for giving everyone a turn;

(2) the attention to individual differences in interest and ability when questions are tailor-made for specific children;

(3) the encouragement of intellectual honesty in your preparedness to deal with disagreements (in procedure 7);

(4) the use of summaries and questions to stimulate thought about sequences of events and the kinds of connections between events (mentioned under the heading, Watch for and Encourage);

(5) the possibilities of adding challenges in the areas of classification, seriation, and number by the kinds of stories you construct and the questions you choose.

The last point suggests a valuable exercise to help you stretch your understanding of the theory and to help build up your stock of thinking activities. Try the next Teacher Task.

**TEACHER TASK 8-9**

---

Pick at least two of the following six areas of knowledge: classification, seriation, number, spatial relations, temporal relations, and conservation. Find or construct a story line that can be used to generate questions to stimulate thinking in the area of knowledge you chose. Describe the story line, describe the props to be used, and list at least five sample questions that allow children to either provide the details of the story or to alter the plot.

Hint: You might think about a simple plot in which, say, Danny searches for his twin sisters, who are late for dinner, and finds two of just about everything (flowers, toys, pieces of furniture) except sisters. What questions could be asked in this story? How about gradually increasing the numbers?

---

### Rope Drama

*General comments.* In addition to the close-knit group feeling and the physical exercise this activity generates, it provides an opportune setting for work on representational ability and the precursors of logico-mathematical knowledge. It also counters egocentric tendencies by combining visual and kinesthetic evidence of others' actions—you can't loosen the tension on the rope just by taking your hand off; others will also have to relax their grip. This is a freewheeling activity that develops spontaneously as you work with it. Here we've suggested some idea starters. Get into the spirit and take off from there.

*Materials.* A piece of rope one-half to one inch thick and about twenty feet long—longer if you have a large group or if you want to tie knots in it for children to hold on to.

*Procedure.* Make the rope into a circle and have the group sit around the outside of it. (If you have fifteen or more children, you may want to use two ropes and have two circles—especially the first time you do an activity of this sort.) Using as much drama and as many sound effects as you feel in the mood for, instruct children to hold on to the rope. For example, "This is a wiggly rope, so you have to reach out fast, whoosh, and grab it quickly, chonk, and don't let it get away" (as you wiggle the wrist of the hand holding the rope). Don't be inhibited about inventing sound effects. They help focus the group on the particular body joints used in the motion and greatly enhance the delight children find in this activity. Begin the activity with variations designed to get everyone used to the way the rope responds to coordinated movements. You might start with everyone's simultaneously raising the rope slowly over the head, down to the waist, and then to the floor. Stepping on or over the rope and swaying back and forth with it make children aware of how others' actions influence the way their section of the rope behaves. Here are some suggestions for subsequent elaborations. (You wouldn't do them all in one session. Pick and choose according to the abilities and interests of your group.)

(1) Work on continuity (infra-logical knowledge) by having the group members move themselves and the rope in a circle; stand still but move the rope in a circle (by passing knots around); and—a harder task—pass people around the circle: with one person replacing his neighbor, that neighbor replacing her neighbor, and so on, for a chain effect.

(2) Work on the understanding of relations (seriation) by using gradations in speed of motions, pretended heaviness of the rope, numbers of body parts touching the rope, and so on.

(3) Emphasize classification by getting children to contribute ideas for how to move the rope when it is
    (a) so heavy you can hardly lift it,
    (b) very lightweight,
    (c) extremely fragile (incidentally, this demonstrates that a slow rate of motion can be used in representing lightweight objects as well as heavy ones, and it focuses attention on other features of the motions involved in moving heavy things).

(4) Work on number and temporal duration as you and the children work out various rhythmic variations (step, step, and lift, for example, or two large slow steps followed by a series of hops set to a phrase such as, "Giants striding; small bird hopping along").

*Watch for and encourage*

*Children's resistance to or acceptance of flexibility* in performing different actions on the same object.

*Variety and ingenuity* in thinking of ideas.

*Adjustment of motions* in response to others' actions (a very egocentric child who doesn't attend to the consequences of others' actions will be thrown off balance when the rope does unexpected things, and may seem uncoordinated).

*Sensorimotor understandings* in the areas of logico-mathematical and infra-logical knowledge, depending on the variations you've used. Some examples are suggested next.

*Classification*—consistency in demonstrating variations of types of movement such as various motions of the wrist or ways to move one's legs while holding the rope between one's knees.

*Serial relations*—finding an action to fit in a previously constructed series (thinking of a way to make the rope higher than one's ankles, for example, but lower than one's shoulders) or demonstrating a seriated sequence of actions (such as making the rope go slower, slower, and slower still).

*Number*—ability to deal with very simple one-to-one correspondences as shown in response to requests for each child to hold on to one knot in the rope, ability to handle rhythmic uses of the rope.

*Spatial relations*—ability to imitate and/or follow instructions about positioning parts of the body under the rope, on the rope, inside the circle, and so on; ability to handle spatial continuity tasks such as passing knots around the circle.

*Understandings on the level of thought* in the areas we have listed. In the area of classification, for example, you might look for children's answers to such questions as, "Are there more ways to move the rope just with your hands or more ways to move the rope in general?" You might ask them to count the total number of variations you've tried out and then the number of ways that involve the hands alone. Be sure to notice spontaneous comments during the activity as well as the answers elicited in discussions before and after the rope motion. Take another look at the Developmental Guideposts in Chapter 6 for more ideas to adapt to this activity.

*Remarks on Rope Drama.* The main part of this activity exercises sensorimotor abilities and provides the kind of physical successes that precede understanding on the level of thought (see Piaget, 1976, 1978). To take full advantage of this potential, it is helpful to concentrate initially on physical features of the activity, with (1) an emphasis on sound effects to make it fun, (2) an exploration of the range of movement with various parts of the body, and (3) a development of group cohesion (usually achieved by giving simple and explicit directions). Later in the same session, or on a subsequent day, children can suggest different motions for the group to explore. If you want to focus on classification, you could encourage suggestions for arm movements only, or for ways to pass a movement around the circle, or for any other category of motion you can dream up. In the process, children will be discovering a variety of spatial constraints, acquiring a sensorimotor understanding of centrifugal force, and developing ways to deal with both.

We suggest devoting different sessions with the rope to different areas of knowledge. One session, for instance, might consist of some giggle-producing warm-ups, a series of tasks involving spatial continuity with varying degrees of cognitive and physical demands, and a few favorite moves to end the activity. Another might focus on rhythms, seriated motions, or classification.

Discussions before, after, and during the break in the rope activity will help in moving the acquired sensorimotor understandings to the level of thought. Because this kind of follow-up is so important in fostering development, we've included the following Teacher Task to get your ideas flowing.

*TEACHER TASK 8-10*

---

List at least six ways to make sure the Rope Drama is a Piagetian activity. Use the format introduced in the discussion of snack-time procedures and outlined here.

|  PROCEDURE | **AREA OF KNOWLEDGE ENHANCED BY THE CHANGE IN PROCEDURE** |
|---|---|
| *Instead of:* | |
| *Do:* | |

Try to include suggestions for how to discuss the movements with children as well as suggestions for how to interact with the rope and suggestions for how, when, and how often to repeat and/or vary the activity.

---

We hope this discussion has convinced you that movement activities have exciting potentials for cognitive development. It will be enormously illuminating for you to apply the kind of analysis for cognitive potentials you've applied here to other movement activities you've tried or have read about.

### Indoor Free-Play Activities

A typical arrangement in preschool and kindergarten programs is to have teachers plan and prepare activities, with children doing the clean-up. There is good reason for this tradition. Teachers use their knowledge of child development and curriculum to plan appropriate and stimulating activities for a variety of interests and abilities, they know what materials are needed and where to find them, and materials that are displayed and ready to use draw children's attention and suggest how they might be used. Children lack the experience needed for planning most activities, and they don't know where to find the necessary materials. Encouraging children to clean up after themselves fosters a sense of responsibility and in a matter of five to twenty minutes achieves, through cooperation, what it would take the teachers alone an hour or more to do. Besides, clean-up times are rich in potential for cognitive development.

There are some beneficial deviations from this arrangement that can be introduced as the school year progresses (change, you'll remember, is a key word for the classroom environment). Children can gradually take larger roles in preparation for favorite activities, such as easel painting. They can progress from getting out brushes to putting up their own paper and to mixing their own paint. Cooperation, spatial judgment, physical knowledge, seriation, classification, number, and physical coordination can all be involved, provided teachers take advantage of the preparation as a valuable activity in its own right. Gathering materials for an activity can be planned into the activity, as in the hospital example discussed in Chapter 7.

In addition to preparing materials for planned activities, children can help do the planning. Early planning efforts include deciding where to play during any particular free-play time and suggesting that favorite activities be repeated. Such efforts involve an understanding of temporal relations and are worth cultivating. After children can stick to a plan for where to start their free-play periods, they can be encouraged to plan a sequence of actions. (Either kind of planning requires an awareness of what activities are available, however, so lists of activities, pictures of the classroom, or even tours around the room might be wise before children are asked to choose an activity.) Requests to have favorite activities repeated can be turned into a planning activity if teachers bring up the requests at group time and explain alternatives, promising to work out the details of when and how to bring back the activity.

As children become more familiar with the classroom materials and the demands of working with other children, they can take a larger role in suggesting new activities and in setting rules for their use. This can be encouraged with interchanges like the following:

> Are you ready to try some new puzzles, or are you still happy with the old ones? You want some new ones? Okay. How about making a special corner for the new puzzles? How do you think we could do that?

or

> Think about what quiet activities you'd like to have out next week and tell us at juice time.

or

Well, if you'd like the plastic blocks again, I guess we could do that. But remember the trouble we had with the towers getting knocked over? How could we make sure that doesn't happen?

The more teachers have discussed their reasons for introducing rules, changing activities, and coordinating the kinds of activities available during the day, the better children can respond to these planning opportunities. Teachers, of course, still have the responsibility to see that the incorporation of children's plans preserves the integrity of the classroom as one that is characterized by activity, change, diversity, and intellectual honesty.

Clean-up after an active free-play period can sometimes seem a bit overwhelming. It needn't be. You just have to get into the right frame of mind. Treat it as an activity in its own right. When you view clean-up as a full-fledged learning experience, you'll find that "sloppiness" can represent progress in psychomotor abilities and a way of handling overly difficult classification tasks, that unfinished tasks may be unfinished only from the adult's perspective, and that reluctance to participate may sometimes reflect the shyness that keeps a child from joining a dramatic-play setting or the "I don't know how" worries that make him or her hesitant about making contributions in the small group.

As an activity, clean-up can have a variety of cognitive, socio-emotional, and psychomotor objectives, depending on how you plan to proceed. Plan ways to make it stimulating, intellectually challenging, and fun. To exercise representational skills, you might use a job chart with pictures of materials or areas of the room and with children's names listed underneath. Number concepts can be reinforced with suggestions about how many items to pick up—for instance, "Each person pick up five things," or "Pick up four blocks, three crayons, two pegs, and one pair of scissors." Even simple mathematical problems can be presented, such as, "If each of you three picks up one block, how many blocks will be picked up? What if Katie picks up two blocks instead of one? What if you each pick up two? Let's do it and find out." Comparisons of more and less can be used when one hand versus two is used to carry small items or when different-sized cartons are used to transport beads back to shelves. You're giving a classification task when you assign someone to pick up only red things or only the hard things with holes in them. And seriation can be combined with classification, in instructions such as, "Pick up all the things smaller than this block."

After you've provided many such experiences, and with a little prompting, children can begin to devise their own pick-up games. They may even be willing to organize into work teams with a leader who sets tasks for the others.

### Creating an atmosphere
### for thinking

Free-play time is uniquely suited to accomplishing two of the goals listed in Chapter 4 for the people in the classroom. First, because children choose what they'll do, when they'll do it, and how long they'll spend at it, free-play time can enhance children's ability and willingness to initiate their own learning experiences. Second, self-confidence is likely to grow in an atmosphere of free choice in which children can tackle a hard problem, retreat to a simpler one, and work their way back up to the harder one at their own pace.

Progress toward these goals doesn't happen automatically in a free-play setting. Some children are overstimulated by a rich array of new materials and the presence of so many other children. Having carefully provided for a variety of activities, teachers now need to help children to become aware of the variety and to choose wisely amidst the excitement of new opportunities and the stimulation of other children's activities. In some cases, a teacher may have to help a child see the need to make a temporary retreat from the hectic pace of a "gang" in order to think about whether the group activity is what that child really wants to do. In other cases, a child may need help joining other children's play. Teachers, especially the "manager," must maintain a constant awareness of opportunities for entry into a group activity and a sensitivity to when children might need help either entering or withdrawing.

Children who are wandering aimlessly or who are "just making trouble" may need help in joining their chosen activity, or they may need help in making the choice. In either case, the first step is to find out. The simple question, "Are you trying to decide what to do?" is nearly always an effective start. If Tanya hasn't decided, she and the teacher may discuss what's available, look at a picture chart of the day's activities, take a tour of the areas, and/or start a joint project, perhaps with one or two other children. It is a good idea to tie suggestions for new activities to a child's previous activities, as in, "You were drawing elephants in small group this morning; maybe you'd like to make one with clay," or "You haven't tried the picnic puzzle for a long time; would you like to try that?" Such comments help the child see ways to think about new activities to try. A tour of the classroom accompanied by a discussion of what children are doing and what kind of help they might need is useful for a child who has trouble joining ongoing activities. One can demonstrate entry techniques explicitly, by, for example, knocking on an imaginary door to the housekeeping area and introducing yourself as a neighbor with a problem, a telephone repairman, or a friend who needs a ride to the doctor.

In helping children join ongoing activities, it is important to find ways that don't interfere with the goal of self-confidence or with the opportunity for children to take the lead in how the activities are carried out. In introducing a new child (and in general, whenever you want to provide a new challenge or stimulate a fading interest), you want first to find out how the children already involved view their activity. That way, you can make your introductions, provocative questions, and subtle suggestions relevant from the children's point of view—and that's the view that counts, after all. If you take the time to observe (and help children do likewise), you can avoid the unwitting disruption of activities you had intended to enhance or extend. In general, the teacher's role is to stimulate, encourage, suggest, wonder, and appreciate, but not to direct and explain.

If you get a chance for prolonged interaction with a child or two, don't make it into a small group. Instead, let the child lead. You can and should try to find out what the child is thinking, provoke new lines of exploration, and make suggestions of various sorts, but be prepared to abandon your line of inquiry if the child does not seem interested. Observe for a while to see what children do find intriguing. (In a small-group setting, you'd be more likely to pursue your line of thought long enough to get children interested or to discover why they're not.) For some useful examples of the kind of interactions we are recommending, see Kamii and DeVries (1976) and Hammerman and Morse (1972).

### Specific suggestions for activities

Planning for free-play time is a demanding job, because of the number of different activities made available simultaneously. In the last section of this chapter, we'll discuss some hints for coordinating activities to provide a play period that is both manageable for teachers and cognitively challenging for children. Here, we'll confine ourselves to looking at each activity individually. The first detailed activity suggestion below is for moments when a teacher can remain in one area of the room, working with whatever children are interested. The second represents the kind of planning that goes into providing cognitive challenges when teachers cannot count on being directly involved in the activity.

### Mystery Pair

*General comments.* This is a version of a "tried and true" activity that you can make into a Piagetian activity. It can be done with one child or with as many as five or so. It is flexible, so that children can leave or enter when they wish—a crucial requirement for free-play activities. That flexibility also makes it a good opening activity if your program is one in which children's arrival time is somewhat staggered.

*Materials.* A collection of pairs of identical items, one item of each pair hidden in a large "mystery bag." You can choose items to emphasize certain features, such as interesting textures, variety of shapes, sounds produced, degrees of flexibility. You can also include a few trouble makers: two sets of blocks of the same size, shape, and texture, but differing in color; or two items that look alike but feel different; or a flat piece of paper and a crumpled one.

*Procedure:*

(1) Invite a few children to sit around a table or rug on which you have placed one item of each pair. Keep the matching items in the mystery bag while you and children explore the materials. Encourage thorough and systematic exploration with questions like those suggested in the Mr. Squishit activity. It will

also help to focus your questions on features that can be discovered tactually: ask about numbers of corners, texture (bumpy, smooth, slippery, fuzzy, hairy), holes, moving parts, and so on—depending on the items you've gathered. Encourage children to say as many things as they can about each item and its similarities and dissimilarities to other items.

(2) Introduce the mystery bag and explain its contents. Without allowing children to see it, remove one item from the bag and let a child feel it behind her back—no peeking! Then you can hold the item hidden under the bag or behind your back while the child tries to find its partner on the table. When the child has made her choice and before you reveal the hidden item, ask her—and the other children—how she decided that that was the right one. If the child points out, for example, that the object has corners, encourage further specificity by commenting on the other items with corners. Ask other children if they think the features the child has mentioned are sufficient to identify the object.

(3) Show everyone the item taken from the bag and compare it to the item picked from the table. If they do not make a pair, help children discuss the differences. Let each child feel the item from the bag while feeling an item chosen from the table.

(4) After children are familiar with this game, you can start using the trouble makers—the items that differ from one another only by visible features or only by tactually discoverable features. If children do not attend to the ambiguity and simply pick one of the possible matches from the table, ask them how they know it's not the other possible one. Discuss what you can and cannot find out by just feeling things.

(5) You can focus attention on classification and relations by choosing items of two or more distinct sorts (for instance, blocks of different shapes and various pieces of fabric); or by supplying four or five different-sized buttons, lengths of Tinker Toy pieces, stiffnesses of paper, or whatever.

(6) An interesting variation on this activity is to do the feeling with one's feet.

*Watch for and encourage*

*Physical Knowledge*—systematic exploration, attention to a variety of features, ability to explain the choices made, decentration (see Chapter 5 if you've forgotten what this means), as revealed by the ability to make correct judgments about the trouble makers.

*Infra-logical Knowledge*—judgments based on topological properties (continuous edges, holes), focus on Euclidean properties (length, angularity).

*Logico-mathematical Knowledge*—spontaneous seriation of items on the basis of some feature, appeal to transitivity in explaining the choice of a matching item, grouping similar objects or discussing similarities and differences (classification), discussions of how many items of a certain sort there are (number) or of whether there are as many items in the bag as on the table (one-to-one correspondence).

*Remarks on Mystery Pair.* This activity description has much in common with the ones we've already seen. Notice especially the following features:

(1) Trouble makers are included to provoke cognitive conflict so as to help children make judgments based on a variety of cues rather than on just the first one they happen to notice—that is, the trouble makers help children decenter.

(2) Questions are used to encourage thorough exploration. In trying to generate appropriate kinds of questions in procedure 1 and in deciding when and how much to follow up on them, remember that the purpose of your questions here is to encourage the kind of mental and physical activity that enhances intellectual development. The questions are used to encourage children to interact with objects in increasingly complex ways (to use their fingers to feel the holes in a block, for example, rather than simply to pass their whole hand over its surface) and to help them make use of this more sophisticated action in their construction of new understandings. A verbal response by the child to the question you ask may or may not be helpful in achieving these goals.

(3) The aim of procedures 2 and 3 is to help children break out of egocentric thinking as they try to convince others of the reasonableness of their choices and as they challenge the choices made by others. Given this aim, it would be appropriate to "play dumb" and ask questions that require more explicit descriptions. For example, when a child claims to have felt a block like the one on the table, you might remark, "But this block has corners" or "two holes" or "a long side."

(4) This activity could be extended to range over other areas of the room if children are asked to add to the collection. Their task would be to find two things (number) that are just alike (classification) and that, say, also have holes (classification), or are longer than this block (seriation) but can still fit in the bag (spatial judgment) or make sounds like castanets (classification). Children could decide on the kinds of things they want to add and then either conduct their own search or give the task to other children.

(5) One set of variations on this activity includes matching sounds, tastes, smells, combinations of such features, or whatever else you can think of. If you use such variations, don't forget to think about the kinds of questions you could use to help children decenter and to be systematic in their exploration of the chosen materials. With older children, you might try some variations with greater

representational demands. Children could be asked to match perceptually dissimilar items (explored tactually) that have the same use. Or you might focus on kinesthetic and proprioceptive perception, by positioning the hand of a child whose eyes are closed and then asking the child to pick out a picture (eyes open now) that shows a hand in the same position.

Do you see why we want to call these activity ideas frameworks rather than daily lesson plans?

### Road Building

*General comments.* Planning free-play activities generally involves preparation for many different potentials in different materials. The choice and arrangement of the materials, together with some hard thinking about thought-provoking interaction strategies, influences which potentials are most likely to be actualized. Here's a sketch of procedures to use for emphasizing spatial concepts in the block area.

*Materials.* Unit blocks, cars and trucks, plenty of floor space.

*Procedure.* Before children arrive, partially construct several roads suitable for different-sized cars and trucks. You may want to start some roads consisting of parallel tracks as well as some solid roads. Put a few vehicles on the roads. Building a small house or two wouldn't hurt either, but don't get too elaborate. (We once got so carried away with our enticing arrangements that there was no thinking room left for children. Fortunately, the problem was solved by a child, who, first to our horror and then to our delight, kicked down all the roads and buildings and then started afresh: building roadways. We had managed to stimulate road building in spite of our bungling, thanks to the wisdom of children.) When children arrive, observe and make yourself available to make comments, ask questions, steady block structures, and the like.

To make it easier for you and your coworkers to interact effectively in keeping with the goals you've set and the materials you've provided, you might want to post some suggestions for interaction strategies in the block area. Your list might look something like the one below.

> Introduce a car that's too wide for the roads already built. Introduce blocks that are too narrow for the cars being used.
>
> Ask how people who live in one area get to another, how long it will take to "drive to the store" or "to drive home again."
>
> Ask about plans for new roads—entrance and exit ramps to throughways, plans for new straight roads to avoid dangerous curves, roads to use for stock car racing, and so on.

Introduce rivers, forests, swamps, mountains, and ask about plans to build roads over, through, and around the areas.

Suggest that children step out of the area (perhaps standing on a chair) to get an overview of the scene.

Take Polaroid photographs of the area and share the pictures with the children.

Suggest making maps of the roads already built, so that the activity could be continued another day—or start drawing a map yourself.

*Watch for and encourage*

*Understandings of Enclosure*—buildings completely enclosed or with doorways, discussion of needed openings for bridges and tunnels.

*Understandings of Part-Whole Relationships*—use of different-sized blocks to make roads of equal width and/or length.

*Distance Judgments*—choosing, in advance, enough blocks to make a road of a specific length, choosing the right-sized blocks and the correct spacing for making tunnels, bridges, ramps.

*Distance Measurements*—use of a length of string, a particular block, or the time it takes to hum "dum te dum te dum" while moving a car along the floor.

*Quantification of Direction*—construction of parallel roads.

*Understandings of the Relation between Duration and Space*—the construction of race tracks of the same length, the use of appropriately placed starting points, the use of staggered starting points with appropriately staggered ending points.

*Advance Planning*—for road building and house construction.

*Conservation of Distance*—discussions of whether a forest added to the side of the road shortens the distance, discussions of how far a car has to drive on a curvy road compared to a straight road, choice of the shortest path when the number of blocks is limited.

*Understandings of Continuity*—construction of different roads to the same place, construction of detours around swamps, houses, and so forth.

**Remarks on Road Building.**   Although road-building activities provide cognitive challenges in all areas of logico-mathematical knowledge, it is wise to plan a given activity with a focus on a single area of knowledge, as in the previous example. That way, materials and interaction strategies can be coordinated in advance to provoke hard thinking. In a free-play area where you can't count on prolonged teacher-child contacts, you need to have stimulating questions and comments on the tip of your tongue. Your chances of enhancing the ongoing activity (rather than making irrelevant, though perhaps friendly, comments) are increased if you've thought about the kinds of thinking the materials have been arranged to provoke. An additional advantage of planning free-play activities with a focus in mind is that you as a teacher are more likely to notice related understandings and questions in other activity areas of the classroom and are better able to provide appropriate intellectual challenges.

Teacher Task 8-11 should help you refine your ability to develop theory-inspired plans with a definite focus. As you can see by now, the road building activity is just one of dozens of activity ideas that are generated by the list of potentials for blocks at the end of Chapter 7.

*TEACHER TASK 8-11*

---

(1) Plan a free-play activity for the block area with an emphasis on your choice of an area of logico-mathematical knowledge other than spatial understandings. Use the Developmental Guideposts in Chapter 6 and the example of blocks at the end of Chapter 7 for ideas on interaction strategies and ways to arrange the area.

(2) Plan a "Seriation Sand Table" for free-play time.
   (a) This partial list of materials may help you get your ideas going:
      sand table with three sections or three large plastic tubs for dry sand, moist sand, and very wet sand
      large drop cloth to put under work area
      coarse sand
      three sifters with different-sized meshes
      three funnels of different sizes
      three sizes of spoons and/or shovels
   (b) In thinking about procedures, plan some specific suggestions for how to arrange materials. For example, to help children notice the possibilities for serial ordering and correspondences, you might group materials by size (small bucket with small shovel and small funnel) or arrange them in a seriated row. Also plan some suggested interaction strategies, as was done in the road-building activity description.
   (c) To generate a list of what to watch for and encourage, use the Developmental Guideposts in Chapter 6 and think about ways to promote activity, intellectual honesty, diversity, and change—the four key classroom characteristics discussed in Chapter 4.

---

Teachers we've worked with have found it extremely valuable to augment their focused plans by adding descriptions of the kinds of thinking to watch for and encourage in the other areas of knowledge. This provides practice in developing ways to apply theory and prepares one for taking advantage of on-the-spot opportunities. The next Teacher Task will get you started on this useful procedure.

*TEACHER TASK 8-12*

---

Add to the two activity plans you developed in Teacher Task 8-10 a list of what to observe for and encourage in areas of knowledge other than the one specifically emphasized. Make sure to keep your suggestions tied to the original activity plan—that is, think about questions and understandings likely to be generated by the materials you've made available.

---

**Outdoor Free-Play Activities**

Outdoor activities and interaction strategies should be planned with as much attention to activity, diversity, change, and intellectual honesty as indoor activities. Quiet activities especially suited for the out of doors (mud pies, water painting on hot cement, bug watching) should be balanced with more boisterous ones such as rope swinging, construction activities, and tire rolling. Such a challenging physical task as building a fort is readily combined with an intellectual task, perhaps figuring out how to make it stay up—if teachers have provided appropriate materials (planks, wooden boxes, old blankets) and have thought through strategies for helping children invent the solutions.

To help children take advantage of the variety available, you may want to announce what's available before going outside. Or, as in indoor free play, charts, verbal reminders, group discussions, and the like can be used. If the weather is unpredictable, vulnerable equipment can be left inside until just before you go outdoors. Then children can help bring it out. A discussion of which equipment gets this treatment, and why, will increase children's physical knowledge.

The cleaning up of outdoor equipment is comparable to clean-up indoors except that the equipment is usually heavier and bigger—materials with many small pieces (puzzles, pegs, beads) are less often available outside. Many of the same intellectual challenges arise for outdoor clean-up as well, though we have found that outdoor equipment more easily lends itself to dramatic-play themes during clean-up. Children can bring their "buses" (trikes) to the garage, bring in the shovels and pails before "quiting time," or pack up the "camping gear" for the next hike. Many activities, such as mud-pie making, digging for worms, or body painting, warrant extra time and require a special place set aside for washing off. If you've worked with groups of young children, you already know that clean-up for the bigger, messier projects has to start earlier than for the others. If you talk with children about the reasons for this, they'll not only cooperate more fully, they'll be thinking about temporal relations, physical knowledge, and even some logico-mathematical knowledge proper (one can classify and/or seriate activities according to the estimated required time for clean-up).

*Creating an atmosphere*
*for thinking*

Outdoor play lends itself especially well to experiences essential for constructing physical and infra-logical knowledge. Because of the more vigorous activity levels and the extra watchfulness required for safety purposes, conversations about expected effects or why things work are often less extensive outdoors than they would be indoors. Quick insights, stimulating questions, and the discovery of fruitful problems for future exploration, however, are not at all infrequent, especially if equipment designed for comparisons, cognitive conflict, and exciting construction challenges is provided.

*Specific suggestions
for activities*

Because you've already had samples of detailed free-play activity ideas, we'll just give one detailed activity framework here to illustrate the unique opportunities available outside. Then we'll suggest some materials for stimulating young children's exploration of natural phenomena, and we will ask you to think about the cognitive potentials in those materials.

**Obstacle Course**

*General comments.* This is a favorite outdoor activity that can also be done indoors with suitable modifications.

*Materials.* Tires, ropes, planks, large wooden crates, cardboard boxes, barrels, mud puddles—anything that strikes your fancy.

*Procedure:*

(1) Using whatever materials you can scavenge and all the ingenuity you can muster, set up an obstacle course. To work on continuity, you can arrange materials so that progress one way is more difficult than another. You can make a linear course with one starting point and one stopping point, you can make multiple entries and exits, or you can make a course that loops back on itself.

(2) The first time you set up an obstacle course, you may have to show children how to get started. After that, there'll be no problem.

(3) Be alert to safety precautions: help children avoid congestion, and help them predict difficult parts of the obstacle course and adjust their movements accordingly.

(4) After you've experimented with a variety of obstacle-course arrangements, children can help design and construct them. You can add an emphasis on classification, by suggesting obstacle courses made only of round things, of flat things, of soft things, and so on. A challenge to both number understandings and flexible problem solving can be provided by requesting that exactly ten items be used. You can work on representational ability by having children draw a blueprint of an obstacle course that's already set up, so that they can reassemble it inside or on another day. Or, as they become more sophisticated in the art of obstacle-course

construction, they can list materials or draw plans for obstacle courses they want to set up.

*Watch for and encourage*

*Physical Knowledge*—ease of navigation through the obstacle course, indicating recognition of structural attributes related to stability; adjustments of motion in anticipation of obstacles (bouncy tires, a long jump); testing for stability when constructing an obstacle course (How systematic is the test?); choice of appropriate objects and arrangements for the obstacle course. (Could any child traverse the course, or is it too difficult? Is it a connected course or a few objects here and there?)

*Infra-logical Knowledge*—interest and ability in copying an existing obstacle course (Are all the pieces copied? Are they in the right order? What kinds of errors are made?), accuracy of distance judgments, use of different routes to the same end on an existing obstacle course, planning different points of access into the construction of an obstacle course, willingness to make and use plans for constructing a course or for traversing an existing one, flexibility in substituting one object for another when given a limit of ten objects, discussion of how long and how difficult the course is, starting from different points of entry.

*Classification*—consistency in choosing objects with some common feature for particular sorts of uses in obstacle-course construction, ability to choose all and only objects with some property (for instance, things that roll) for the construction of an obstacle course.

*Relations*—construction of "staircases" with five or more levels; spontaneous use of serial correspondence, as in putting the biggest tire with the biggest plank, the middle-sized tire with the middle-sized plank, and so on; insertion of an object of the appropriate height to add a step where the gap is too high.

*Number*—spontaneous comments about numbers of items, how many children can be on the course; suggestions for limiting the number of children on the course; responses to teacher-set limits on the number of children.

**Remarks on Obstacle Course.** This activity framework illustrates a general sequence strongly suggested by Piaget's theory: the shift from a heavy emphasis on sensorimotor activity to an emphasis on mental activity within the same framework. Initial obstacle courses are prepared by teachers, with the challenge to children being the physical mastery of those obstacles and the making of on-the-spot judgments about how to overcome one. Later, obstacle courses are planned by children, with increasing encouragement to plan further and further ahead, to exercise their logico-mathematical and infra-logical understandings, and to increase their understanding in the area of physical knowledge. Later obstacle courses may also introduce new and more difficult sensorimotor challenges, only to be followed by even more complex demands on the level of thought.

*TEACHER TASK 8-13*

---

Plan an activity for outdoor free-play time using the format for plans in this chapter.

(1) Under the heading "General Comments," explain why the activity is particularly suitable for outdoor free play.

(2) Use Chapter 7 for help in choosing theory-based procedures.

(3) The guideposts in Chapter 6 will help you generate a list of what to watch for in each of the three areas of knowledge. Try to be as comprehensive as you can; look for understandings in each of the areas within infra-logical and logico-mathematical knowledge.

(4) Indicate how you would change the activity to (a) add more difficult sensorimotor demands, and (b) increase challenges for infra-logical and logico-mathematical knowledge.

---

### Exploring Natural Phenomena

Here is the list of materials we promised earlier. As you read through the list, think about the cognitive potentials in each material and jot down any ideas that come to you for emphasizing understandings in the different areas of knowledge.

*Wind:* streamers and scarves, kites, pinwheels of different sizes and materials, paper airplanes, soap bubbles, lightweight beach balls.

*Gravity:* planks used as inclined planes with varying degrees of incline; balance boards; hillsides used for rolling tires, for sledding, and for running; tire "pendulums" (tires suspended from a tree or swing set by stiff ropes); construction materials (wooden crates, barrels, planks, large wooden blocks, slices of old tree trunks); simple pulleys; rope.

*Fluid Dynamics:* mudholes, artificial streams made with old eaves, troughs, or with a bent metal garden border, ponds made with washtubs or with a sheet of plastic lining a hole dug by you and the children, pieces of hose for siphoning, buckets, containers with holes punched at different heights along the sides, tires with water inside for rolling. (Why doesn't the water spill out? Why does it always stay at the bottom as the tire rolls?)

*Flora and Fauna:* shovels for digging worms, grubs, and so on; insect cages and nets; sturdy, wooden or plastic-edged, magnifying glasses; a section of the play yard devoted to native plants and wildflowers; a garden.

*Light and Heat:* colored cellophane viewers; prisms; wood, concrete, and metal surfaces to compare in sun and shade; scarves, banners, puppets, and the like, for shadow dancing.

*Remarks on Exploring Natural Phenomena.*  Many of the materials suggested are not part of standard school equipment but can be improvised easily. Swings on ordinary swing sets can be replaced by rope ladders and tire swings or made more intellectually stimulating by adjusting the swings to provide a variety of heights. Homemade plank and crate ramps can complement standard metal slides. Children can help start a wild-flower garden in a corner of the yard. Old tires can be obtained from a local gas station or tire dealer. Forages for equipment can become exciting field trips for small groups of children or, occasionally, for the whole group.

As the school yard accumulates materials with rich potentials for infra-logical and physical knowledge, you may find the outdoor time the most intellectually stimulating part of the day. As you gather equipment, you'll undoubtedly conjure up new ideas for materials and their uses. If you're like the teachers we've known, you'll also find yourself integrating indoor and outdoor times so that the activities are complementary. Activities indoors will pursue interests developed outside, and vice versa.

## PUTTING IDEAS TOGETHER:
## AN INTEGRATED CURRICULUM

So far, we've looked at some specific activities and their potentials for stimulating intellectual development, but we haven't begun to describe the diversity of kinds of materials and subject areas you'll want your classroom to provide.

Nearly everybody agrees that variety is important, and most people construct similar lists of the kinds of variety they value, but why is variety so important? Many different reasons have been offered. For instance: new experiences encourage new interests; different materials require different kinds of physical coordination; everyone in our culture should be familiar with a certain variety of aesthetic experiences. Our theory adds one more reason. Diversity is a key word for the subject areas in the classroom because, just as individuals differ in developmental level and pace, so they differ in other abilities or interests that influence what kinds of subject matter stimulates their logico-mathematical thought processes. The child with an extremely good ear who is sensitive to tone differences and subtle rhythmic variations may develop in the three kinds of knowledge more enjoyably through musical activities than through climbing activities. Another child may miss the tonal qualities that make music such an intense pleasure for the first child (though the second may still enjoy singing games) but be fascinated by living things. A variety of subject areas allows for individuals to develop intellectually in areas of particular interest to them.

It is important to have a representative showing of different subject-matter areas and to be prepared to provide intellectual challenges in each of them. Not every day, of course. Sometimes an area will be used primarily for aesthetic purposes, for practice in motor coordination, or for exploring some emotion. Nonetheless, if the diversity of areas is to serve the needs of individual interests, we must spend some time putting the theory to work in each area.

### Planning for Diversity

A list of areas and illustrative materials generally available in good early-childhood programs is this:

*art and construction:* paints, paste, scissors, clay, drawing materials, pipe cleaners for construction, easels
*music and dance:* records, tape recorders, instruments, scarves and capes for responding to music
*science:* plants, pets, boxes of things to explore, water tables, sand, flashlights, scales, rulers
*large motor:* large blocks, ride-on trucks, wheelbarrows, climbers, woodworking bench
*small manipulative:* pegs, puzzles, beads, small construction toys
*dramatic play:* dress-up clothes, props (for instance, accessories for fire fighters and post-office workers), housekeeping accessories, dolls, stuffed toys
*books:* picture books, reference books, favorite stories

In grade schools, these areas are frequently replaced by such categories as language arts, social studies, math, reading, and physical education. Later, the divisions might be art, history, algebra, chemistry, and so forth. The change in how the subject area divisions are made reflects a changing emphasis but does not eliminate basic kinds of learning. Older children are exercising small-manipulative skills as they practice writing or handling beakers and flasks. Young children are working on reading (or prereading) skills as they draw pictures to represent procedures for cleaning the guinea-pig cage and as they look for their names on an activities chart. The foregoing list has served preschools well because it emphasizes areas where interest is high and progress is most noticeable in two- to five-year-olds.

In earlier chapters, we mentioned the need to provide a balance of activities that enhance each of the three kinds of knowledge and their subdivisions. Here we are emphasizing a new variable: different subject-matter areas. Most subject-matter areas have potentials for all three kinds of knowledge, but the potentials are not always consciously recognized and elicited. If you spend some time thinking about potentials in each of the areas, and devise ways to increase their chances of being put to use, you will find your time well spent.

It is very helpful to do your planning on a chart, so that you can see at a glance what kinds of knowledge you have provided for, what areas need constant teacher attention during free play, and how you have distributed teacher guidance and emphasis on different kinds of knowledge among the different subject-matter areas. You can use group times to make sure teacher-initiated activities emphasize

**CHART 8-2   Planning for Balanced Diversity in Group Activities
Sample Plan for a 4-Day Week**

|  | LARGE GROUP | SMALL GROUP | JUICE TIME |
|---|---|---|---|
| *Monday* | Story Construction— emphasis on *representa- tion* using theme based on Squish It activity | *Classification—small- manipulative* activity (Squish It) | *Number*—independence of size and number (choice of one large cracker or two small ones) |
| *Tuesday* | Rope Drama—emphasis on *large-motor* skills (stretching and balance) | *Relations—music* activity using different-sized drums (tone and rhythm) | *Number*—"buy" snacks (2 popsicle sticks for a slice of apple) |
| *Wednesday* | *Dramatizing* emotions— how would you look (stand, walk) if you were sad (angry, happy)? | *Representation—art* activ- ity constructing clay people | *Conservation*—using a measuring cup to serve juice in different-sized cups |
| *Thursday* | Introduction of pet snake —emphasis on *physical knowledge* concerning care and handling | *Conservation—science* activity measuring things in the room with strings, sticks, spoons, and so on | *Conservation and Physical Knowledge*— discussion of what hap- pens to the sugar cube when you add it to lemon-flavored water |

different kinds of knowledge in a diversity of subject areas. Chart 8-2 shows variety planned into large-group, small-group, and juice-time activities for a four-day week. Chart 8-3 shows variety planned into free play activities for one day. You may want to use a single chart to display all the plans for a given day (free play, group times, and snack time all included) in order to see what kind of thinking space you'll have during the day. Some signaling device, such as a *T* for "teacher required," next to any activity that requires close attention will help you see what kind of a day you've planned for yourself and the rest of your staff.

### Thinking Room for Teachers

If teachers are to be able to observe children's thinking and to follow through on ideas and questions, they need thinking space during the day. They need oppor- tunities for getting an additional piece of equipment, for writing a quick note to themselves, and for quickly thinking through the feasibility of an on-the-spot modification in the day's plans. There are two ways to use your charts of the day's activities to provide yourself with some thinking space. The first is to rethink some of the plans in order to reduce the teacher attention required; the second is to think through some possible follow-up strategies ahead of time.

**CHART 8-3  Planning for Diversity in Free-Play Activities**
**Sample Plan for One Day in a Classroom with Three Adults**

| SUBJECT MATTER | ACTIVITY |
| --- | --- |
| *Science* | *Physical Knowledge (cognitive conflict):* tasting station—things that look alike but taste different (powdered sugar, baking soda, baking powder, flour; water, vinegar, corn syrup) |
| *Music* | *Serial Correspondence (length and tone):* xylophones that can be taken apart and put back together again |
| *Art and Construction* | *Preconservation (weight):* play dough and balance scales—make dough people, weigh them, and then see what happens when you make them fatter; weigh short, fat worms, then roll them to make them longer and skinnier, and check effects on the scale |
| *Large Manipulative* | *Spatial Relations (topological):* construction of a "city" using large blocks and huge cardboard boxes<br>obstacle course outside set up with "hills" of different sizes, bridges, "streams" to jump over, and so on |
| *Dramatic Play* | *Temporal Relations:* camping—packing, hiking (outside on obstacle course), setting up camp<br>*Number:* equipment store inside (with tickets to purchase supplies) |
| *Small Manipulative* | *Classification:* beads (sorted by size and color), strings of different lengths<br>pegs (sorted by size and color) and pegboards<br>puzzles<br>geoboards (boards with regularly spaced nails and rubber bands to stretch between nails) |
| *Books* | Stories about trips, especially camping<br>Nature books—plants, animals, stars<br>Some old favorites |
| *Outdoors* | *Spatial Relations:* obstacle course (see description above)<br>*Preconservation (weight):* seesaw (extension of weighing activity in art area)<br>*Seriation and Physical Knowledge:* ramps of different lengths all starting from the same height |

1 adult stays with science activity (can keep an eye on small-manipulative area)
1 adult moves from area to area indoors
1 adult outside

To reduce the need for teacher attention to an activity area without reducing the variety of subject matter, you can either replace the activity with one that doesn't require an adult or you can adjust it so that children can handle it alone. Finger painting might be replaced by crayons and paper, for example, or by play dough. The tasting station (from Chart 8-3) might be replaced by sturdy magnifying glasses and a box of nature objects to explore.

If, for various reasons, you want to keep the original activity, you can simplify it so that children can handle it alone or you can adjust the timing of the activity. To simplify a paint-mixing activity, for example, paints might be premixed rather than mixed by children, but a small pitcher of water could be available for thinning the paint. You might also want to reduce the number of materials available in, say, the small-manipulative area. Sometimes you can keep all the original activities as planned by starting them at different times. If only two adults were available on the day for which the activities in Chart 8-3 were planned, outdoor free play could come after indoor free play, and the camping activity could focus on trip preparations and short "practice hikes" until outdoor free-play time. Or you could preserve the indoor-outdoor flexibility and put the tasting station outside.

Our second suggestion for obtaining thinking space was to think through follow-up possibilities in advance. As you probably noticed, some follow-up activities were built right into the plans on Chart 8-3. The obstacle course outside was set up with the camping activity in mind. The seesaw was put out to provide opportunities for comparing its action to that of the balance scales. Geoboards provide a nonstandard opportunity to compare length and tone.

The xylophone activity could be extended by comments on the sounds rubber bands make on the geoboards in the small-manipulative area. (If this intrigues children, you might want to discuss with them plans for some xylophone or stringed instrument constructions later in the week.) Think about future activities that compare tones and length (or height): you might try different levels of water in soda pop bottles or invite a recorder player to bring in a range of instruments for a large-group demonstration.

The play dough weighing activity lends itself to a variety of other materials. If the scales are brought to the snack area, children might test for changes on the scale when a napkin is crumpled or a cracker is broken. If extra scales are available, the scales and play dough might be integrated into the dramatic play area as "food" is weighed out for backpacking expeditions. Preoperational children are unlikely to focus on conservation of weight here, but they will be acquiring valuable experience as they notice whether the scales do or do not go down when they change the condition of each object.

If camping becomes the activity of the day, you might want to take a small group of children on a nature walk or a short hike on a nearby hill (or staircase). You can use the nature books available in the story area to initiate discussions of what you'd see on a camping trip. Perhaps the city being constructed in the block area will become home for weary campers.

Having spent thirty minutes or so thinking through connections among the activities you've planned, you are likely to make appropriate comments and extensions during the day. The ideas will be in the back of your mind even if you haven't written them down. Just to give you practice in actually putting it all on paper, though, try the next Teacher Task.

**TEACHER TASK 8-14**

(1) Using a chart with entries for each of the seven subject matter areas shown on Chart 8-2, entries for group times, and a separate entry for clean-up strategies, plan two days' worth of activities for a classroom you are familiar with. (Some people find it easier to plan with a theme in mind—a circus, a focus on animals, or whatever. Such themes are usually more motivating for teachers than for children, but teachers are a part of the classroom too, and if it helps you generate ideas, go ahead.)

(2) Examine the activities for potentials in the different areas of logico-mathematical knowledge. Have you got a good balance? If not, think about ways to shift the emphasis in the various subject matter areas without putting in entirely new activities.

(3) When you've got a tentative plan, note whether or not a teacher is required in each of the free-play areas. If there aren't enough teachers to go around with one left free to be the manager, adjust the activities. Either move them to different times or adapt them so that a teacher's presence is not required.

(4) Finally, list as many ways as you can to follow up on the activities you've planned. Think about comments you might make during small-group times, large-group sessions, and snack time. How might materials or ideas from one activity be put to use in another?

### Planning for Change

Although long-term planning is important in early-childhood programs, we will say little about it here. The charts at the end of Chapter 4 and the Developmental Guideposts in Chapter 6 will help you sketch out tentative long-term plans. Unless you have had considerable experience both with young children and with applying Piaget's theory (and even when you have had such experience), it is wise to let new plans grow out of the careful observations you make and the hard thinking you do about current classroom activities. You can plan themes (such as health, circus, animals) well in advance, of course—that's not the kind of content or sequence about which Piaget's theory has anything to say—but you wouldn't want to evade children's sudden preoccupation with serial correspondences just because you had scheduled that area of knowledge for next April.

As you work through your own daily activity plans and become increasingly familiar with the Developmental Guideposts and the suggestions in Chapter 4, you will quite naturally work on understandings such as spatial continuity early in the year (or with younger children) and reserve complex reproductions of linear order for the more advanced. You will look for consistent sorting before you suggest horizontal reclassification tasks. You will gather evidence for understandings of one-to-one correspondence before you try cognitive conflict in number-conservation situations. Careful observation and constant assessment of how you're doing will be your guides to future planning. Chapter 9 gives some pointers for ways to keep track of how you're doing, so that appropriate future activities can be planned.

## SUMMARY

The two recurrent themes in this chapter have been that intellectual abilities develop—they are not learned, and that development can be enhanced by a well-designed environment. We began by exploring the difference between learning and development, using training research as an illustration of how the issue has been viewed and of why the distinction is important.

Next, we studied ways to use Piagetian theory to enhance intellectual development during different parts of the school day; we looked at juice time, small-group time, large-group time, free-play time indoors, and free-play time outside. For each of these, we suggested ways to incorporate ideas drawn from the theory into the procedures used and into the creation of an environment for thinking. After discussing a variety of hints for stimulating thought in each time period, we looked at one or more detailed descriptions of activity ideas. We took activities familiar to most experienced teachers and demonstrated how subtle shifts in focus, careful choices of materials, and attention to the interaction strategies discussed in Chapter 7 could maximize their potential for thinking activities. In discussing activities, we drew heavily on Chapters 6 and 7 to show us the connection between Piagetian theory and the kinds of responses children were likely to make. We paid particular attention to strategies that would both stimulate thought and elicit information about the child's level of development.

Finally, we took a brief look at how to put ideas together so that the theory showed itself in different subject-matter areas and throughout the school day. Here, as elsewhere, we avoided attempts to teach intellectual abilities and concentrated on ways to stimulate their development by providing a classroom environment characterized by activity, change, diversity, and intellectual honesty.

As usual, the Teacher Tasks were an integral part of the material presented.

## REFERENCES

HAMMERMAN, ANN, and SUSAN MORSE. "Open Teaching: Piaget in the Classroom," *Young Children, 28,* no. 1 (1972), 41–54.

KAMII, CONSTANCE, and RHETA DeVRIES. *Piaget, Children, and Number* (Washington, D.C.: National Association for the Education of Young Children, 1976).

MODGIL, SOHAN, and CELIA MODGIL. *Piagetian Research: Compilation and Commentary, Volume 7: Training Techniques* (Windsor, England: NFER Publishing Company Ltd., 1976).

PIAGET, JEAN. *The Grasp of Consciousness: Action and Concept in the Young Child,* trans. Susan Wedgwood (Cambridge, Mass.: Harvard University Press, 1976 [first published in French, in 1974, under the title, *La Prise de Conscience*]).

PIAGET, JEAN. *Success and Understanding,* trans. Arnold J. Pomerans (Cambridge, Mass.: Harvard University Press, 1978 [first published in French, in 1974, under the title, *Réussir et Comprendre*]).

SAUNDERS, RUTH A. "Classification Abilities in Young Children: Longitudinal Effects of a Piagetian Approach to a Preschool Program and to Teacher Education" (Doctoral dissertation, University of Wisconsin, Madison, 1976).

SKINNER, B. F. *Science and Human Behavior* (New York: Macmillan, Inc., 1953).

WOHLWILL, JOACHIM, V. DEVOE, and L. FUSARO. "Research on the Development of Concepts in Early Childhood." Final Report, National Science Foundation Grant G5855. Pennsylvania State University, January 1971.

# 9

# EVALUATING
# THE
# PROGRAM

## INTRODUCTION: THE *WHY'S, WHAT'S,*
## AND *HOW'S* OF ASSESSMENT

Having worked through the preceding chapters and attended to the Teacher Tasks, you have, no doubt, become quite familiar with the ways of the theory beast; we hope you have even begun to tame it. If so, you are ready to take stock of your progress. This chapter is designed to help you begin your search for ways to assess the extent to which the environment you have created (or the one you have stepped into) *is* what you want it to be and *does* what you want it to do for children.

In evaluating how well you're succeeding at the kind of teaching you've decided to do, you'll need to look at three major areas: (1) descriptions and judgments of the classroom environment—both physical and social, (2) the effects of the environment—particularly on the activities and accomplishments of children, and (3) your own teaching behaviors—and those of your colleagues. In this chapter, we'll be concentrating on the first two of these. Apart from a few suggestions, the issue of how to look at what teachers are doing will be reserved for Chapter 10.

The hints and techniques discussed in this chapter will be most useful to you if you refer to the discussions in Chapters 4, 6, and 7 and to your thoughts in re-

258

sponse to those chapters. As usual, this chapter offers hints and techniques to be incorporated into what you already know: it is a discussion of the ingredients of good evaluation rather than a set of recipes.

### Why Should We Assess?

As you've probably gathered from your reading so far, and as many researchers have pointed out (see, for example, Ball, 1975; Kamii, 1971; and Sigel, 1975), assessment of early-childhood programs is extremely difficult. It is difficult because (a) we are often unsure of how to formulate precise goals; (b) there are few, if any, available assessment tools that we believe can reliably measure what we want measured; (c) many of the goals we have for children are long-term goals and cannot be adequately measured until many years after the school experience; and (d) neither Piaget's theory nor other theories of personal and social development have yet been able to offer a detailed, step-by-step sequence of developmental accomplishments within the preoperational period. (In fact, Piaget's theory tentatively suggests that there may be no clear within-stage sequence that is invariant from child to child during the preoperational period.)

With all these difficulties, why do we bother with assessment? We bother with it because we *do* have goals for children, for ourselves, and for the classroom environment—however vaguely our goals may be formulated—and we want to make sure our efforts are bringing us closer to those goals. We want to know more than we can learn from simplistic measures of achievement or developmental progress (as determined by some arbitrary standard), more than we can learn from expressions of parental satisfaction, more than we can learn from our own feeling that the classroom is a productive, happy place. These things are important, but they tell us merely that something we're doing is right. We need to know more than that. We need to know specifics, so that we can make appropriate changes in accordance with the changing needs of children and so that we have some rational control over the effects of our behavior on the environment.

Incidentally, responsible parents, administrators, and funding agencies also refuse to accept vague statements of success in their demands for tangible evidence of the value of the program. To satisfy them as well as ourselves, we need both a direct description of the environment and an assessment of the effects the environment has had on children's development.

Fortunately, the important task of assessing programs is not as impossible as it may seem from the preceding comments. After all, we come to the assessment task with theoretical knowledge and a wide variety of abilities: we have a fairly good idea of what kind of social interactions we hope to see in the classroom (both among children and between children and adults); we have some idea of what to look for in assessing the physical environment (see Chapter 4); we have some understanding of developmental processes, so that we can look at the effect the physical and social environment has had on children's development (see Chapter

6); and, most importantly, we know that we have to look for optimal combinations of features rather than at simple lists. Our real problem is how best to apply our knowledge and skills to the assessment task.

## What Should We Assess

Although our theory has given us some special guidelines for deciding what and how to measure (Chapters 4 and 6), there are a number of theory-independent concerns that affect what we decide to measure. These concerns are not irrelevant to the theory; they are merely independent. That is, they arise no matter what theory guides the program. One of the most fundamental concerns is the issue of what we want the measurements for. What do we hope to gain from the information we gain? How will we apply the information? Specialists in program evaluation (for example, Suchman, 1967, and Scriven, 1967) have distinguished two basic types of evaluation according to the kinds of uses most likely to be made of the results. The kinds of evaluation are called *summative* and *formative*.

### Summative evaluation

Summative evaluation is an assessment of the overall effects of the program. Here the interest is in the intended (and unintended!) effects of the program as a whole. We want to know the conditions under which the effects arise (and for whom), as well as how long effects last and when they show up. For example, we might seek information about the overall effects of the program on the children's stages of cognitive development and/or their ways of approaching intellectual challenges. Or we might look at the indirect effects the program has had on the personal and social development of the children's siblings, on the group feeling among the parents of the children in the program, or even on community attitudes toward the needs of young children (as illustrated by the provision of high-quality community playgrounds and parks, for example). We might try to find out whether the effects of the program are lasting and whether there are any delayed effects of the program—effects that don't show up at all until well after the children have left the program (ease in learning long division, perhaps, or a special adeptness in handling science courses).

You may already be familiar with studies comparing the effects of different preschool programs, such as that by Miller and Dyer (1975). This is an example of summative evaluation. Such evaluation is rarely handled by the classroom teachers, thank goodness—there's more than enough to do without that! However, it is vital that teachers understand the general nature of summative evaluation and are aware of its problems and limitations. When funding agencies, parents, or administrators try to sell you a program by using impressive-sounding facts and figures on IQ gains or achievement-test scores, it is good to remember these three caveats: (1) Many such tests are not very reliable with young children (so that it's difficult to tell when children have shown what they are really capable of, when they're depending on mere intuitions—about which they'll change their minds momentarily—and when a poor performance is due to shyness, reluctance to cooperate, shifts of attention, or even the need for toileting). (2) The effects of a program may not be long-lived. (3) Impressive-sounding gains *may* have been purchased at the expense of deeper understandings (remember Piaget's warning about the detrimental effect premature verbal facility can have on the process of genuine understanding).

The point of the reservations just expressed is not that summative evaluation is worthless. On the contrary, such research makes a vital contribution to our growing understanding of children's learning and development. The point is that meaningful evaluation is extremely difficult and the science of program evaluation is still young. Each study has to be examined with care to see whether the kinds of effects *you* think are important were assessed, whether adequate controls were used, and what important possible outcomes were ignored. The need for you to take this kind of critical stance toward research results is part of the reason we asked you to go to all the trouble of listing your goals and expectations for children, back in Teacher Task 4-1. What you have learned of Piaget's theory so far and a thoughtful look at some of the *how's* of assessment discussed later in this chapter should give you some ways to critically examine studies.

*TEACHER TASK 9-1*

Suppose an evaluating team has sought your approval for a proposed assessment of the early-childhood program you work in (or of some program you have experience with). The plan, you are told, is to measure a variety of skills and abilities of children entering the program in the fall and to repeat the same measurements in the spring. Team members explain that children will be assessed individually on reading-readiness skills, mathematical knowledge, motor coordination, and social awareness.

Make a list of questions you would want answers to before you would give your consent. In making your list, remember to consider demands made on staff and parents as well as children, goals you have for the classroom (based on your understanding of Piagetian theory), different ways of obtaining the same information, and the intended uses of the evaluation results. (Don't be shy about writing down *all* your questions. For instance, the question, "If children don't show significant gains, will I be fired?" is perfectly legitimate!)

The list of questions you generate should help you focus on the parts of this chapter most relevent to your concerns. In addition, if you revise the list as you read, you will develop an intelligent and informed response to outside evaluation requests and a tool for deciding among several such requests, should they be made.

*Formative evaluation*

Because formative evaluation is the kind of most direct concern to teachers in the practice of their profession, it is the kind we'll be discussing in most of the rest of this chapter. Formative evaluation provides feedback to teachers about what they're doing and the effects they're having on children while the program is still in operation. Its purpose is to help one decide how to adjust the environment (including teacher behaviors) so as to better achieve the goals one has already set, or, sometimes, to show where new goals need to be set.

Although most discussions of formative evaluation focus on sequences of learned information and sequentially acquired abilities, this is hardly a necessary feature of good formative evaluation. True, before they were fully acquainted with the theory, many good Piagetian scholars (for example, Kamii, 1971) looked at formative evaluation in terms of sequential acquisitions, but it has become increasingly clear that such approaches are given the cold shoulder by Piagetian theory. If you take a minute to think back on the comments about the process of development (particularly in Chapter 2), you'll have no trouble sympathizing with the theory's point of view. The knowledge we're interested in doesn't come bit by bit. It comes with surges, regressions, brilliant intuitions, and hesitant reconsiderations. The kind of formative evaluation that will be most useful to those who've made friends with Piagetian theory will assess the classroom environment (both physical and social) and the kinds and amounts of thinking done by the children in it in terms of what Piaget's theory suggests is most conducive to optimal intellectual development.

Because there are few instruments available for assessing what we want to assess, teachers must rely largely on their own hard thinking to find ways to evaluate the results of their efforts. Most of the rest of this chapter is designed to help you develop your own ways to assess what you're doing. We'll be looking at ways to assess the classroom environment both when children are present and when they're not, and we'll delve into some problems and techniques involved in assessing the effects of the environment on the people in it.

## How Should We Assess?
## Some Preliminary Cautions

In any attempt to assess our own situation or to help ourselves grow as teachers by changing the way we do things, it is important to be aware of some general problems of assessment. We'll look at five important problems that plague everyone doing evaluation, no matter how sophisticated they've become. Only constant vigilance can save us from making the five mistakes discussed next.

*Mistake 1: letting preconceived notions*
*blind us to important facts*

We've already discussed the fact that certain uses of theory can blind us to what is really going on in our classrooms or to how a child thinks and feels (see Chapter 1). Subjective impressions of children, being so heavily influenced by our own attitudes and experiences, are considered particularly vulnerable to the blindness. Prejudices enter as we unconsciously make use of our notions of how children should behave, our own childhood experiences with what is considered "nice" and what isn't, our values about people of all ages, and our beliefs about what child behaviors lead to what adult personalities and habits. One and the same behavior, spitting into the drinking fountain, say, may be regarded as the precursor of a disgusting habit, as a childish expression of emotion, as a flagrant violation of unspoken rules, or as a brilliant piece of experimentation—depending on who's observing the behavior, why the observation is being made, and what other observations have been made of the same child. This variation in descriptions of behavior is not necessarily bad. Our special interests *should* influence what behaviors we look at and how we interpret them—that's how we put our theory to work—but they should not preclude our noticing other details or listening to observers with other views.

The task of freeing ourselves from the influence of unwanted biases is extremely difficult and is certainly not alleviated by the fact that our skepticism toward the recommendations of so-called impartial observers is frequently justified. We need to assess the way things are in terms of the way we, guided by our thoughtful conversations with our theory, want them to be. A comment such as, "You have too many blocks!" either tells us what we already know (we are perfectly capable of counting the number of blocks we have available) or is a judgment relative to some theory (too many blocks for what? relative to what?). Is the number of blocks we have at all important to our judgments of the classroom environment in terms of goals and values influenced by Piagetian theory? Maybe the proportion of space or time devoted to block activities is more important. Or maybe we should look instead at how teachers and children interact in block play. We cannot prevent our wants from biasing our perception of the way things are by pretending our wants don't exist. What we need are ways to be objective once we've let our theory help us (a) determine what our wants are and (b) identify features of the environment it would be most profitable to look at.

Discussions of informal assessment in the form of teacher discussions, notes jotted down during the school day, or journals kept on a daily or weekly basis, tend to emphasize the danger of bias in subjective evaluations and to urge careful attention to the distinction between observation and inference. We agree that subjective evaluations are vulnerable. But so are the seemingly sophisticated observation scales and standardized tests. We can't avoid the danger of prejudiced reports merely by using commercially available scales and tests. Indeed, an overdependence on such tools can lead one right into the next two mistakes.

*Mistake 2: making judgments based
on instruments (tests or observation
procedures) that are unreliable
or invalid*

An *unreliable measure* is one that does not give an accurate measurement of whatever it is designed to measure. The shimmering look of the highway on a hot day, for example, is not a reliable measure of whether or not there's water on the road ahead. Many carefully constructed tests designed to measure intellectual capacities fail to provide reliable measures when they are used with young children. If you've worked with preschoolers, you are well aware of some of the reasons for this unreliability—frequent shifts of attention, for example, or lack of concern about showing what one can do on such tests.

An *invalid measure* can be generally characterized as one that fails to measure the trait, ability, or skill that it purports to measure. We may think we're measuring a child's level of understanding of some physical phenomenon, for instance, when in fact all we have is a measure of that child's knowledge of certain English expressions. (This was part of the point made in Chapter 7 about the experiment of blowing up a balloon under a book and teaching about air pressure.) John Holt (1969), vigorously speaking out against the misuse of testing in schools, has pointed out that what many tests actually test is children's ability and willingness to play the game of finding out what the tester wants, discovering the "trick" questions, and engaging in a personal duel with the tester. Where this happens, the test gives an invalid measure, regardless of whether or not the test has the potential for assessing what it was designed to assess.

In choosing and developing whatever tests, observation procedures, or interview techniques we'll use in assessing the progress of ourselves and the children we teach, we'll want to take great pains to make our procedures and instruments reliable and valid, both potentially and as used in practice.


*Mistake 3: neglecting important variables
because there is no quick and easy way
to measure them*

Anyone who's been at all sympathetic to the views presented in the previous eight chapters is already on the lookout for this kind of mistake. Just to further sensitize you, here are some tips for avoiding the slippery slide into one or more versions of this mistake:

(a) If you think something is important to keep track of, it probably is. Resist the temptation to rationalize away its importance.

(b) If you think certain observations should be made, interviews given, or tests administered, make arrangements to do them right away. It is all too easy to plan to take care of such things next week or next month—neither of which seems ever to come in the ordinary course of events (or else it comes too late, when what you wanted assessed is no longer there to be assessed).

(c) When observations need to be made, take the time and effort to do them, even when you think a better job could be done if only you had extra help, more time, a more sophisticated technique, or whatever.

(d) Do your utmost to be intellectually honest about the objectivity of your measures, the care with which observations are made or measurements taken, and the interpretation of the information you've gathered. Hastily made measurements can often provide useful information (though one wouldn't put as much faith in them as in those carefully done). Information from a variety of sources can help you decide how accurate your information is. If you see some interesting results based on some fairly rough-and-ready procedures, you can use other, more re-fined, procedures to test out the insights so gained. Keep the initial results, but make a note of whatever qualifications need to be made, and then supplement the findings with other procedures (later observations, parents' comments, interviews, and so forth).

(e) Take the time and mental energy to develop clinical interviewing proce-dures, to devise ingenious observation schemes, and to share information and ideas with other staff members, parents, and any other people who work with your chil-dren or your classroom.

### Mistake 4: misusing numerically organized information

Suppose you have devoted much of your theory-inspired planning to activi-ties in the block area, but you wonder whether you are unconsciously discriminat-ing against the girls in your classroom. Sex-role stereotypes may be keeping girls away from the block area. If so, you will want to concentrate either on changing their attitudes or on more conscientious planning for the activities they accept as appropriate. A visitor in the classroom has graciously offered to observe the block area this morning. According to the observation report, there were six boys and three girls who made use of the area. Do these data tell you anything about the adoption of sex-role behaviors in your classroom? Clearly, more information is required before you can make a judgment.

First, there is the problem of what the observed numbers should be compared to. If your class has fifteen boys and only seven girls, then approximately equal *proportions* of its girls and of its boys were in the block area (slightly fewer than half in each case). Here, the larger *number* of boys in the area is not a valid measure of differences in behavior due to adoption of sex roles.

A related problem involves the reliability of a one-day observation period. If the relative proportion of boys to girls had been reversed on the previous day (assuming, now, equal numbers of boys and girls in the class), this morning's count is not a reliable indicator of sex-role adoption.

Issues of validity and reliability—in the foregoing cases, of what should be counted, how many times to observe, and how long each observation should be—are thorny ones. To make decisions about these matters, it is helpful to spend some time playing devil's advocate. Temporarily set aside your own preferred hypothesis, and badger your brain until you have a long list of alternative explanations for the observed results. For example, perhaps there is a group of girls who would have dominated the block area if their ringleader hadn't taken up with such dedication her recent interest in the new twenty-five-piece puzzle. The fact that the boys in your classroom dominated the block area this morning may not have had anything to do with the adoption of sex-role stereotypes. And, then again, it just may have. The point is that the discovery of a correlation does not tell you the cause of the correlation.

After playing devil's advocate, switch back into your own perspective. Examine the list of possible explanations and eliminate those you already have evidence against. Those that remain will warrant further testing. They can be a great help in guiding subsequent observations. You may still have a good way to go before being satisfied that you've found the right answer, but you've eliminated some alternative explanations and you can now focus your observations on testing specific explanations.

If you've followed the suggestions thus far and are still undecided about how much faith to put in your answer, and if you think the question you're asking is a very important one, worth the time it will take you to follow up on getting an answer, it is wise to turn to experts in evaluation and assessment. There is much more to be said on the use and misuse of numbers and statistics than can be said in a book such as this one, and unless you're seriously interested in research, you won't want to spend the months it would take to get familiar with the ins and outs of experimental design and data analysis. The references given at various places in this chapter can point you in some profitable directions, but they only tap the surface of a huge field of study.

*Mistake 5: letting evaluation concerns
dominate the classroom environment
(letting the tail wag the dog)*

To avoid this mistake, temper the foregoing admonitions, about the importance of taking the time and effort to evaluate, with a healthy perspective on why the children are in your classroom in the first place and what your goals are. The evaluation you encourage should be *relevant to your goals* and should not interfere unduly with the attainment of those goals. High-pressure testing procedures, for example, even if they are valid and reliable measures of some ability you aim to enhance, may undermine the goal of having a noncompetitive classroom atmosphere. Some other way to measure the ability should be sought.

In general, you can expect there to be many more things you'd like to assess than can possibly be assessed. In choosing what and how to assess, you'll have to consider the temperaments of your fellow staff members, your own interests, the requests of parents, and advice from Piaget's theory—all these in addition to the amounts of available time, energy, money, and know-how. Because these factors vary in importance from one situation to another, we can give no easy guidelines for your decision making. The main thing is to *get started!* Develop some habits of observation and inference, of hypothesis generation and testing, of jotting down notes and looking at them later, of summarizing and commenting on your own teaching behaviors. Decisions about exactly what and how to evaluate can be revised as you go.

**TEACHER TASK 9-2**

Here are some questions to ponder:

(1) Suppose you want to know whether Paula has the notion of one-to-one correspondence. Which of the following procedures is likely to give the most *reliable* information? Why?

    (a) parents' anecdotes about Paula's ability to count

    (b) video tapes of Paula's play with blocks and toy animals

    (c) conversations with Paula in the block corner about numbers of blocks

    (d) having Paula count her fingers, your fingers, her toes, and so on

(2) What, if anything, could be done to improve the reliability of each of these procedures?

(3) To what extent does a child's expertise in writing her own name provide a *valid* measure of her understanding of the between-ness relation?

The bulk of this chapter is intended to provide you with a variety of ideas about formative evaluation. You won't be able to make use of all the ideas—at least not right away. Our purpose is to give you a sample of techniques to choose from. Starting from what interests you, what is most feasible, or from whatever a chance page opening dictates, you can apply our suggestions and then go on to exercise your own ingenuity in refining, elaborating, and developing new ideas for use in your own situation.

## CHARACTERIZING THE CLASSROOM ENVIRONMENT

There are important features of the classroom environment that can only be adequately assessed when children are present. In this group are such features as the quality of child-child interactions, the quality of teacher-child interactions, and the amount of crowding in a particular area of the room. There are other features that can be examined when children are not present. Such features can be noted, recorded, and evaluated in terms of their potentials for enhancing the goals you've set. Among these features are the number and arrangement of private spaces, the quality and quantity of art materials, and the amount of challenging climbing equipment. Examining both kinds of features will help you determine whether the classroom you're assessing is what you want it to be.

As in any kind of description, your record of the classroom environment will be selective. Your own interests, augmented by your acquaintance with Piagetian theory, will focus your attention on some features to the exclusion of others. Some of the features you notice, you will have the time and inclination to record. Others will be briefly noted and then forgotten. How do you make sure that important features get noticed and that the records you make will be useful? This is an important and interesting question, and one to keep constantly in mind regardless of how long one has been concerned with evaluation.

Before we call upon the theory (you knew that was coming!), there are two rather obvious, but often ignored, principles we should pay attention to. First, it is a great help to have done some thinking in advance about what you want to know, what kinds of evidence to look for, and when to do the looking. Second, decisions about recording should be made in advance. For example, if you plan to make lists or use charts, set them up before you go into the classroom. Then all you have to do is to fill in the blanks. Because the kinds of information you can get and the time constraints on recording information differ markedly according to whether or not children are present in the classroom, we'll look at the application of the two principles just mentioned in two different ways: first, in evaluating the classroom when children are *absent*; second, when children are *present*.

### Evaluating the Classroom Environment
### When Children are Absent

Although the environment must be evaluated in terms of the way children and adults interact in it and with it, useful observations can be made when children are not present. One can evaluate the selection and arrangement of materials, the arrangement of space, the quality of the lesson plans, and, in staff discussions after children leave, the use children made of space and materials. Insofar as you are guided by Piaget's theory, you'll be looking for evidence that the classroom exemplifies the four key words discussed in Chapter 4. The key words, you remember, were activity, change, intellectual honesty, and diversity.

*TEACHER TASK 9-3*

(1)  Go over the charts at the end of Chapter 4. Make your own list of things to look for when children are *not* present. Make another list of things that can be observed only when children are present.

(2) Now sort through your lists and from each one pick three or four features that are of most interest to you with respect to the classroom you work in (or the classroom you have access to).

(3) Spend one week keeping records of those features. During the week, make notes to yourself about the record-keeping problems you confront and about problems you foresee.

(4) At the end of your week of record keeping, take an hour or two to think seriously about these two questions: What did you learn about the classroom and/or the people in it? How can you constructively use what you've learned?

There are two important times for assessing the classroom environment without children in it. First: before children arrive each day, or at the beginning of each week (whenever you make major changes in plans or materials), you can assess the potentials of the environment you have prepared. The amount and quality of materials available, the lesson plans you have thought through, and your own readiness to lead (or follow) activities through a variety of on-the-spot modifications are all important indicators of the potential benefits of the environment. Second: after children leave, you can evaluate in a very general way which potentials were realized—and to what extent. Again, this can be done on a daily or weekly basis.

### Before children arrive
### —a classroom once-over

One of the first tasks before children arrive each day is to get down on your hands and knees and check out the room and the outdoor play area from a child's point of view. This is vital; what is accessible and inviting from the perspective of a human being over five feet tall may not be so for someone only three feet high. Test the view from different areas of the classroom. Can you see other activities? Do you have enough room to work? to invite a friend to join you? Is there a place in the room where you could go to be by yourself and still be able to peek out to see what is going on? Does the road-building setup in the block area invite thoughts about spatial continuity? Can you reach materials you might need for artwork, for building roads, for taking an imaginary trip across the ocean?

As you go through the final countdown before children enter the classroom, keep the charts from Chapter 4 in mind. The central column on each chart indicates features of the physical environment that are worth your attention. Those charts give you clues about the *kinds* of features to look for—adequate supplies, plenty of space, systematic storage of materials, and so on—and they give you some indication of the *purposes* for having those kinds of features. What they don't tell you is how to know when the features are adequately represented in your classroom.

In some cases, your on-the-spot judgment will give you the answer. If you sit on the floor so that your head is child-height, and mentally picture the children going through the daily activities, and if you make your mental picture vivid enough to include the personalities of the children, you are in a good position to judge how adequate the arrangement of materials and furniture is.

For judgments about other features that affect your classroom environment, a more systematic, preplanned examination is called for. This involves the use of detailed lesson plans, making lists and charts, setting up observation schedules, and making careful records of the changes in the environment over time. This kind of examination can be done whenever time permits: after children leave, before they arrive, on teacher workdays, or (if your situation permits it) during nap times. Before we grapple with the problems and potentials involved in such types of examination, however, there's one more task to be done in those few moments before children arrive each day.

While you're taking stock of the environment, set aside a moment to take a critical look with your own needs in mind. To conscientiously apply Piaget's theory, you'll need some thinking space yourself. Sit down in areas of the classroom where you think you'll be needed, and then look around. Can you see other areas of the classroom where children are likely to be working? If you can't, you will probably want to rearrange some furniture—or at least make a mental note to let other staff know when you're in that area so that they'll be keeping an eye on the areas hidden from your view. Four other questions to ask yourself are: (1) Do you know where materials are for possible expansion of activities, and can you get to them easily? (2) Do you have note pads available in different parts of the room (or in your pocket), so that you can jot down observations and questions? (3) Do you know where other staff members plan to be in the room and what kinds of activities they're going to be responsible for? (4) Can you see suggestions for inter-action strategies you've posted in various activity areas?

If you're satisfied for the present with your countdown procedures, you are ready to tackle a more thorough analysis of the classroom environment. A thorough analysis can be undertaken at a variety of times, depending on your class schedule and your preferences for early rising, fast getaways after children leave, or off-hour visits to the classroom. For convenience, we'll divide this kind of analysis into two rough, and overlapping, groups, according to whether it is focused on what potentials there are in the environment or on what potentials were actually exploited by the people in the classroom. First, we'll look at what potentials there are in the environment as a before-children-arrive kind of evaluation. The second group will be taken up in the discussion of evaluation after children leave. In both cases, a major concern will be how to deal with the wealth of information available.

### Before children arrive
### —a careful analysis

What does a Piagetian classroom look like before children arrive? We know that it should have potentials for intellectual challenges in the areas of classification, seriation, number, spatial relations, temporal relations, and conservation. And we know it should contain the kinds of materials that promote the active construction of knowledge. This suggests that we ought to look for arrangements that suggest intriguing questions in the areas of logico-mathematical and infra-logical knowledge. We also ought to look for materials that promote intellectual honesty and the kinds of activity our theory suggests will lead to intellectual growth. Let's look first at some ways to analyze the potentials for active construction of knowledge. Then we'll turn to the particular areas of knowledge.

From Chapter 4, we know that active construction of knowledge is promoted by materials with multiple solutions, materials that suggest cooperative play, and materials that can be used without a teacher's constant demonstration. Materials that promote an atmosphere of intellectual honesty include self-correcting materials and materials with tolerance for error (the latter including such items as unbreakable toys, easily alterable equipment, and nontoxic equipment). You can get a rough estimate of how conducive your classroom environment is to active construction of knowledge by looking at the kinds of materials available. Look back at the charts in Chapter 4 to generate categories of materials to notice. Then go through your classroom and generate lists like that in Sample 9-1.

Once you've set up your lists, you can look for proportions of various types of materials available each day. One easy way to keep track is to use one piece of paper for each day (or week), with the categories listed at the top. Then simply list each of the materials available on that day according to which category (or categories) it fits. Your list would look something like Sample 9-2.

**SAMPLE 9-1  Materials and Their Potentials**

| MATERIALS THAT SUGGEST MULTIPLE SOLUTIONS | MATERIALS THAT SUGGEST ONE RIGHT ANSWER |
|---|---|
| boxes of miscellaneous materials (such as prisms, magnifying glasses, kaleidoscopes) for children's explorations | A set of materials for use by the teacher in demonstrating specific properties of light |
| Blocks, Tinker Toys, Lincoln Logs | Form puzzles, stacking towers |
| Easels, paints, clay, finger paint | Coloring books, step-by-step art activities |
| Blocks and amorphous forms in housekeeping area | Only special dishes and furniture in doll corner |
| Battery boards for experimentation | Mechanical toys (for example, pull a string to make it talk) |
| Records with suggestions for improvisation, a variety of music forms | Records with specific instructions (for instance, calisthenics) |
| Moveable large-motor equipment (for instance, planks, boxes, ladders, ropes, A-frames, tires) | Permanent equipment (for example, swing set, slide—especially in conjunction with the absence of other types) |
| Stories with no answer, a wide variety of books | Books with a definite message about the acceptable way, all books having similar conclusions |
| Materials out at children's level | Materials up on teacher's shelves |

SAMPLE 9-2  Types of Materials Available to Children (Arranged by Category)

| ENCOURAGES MULTIPLE SOLUTIONS | SUGGESTS ONE RIGHT ANSWER | REQUIRES OR SUGGESTS USE WITH MORE THAN ONE CHILD | GENERALLY EXPECTED TO BE DONE ALONE | REQUIRES TEACHER HELP | SELF-CORRECTING |
|---|---|---|---|---|---|
| Unit blocks | | Unit blocks | | | Unit blocks |
| Woodworking | Wooden puzzles | | Woodworking | Woodworking | Wooden puzzles |
| | | | Wooden puzzles | | |
| Dramatic play —fire-fighter hats, hoses, and so on | | Dramatic play | | Dramatic play (my kids still need lots of help with disputes, and this is a particularly volatile area for them) | |
| Art area— colored chalk on wet paper | Alphabet Lotto | | Art area | Art area | Alphabet Lotto |
| | | | Alphabet Lotto (my kids seem to use it as a puzzle —not yet ready to make a game of it) | | |

Don't forget that the outdoor space you have is an important part of your classroom. You might want to keep separate lists for indoor and outdoor activities. This will enable you to see clearly how well your use of outdoor space contributes to your goals for the total school environment.

When you have generated a list accommodating the goals suggested by the theory as well as those of particular concern to people with an interest in your program (administrators, parents, licensing personnel, funding-agency representatives, and the like) and you have faithfully categorized the available equipment according to your best judgment as to how it will be used by the particular children you have in your classroom each week, you will want to see the pattern in what you've been doing. After you've collected four or five weeks' worth of charts, try counting the number of entries under each column for each week. A chart with the categories listed at the top and the weeks listed along the side can then be filled in with the numbers you get. If you're up to the task, graphing the changes will bring them more dramatically into focus.

Now you're ready to ask yourself some questions. Which columns (or graphs) show an increase over time, which ones show a decrease, and which ones remain constant? Does the change (or lack of it) fit with what you know about development—based, of course, on Piaget's theory? If you're dissatisfied with what you see, you might want to devote more time to conscious planning of the physical environment. If you like what you see, you might record a few sentences explaining the rationale behind the pattern. This is helpful for later assessments of the year's progress and for explaining your program to interested parties.

A few quick sketches of how materials were arranged wouldn't hurt either. Once you've mapped out a basic organization of the classroom, all you'll need to do will be to indicate innovations as they occur. These records can be invaluable in later attempts to analyze why activities went the way they did—important information to have if we want to use past experience in preparing better environments. If you haven't made room diagrams before and want a few examples to stimulate your own ingenuity, either of the following two sources would be worth consulting.

KRITCHEVSKY, SYBIL, and ELIZABETH PRESCOTT, with LEE WALLING. *Planning Environments for Young Children* (Washington, D.C.: National Association for the Education of Young Children, 1969).
SARGENT, BETSYE. *The Integrated Day In An American School* (Boston: National Association of Independent Schools, 1970), pp. 4–9.

For help in maintaining the ties between your record keeping and the theory, try arranging the information you gather so that it reveals the way your classroom exhibits the four key aspects of an optimal environment for development—activity, intellectual honesty, diversity, and change. The use of the charts from Chapter 4 will help you combine the categories you've set up into those that enhance an atmosphere of intellectual honesty, for example, and categories that are either neutral or negative with respect to intellectual honesty. A similar procedure can be used for those that promote activity. You can get a measure of diversity by checking for entries under each of your original categories. If you have several categories that are not represented on a particular day (or during a particular week), you may not be providing enough diversity. The importance of providing diversity, remember, is to meet the different needs of the many individuals in the classroom at any given time. To the extent that it is possible, we want to make opportunities available to each individual whenever he or she is ready for them. Various kinds of change can be assessed by comparing the numbers of items—and the *kinds* of items —under each category from week to week.

*TEACHER TASK 9-4*

(1) First make a list of the materials that are presently available to children in the classroom where you work. Now sort your list into two categories: materials you think are most enjoyable and hold the most potential for solitary play (or one-to-one interaction between a teacher and a child) and those whose potentials are best realized in cooperative play. Finally, draw a diagram of the classroom and indicate where the materials are.

(2) Pick several of the materials as focal points for observation over the next week. Record how frequently each material is used by one child alone and how frequently it is used by two or more. If you or other staff members have made special efforts to get children to work together on particular activities, make a note of it.

(3) Now you're ready to make use of the information you've gathered. Sit down with your lists from (1), your frequency counts from (2), and, if possible, your coworkers. Ask yourself whether you have an optimum balance between solitary and cooperative play. If you do, sketch out a plan for maintaining the balance. (Remember, change will be required to maintain balance: children will lose interest in particular materials, solitary investigative play may develop into cooperative ventures, and so forth.) If you feel you do not have an optimum balance, consider changes in (a) the materials available (were your hypotheses correct about which materials had which potentials?), (b) the arrangement of materials (it may be only the lack of space that makes an activity a solitary one), or (c) the kinds of interactions teachers are using (suggestions such as, "Find a friend to work with you on the Lotto game" can do wonders).

(4) Use the thinking and fact-gathering you've done to make your classroom be what you want it to be.

If the procedures discussed so far seem to you to be missing a lot of important information, you're right. One way to augment them without yet turning to assessment techniques for use after children leave each day is to examine your lesson plans. The teacher's behavior, after all, is a major force influencing how materials are used. What a teacher does can change solitary play materials into group activities and one-answer games into multiple-solution challenges.

Although we do not always carry through with our intentions, what we do or do not plan to do affects what we actually accomplish. If we make careful lesson plans and make a conscientious effort to meet the goals we set for ourselves, then our lesson plans can be a useful indication of the kind of environment we have created. We must not let ourselves get carried away with this kind of assessment, however. As every teacher knows all too well, there is no guarantee that what is in one's lesson plans will occur in the classroom, nor that what is left out of lesson plans will not occur. With this caution in mind, we can take another look at the detailed lesson plans we discussed in Chapter 8. Such plans can help us to evaluate the environment we provide as well as help us to create that environment. In the lesson plans that have accumulated over a period of several weeks, we will want to look for the following kinds of things.

(1)  Evidence that the theory has been put to work throughout the classroom—activities planned with a *variety of methods* (peer demonstrations, free exploration, stories told with objects, teacher questions, and the like) and a *variety of materials* (to be smelled, touched, tasted, seen, and heard) for *each* area of knowledge.

(2)  Evidence that children with a preference for a particular kind of activity will get a variety of intellectual challenges—use of the *same materials* for a *variety* of goals and activity plans.

(3)  Preparation for a variety of goals and different kinds of responses—alternative materials listed, questions and explanations thought out, provision for a variety of developmental levels.

(4)  A rough sequence of goals in each area of knowledge throughout the year (for instance, emphasis on conservation of substance comes after predictions of "how much"). Chapter 6 gives guidance here.

(5)  Careful plans for free-play time as well as for special activities.

(6)  Provision for lots of physical and mental activity on the child's part rather than an emphasis on teacher demonstration.

(7)  Explicit provision for peer interaction with either teacher verbalizations to help children focus on peers or with activities that require two or more children.

(8)  Activities with multiple solutions.

(9)  Provision for choices in activities—for instance, choices of which kind of juice to have, choices of whether or not to visit a new place.

It is important to add to this kind of assessment some way to monitor the provisions made for children's invention and application of understandings of spatio-temporal relationships, number, classification, and seriation. Although this task can be approached by assessing arrangements of materials (rather than their mere presence or absence) and judging the cognitive demands implied, it is more naturally approached through actual and/or intended teacher behaviors. If you have followed the suggestions in Chapters 7 and 8 and have recorded in your lesson plans potentials for practice and challenge in these logico-mathematical areas of knowledge, it will be easy to count up the number of opportunities you hoped to provide in each area. If you find that 70 percent of your activities are dominantly concerned with classification, 62 percent involve potentials for increasing number understandings, but only 2 percent have potentials for augmenting children's understandings of spatio-temporal relationships, you will want to look again at Chapters 6 and 8 and to rack your brain for ideas on ways to fill in the gap. (Don't worry if your percentages don't add up to 100. They won't. This is because many of your activities make valuable contributions to several areas simultaneously.)

We've discussed a number of kinds of record keeping, not all of which you'll have the time to do. But even if it were possible to do them all, crucial information would still be missing. What's lacking is an account of how our plans and carefully prepared environment fare under the challenges of the day. For this information, we need to do some evaluation after children leave.

### After children leave—
### a classroom once-over

There are two sources of information that are most profitably exploited immediately after children leave each day. One is the physical condition of the classroom. In using this source, we feign ignorance and pretend to come to the scene as naive as a group of Martians just landed in the school yard. In using the second source, our own memories and notes, we do just the opposite. We piece together everything we can from our own experience as part of the activity in the classroom.

Let's take a closer look at the first source. To get an indirect measure of what materials have been used and how they've been used, you might dispense with clean-up time one day each week. Then, after children leave, you can record such information as which materials are off the shelves, suggesting that they have been used; which materials are out in ways suggesting that several children have used them at one time; or which materials have been moved away from their usual storage areas and into other activity areas, suggesting that children have integrated different areas of the classroom or have found an arrangement of materials more suitable to their needs than the one you had originally set up. Pictures made by children and written observations left by teachers are also fair game in using this source of information.

The method just suggested is the kind preferred by many experimentalists who distrust the subjectivity they see in clinical assessments. You will undoubtedly want to add to the descriptions of the classroom your own professional judgment about how materials were likely to have been used—for what purpose and at what developmental levels. In this procedure, it will add to the objectivity of your characterizations if you imagine yourself more as an outside professional called in to examine the evidence than as a naive stranger. If you are part of a teaching team, each member of which spent time in different areas of the classroom, no pretending is needed. You can each examine the areas handled by other teachers. It is an eye-opener to compare the assessment made by the noninvolved teacher to that made by the teacher who worked in the area. (If there is an explicit disagreement about what went on, whose description would you believe? Why?)

The kind of information we've been discussing will only be useful to you as formative evaluation, of course, if you use it to help form your program. The next Teacher Task is designed to help you start thinking about how to make good use of this type of information.

*TEACHER TASK 9-5*

For the last four weeks, teachers in a preschool classroom have been keeping records of the condition of the classroom just after children leave each day. Early in the observation period, the block area seems to have been largely untouched, but for seven of the last ten days, it has been what one teacher describes as a "disaster area"—blocks piled here and there, small blocks strewn about the room or just tossed into the shelves, and so on.

When the teachers sit down to discuss their observations, they conclude that (1) children are showing more interest in the block area than before but that (2) little constructive play is occurring (this is corroborated by anecdotal evidence collected while children were present) and that (3) cleaning up the block area is a hassle. Teachers resent the chore and children avoid it. Because of (1), removing the blocks is not an option. Instead, some way must be found to meet both of the goals: to increase the amount of constructive play and to make clean-up easier. Discuss with one or more colleagues how you would go about trying to meet these goals. Think about

(a) observations that would be helpful in better understanding the problem and/or in monitoring progress toward resolving it.

(b) the arrangement of blocks within the block area. (For instance, is there enough room for storage? Is it clear where each block goes? Are blocks of different sizes and shapes easily recognizable on the shelves?)

(c) the relation of the block area to the rest of the classroom activities and traffic patterns.

(d) the kinds of rules that might help meet both goals simultaneously (for example, rules concerning who picks up what and when, or rules about how many children play in the block area and when).

(e) specific activity plans for the block area and the appropriate arrangement of materials. (The section on learning potentials in blocks in Chapter 7 may be helpful.)

The second source of information to be obtained right after children leave the classroom is your own observations, whether stored on organized charts, on odd scraps of paper, or in your memories of what happened when, why, where, how, and with whom. You can keep this information from slipping away from you by making use of it in staff discussions each day and by organizing it in written form for future consultation.

If you are lucky enough to work with other staff members and to have a few moments to discuss the day with them right after children leave, sharing anecdotes and impressions of the day can have a considerable impact on your program. If you observed David making tickets for his "train" in the block area but didn't get a chance to notice what he did with them, bring up the incident. Maybe someone else saw the distribution, and together your observations can reveal David's complex representational and numerical understandings. Or maybe you're planning a sorting activity using a "junk" tray (see Kamii, 1973) and want some clues about Saul and Melissa's use and understanding of classification schemes. Ask other teachers if anyone noticed what they did with the flannel board figures when they tired of retelling the story of Goldilocks. The results of sharing ideas and observations can go immediately to work in your plans for future activities. These results can also give you a guide for what kinds of observations to make. If no one saw the end of David's ticket making, you might try to find time tomorrow to talk to him about it—to probe his number understandings by asking about what he did, and might do; about the consequences of having distributed them one way rather than another; and so forth.

Staff discussions are good times for brainstorming, too. If you've had a rough day and can't figure out what went wrong, others can help you think of possible explanations and ways to avoid a repeat. If the day has been terrific, the group can make suggestions for keeping things on the upswing. And don't forget the value of a group for helping you generate helpful questions for getting information from some other good sources—parents or student observers, for instance. Daily staff discussions can have immediate and favorable effects on room arrangements, teaching tactics, activity plans, and observation priorities—all of which can be modified before children walk through the classroom door the next time.

Some effects take longer to produce (and to notice) than others. Long-term effects may be missed in daily discussions, but they usually make an appearance where written records are kept. Although much of what ought to be recorded takes careful analysis and can be put off until later in the day, it is a great aid to make a few notes right away. To be sure you find time to make some written records that will still make sense to you weeks later when you need them, you might make it a habit to write brief comments on each lesson plan, on a diagram of the classroom arrangement for the week, and/or on memos about teaching duties and responsibilities of the different members of your team. These plans and diagrams are likely to be near at hand and are also likely to be looked at later in the year when you're doing a bit of long-range evaluation and planning.

You already have a good idea of what kinds of quick notes to take (or you will, if you take a moment to hink about it), but just as a reminder, don't forget to include general comments about (a) how many children participated and why, (b) the level of interest, (c) the kind of social interactions promoted by the activity, (d) variations and augmentations you *did* use or *could* use some other time to either improve the activity or extend it, (e) your impressions about the cognitive challenges made by the activity for the particular children involved, and, finally, (f) any surprises. It has been our experience that general comments of this sort often overlook particular achievements and difficulties of individual children. A general reaction to a small-group activity, for example, might be, "They liked the activity and found it fairly easy." The problem is, who are "they"? Did every single child involved find it fairly easy? Or was it only three of the four? Or was it only a talkative twosome, the pair who usually makes the greatest impression? To zero in on exactly who did what, you'll want to rely on a more careful and time-consuming assessment.

### After children leave
### —a careful analysis

One of the most common aids to reflection on the day's activities is the keeping of a journal. Although few teachers we know can manage to write in their journals every single day, daily entries are something to aim for. No matter how brief the entry, if it's in writing, it is preserved for future pondering. Furthermore, the pressure to write something stimulates at least a minimal evaluation of the day. One has, if nothing else, the task of deciding what is worth recording.

There are many different ways to organize a journal. A journal organized simply by date tends to be most useful for insights into yourself as a teacher. To make the journal more of an integral part of planning and evaluation, try organizing it by children rather than by date. Leave a section for each child, with room for anecdotes as well as for the results of testing procedures, scheduled observations, health information, and so on. Then date the entries as you make them. Your sections on Oscar, for example, might have a description of a number activity, dated September 23; a discussion of a dispute he had with Vinh, dated October 1; a transcript of his comments on an elaborate drawing, dated October 2; and a blow-by-blow account of his triumph over the twenty-four-piece puzzle, dated October 12. Scraps of paper with observations made during class time (by you or other staff members), various drawings of his, some notes to yourself about a clinical interview you're planning to conduct, and a parent-information sheet may all be part of the section for Oscar.

Another way to arrange your journal is by kinds of activities or areas of the room. Include sections for the art area, the blocks, the science center, the book corner, the dress-up area—whatever the areas are in your classroom. A journal of this sort can be extremely helpful in making decisions about the physical environment, especially if you're careful to record information such as how many children were in the area (and who they were); what kinds of use they made of the area; how much integration there was between this area and others; the effects of changes you've made in the area; the effects of teacher presence and activity in the area; and ideas for later arrangements, adjustments of materials available, teacher interactions, and so on. As in a journal arranged so as to highlight the progress made by individual children, you won't have an entry for each section each day. You might concentrate on the block area for a week and then switch to the art area. Or maybe you want information on the block area every week. In that case, make sure there's at least one entry under "Blocks" each week. You needn't make your entry on the same day of each week, though it might help you remember to get the entries you need.

A third way to organize your journal—and a very helpful way if you're trying to further your acquaintance with the theory—is to use sections for the areas of knowledge discussed in Chapter 6. This arrangement will pose a real challenge for decisions about where to record various observations and anecdotes, but the time you spend analyzing the episodes to determine whether they reveal more about classification abilities than they do about seriation will serve you well. You'll be doing some deep thinking about what the children were doing and what you've learned about their developmental levels. There's bound to be considerable overlap in the categories appropriate for a given activity anyway, so a few misplaced descriptions won't hurt. One way to choose a section when several seem appropriate is to base your choice on the ideas you've gotten from the episode. If it inspired thoughts about other classification activities, put it under "Classification"—and jot down those other ideas too! As with the other kinds of journal organization, date each entry. If you include answers to "Who?," "Where?," and "With what materials?" in your descriptions of episodes, this kind of journal will give you much of the information provided by the second kind we've described.

As you can see, there are a variety of helpful ways to organize a journal. The organization you use depends on your interests and what you feel most comfortable with. You may use one kind of organization for a month or two and then switch. It may even be manageable for you to keep two kinds simultaneously. However you arrange topics, keep in mind that we're still talking about recording after the fact. A journal is a record of what you can *remember*—with the help, perhaps, of some hastily scrawled observations and the comments made in staff discussions. If some kind of organization jogs your memory better than others, use that one.

One more word about journal entries, and then you can concentrate on the Teacher Task you know is bound to come. Human memory being what it is, you're sure to have reservations about such things as whether Sheila was actually involved in the building of the "boat" as well as in the "riding," or whether Kim had initiated the comments about relative weights of paint in different jars or just responded to Mrs. Trien's prompting. That's all right. Qualify your descriptions where you are uncertain. Use question marks, or phrases such as, "I think Sheila also helped build the boat. If so, she took part in an elaborate planning scheme involving the assignment of duties, disputes and resolutions concerning appropriate materials, and the making of 'blueprints' (see attached observation notes taken by Collin)." Having written such a description, you can ask Collin, when you next see him (or others who may have been watching) if they remember Sheila's being there. The journal is a record for *you* to use in maintaining the kind of environment you want. It needn't be carefully edited for possible exposure to the public eye. Okay, dig into Teacher Task 9-6

### TEACHER TASK 9-6

If you have never kept a journal or are new to teaching, start with the first of the tasks below. If you are more experienced in either journal writing or teaching, you may want to begin with the second task.

Task 1

Keep a journal for three weeks, each day writing down the *one* best event of the day and the *one* worst event. These events can be anything from meaningful glances and brief comments to prolonged episodes. They can be things that happen to you or things that happen to someone else. They can be things *you* do (or refrain from doing) or things *others* do.

Week 1: Write down whatever events qualify.

Week 2: Each day, concentrate on the event that made *you* feel the best and the event that made *you* feel the worst.

Week 3: Pick another person—a teacher, a child, a parent—and concentrate on events you think were the best and worst for that individual.

At the end of each week, look over your journal for patterns. Think about what you can learn about yourself, the kind of environment you're in, and the way it affects other people. If possible, share your reactions with someone else.

Task 2

Pick one area of logico-mathematical or infra-logical knowledge from Chapter 6. Each day for one week, make at least one entry relevant to your chosen area. Make your entries as detailed as you can, and jot down any related ideas that come to you.

At the end of the week, make a list of what you want to know about children, teaching strategies, or the classroom environment that would be relevant to ideas and questions that came up in your journal. What details do you wish you had included in your entries? What further information gathering is needed?

Plan three small-group activities based on what you've learned from your journal and on what questions and ideas your journal keeping has generated.

## Evaluating the Classroom Environment When Children Are Present

### What to observe

Observation of the classroom in operation is the best source you have for answering the question of whether the classroom is what you want it to be and does what you want it to do. If you have made use of the time when children are not present to evaluate and record materials, room arrangements, and lesson plans, you can devote all those precious moments of observation time while children are present to watch and record the behavior of the people in the classroom. You'll want to watch for features of the social environment (interactions among the people in the classroom) as well as for features of the effective physical environment (those features that teachers and children actually respond to). It is fairly standard in books on observation techniques to recommend that observations be

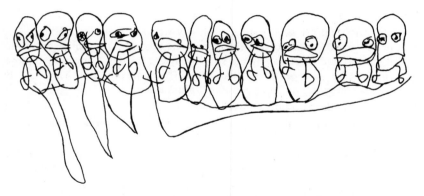

made of children's interactions with *materials,* their interactions with other *children,* and their interactions with *adults* in the classroom (see, for example, Cohen and Stern, 1978; Lindberg and Swedlow, 1976).

It helps to keep these three categories of interactions in mind as you make decisions about what to observe. You may notice, for example, that you have many intricate examples of Carmen's social behaviors but that you have no idea of how well she can handle herself on the obstacle course or of what she does in the science area. As you begin to know Carmen better, you will undoubtedly want to combine the categories. Then you can compare, say, Carmen's use of the science area when she's alone to her use of the science materials when other people are present, or perhaps you'll want to investigate her social adeptness as revealed in the presence of both adults and other children to that when she is interacting only with other children.

Our theory has no quarrel with dividing interactions into these three categories. It reminds us, however, that our knowledge and questions about cognitive development will influence what specific things we look for in each category. As we've already seen, our knowledge of theory will help us find alternative ways to analyze a situation. (Remember the episode with Jessica and Josh in Chapter 2, p. 21.) In social interactions, we can look for evidence of egocentrism, centration, and figurative ways of knowing. (If you've forgotten just what these amount to, check Chapter 5.) Interactions with materials can reveal much about a child's operative ways of knowing: about logico-mathematical and infra-logical knowledge and about the present state of equilibrium and disequilibrium in the child's understanding. The Developmental Guideposts in Chapter 6 are some explicit answers the theory beast has given us about what to observe in these areas. There are some implicit answers, too, which you have been discovering as you've thought about what behaviors would constitute evidence that the classroom exemplifies the four key words: activity, change, intellectual honesty, and diversity.

In addition, to make full use of Piaget's theory, we will frequently have to combine categories. Our understanding of a child's use of materials often depends on the social interactions that occur while the materials are being used. Discussions among children while they work with materials often influence both the way materials are used and the kinds of insights we gain into children's understandings. We may want to intervene ourselves to ask questions, make suggestions and counter-suggestions, and move the materials in various ways in order to elicit the uses of the material that will show us how the child is thinking. (This isn't always the case, of course. Sometimes we'll be looking for evidence of independence and variety in children's spontaneous uses of materials.) The observation exercise shown in Sample 9-3 can give you a start on your own organization of what to focus on as you make observations.

**SAMPLE 9-3** *AN EXERCISE IN ANALYZING CHILDREN'S RESPONSE TO MATERIALS*

*Step 1.* Select an activity or material (such as art, small manipulative, pets, large motor, dramatic play).

*Step 2.* Prepare five recording sheets. For the observation described in Step 3, you'll need *two* like this:

Child being observed _____    Date _____
Activity _____    Observer _____
Observation started _____; ended _____

*Approach*
How Initiated    |    Affective Qualities

*Departure*
How Initiated    |    Affective Qualities

*Comments on Child's Thinking* (inferences based on observations above)

For the observation described in Step 4, you'll need *three* like this:

Child being observed _____    Date _____
Teacher being observed _____    Observer _____
Activity _____
Observation started _____; ended _____

| Description of interaction | How interaction helped or hindered child's use of material | Other potentials in the activity | How potentials could be realized |
|---|---|---|---|
| | | | |

*Step 3.* (a) Observe two children's approaches to and departures from an activity. In each case, note whether the approach and departure are self-initiated, teacher-initiated (verbal or nonverbal) or other-child-initiated. Describe the affective qualities of the approach and departure (for example, eager, purposeful, hesitant, angry).

> (b) Using Piaget's theory, explain what your observations tell you about how each child is thinking (for instance, evidence for egocentrism, level of classification, spatial concepts).
>
> Step 4. (a) Record three teacher-child interactions within the activity.
>
> (b) Comment on how each of the interactions enhanced or detracted from the child's use of that activity in terms of Piaget's theory.
>
> (c) Describe some of the potentials in the activity relevant to theory-guided goals.
>
> (d) Discuss how the potentials might be more fully realized. (Think about teacher behaviors, timing of activities, groupings of children, and arrangements of materials.)

### How to observe

There are two major kinds of observation that concern us in assessing the environment. The first kind has been mentioned throughout the previous chapters and is an integral part of all good teaching. It is the kind of observing you do as you interact with children. The second kind is observation without interaction. As a thinking teacher, you'll be making both kinds of observation. Sometimes an opportunity will arise spontaneously and your task will be simply to make use of it while it is there. At other times, observation opportunities will be planned. In the latter case, you'll have ample time to make decisions about how to focus your observations, where and when to make observations, and how to record what you observe. The effort you put into making these decisions for planned observations will serve you well when spontaneous opportunities arise. Because decision making in spontaneous situations is largely a matter of applying what you do at greater leisure when you plan your observations, we'll focus our discussion on decision making when observations are planned and will restrict ourselves to just a few words about how to manage spontaneous observations where that differs from planned ones. Also, since the decisions you make depend on whether observations are made with or without observer-child interactions, we'll address the issues separately for each kind of observation. We'll use the clinical interview (Piaget's *méthode clinique*) as our model for observations with interaction. For observations without interaction, we'll rely heavily on traditional sources for early-childhood programs.

### Observation with interactions: the clinical interview

*Focus.* The "méthode clinique" is particularly well suited to eliciting evidence of children's underlying intellectual organization (their cognitive structures and the states of relative equilibrium and disequilibrium). In addition, a well-conducted clinical interview is a valuable intellectual experience for both the interviewer and the child. The interviewer learns something about the child's ways of thinking; the child thinks deeply, and often in new ways, about an intriguing problem. A successful clinical interview depends on two features of the interviewer, neither of which is easy to come by: (1) having a clear idea of what kinds of evidence it would be helpful to elicit, and (2) maintaining a focus on eliciting evidence of that kind.

The more intimately you are acquainted with the theory, the more you are likely to embody the first feature. For starters, make use of the Developmental Guideposts (Chapter 6) and do plenty of hard thinking about what various responses might tell you about a child's intellectual organization. A look through the interviews in some of Piaget's own works is also well worth the time and trouble. While you're thinking about responses, consider differences in the kinds of evidence you'd get if you used various kinds of questions and materials. For example, Piaget used clay to investigate children's understandings of substance conservation. Would sand work as well? And suppose a child claimed that a ball flattened into a pancake now contains more clay. Compare the likely responses to these two questions:

(1)  Why does this have more?
(2)  Well, a little girl told me yesterday that she thought that they had the same amount. How would you explain things to her?

As Piaget has pointed out (1929), becoming an expert at clinical interviewing is no easy task. Only extensive practice will help you overcome the use of clumsy and/or leading questions, the tendency to ververbalize, and the haphazard application of preconceived ideas. Preconceived ideas, especially ideas of what kinds of evidence are most needed, are what guide your inquiry. However, without considerable flexibility, guided by sensitivity to children's varying approaches to the issue, the preconceived ideas will lead you astray. What you want them to do is to help you maintain the focus of the interview—the second feature of a successful interviewer—without forcing the discussion into the superficial and destructive game of "Tell me what I want to hear." As you work on conducting clinical interviews, you'll develop your own personal style and strategy. To get you started, here are some basics of conducting good interviews:

(1)  *Establish rapport before you begin the interview.* Remember, you're finding out what another human being thinks about things, not simply checking off answers to a list of questions.

(2)  *Choose materials and settings likely to elicit the kind of thinking you're interested in.* Children's responses vary according to social goupings as well as in response to different materials and instructions.

(3)  *Give children time to think.* Resist the urge to rephrase a question or handle materials immediately after you've posed a problem. A rephrased question is often interpreted as a completely new question. The child's attention is then taken off the problem at hand and turned to processing the sentences you utter.

Nervous handling of the materials may make the child think you are impatient for an answer. In such a case, you may get quick answers for answering's sake, which is hardly a good indication of what the child really thinks.

(4) *Start with questions at early developmental levels and work up to what you estimate will pose a conceptual difficulty.* For instance, you might ask about the distance between two toy houses and the distance between windows before you ask about the distance between them when a tree is put between the houses.

(5) *Vary the use of open-ended questions and closed questions.* Open-ended questions, such as, "What do you think will happen now?" give children a chance to say what's on their minds. Closed questions, such as, "Which doll has more pennies?" help focus the discussion and provide a context for subsequent open-ended questions.

(6) *Ask children to explain the reasons they have for thinking what they do.* In the earlier example, of flattening a clay ball into a pancake, an interviewer might respond to a child's claim that the pancake had more clay with, "Now, how did that happen, I wonder?" or "That's interesting. Do you think it works for oranges, too? If I squash an orange, will I get more to eat?" In cases where children have changed their minds, pointing out the conflicting answers may elicit children's reasons for thinking as they do. You might say, "First you thought they were the same and then you said this one had more. What do you think now? Why did you decide this is the right answer?"

(7) *Remember to make use of nonverbal questions and suggestions.* You can show surprise, interest, or uncertainty by facial expressions. You can share the child's delight in a discovery with a hug and an expression of your own delight. You can move materials so that new features are made prominent. To test the strength of a child's convictions, you can even resort to sleight-of-hand techniques. A standard test of a child's conservation response, for example, is to surreptitiously remove a piece of the clay in the process of flattening it. Similar sneaky strategies can be used in problems of numerical equivalence.

(8) *Watch for nonverbal indicators of children's thinking.* Both surprise and lack of surprise give valuable information. You learn something about Cynthia's egocentrism, for example, when she shows no surprise after having looked through a small window into a dollhouse, walked to the other side of the table to look in again, and seen exactly the same view as before—the doll house having been inconspicuously rotated so as to give her the original view. In less devious manipulations, it is often children's surprise that tells us what they think. A five-year-old who thinks a change of shape involves a change in weight and who understands the use of scales will be surprised to see that the readings on the scale stay the same. You can also use children's actions as a guide to their thoughts. Find out Hoang's under-

standing of number relations by asking him to change two unequal groups of objects so that each group has the same amount. Then watch what he does. Does he add or remove any objects? Does he rearrange the objects—stack them, move them apart, move some together?

(9) *Use suggestions and countersuggestions.* Positive suggestions are usually attempts to help the child see problems in the solution that's offered. For example, in Piaget's interviews on children's concepts of space (Piaget and Inhelder, 1956, p. 156), he encouraged children to step back so they could see the whole line of pegs they'd constructed. Countersuggestions are often helpful in eliciting the degree of conviction with which a child holds a certain view. You can use claims about what other children have said or you can claim to hold an opposing view yourself. Your own claims to opposing viewpoints are most valuable when they border on the ridiculous. If the child is sure you're joking, you can share a laugh and then ask for an explanation of why your suggestion is so ridiculous. If Nicole hasn't quite decided whether or not to take you seriously, she is inspired to reexamine her reasons for thinking that her answer is adequate—and she may be motivated to explain why she's right and you're wrong.

(10) *Don't be afraid to follow children's lead when they take up seemingly unrelated issues.* There's always the chance that what seemed to be a tangential concern might give you precisely the information you wanted. If not, you can explore the child's topic until you're convinced that it's not helpful to your understanding of the intellectual structures you're investigating. Then make use of what's been said to get back to the issue you started with. If you're using groups of blocks, paper cups, and toy cars to explore Henry's number understandings, for example, and Henry wants to talk about the cars he has at home, you can let him tell you about his own cars and then verbally match up the cars you've gathered with the ones he describes—"Here's a car to be a partner to your Tonka truck; here's a car to go with the jeep . . ."

(11) *Remember to generate hypotheses about thoughts children might have about related problems. Then put your hypotheses to the test.* Be prepared to fill in the blanks in questions of this sort:

Suppose _____; then what would happen?

If it works the way you say, then _____. What do you think?

Would it work if we _____?

**TEACHER TASK 9-7**

Work on your ability to conduct a clinical interview by applying the preceding eleven guidelines to several mini-interviews, short conversations of five minutes or so.

In preparing for the interviews, *first,* pick an area of knowledge to study (such as spatial understanding, number, relations). *Second,* review your understanding of development in that area. *Third,* using your general feel for the abilities of the children you'll be interviewing, select materials and formulate procedures (questions, comments, tricks) to use for eliciting the information you want. In planning your procedures, don't forget to consider where and when you'll be conducting the interviews. *Fourth,* write down the kinds of responses you think you'll get from the children you plan to interview. *Finally,* devise a scheme for recording results. Video taping would be ideal, but audio recorders and paper and pencil can be made to do marvelous things.

Before you conduct the actual interviews, it will be extremely helpful to try out your procedures and to discuss the results you expect with adults who know about children.

As you conduct the mini-interviews, feel free to modify your procedures. If you find five minutes much too short, extend your conversations. Eliminate questions that seem merely to confuse children about what you want to know. Develop new ways of phrasing questions and vary the materials you've chosen, as circumstances dictate. You may also find yourself developing more efficient ways of recording the interviews.

When you have finished the interviews, consider the following three questions:

(1) What aspects of your interviewing strategies need the most work?
(2) How will you go about improving them? Do you need more information? more practice? more confidence? more cooperation from other teachers?
(3) What have you learned about the children you interviewed and about development in general?

Finally, jot down ideas you'd like to pursue—specific answers offered by children, ideas about variations on materials and procedures, other kinds of understandings you'd like to explore and so forth.

Teacher Task 9-7 is one of those activities that can be repeated frequently with infinite variation and that constantly yields new benefits for your teaching techniques as well as for your assessment skills and for your knowledge about the children you work with.

Most of the observations you make while interacting with children will be shorter and less single-minded than the clinical interview. Frequently, you'll be combining your efforts to assess children's present levels of understanding with your efforts to lead them to new understandings. Usually, the two efforts enhance each other, but in those cases where they conflict, you'll have to know what your priorities are. If leading children to new understandings takes precedence in a particular activity, you'll have to sacrifice some opportunities for, say, pursuing Jeremy's intriguing comments on temporal ordering. If observations are badly needed, you may have to sacrifice some prime on-the-spot teaching opportunities. In either situation, you are better off if you know just what your priorities are and if you've thought about ways to incorporate both kinds of effort.

Careful lesson planning, with an account of *why* you're doing the activity, will help you establish and stick to your priorities without sacrificing any more than you have to. In planning activities, take the time to think about what kinds of questions are likely to be useful in different kinds of activities. Large-motor activities, for example, lend themselves to the making and immediate testing of predictions (though they do not encourage thoughtful evaluation of a variety of different predictions). Conservation questions are likely to arise at the sand and water tables. The art area lends itself to discussions of representation. New, unfamiliar materials are likely to evoke descriptive comments rather than analytical ones. Familiar materials and activities can encourage new solutions to old problems —particularly when a novel material is added to the old, familiar ones.

Careful planning will also help you focus your observations, thus making you a more efficient observer. You'll have thought about important follow-up questions and ways to elicit a child's thoughts about different aspects of the activity (instead of waiting for the subject to come up).

Interactions with several children at once pose few additional problems. The main drawback is that it is difficult to sort out who thinks what. Children may echo one another or let one child lead the discussion. The main advantage is the opportunity to see children's social interactions and the joint problem-solving that can occur in such interactions. You can make use of conflicting opinions by pointing out differences in a nonevaluative way. Avoiding such comments as, "Look, everyone, Vishnu's got the right answer," you can focus attention on the variety of answers suggested and on the examination of each one. You can ease tensions when one child has suggested an answer everyone else recognizes as wrong, by using a little playfulness. "What if you really could lift up houses?" you might ask. "What would you be like? Why can't you lift up houses, anyway? Could you get something to help you lift a house?"

*Where and when.* Clinical interviews, or modifications thereof, can be conducted just about anywhere and at just about any time during the school day. Three considerations to bear in mind when deciding on a time and place for a clinical interview in your own situation are: (1) make sure you have the opportunity to observe carefully and to make the desired records, (2) minimize the amount of interference (friendly or otherwise) from children not officially part of the interview, and (3) work with children when they are in an appropriate frame of mind.

A quiet corner of the room with an electrical outlet for a tape recorder, and maybe a shelf or a small divider partially screening you from the rest of the classroom, is a good arrangement. It minimizes potential distractions while allowing you quick access to the rest of the classroom should an emergency arise. If you have the necessary space and staff, you can furnish another room, a corner of the hallway, or a large broom closet with a rug or table and chairs or climbing apparatus, and so forth, with the choice of place and equipment depending on the environment you want for the particular interview you're conducting. You might also choose a part of the day when extra teacher time is available: when a classroom volunteer is around, when the free-play activities are all ones that require a minimum of adult supervision, when some of the other children are napping, or before the majority of children have arrived (during the early-morning hours at a day-care center, for instance). Preschool teachers are famous for their ingenuity. If you want to conduct a clinical interview, you'll manage to find a place and a time that works in your situation—and it will probably be different from any of the specific suggestions we've given!

Finding a time and place for spontaneous versions of the planned clinical interview is usually not a problem. You look for children doing interesting things, you wait and watch to get acquainted with the nature of their activity (making a few notes to yourself on one of those pads of paper you've placed around for just such purposes), you ask to join the activity (verbally or nonverbally), and you begin to wonder out loud, to make predictions, to discuss thoughts, and finally to ask questions fairly directly.

In both the spontaneous and planned versions of the clinical interview, you'll want to adjust your actions to the individual children involved. Some children, particularly when school is still new, may be reluctant to leave the room. Others won't be able to concentrate unless the classroom activity is out of sight and hearing. Some children may work well in groups; others may vie for attention, get caught up in trying to impress the others, or become shy and withdrawn when in a group situation. Timing will also vary from child to child. Avoid requesting a clinical interview with a child whose favorite group activity is just beginning, or with someone who's just made a new friend. If your interview has been well planned, you know that you have a valuable experience to offer children. Use your good judgment to decide when that experience will be most beneficial for you, the child interviewed, and the rest of the class.

*Keeping records.* The kinds of records you will want (and be able to get) while you are interacting with children will depend on whether you are trying to record the interactions themselves or whether you are interested just in what children are doing. To record interactions, it is an immense help to have a tape recorder. (A video tape with someone to run it would record much more than an audio tape, but a small audio cassette recorder is a lot easier to get.) If you manage to get an audio tape of your interactions, make sure to listen to the tape as soon as possible after the interaction. Then, while the experience is fresh in your mind, you can make notes about what materials you were looking at, what nonverbal behaviors accompanied the discussions, which voice is whose, and the like. As you get used to taping yourself, you may even find yourself developing the habit of making your comments to children identify the child, the materials used, and the behaviors. If you take the time to acquire this art, it will serve you well as you use the tapes to help you know better both yourself as a teacher and the children you work with.

If you don't have someone to make video tapes of your interactions, you don't have an extra observer to make notes, and you haven't been able to get a hold of a tape recorder, you can still keep some running records on what you're doing. Take a pad of paper with you and jot notes to yourself as you work with a child.

In a small-group activity, you may even want to use an evaluation card like the one in Sample 9-4. If asked about the writing you are doing, you can explain the truth to children: you are writing down things you want to remember about what's happening in school. Intellectual honesty does not require you to go into great detail about Piagetian theory and all your motivations for making written records.

**SAMPLE 9-4** *EVALUATION OF SMALL GROUP ACTIVITY*

Date: May 12, 1981
Teacher: G.
Activity: Squish It

TO WATCH FOR:

| Names of Children in Group | gets all of the squishable things together | picks objects that feel the same | picks objects used for the same purpose | uses ideas of other children and makes suggestions | makes hypotheses about squishability and tests them | is confused about the re-sorting task | Comments |
|---|---|---|---|---|---|---|---|
| Wayne | | | | | | | |
| Theresa | | | | | | | |
| Inja | | | | | | | |
| Ellen | | | | | | | |

If you are busy teaching and you want to record events that do not involve your own interactions with children—the distribution of children among the different areas of the classroom, for instance—you can enlist children's help. Some programs make it a part of their free-play routine for children to "sign in" when they go to an area. In other classrooms, children plan where they are going to work during free-play times and then indicate their chosen areas at the end of group planning sessions. In still other programs, after the free-play time is finished, children discuss who played where. Whether or not you have this kind of help from children, you might want to make your own calculations about what's going on. A timer could be used to help you make systematic observations of who is in what areas. Set the timer for five-, ten-, or fifteen-minute intervals. Each time it sounds, list which chil-

dren are in each area. (Incidentally, since we're discussing observations with interactions here, it is fair to ask those children you know are using an area whether
some other child, about whom you are unsure, is also using it.) A chart with the
different classroom areas identified and space for listing who's in what area each
time the alarm goes off will make the recording task go faster.

*Selected references to help*
*with clinical interviews*

ALMY, MILLIE, and CELIA GENISHI. *Ways of Studying Children,* rev. ed. (New
York: Teachers College Press, 1979).
COPPLE, CAROL, IRVING E. SIGEL, and RUTH SAUNDERS. *Educating the
Young Thinker: Classroom Strategies for Cognitive Growth* (New York: D.
Van Nostrand Company, 1979).
INHELDER, BÄRBEL, HERMINE SINCLAIR, and MAGALI BOVET. *Learning
and the Development of Cognition,* trans. Susan Wedgewood (Cambridge,
Mass.: Harvard University Press, 1974).
KAMII, CONSTANCE, and RHETA DeVRIES. *Physical Knowledge in Preschool
Education: Implications of Piaget's Theory* (Englewood Cliffs, N.J.: Prentice-
Hall, Inc., 1978).
PIAGET, JEAN

Read any of his books whose titles begin with the words "The Child's Conception
of . . ." (for example, *The Child's Conception of Physical Causality*). Also helpful
for their examples of the use of materials to raise questions and pose problems are
the following:

PIAGET, JEAN. *The Grasp of Consciousness: Action and Concept in the Young
Child,* trans. Susan Wedgwood (Cambridge, Mass.: Harvard University Press,
1976 [first published in French, in 1974, under the title, *La Prise de Conscience*]).
PIAGET, JEAN. *Success and Understanding,* trans. Arnold J. Pomerans (Cambridge, Mass.: Harvard University Press, 1978 [first published in French, in
1974, under the title, *Réussir et Comprendre*]).
INHELDER, BÄRBEL, and JEAN PIAGET. *The Early Growth of Logic in the
Child,* trans. E. A. Lunzer and D. Papert (London: Routledge and Kegan Paul,
1964 [first published in French, in 1959, under the title, *La Genèse des
Structures Logiques Elémentaire*]).

*Observation without Interaction*

Although there is much to be said for and about observation without interaction, we will say very little here. Because there are already many good sources
of observation techniques easily adaptable to classrooms influenced by Piaget's
theory, we will limit ourselves to some theory-inspired suggestions for what to
focus observations on and a list of recommended references.

Observations without interaction are particularly useful for getting answers to questions such as these.

(1) Which materials are the most or least used? Or which *kinds* of materials are the most and least used (as categorized by lists of materials that contribute to intellectual honesty, activity, change, and diversity)?

(2) Who initiates dramatic play more frequently, children or teachers?

(3) Where in the classroom do children spend the most time? engage in the most social interactions with other children? make and test predictions most frequently? fight the least? make the most constructive use of materials?

(4) How often do teachers help children work out solutions for themselves?

(5) What kinds of problem-solving do children engage in?

(6) How do teachers help a child think through a problem?

(7) What do children do with a material when a teacher leaves after having helped them think of ways of using it?

(8) What are the adults in the classroom doing: how much housekeeping, how much communicating with one another, how much interacting with which children, how much moving about the room?

*Selected references to help*
*in devising recording forms*
*and in focusing observations*

Examples of recording forms and guides for focusing observations can be found in any of the following books:

BARKER, ROGER G., and HERBERT F. WRIGHT. *Midwest and Its Children; the Psychological Ecology of an American Town* (Evanston, Ill.: Row, Peterson and Company, 1954).

BOEHM, ANN E., and RICHARD A. WEINBERG. *The Classroom Observer: A Guide for Developing Observation Skills* (New York: Teachers College Press, 1977).

ROWEN, BETTY. *The Children We See: An Observational Approach to Child Study* (New York: Holt, Rinehart and Winston, 1973).

SHURE, MYRNA BETH. "Psychological Ecology of a Nursery School," *Child Development,* 34 (1963), 979–992.

## THE EFFECT OF THE CLASSROOM ENVIRONMENT ON THE PEOPLE IN IT

Suppose the classroom is just the way you think it should be. What is the effect of the carefully cultivated environment on the children and adults in it? This question has three parts: how does the environment affect the activities of people while they're in the classroom? How does the environment affect people's present abilities (whether or not they use their abilities in typical classroom activities)? Finally, how has the environment affected what people are able to do and interested in doing when the school year is finished? The first part of the question calls for observation and analysis of the activity in the classroom. The second part can be answered with the kinds of tests, interviews, and observations appropriate for formative evaluation. The third part requires summative evaluation.

All of the parts ask for causal connections. Unfortunately, it is extremely hard to establish cause-and-effect relations in questions of this sort. Even if the children in your classroom are more inquisitive, more self-reliant, and more social than they were when the year started, this is not clear evidence that this happy state of affairs was caused by the environment you've created. Maybe you're seeing a delightful side effect of some other cause (a change in the general prosperity of the area, for instance, or the introduction of a baby-sitting exchange). It takes some massive research designs and sophisticated techniques to make a convincing case for causal connections between educational environments and human progress. If you wanted to undertake such a study, you'd need to call in expert help and apply for government grants. Even with imported expertise in evaluation and with ample funding, your question cannot be properly answered unless you know what effects you hope to find. Experts can help you decide how to eliminate and/or compensate for extraneous variables (contaminating influences), but they cannot tell you what it is you want to know about.

Because the option of outside expertise and a major research project *may* open up for you and because you can establish some interesting correlations even if you can't prove causation, it is worth seeing what kinds of answers would be relevant to each of the three parts of our question: the effects on activities, the effects on abilities, and the effects on later functioning.

### Effects on Activities

Whether you're interested in the effects of the environment as a whole on the quantity and quality of various kinds of activities (a kind of summative evaluation) or in the effects of various changes in the environment on kinds of activities (a kind of formative evaluation), observation is the key to discovering relationships between the environment and its effects on what people do.

If you're interested in the effects of the environment as a whole and are in general agreement with the goals discussed in Chapter 4, the observations you'll be interested in will be those that contribute to your knowledge of (a) how the environment has contributed to the achievement of the six goals for people, and (b) to what extent the environment is self generating—that is, to what extent it encourages activities that maintain its features of activity, intellectual honesty, change, and diversity; and to what extent it encourages activities (such as excessive competitiveness) that destroy these features.

In looking at the extent to which the environment as a whole is self-generating, you'll want to know the answers to questions such as these: do the activities show that the people in the classroom are contributing to the atmosphere of intellectual honesty? For which people is this the case? Are the people in the classroom actively constructing knowledge? Are they active socially, physically, and intellectually? Do people's activities change over the course of the year, and is this because of the way people in the classroom are responding to materials and to one another? Are the activities of individuals diverse? Do different people do different things, in different ways, and with different degrees of understanding? For deciding what specific behaviors to observe for answering such questions, go back over the charts at the end of Chapter 4 and start making yourself a list. You'll soon discover, if you haven't already, that the suggestions on the charts need a lot of refinement and added detail if they are to provide you with specific behaviors and activities to look for.

*TEACHER TASK 9-8*

---

(1) Pick one of the goals for the classroom (such as "an atmosphere of intellectual honesty") and think about what behaviors would be indicative of progress toward that goal.

(2) Make three sets of lists of behaviors to look for. Make one set for children, one set for teachers, and one set for parents. In each set include behaviors you think contribute to the goal you chose and behaviors you think detract from that goal (whether or not they contribute to some *other* goal you think important).

(3) Devise a systematic way to observe for the behaviors you've listed, and construct a chart for recording your observations. For example, you might spend ten minutes observing parent behaviors (as they bring children to school), ten minutes observing children, and then ten minutes observing teachers. You could repeat this cycle every third school day for several weeks before you sit down to take stock of the information you've gathered.

(4) Make observations according to the schedule you've devised. As you observe, refine and modify your lists of behaviors until you're satisfied your observation instrument gives you a valid and reliable measure of how well the classroom is progressing toward the goal.

---

In investigating the contributions of the environment as a whole on the goals for people, you'll want to decide which behaviors and activities are indicative of each goal. Try constructing an observation scale (with the help of experts, if you can get it) for measuring behaviors. Or construct a general description of the kinds of behaviors you think are relevant, and evaluate your classroom several times during the year. The use of a rating scale and brief written examples of behaviors that you see or infer will be helpful in making comparisons later. Sample 9-5 shows what such an evaluation form might look like.

In assessing the effects of the classroom environment, remember that the adults as well as the children in the environment are affected by it. Interviews, questionnaires, and even informal discussions can be used to find out how adults respond. You'll want to know, for example, whether the environment that you think is terrific for children is so much of a drain on the energy of the adults involved that teachers (including yourself) will "burn out" in several months, or in a year. Are the adults comfortable in it? Do they like the experience of being in the classroom? Are they learning about children, intellectual development, and the effects of different interactions? Are adults drained or exhilarated by the class day? We'll explore some ways to answer these questions in Chapter 10.

**SAMPLE 9-5** *EVALUATION OF THE GENERAL CLASSROOM ENVIRONMENT: THE ACTIVITIES OF THE PEOPLE IN IT*

---

Date _____

Observer _____

*Goal 1:* Self-Confidence                1  2  3  4  5

Children and adults are confident in initiating, and responding to, social overtures. They tackle physical challenges with self-assurance and are willing and able to try out their own ideas.

*Comments and/or Examples*


*Goal 2:* Empathy                1  2  3  4  5

Through both verbal and nonverbal means, teachers show sensitivity to the emotions, special skills, and understandings of one another. Teachers are able to work as a team. In the way they arrange the environment and interact with children, teachers express understanding of children's feelings, interpretations of events, and physical limitations. Children listen to one another and make judgments about how others feel and think about things. They anticipate the wishes of others, as indicated in passing materials to one another and in sharing.

*Comments and/or Examples*


*Goal 3:* Taking Responsibility for Own Learning        1  2  3  4  5

Teachers find and read books on child development, Piagetian theory, and teaching; they suggest and try out new techniques; they generate hypotheses and test them; they ask questions of other staff members; they make observations of children, other teachers, and themselves; they visit other programs. Children explore materials, experiment, ask questions, and generally engage in self-motivated, constructive activity.

*Comments and/or Examples*

*Goal 4:* Interest in Alternative Ways of Doing Things      1   2   3   4   5

Teachers try out new materials, room arrangements, schedules, and teacher strategies. They ask for, and listen to, suggestions from other teachers, parents, and other professionals. They look for variations in the way children solve problems, they point out the differences, and they encourage the search for a variety of methods. Children use the same materials in a variety of ways; they solve problems one way and then try out a different solution for the same problem. Children ask others about how they're solving a problem or using an activity and tell others about different ways of doing things.

*Comments and/or Examples*

*Goal 5:* Critical Thinking      1   2   3   4   5

Teachers and children build on the ideas of one another, test the predictions they make in a systematic way, and apply the logico-mathematical and infra-logical understandings they have to the analysis of problems they meet. Staff discussions show teachers asking for evidence, suggesting alternative analyses, using charts and observation scales, and incorporating new ideas into future lesson plans. Use of materials in the classroom is often collaborative. Children and teachers are persistent in their attempts to find answers.

*Comments and/or Examples*

*Goal 6:* Flexibility      1   2   3   4   5

Teachers and children adapt easily to changes in schedule, activities, and materials. They adjust their plans and behaviors to the size of the group they're in, differences in content, obstacles (such as bad weather) to previous plans, and the particular people they're working with. For example, children discuss how to use the block area when it is crowded; teachers and children think of alternate materials to use if the planned type of finger paint runs out; children make useful combinations of materials from different areas of the classroom.

*Comments and/or Examples*

Note:   Explanation of Rating Scale in upper right-hand corner of each goal.
        Activities and behaviors consistent with the goal occur
        1—almost never
        2—occasionally
        3—often
        4—very often
        5—almost always

The way we've posed the questions we've been raising so far suggests a concern with summative evaluation. If you want to use the answers to such questions to influence what you do in the next week, you'll want formative evaluation. For this purpose, supplement the foregoing suggested procedures with descriptions of specific features of the environment. Then you can look at the correlations between changes in those features and changes in the activities of people in the classroom.

### Effects on Abilities

Since abilities can only be inferred from actual performances, assessing abilities should be done under optimal conditions—conditions in which performance is a relatively straightforward expression of ability, unhindered by shyness, reactions to a frightening room, difficult vocabulary, unfamiliar materials, or anger left over from a dispute with a friend. Abilities can be inferred from observations made of behaviors in the classroom, from clinical interviewing procedures, from information gleaned from discussions with other adults who know the person (such as parents or friends), and from standardized tests.

We've already explored some of the problems and potentials in the first two methods. Let's take a brief look at the third and fourth methods as they bear on the children in the classroom.

#### Information from other adults

In our earlier comments on making use of staff discussions, we mentioned the need to think about questions for eliciting information from people who know the children you work with. Various kinds of questions, questionnaires, information sheets, home visits, and conference arrangements can be used to obtain information about children's abilities. (Apart from some comments on conferences in Chapter 10, we'll leave the investigation of such procedures for obtaining information up to you.)

The major advantage of asking others about what a child has done, or seems to be capable of doing, is that one can get beyond the relatively limited sample of times and contexts supplied by the classroom. Different abilities emerge in different contexts. Comments a child has made at bedtime or on a cross-country trip with the family can reveal remarkable insights or interesting confusions that are not revealed in the classroom. The major disadvantage of getting information from other adults is that you have to rely on what they can remember. Like you, they will have their own interests, beliefs, and attitudes to influence what they notice, what interpretations they make, and what features they remember. They may ignore or forget details that are crucial to the testing of hypotheses you have about a child's abilities. Think back to your own observations of children, made before you were acquainted with Piaget's theory. You undoubtedly noticed fewer—or at least different—details than you do now.

Fortunately, the disadvantage in using other adults as an information source can be overcome—and by precisely the methods you've used to make your own observations more useful and more accurate. As you meet with them, discussing theory and observation, asking probing questions to uncover details in the incident being described, or asking for concrete examples to support inference made, the adults will have opportunities for inventing and discovering ways to make their own future observations more useful to you. They'll be doing their own thinking about what details to look for in future observations. A delightful side effect is that the more they know about children and intellectual development, the more enjoyment they will get from observing and analyzing what the children are doing.

### Information from standardized tests

We've already expressed some reservations about the use of standardized tests on young children. We said that they often fail to measure the abilities we want measured and that, regardless of how well they are constructed, it is hard to get a reliable measure when they are used with young children. Researchers are well aware of these two problems and have made some progress in overcoming them. Nonetheless, of the hundreds of available standardized tests for young children (more than 900 in 1973, according to Henry Dyer, 1973), practically none assesses the abilities of most concern to our theory. Recent efforts toward constructing Piagetian-based measures (see the review of such attempts in Modgil and Modgil, 1976) have tended to result in ways to assign stage designations to children rather than to reveal degrees of flexibility and efficiency in children's use of the thought processes that will eventually lead to the construction of the various stage-characteristic logico-mathematical structures.

If you decide to use standardized tests in assessing children in your classroom, be sure to take two precautions: look at the test carefully to see what it measures, and make sure that the administration of the test is a pleasant experience for children and is not a waste of their time. Remember, a child's time is precious too, just as yours is—this in spite of the fact that you're more aware of the actual passage of time than a child is.

### Effects on Later Functioning

Although the preschool years are valuable in themselves, they are also important for their potential impact on future development. A good preschool environment ought to have some beneficial influence on later learning and development as well as on present abilities and behaviors. And it undoubtedly does have some such influence. The question is, *what kind* of influence, and *how much* influence?

Researchers interested in Piagetian theory and in preschool education have long been emphasizing the need to look for long-term effects of preschool programs. There is little consensus, however, on what kinds of effects to look for.

Should we look at career success? at level of highest academic achievement? at social accomplishments? at general adjustment to whatever life-style the individual has?

Although these questions as yet have no answers, there have been a few plausible suggestions. David Hawkins (1965) has stressed the importance of the experience of "messing about" for understanding college physics. Constance Kamii (1972) has speculated that early experiences might affect the stability of formal operations (the thought structures characteristic of the last developmental stage of logico-mathematical knowledge). Eleanor Duckworth's work (1973) points to influences on the general approach to problem solving, self-initiative, and group collaboration. Schweinhart and Weikart (1980) find academic and social benefits still being reaped when former preschoolers have reached the ripe old age of fifteen years.

If you want feedback on how the children who have been in your program function later on, you can use these suggestions, the goals for people (from Chapter 4), and even some of the Developmental Guideposts from Chapter 6 to develop a questionnaire. Parents, grade-school teachers, friends, and the like might be persuaded to fill it out—or you could use it yourself as a guide for interviewing children a year or more after they've left your program.

## SUMMARY

In this chapter, we began our exploration of program evaluation with a brief discussion of what evaluation could do for us. We distinguished between *summative evaluation,* a sort of "summing up" of the overall effects of the program, and *formative evaluation,* a continuing attempt to assess and modify the program as it evolves. Because of its immediate application to teaching concerns, formative evaluation was the focus of most of the rest of our exploration.

After reminding ourselves of the dangers inherent in blindly trusting standardized measures and having recognized how few standardized measures there are for the kind of formative evaluation our theory beast insists upon, we found ourselves face to face with the need to be our own researchers—to do our own setting of goals and our own construction of ways to assess progress. We then plunged right in to the sea of observation techniques and guidelines, taking care to think about the *validity* and *reliability* of the various procedures.

In looking at ways to characterize the classroom environment itself, we explored various counting and categorizing procedures relevant to the goals our theory led us to in Chapter 4. We divided our exploration into the examination of those procedures designed for use when children are not in the classroom and those designed for use during the school day. In investigating the latter, we devoted considerable attention to techniques of observation with interaction, using the clinical interview as our model, and we touched on observation without interaction. We also surveyed the rich source of information found in more anecdotal methods—journals, comments jotted down during the school day, and staff discussions.

Our exploration of ways to discover the effects of the environment on the people in it was directed primarily toward formative assessment of children. We did, however, get a brief glimpse of the directions one might take in summative assessment. A discussion of the effects of the environment on adults was reserved for Chapter 10.

Throughout our examination of assessment techniques, we kept an eye on ways to incorporate the procedures into real-life teaching situations. A variety of exercises (Teacher Tasks) were directed toward developing general skills in assessment techniques while stimulating the discovery of methods most amenable to the particular interests, abilities, and situational constraints of each individual.

In the course of our inquiry, it became clear that the single most important directive in the area of evaluation was *no procrastination allowed!* One has to start from exactly where one is—from one's present limitations, present interests, present abilities, present situation. With practice and the accumulation of the wisdom that comes only from experience, evaluation will become a regular part of one's teaching.

## REFERENCES

BALL, SAMUEL. "Problems in Evaluating Early Education Programs," in *Evaluation of Educational Programs for Young Children,* ed. Richard A. Weinberg and Shirley G. Moore (Washington, D.C.: The Child Development Associate Consortium, 1975).

COHEN, DOROTHY H., and VIRGINIA STERN. *Observing and Recording the Behavior of Young Children,* 2nd ed. (New York: Teachers College Press, 1978).

DUCKWORTH, ELEANOR A. "The Having of Wonderful Ideas," in *Piaget in the Classroom,* ed. Milton Schwebel and Jane Raph (New York: Basic Books, 1973).

DYER, HENRY S. "Testing Little Children: Some Old Problems in New Settings," *Childhood Education, 49,* no. 7 (1973), 362–367.

HAWKINS, DAVID. "Messing About in Science," *Science and Children, 2,* no. 5 (1965), 5–9.

HOLT, JOHN C. *The Underachieving School* (New York: Pitman Publishing Corporation, 1969).

KAMII, CONSTANCE. "An Application of Piaget's Theory to the Conceptualization of a Preschool Curriculum," in *The Preschool in Action: Exploring Early Childhood Programs,* ed. Ronald K. Parker (Boston: Allyn and Bacon, 1972).

KAMII, CONSTANCE. "A Sketch of the Piaget-Derived Preschool Curriculum Developed by the Ypsilanti Early Education Program," in *Early Childhood Education,* ed. Bernard Spodek (Englewood Cliffs, N.J.: Prentice-Hall, Inc., 1973).

KAMII, CONSTANCE. "Evaluation of Learning in Preschool Education: Socio-emotional, Perceptual-motor, and Cognitive Development," in *Handbook on*

*Formative and Summative Evaluation of Student Learning,* ed. Benjamin S. Bloom, J. Thomas Hastings, and George F. Madaus (New York: McGraw-Hill, 1971).

LINDBERG, LUCILE, and RITA SWEDLOW. *Early Childhood Education: A Guide for Observation and Participation* (Boston: Allyn and Bacon, Inc., 1976).

MILLER, LOUISE B., and JEAN L. DYER. 1975. "Four Preschool Programs: Their Dimensions and Effects," *Monographs of the Society for Research in Child Development,* vol. 40, nos. 5–6. Chicago: University of Chicago Press.

MODGIL, SOHAN, and CELIA MODGIL. *Piagetian Research: Compilation and Commentary, Volume 4: School Curriculum, Test Development* (Windsor, Berks., Great Britain: NFER Publishing Company Ltd., 1976).

PIAGET, JEAN. *The Child's Conception of the World,* trans. Joan and Andrew Tomlinson (London: Routledge and Kegan Paul, 1929 [first published in French, in 1926, under the title, *La Représentation du Monde chez l'Enfant*]).

PIAGET, JEAN, and BÄRBEL INHELDER. *The Child's Conception of Space,* trans. F. J. Langdon and J. L. Lunzer (London: Routledge and Kegan Paul, 1956 [first published in French, in 1948, under the title, *La Représentation de l'Espace chez l'Enfant*]).

SCHWEINHART, LAWRENCE J., and DAVID P. WEIKART. 1980. "Young Children Grow Up, The Effects of the Perry Preschool Program on Youths Through Age 15," *Monographs of the High/Scope Educational Research Foundation,* vol. 7. Ypsilanti, Michigan: High/Scope Press.

SCRIVEN, MICHAEL. "The Methodology of Evaluation," in *Perspectives of Curriculum Evaluation,* ed. Ralph W Tyler, Robert M. Gagné, and Michael Scriven (Chicago: Rand McNally, 1967).

SIGEL, IRVING E. "The Search for Validity or the Evaluator's Nightmare," in *Evaluation of Educational Programs for Young Children,* ed. Richard A. Weinberg and Shirley G. Moore (Washington, D.C.: The Child Development Associate Consortium, 1975).

SUCHMAN, EDWARD A. *Evaluative Research: Principles and Practice in Public Service and Social Action Programs* (New York: Russell Sage Foundation, 1967).

# 10               BECOMING

## WAYS OF BEGINNING

We hope you have come to share our view of Piagetian theory, not as a hateful beast or a heavy burden, but rather as a valuable beast of burden. The Teacher Tasks scattered throughout the chapters were designed to help you develop your own unique relation with the theory, so that it works for you in your teaching environment. This chapter contains a few hints to help you enhance and maintain the healthy and productive relationship we hope you've acquired.

The hints we give flow from our conviction that the nine principles articulated in Chapter 3 extend beyond childhood and apply to adult understanding. Understanding theory is not a matter of accumulating facts (Principle 4) and becoming facile with theoretical jargon (Principle 7). It is a matter of active construction (Principle 8), in which we reorganize our ways of responding to children (Principles 1 and 2). We are best able to acquire understanding when we are allowed to move at our own pace (Principle 3) and when we work in an intellectually (Principle 5) and socially (Principles 6 and 9) supportive environment.

One of the major problems cited by teachers we've worked with is the difficulty of creating and maintaining a supportive environment for investigating and applying Piagetian theory in their own classroom situations. The suggestions in this chapter are to help you create the kind of environment in which you can continue to grow.

### Taking the Risk

Whenever you set out to change yourself and your surroundings, you run the risk of making things worse than they were before. Moreover, it takes time and a good deal of patience and hard work before the theory becomes an integral part of your teaching—before it has its optimal value for you. You are aware of this, having already faced it in working through this book. Others share your concerns, sometimes too much. Long after you're convinced that the change is necessary and for the better, others will be challenging the values you express, questioning whether the means you propose will lead to the desired ends, placing obstacles in the way of progress, criticizing your classroom environment, and asking searching questions about the theory for which there are at present no answers. You will be backed against the wall with repeated requests to show how you know that you're doing the right thing (and some of those requests will come from your own mouth). Neither you nor your challengers will be satisfied with the obvious and equally unanswerable counter-challenge, "How do you know I'm not?"

Unless you are prepared for such discouragement, it can significantly impede your progress and the joy you find in making it. There are a variety of strategies for fighting discouraging influences before they get you down. Let's look at three.

First: find a support group—people with whom you can share your discoveries and puzzlements, people who are generally sympathetic to what you're doing and willing to help you do it, people who give *you* the kind of support *you* need. A fellow teacher, a parent, or even a friend or relative with no specific role in early education can be your support group.

Second: take the offense in meeting the opposition. Spread the word about potentials in various activities and the purposes for various strategies *before* people begin to cluck their tongues over what goes on in your classroom. The more you have explained what you're trying to do, the less likely you are to collect misdirected negative comments, which are not only unhelpful, but downright discouraging. Make a special effort to share your observations and insights into children's understandings and the effects of various teacher strategies on them with people who are likely to visit your classroom. If possible, find some time to analyze incidents with people who observe you. Remember, you have been growing in your powers of theory-guided observation; they may still be at the level of observation reports such as, "The children played for forty-five minutes and then sang songs." Or maybe they're guided by a totally different theory. In either case, it will be of help to both of you if you can find time to provide this service. You may even get some constructive criticism as a result of it—observations and suggestions made with *your* goals in mind. Some examples of lesson plans, especially if they include a description of the kinds of behaviors you are trying to elicit, can be posted or distributed to those who will have access to your classroom. A short written description of your goals and methods can also be very helpful.

Third: make use of your allies—the parents of the children you teach and the various adults (volunteers, cooks, and so forth) who participate in the classroom. If you share your growing knowledge with such people, they can help collect evidence for how well you are creating the environment you want. They can supply observations and anecdotes, they can help visitors understand what's going on, and they can help both you and themselves appreciate more fully the changes you're making. Not all of their comments and observations will be soothing to your ego, of course. Appreciate the good comments, take the negative comments in stride, and use the comments that indicate a lack of understanding as a guide to the kinds of points you'll want to make in explaining yourself to less-sympathetic audiences.

The use of strategies such as the three we have mentioned will not eliminate the risks involved in changing things, but they will help to minimize them. It is also useful to be aware of some of the common ailments that are likely to plague you as you work out your relationship with the theory beast.

### Some Common Ailments and Suggested Remedies

The four ailments most commonly plaguing us and the teachers we've worked with are these: putting your foot in your brain, feeling inadequate and not "up to the job," judging new goals and methods by old standards, and putting a puppet in your place. We'll look at each of these ailments and their symptoms as well as at some suggested remedies.

*Putting your foot
in your brain*

*SYMPTOMS:*

Repeated use of words such as "I can't" or "We can't."
Reluctance to acknowledge the possibility of alternative ways of doing things.
Holding on to a preconceived notion of what things must be like.

*SUGGESTED REMEDIES*
*AND PREVENTIONS:*

(1) When you're feeling on top of things and ideas are flowing, write down all the alternative ideas you can. When your foot is in your brain, blocking the generation of new ideas, your list can help you get your foot out.

(2) Sit down with other people. State your goal and the obstacles you see, as clearly and neutrally as possible. (It may help to write this down.) Then brainstorm for a while. Think up as many alternatives as you can, no matter how crazy they are. If this hasn't already gotten your foot out of your brain, try the next remedy.

(3) By yourself, or with other people, pick one of your reasons for thinking you can't do whatever it is you're concerned about. Show why that reason does not apply. You can use whatever imaginary situations and silly arguments you wish. The purpose is to get you back into the habit of thinking positively—to get your foot out of your brain, so that it can finish the problem-solving task you've set it.

### Feeling inadequate

*SYMPTOMS:*

This ailment expresses itself with symptoms like those for the first ailment, but the attitudes tend to be directed toward oneself. This ailment often follows periods of intense enthusiasm and great ambitions, especially when time, effort, and/or personality estimates have been left out of the statement of goals.

*SUGGESTED REMEDIES*
*AND PREVENTIONS:*

(1) You can dispel many of your self-doubts by looking at the facts. Look at records you've made of the changes you've brought about in the classroom, of what parts you've read of various books, of the kinds of observations you've made, of the kinds of interactions you've had with other staff. A journal is a valuable weapon against this ailment, especially if you remember to note your accomplishments. (Such an entry might read, "Today I got interiorization and internalization straightened out. Hurray!")

(2) Divide a piece of paper into two columns. In the left-hand column, list as many of your teaching or learning behaviors as you can. Apply your observation/inference skills in making your list as neutral and noninferential as you can. When you've got a good-sized list of various kinds of teaching behaviors (or learning behaviors, if getting acquainted with the theory is what discourages you), you can begin work on the right-hand column. Opposite each item in the left column, write

some inferences about what skills, abilities, and potentials for later development each behavior shows. Only positive inferences are allowed!

(3) If you know others who are attempting to tame the theory, share your doubts with them. They have surely felt the same way about themselves, and they can often recognize your assets better than you can.

### Judging new goals and methods
### by old standards

*SYMPTOMS:*

A nagging suspicion deep down that a really good teacher, even one guided by the theory beast, has a quiet classroom, with dutiful children focusing their attention on the inspiring behavior of the teacher.

Fantasies of asking the perfect question, of creating the ideal classroom, or of becoming the paradigm Piagetian teacher for other teachers to imitate.

Criticizing yourself for slow progress or lapses in performance.

Allowing traditional tests and observations to be the only, or the most important, measure of the success of your classroom.

*SUGGESTED REMEDIES*
*AND PREVENTIONS:*

(1) Carefully work through the charts at the end of Chapter 4 and the Developmental Guideposts in Chapter 6. Write your own list of materials, behaviors, and events that are good indicators of intellectual *activity* and *development* in a preschool or kindergarten classroom. Make a separate list, as detailed as you can, of materials, behaviors, and events that indicate a lack of intellectual activity and development. Now look for how many of the indicators on each list are truly compatible with a classroom in which the teacher is the primary focus of attention. Regardless of how many you find for each list, you will have been reminded to judge your teaching by what's happening in the classroom rather than by some preconceived notion of perfection.

(2) At the front of your journal, your lesson-plan folder, or even your wall— wherever you're likely to see it frequently—write the words, "Have I done the right thing?" Cross out those words and under them write these three questions in bold letters: "What exactly did I do? What was the outcome? What kind of further action will be likely to produce the effects I wanted?" Whenever you find yourself asking if you've done the right thing, dreaming of the perfect lesson, or criticizing your own progress, look at those three questions and focus on answering them.

(3) Keep records of what goes on in the classroom, using hints from Chapter 9 if you like, and *use those records.* When people ask how things are going, show them some anecdotes and observations.

*Putting a puppet*
*in your place*

*SYMPTOMS:*

A feeling of artificiality.

A feeling of frustration and helplessness in situations (especially those concerning management or discipline) where you previously had no trouble.

A tendency to create imaginary versions of yourself either of this sort—you can squeeze thirty-seven hours of work into eight and handle even the most difficult disputes with miraculous insight and tact—or of this sort—you can scarcely read, much less understand, anything theoretical, and you clunk around the classroom like an oversized marionette, misinterpreting children's behaviors and uttering meaningless phrases.

*SUGGESTED REMEDIES*
*AND PREVENTIONS:*

(1)  When you find your behaviors awkward and out of place, take the time to rethink why you're using those behaviors. What are you trying to find out with a particular question? What message were you trying to get across? Do you think your behavior achieved your aim?

(2)  Look for opportune times to try out your new techniques. Concentrate only on small-group times, for example, and don't feel obligated to make every comment and question fit into some clinical-interview scheme. When you see a chance to probe a child's understanding of classification, do so. And record the episode! If discipline scares you, try out new techniques in specific, well-defined settings (small groups, juice time, outdoor play) and fall back on your old techniques everywhere else.

(3)  Keep records of your changing self—changes in your understanding of theory, your goals and attitudes, your repertoire of teaching strategies, your observations and inferences. Look in your records for plateaus as well as spurts, and remember, confusions and regressions are a necessary part of your progress. The particular way you progress, the particular confusions and partial resolutions you encounter, are a part of you. Nearly every teacher we've worked with, including ourselves, has gone through a period of holding back and a period of bombarding children with a spate of questions, before finding an equilibrium.

## FEELING AT EASE WITH THEORY

One of the big stumbling blocks in the way of developing a fulfilling relationship with Piagetian theory is the tendency to get so bogged down in theoretical terms that one either settles for verbal facility instead of understanding or gives up in disgust, convinced that the benefits of understanding the theory are not worth the cost. There are two ways to avoid this stumbling block—both equally important. One way is to read secondary sources that make an explicit attempt to tie theory to practice or to explain theoretical terms in concrete ways. The other way is to go straight to the master, but to concentrate on those writings that have the most obvious implications. Let's look at the second way first.

### Reading Piaget's Own Works

Coming, as he does, from an experimental perspective, Piaget has tied his terms, generalizations, and hypotheses to specific situations. Many of his books are filled with examples of the adult-child interactions from which his theory originated and with which it grew. Among those that have been most popular with the teachers we know are the following. (Full references are given at the end of this chapter).

> *The Child's Conception of Space,* Piaget and Inhelder (1956).
> *The Language and Thought of the Child,* Piaget (1959).
> *The Early Growth of Logic in the Child,* Inhelder and Piaget (1964).
> *The Child's Conception of Number,* Piaget (1952).
> *Play, Dreams, and Imitation in Childhood,* Piaget (1951).
> *The Moral Judgment of the Child,* Piaget (1932).

There are others of a similar nature, such as Piaget's later works, *The Grasp of Consciousness* (1976) and *Success and Understanding* (1978), and others that you'll find as you begin to explore library shelves. Harder for our teachers to read, maybe because these books are less helpful as a direct source of ideas for classroom strategies and activities, but nonetheless fascinating and useful in conveying basic ideas and explaining theoretical terms, were the following, all by Piaget:

> *Psychology and Epistemology* (1971b).
> *The Psychology of Intelligence* (1950).
> *The Child and Reality: Problems of Genetic Psychology* (1973).
> *Genetic Epistemology* (1970).

To really get the feel of Piaget's approach to intellectual development and that tremendous insight he had into how to get children to show him how they thought, you have to read the originals. The more the better, but it will suffice for getting the spirit to

(1) Read thoroughly one of Piaget's books from the first list. Do plenty of rereading and puzzle over confusing passages until you can make sense of them.

(2) Read cursorily at least two other books by Piaget. This means that you can skim much of the book, but do pause occasionally to savor a particularly de-

lightful exchange with a child. Focus on summary statements and explanations. Any of the books in either of the lists above is a good choice here. If you have biological leanings, try Piaget's *Biology and Knowledge* (1971a). It is hard, but it will open up new insights into Piaget's approach.

(3) Use the understandings you've gained by doing this reading. Spend an hour or more explaining, in your own words and to someone else, the major ideas you found in the book you read thoroughly. Then point out implications for teaching. Be sure to think about and discuss the next three questions. It will be a considerable help to have already tried out with children some of the ideas you've read about.

(a) What ideas or implications are there for verbal and nonverbal questioning strategies?

(b) What ideas has the book generated for kinds of activities or ways of doing activities?

(c) How can you use insights from the book to help you understand what kinds of thinking go on in the activities you already use with children? (In other words, what have you learned from the book about formative evaluation strategies?)

Now make use of your answers in your interactions with children.

### Reading about Piaget's Theory

Some people find it helpful to read secondary sources as they read Piaget's work—to go back and forth from one to the other. Whether you do it that way or whether you prefer to read them sequentially, make sure you look at some sources other than Piaget. There are some that are just too good to be passed up. Despite the increasing number of books that describe and explain Piaget's theory, we still recommend Ginsburg and Opper's *Piaget's Theory of Intellectual Development: An Introduction* (1969), to be read through, and Flavell's *The Developmental Psychology of Jean Piaget* (1963), to be used rather as a reference book or handbook. Our top recommendations for guides to theory based activities are the following:

*Constructive Play: Applying Piaget in the Preschool,* Forman and Hill (1980).
*Physical Knowledge in Preschool Education: Implications of Piaget's Theory,* Kamii and DeVries (1978).
*Piaget, Children, and Number,* Kamii and DeVries (1976).

Several other works that deserve mention but that for various reasons are not given top priority are Copple, Sigel, and Saunders, *Educating the Young Thinker: Classroom Strategies for Cognitive Growth* (1979), which is somewhat removed from orthodox Piagetian theory; *Educational Implications of Piaget's Theory*, a collection of essays edited by Athey and Rubadeau (1970), which is somewhat dated by the interpretations of theory offered in various articles; and Smilansky's *The Effects of Socio-Dramatic Play on Disadvantaged Preschool Children* (1968), which is very helpful for representation but hard to get hold of.

Of course, our list reflects our own biases. In the long run, you'll have to decide what's most worthwhile, but if you've looked at all of our recommendations, you'll have a solid start. You'll be able to make up your own mind about what you find in the bookstore or on library shelves. To give you some more sophistication in the search for additional information regarding what Piaget's colleagues think about the theory and its application, the following two works are excellent:

*Learning and the Development of Cognition,* Inhelder, Sinclair, and Bovet (1974).
*Piaget and His School: A Reader in Developmental Psychology,* ed. Inhelder and Chipman (1976).

As you work through your choice of readings, remember to continually test your ideas and understanding by applying what you've read to your work with children. Return from time to time to books you've already read. Insights you've gained from later readings and interactions with children will alter the interpretations you make of those first readings in ways that will excite and delight you—at least, that's the way it's happened with us. New insights will also influence the kinds of ideas you have for sparking up old lesson plans or modifying plans you find in activity books.

Let's look now at some ways of making sure the theory is let out of the books and into the classroom.

### Using the Theory

*Lesson-plan warm-ups*

For many people, the most difficult part of applying the theory is thinking of activities to apply it to. Others are brimming with ideas for activities, but they freeze whenever they try to work with the theory. If you are someone who has a hard time getting ideas in the first place, these four strategies may help.

(1) Think about the activities you enjoy doing. Do you like cooking, going to the beach, fishing, running, painting, gardening? What is it about these activities that you like? (For example, maybe what attracts you to gardening is the bright colors of the flowers you grow, or maybe you like the feel of damp earth.) Ask yourself what a child might enjoy about the activities you like. Pick a feature of one of the things you like to do and develop that feature into an activity plan. The

big danger here is to be overly ambitious. In developing your activity, remember to keep children's size, strength, stamina, coordination, and level of intellectual development in mind.

(2) Activity books are a good source of rough ideas for activities. Since most such books are not written with Piagetian theory in mind, the activities will require some alteration. Thumb through a book and pick an activity that strikes your fancy. Get the suggested materials, ask yourself the questions recommended for children, and see if your interest is piqued. If so, you have an activity to develop and modify as you apply principles from the theory. If not, spend some time just exploring the materials. As you touch, taste, smell, look at, and listen to the materials, ideas for related activities and other materials to liven things up will come to you.

(3) Talk to other people about what children's favorite activities are. Teachers, parents, and older siblings are good sources of information. Try to figure out what it is about the activity that children enjoy. This will help you to expand the activity into other related areas.

(4) Observe children at play—doing art projects, building with blocks, digging in beach sand, and so on. Record their comments and questions related to the different areas of logico-mathematical knowledge.

Once you have an activity idea, you can put the theory to work. The chief value of the next three suggestions is that they serve as warm-ups for applying the theory, though they can also help generate ideas for activities.

One valuable warm-up is to go to a preschool or kindergarten (or spend some time in your own classroom) and play with the materials yourself. Think about which activities or materials attract you first, which ones hold your attention the longest, and why. What did you do with the materials? What problems did they present you with or did you set for yourself? Did you like handling the materials?

A second warm-up is to pick a simple material, such as play dough, soapsuds, sand, or paper. Spend at least thirty minutes (an hour is better) exploring the material as thoroughly as you can. What can you do *to* it? What can you do *with* it? What stories can you tell about it? Think of ways to help children discover what you've discovered about it and about ways to find out about it.

Our third suggested warm-up is to pick one of your favorite activities, or one you'd like to try, and write it up in the format given in Chart 10-1. Now put the theory to work. Keeping in mind the nature of the activity as you've described it (the particular location, the exact colors and textures of the materials, the procedures to use and so forth), list behaviors that you could easily see or elicit without disrupting the activity and that reveal understandings, confusions, or just interest in the various areas of logico-mathematical and infra-logical knowledge. Try to list behaviors in each of these areas: classification, relations (seriation), number, space,

**CHART 10-1**  *ACTIVITY PLAN FORMAT*

---

*Brief Description of the Activity:*

*Main Objectives for Children:*
(Be honest and explicit about what you really want them to get out of the activity, whether or not it is related to the theory)

*Main Objectives for the Teacher:*
(Make these personal. What do you want to work on in yourself?)

*Location:*
(Inside or outside? Where in the classroom? When during the day—small group, free play?)

*Materials:*
(Be very specific, and think about why you're using these particular materials.)

*Procedure:*
(Make this as detailed as you can. What questions will you ask? How will you respond if children exhibit various misunderstandings?)

*What to Watch for in terms of the Theory:*

---

and time. You may also want to consider the use of specific verbal or nonverbal strategies for eliciting information, without interrupting the activity. Some strategies can be used during the activity itself. Others might involve a discussion of the activity after it is over—at snack time or in a quiet moment with a single child during free play, for instance.

The last two exercises bear frequent repeating with new materials and activities. Our teachers wrote up lesson plans like that in the last exercise for the first six to twelve weeks that they worked with the theory. Putting the theory to work in each of the areas of logico-mathematical knowledge was an especially grueling experience but was universally applauded as the single most helpful exercise for integrating theory with practice. And no wonder! As you search your brain for the tie between your activity and the theory, you find yourself adjusting your choice of specific materials, subtly altering your procedures, and making notes to yourself about how to observe for and/or elicit children's understandings in the different areas of knowledge. You find yourself trying out new strategies, gathering ideas from the responses they encourage, and observing more details about children's understandings than you ever thought possible. It has been our experience that after an initial slowness (lasting anywhere from one to eight weeks), the ideas come so thick and fast that one can't possibly write them all down.

At this stage, you are ready to develop a more careful theoretical focus for your activity plans. Without losing the observational alertness you've developed and the readiness to respond to a child's fascination with an unplanned aspect of the activity, you can concentrate on ways to guide the activity toward a specific goal related to the theory.

### Developing a focus
### for your activity

It is one thing to have thought of a variety of potentials for an activity. It is quite another to get any of the potentials realized. To help the hoped-for happen, you have to be able to follow up on promising leads. And you have to be able to direct attention to the features of an activity that will fascinate and intrigue once they are properly noticed. It is not enough simply to display the features or to refer to them. They must be set in a context so that they present a puzzle that the children see as clamoring for a resolution.

You can help yourself choose a focus while you work on refining your abilities to follow up and direct attention if you take the time and effort to actually write out strategies you could use to enhance the potentials you listed in doing the last exercise. For each area (classification or relations, for example) think of yourself doing a clinical interview. Think about questions, comments, gestures, additional materials, and, yes, even sleights of hand, that can be used to make the activity an exciting and informative one for both you and the children involved. You will probably find that this is easier to do for some areas than for others, given the activity you've planned. Use the area for which you have the most ideas, or the most connected ideas, as your focus. You may want to adjust your written activity to accommodate this emphasis.

Now you are ready to do a simulation study. Find a friendly coworker or two to help you, and explain the activity in detail. Invite them to pose problems for you to solve. Suppose, for example, that a crucial piece of equipment breaks or has been left at home. What if too many children join the group? How will you handle Rose's desire to tell everyone about her new hamster (which you didn't realize was in the shoe box she brought to school and is now under her hat)? Think of the kinds of situations most likely to arise in your classroom. As you are presented with each problem, try to solve it in a way that enables you to maintain (or regain) your main focus. Make a note of how the materials and your behaviors enhance or interfere with the aim of the activity. Don't forget to think about what to observe for when you do the activity in the classroom.

After making any necessary changes in your activity plan, you are ready for the real test. Take the activity into the classroom and try it out. Whether or not the activity you've chosen is a familiar one to you, the concentration on working with the theory may make it a little scary. Don't hesitate to do what you can to make things easier for yourself. The first time through, it is a good idea to work with children you think are the most cooperative or the most likely to be patient with your starts and hesitations. Regardless of how much advance thinking you've done and how many precautions you've taken, there will most certainly be surprises. When you're caught off guard and the theory beast isn't whispering any hints in your ear, it is no shame to fall back on some old standbys. Many of the techniques you used before you met the theory are not only compatible with your new approach, they actually enhance it. They don't have to be avoided at all costs just because you don't yet know quite how they fit in.

When you've finished the activity and have some time for reflection, you are ready to broach the question, "Where do we go from here?" It may help you to compartmentalize your thinking this way: (a) look at how children respond to your activity, (b) think of how the activity fits into the stream of things, and (c) examine your own behaviors. What you're looking for in the first two compartments are behaviors that you can use in deciding what to do tomorrow—how to modify or extend what you've already done. We've already had a look into the first two compartments (in Chapters 7, 8, and 9). Let's look at the third as we discuss the general issue of self-evaluation.

## KEEPING ON TRACK

As in the other areas of evaluation we've discussed in this book, formative evaluation is the main concern in assessing oneself and other adults in the classroom. It is of little use to categorize oneself and other adults as "great teachers" or "good people." We want to know what a person believes and does, how those attitudes and behaviors affect the people in the classroom and the general classroom environment, and whether (and how) the attitudes and behaviors could be modified or replaced. If we like the way things are going in the classroom, then we want to maintain whatever attitudes and behaviors are responsible for keeping things that way.

### What to Look At

The first task in evaluating oneself is to decide what kinds of behaviors and attitudes to look at. In Chapter 7, we described a number of specific interaction strategies likely to create the classroom environment favored by our theory. Chart 10-2 is a reminder of the kinds of strategies discussed there. The chart does not provide an exhaustive list of behaviors to observe. Notice in particular the omission of undesirable behaviors. Here, as elsewhere, we encourage you to focus on what you are doing right. Your own experience in applying theory and another excursion through Chapters 4, 6, 7, and 8 will provide additional examples of specific behaviors you'll want to observe.

**CHART 10-2** *EXAMPLES OF TEACHER BEHAVIORS TO OBSERVE*

---

**USE OF MATERIALS**

(1) Provision of materials that suggest open-ended uses—for instance, materials that could be used for a variety of parts (an airplane wing, a propeller, and so on).

(2) Provision of cognitive conflict—for example, Silly Putty introduced when solids and liquids are being compared.

(3) Encouragement of intellectual honesty and peer interactions—for instance, adoption of a child's procedure for constructing something.

**VERBAL INTERACTIONS**

(1) Use of thought-provoking strategies in problem-solving episodes. For example:

    (a) Clarify a problem and help children see the question, but don't solve it.

    (b) Draw attention to features or actions that children seem to have ignored (using "I wonder" statements, as suggested in Chapter 7).

    (c) Suggest a large list of alternatives and let children decide which to use.

(2) Use of open-ended questions—such as "What else?" questions from Chapter 7.

(3) Provision for cognitive conflict—for example, comments such as, "I'm taller than my mother" when children are equating height with age.

(4) Use of comments and questions to help children clarify, focus, and communicate their thoughts.

(5) Use of comments to reinforce thought processes rather than products.

(6) Suggestions that children turn to one another for help; requests for advice and opinions from children.

(7) Requests for different views on a topic; suggestions of various other views.

**OTHER BEHAVIORS**

(1) Interest in children's "wrong" answers and inefficient strategies.

(2) Provision of genuine choices.

(3) Observation of ongoing activity before making suggestions.

(4) Modeling of search strategies, correction of mistakes, and systematic approaches.

(5) Helping children set appropriate classroom rules.

---

In developing or refining new strategies, you may want to monitor one or more of the behaviors in Chart 10-2. Suppose, for example, that you think you have a tendency to initiate activities without due consideration for what children are already doing. You may want to focus on timing, the use of open-ended questions, and observation of ongoing projects. Or suppose that you want to acquire and practice some verbal techniques for redirecting activities. You will want to know how you are doing things now, the effects of your behaviors on children, and how you might refine, augment, or replace your present strategies.

Getting an accurate description of what you're doing is not easy. There are a variety of techniques, however, that can make the task manageable. In the next section, we'll look at ways to gather information about specific behaviors as well as about general areas that require further work.

## How and Where to Look

### Observations

Many of the guidelines discussed in Chapter 9 for observing children apply to observations of yourself. There are special problems, though, in observing yourself. For one thing, you can't step out of the ongoing activity to watch what's going on when you are the part of the activity you want to watch (though you frequently can take a moment to jot down a note about what you did or to make a short entry on a chart). A more sensitive problem is the tendency we all have to confound what we planned to do or wished we had done with what we actually did. Apart from maintaining an awareness of that danger and conscientiously trying to be objective, there are two specific strategies you can call upon. The first is to persuade another person to observe you in action. The second is to make video or audio tapes of yourself.

If you choose the first option, it will be helpful to have set a focus for the observation (such as, "Concentrate on my use of open-ended questions") and/or to request frequency counts (such as, "How many times during the small-group session did I wait five seconds or more for an answer before I rephrased my question?"). Having a particular behavior monitored is valuable for several reasons: it is less threatening than being watched for general "good" teaching behaviors, it tends to heighten your own awareness of what you're doing, and it can give you useful information with which to make your own judgments about how to modify your behaviors. If you're searching for new strategies to use, a discussion with the observer, with the data in front of you, can generate new ideas to try.

If you choose the second option, your initial focus need not be so specific. You may decide, for example, to record events during a particular activity, during a specific time of day, or in a particular area of the room. If you have the necessary equipment, you might even try carrying a portable, battery-operated tape recorder with you, so that you can record your comments as you move about the room. After the recording is finished, you can listen to (and/or look at) the tapes with a specific question in mind. If you have never seen or heard yourself on tape before (this is particularly true of video tapes), it will take several viewings before you can concentrate on specific strategies. Many people prefer to see or listen to a tape by themselves before they discuss it with others. That way, they can rid themselves of the irresistible tendency we all have for our first reactions to be monopolized by concerns about the way we look, our nervous habits, peculiarities of our voice quality, and so on, before they discuss the episode with coworkers, who are, for the most part, blithely unconcerned about any of that.

When you are ready to view the tape from the perspective of an impartial observer and/or to have others view the tape, you can treat the tapes much as you would an ongoing event to be observed. The big advantage, of course, is that you can replay the tape to check your observations and you can show the tape at convenient times to others who may notice very different behaviors in it than you do. A tape is also very useful if you're trying to increase the accuracy of your on-the-spot impressions. Compare the reactions you had to an event while participating in it to what you see or hear on tapes. Some particularly revealing questions can be tested in this way. (1) Who was manipulating the materials, you or children, and in what way? (2) Exactly what suggestions did children make, and how did you rephrase them? (3) Which children said what?

### Written records

The historical approach can be a valuable addition to your self-evaluation methods. Your activity plans, your written observations, and your journal can reveal changes you've made or gaps in your progress of which you have been completely unaware.

Changes in the amount of detail and the kinds of focus written in activity plans can indicate growth in your understanding of theory, increased acquaintance with the needs and interests of the children in your classroom, and the acquisition of new teaching strategies. A look at your written observations can corroborate the conclusions you draw from an examination of activity plans. You will also see progress in the attention you've paid to theoretically relevant details and your ability to elicit the kinds of observations you want. It will be very helpful to you in deciding what information you want and what changes you want to make in yourself if you take note of how many observations you have on each child and adult in the classroom, the kinds of activities for which you have written observations, and the content of your observations. Have you made note of spatial understandings but ignored physical knowledge, for example? Are there some children for whom you have no written observations?

A look at your journal can fill out the picture. It will show you something about your attitudes as well. Look in your journal for the expression of intentions to try out new strategies, use new activities, and extend your application of theory. Which children are mentioned most frequently, and in which contexts? Is there evidence in your journal of your attempts to work with other staff and with parents? (Incidentally, parent meetings provide you with an excellent opportunity to test your understanding of theory. There's nothing like having to explain it to someone else.) Do your entries suggest that you are running yourself ragged?

*General evaluation*

At least twice a year, devote a week to extensive assessment, using all the techniques mentioned above. Evaluate your progress as manager of the environment, the kinds of interactions you engage in with children and staff, your attitudes toward work, the expertise you've been developing in observation and inference, and your understanding of theory.

If you find yourself dissatisfied with how things are going, work on ways to change your situation so that you can get things done. Do you have thinking space? If not, how can you get it? Think about the techniques suggested in previous chapters—for instance, making lists on the wall, a morning checklist, or changes in room arrangement, carefully balancing activities so that you can concentrate on one, soliciting classroom volunteers or aides, and so on. In addition, changing your situation will most likely require close collaboration with the rest of your staff.

## WORKING WITH OTHER ADULTS

In this chapter, and throughout the rest of the book, we have made passing references to the importance of working with other adults: we have mentioned the need for good teamwork in the classroom, the value of sympathetic coworkers, and the benefits of doing various Teacher Tasks with other adults. A good working relationship with other adults, however, does not come automatically. Nor is it a matter of luck. Some concerted effort and special expertise is required. It will probably come as no surprise to you to learn that we think Piaget's theory of children's intellectual development has a very natural extension to adult knowledge. In this section, we'll be putting the theory to work in exploring ways to work with other adults.

As you recall, in Chapter 4 we were careful to construct a single list of goals for *all* the people in the classroom, regardless of age or status. It was not so obvious, perhaps, that the key words for the classroom environment should also characterize the teacher's environment. Here's why we think they do. It is part of Piaget's theory about the nature of knowledge in general, regardless of age or species, that (a) knowledge is acquired actively rather than passively (hence, *activity* is a key word); (b) at each moment, the nature of the activity involved depends both on one's present knowledge and on the match between the environment and that understanding (hence, *change* is a key word); (c) different individuals, since they have had different experiences, have different knowledge to bring to an environment (hence, *diversity* is a key word); and (d) intellectual honesty is a requirement of any kind of cognitive advance (hence, *intellectual honesty* is a key phrase). Adults may not be developing basic cognitive structures, the way children are, but they are certainly constructing new interpretations and acquiring new abilities. If we want to establish a healthy, evolving intellectual climate, we'll want to make sure the working environment for adults is characterized by activity, change, diversity, and intellectual honesty.

### Activity

It is amazing how much apparent apathy and discontent comes, not from the rejection of theory, but from the lack of opportunity for active participation. To forestall this unhappy situation, we can take a hint from work with children and find ways to get every staff member, volunteer, and parent helper to become actively involved. People with little experience can contribute to lesson plans by suggesting general ideas and materials that you and the group refine and elaborate in ways suited to the theory. They can observe the number of times you talk to a particular child or the number of children in the art area. More experienced people can contribute proportionally more. If you are one of the inexperienced people yourself, don't be shy about suggesting an activity idea and then asking for help in making it work. To maximize activity in staff discussions, we have found the following techniques helpful:

> Explore materials: for instance, have a play dough-making session and spend time exploring what can be done with it.
> Explore values: there are some good suggestions for how to do this in Simon, Howe, and Kirschenbaum (1972).
> Brainstorm: for example, think of a variety of different ways to arrange the science area, to stop a spitting epidemic, or to elicit number understandings.
> Work together on Teacher Tasks from this book.

### Change

As the group evolves, different staff members will grow in different ways. You can take advantage of new potentials different members have to offer by incorporating change into the work routine. Teachers may take turns being head teacher or being responsible for particular subject-matter areas. Different staff members may take more responsibility for areas that become interesting to them, they may suggest new goals to work toward, and they may implement new classroom rules. Think about change in staff discussions, too. Is one person dominating most of the discussions or making the important decisions? If so, you might try rotating the responsibility for leading the discussions. This is a way of giving people (including yourself) room to change—a way to break out of an established pattern.

### Diversity

To provide for diversity in the adult environment, there must be provision for activity at different levels and for different interests simultaneously. Some people may not have activity ideas, but they seem to have an instinctive knack for keen observations; others will have ideas for strategies, but not for interesting new materials to try them on. Staff meetings can be adjusted so that different members lead discussions on topics they think they are best able to handle. Of course, if diversity is really to characterize the environment, they have to be allowed considerable freedom in how to conduct the discussions.

It is one thing to be open to a variety of contributions and quite another to effectively communicate that openness. One technique you might try (either individually or as a group) is to generate a list of possible contributions. Then different members of the group can make tentative commitments to specific items on the list, making sure that all the needed teacher responsibilities are covered. Such a list might have entries such as these:

> Generate activity ideas (find activity books, and so on)
> Point out connections between theory and activities (and strategies)
> Play the role of resident expert on classification—or number or infra-logical knowledge, for instance
> Lead discussions on mechanisms of developmental change and appropriate strategies for interactions
> Work with parents
> Decide on weekly focus of observations
> Make observations

Since you can expect people to change at different rates, the commitments will have to be reassessed periodically. Some people will be taking the lion's share of the responsibility while others develop new skills and confidence. Later, the roles may be reversed. Even if you are an experienced teacher, for example, it might be invaluable to you to have someone else take over the coordination responsibilities for a week or two while you work on clinical-interviewing skills.

### Intellectual Honesty

We have reserved for last the discussion of the environmental feature that makes all the others work—namely, the atmosphere of intellectual honesty. We'll discuss here some techniques that have worked for us in creating an environment conducive to staff cooperation and active, fulfilling participation.

Discussions of values can be an effective way to get group members to know and respect one another and to appreciate individual differences. We have usually tried to schedule such discussions early in the school year and at varying intervals throughout the year. That way, unnecessary tensions arising from uncommunicated differences in values can be avoided. In addition, classroom episodes will often stimulate spontaneous discussions of values for children, teachers, and the classroom environment. To get such discussions started, you may want to play with some forced-choice questions of this sort: "Is it more important for five-year-old children to learn to write their name or to learn how to make friends?" or "When teachers think a child is not telling the truth, should they confront the child with their suspicions or should they let it pass?" Another method is to have each person write five goals for young children. Either strategy works best when followed by a sensitive discussion of answers in which the emphasis is on people's reasons for their choices and not on which options (or which goals) are the right ones. To establish an atmosphere of intellectual honesty, it is helpful to use these ground rules: (1) No one has to answer. A pass is perfectly acceptable. (2) You can change your mind at any time.

Three techniques that will help the group focus on specific behaviors and their consequences, rather than on simple, good/bad value judgments, are (1) discussions generated by reading Farson's "Praise Reappraised" (1963), a thought-provoking article pointing out some of the dangers in using praise; (2) discussions generated by reading Piaget's theory; (3) variations in the use of the technique called Proud Whip, a procedure in which people verbalize one aspect of themselves or their behavior that they're proud of. The third technique is a particularly effective one, but is hard to do. Every teacher we've ever worked with has been more willing to engage in self-criticism than in self-praise. Yet, if, as we have suggested, the way to make progress is to build on a strength rather than to try to remedy a defect, we want to focus on our good points, on the features of which we can be proud. Variations on this third technique include focusing on some feature of your teaching *this morning* or on a feature of your record-keeping *this week*.

A technique that is invaluable, but only after the group has been working together for a while and has developed an ability to look at specific behaviors and their consequences, is to have each person characterize another staff member. Each person can write down one teaching characteristic of the person next to him or her and then hand that person the written comment. Discussion of written comments is optional. A more challenging version of this is to have each person write one strength and one weakness of another staff member's teaching. These activities can be temporarily hard on the ego, but they are of tremendous help in learning how others perceive you, in understanding what values others hold, and in paving the way for fruitful group analyses of observations and video tapes of teaching behaviors.

In general, we have found that staff and parent discussions are most profitable when there is a focus—a question or an issue that is to be addressed—and when the group concentrates on what *is* or *might be* rather than on what *should have been*.

## LAST WORDS

We have devoted this final chapter to a variety of suggestions for how to cope with problems that arise in attempts to incorporate Piagetian theory into the classroom. As is our usual procedure, we have left much of the hard thinking and decision making up to you. We had to. In the final analysis, you are the only one who can adequately assess your own situation and choose what is best for you. We hope we have provided enough signposts and makeshift bridges to make your travels with the theory beast both exciting and successful.

## REFERENCES

ATHEY, IRENE J., and DUANE O. RUBADEAU, eds. *Educational Implications of Piaget's Theory* (Waltham, Mass.: Ginn-Blaisdell, 1970).
COPPLE, CAROL, IRVING E. SIGEL, and RUTH SAUNDERS. *Educating the Young Thinker: Classroom Strategies for Cognitive Growth* (New York: D. Van Nostrand Company, 1979).
FARSON, RICHARD E. "Praise Reappraised," *Harvard Business Review, 41,* no. 5 (1963), 1–7.
FLAVELL, JOHN. *The Developmental Psychology of Jean Piaget* (New York: D. Van Nostrand Company, 1963).
FORMAN, GEORGE E., and FLEET HILL. *Constructive Play: Applying Piaget in The Preschool* (Monterey, Cal.: Brooks/Cole, 1980).
GINSBURG, HERBERT, and SYLVIA OPPER. *Piaget's Theory of Intellectual Development: An Introduction* (Englewood Cliffs, N.J.: Prentice-Hall, Inc., 1969).
INHELDER, BÄRBEL, and HAROLD H. CHIPMAN, eds. *Piaget and His School: A Reader in Developmental Psychology* (New York: Springer-Verlag, 1976).
INHELDER, BÄRBEL, and JEAN PIAGET. *The Early Growth of Logic in the Child,* trans. E. A. Lunzer and D. Papert (London: Routledge and Kegan Paul, 1964 [first published in French, in 1959, under the title, *La Genèse des Structures Logiques Élémentaire*]).
INHELDER, BÄRBEL, HERMINE SINCLAIR, and MAGALI BOVET. *Learning and the Development of Cognition,* trans. Susan Wedgwood (Cambridge, Mass.: Harvard University Press, 1974 [first published in French, in 1974, under the title, *Apprentissage et Structures de la Connaissance*]).
KAMII, CONSTANCE, and RHETA DeVRIES. *Physical Knowledge in Preschool Education: Implications of Piaget's Theory* (Englewood Cliffs, N.J.: Prentice-Hall, Inc., 1978).
KAMII, CONSTANCE, and RHETA DeVRIES. *Piaget, Children, and Number* (Washington, D.C.; National Association for the Education of Young Children, 1976).
PIAGET, JEAN. *Biology and Knowledge,* trans. Beatrix Walsh (Chicago: The University of Chicago Press, 1971a [first published in French, in 1967, under the title, *Biologie et Connaissance*]).
PIAGET, JEAN. *The Child and Reality: Problems of Genetic Psychology,* trans. Arnold Rosin (New York: Grossman Publishers, 1973 [first published in French, in 1972, under the title, *Problèmes de Psychologie Génétique*]).
PIAGET, JEAN. *The Child's Conception of Number,* trans. C. Gattegno and F. M. Hodgson (London: Routledge and Kegan Paul, 1952 [first published in French, in 1941, under the title, *La Genèse du Nombre chez l'Enfant*]).
PIAGET, JEAN. *Genetic Epistemology,* trans. Eleanor Duckworth (New York: Columbia University Press, 1970 [first published in French, in 1970, under the title, *L'Épistémologie Génétique*]).
PIAGET, JEAN. *The Grasp of Consciousness: Action and Concept in the Young Child,* trans. Susan Wedgwood (Cambridge, Mass.: Harvard University Press, 1976 [first published in French, in 1974, under the title, *La Prise de Conscience*]).

PIAGET, JEAN. *The Language and Thought of the Child*, 3rd ed. (revised and enlarged), trans. Marjorie and Ruth Gabain (London: Routledge and Kegan Paul, 1959 [first published in French, in 1923, under the title, *Études sur la Logique de l'Enfant*]).

PIAGET, JEAN. *The Moral Judgment of the Child*, trans. Marjorie Gabain (New York: Harcourt Brace Jovanovich, 1932 [first published in French, in 1932, under the title, *Le Jugement Moral chez l'Enfant*]).

PIAGET, JEAN. *Play, Dreams and Imitation in Childhood*, trans. C. Gattegno and F. M. Hodgson (London: Heinemann, 1951 [first published in French, in 1945, under the title, *La Formation du Symbole chez l'Enfant; Imitation, Jeu, et Rêve, Image et Représentation*]).

PIAGET, JEAN. *Psychology and Epistemology*, trans. Arnold Rosin (New York: Grossman Publishers, 1971b [first published in French, in 1970, under the title, *Psychologie et Épistémologie*]).

PIAGET, JEAN. *The Psychology of Intelligence*, trans. Malcolm Piercy and D. E. Berlyne (London: Routledge and Kegan Paul, 1950 [first published in French, in 1947, under the title, *La Psychologie de l'Intelligence*]).

PIAGET, JEAN. *Success and Understanding*, trans. Arnold J. Pomerans (Cambridge, Mass.: Harvard University Press, 1978 [first published in French, in 1974, under the title, *Réussir et Comprendre*]).

PIAGET, JEAN, and BÄRBEL INHELDER. *The Child's Conception of Space*, trans. F. J. Langdon and J. L. Lunzer (London: Routledge and Kegan Paul, 1956 [first published in French, in 1948, under the title, *La Représentation de l'Espace chez l'Enfant*]).

SIMON, SIDNEY B., LELAND W. HOWE, and HOWARD KIRSCHENBAUM. *Values Clarification: A Handbook of Practical Strategies for Teachers and Students* (New York: Hart Publishing Company, Inc., 1972).

SMILANSKY, SARAH. *The Effects of Socio-Dramatic Play on Disadvantaged Preschool Children* (New York: John Wiley and Sons, 1968).

# INDEX